SHAPE IT! 2

CB082251

TEACHER'S BOOK

WITH DIGITAL PACK

Alice Copello

with Simon Cupit

CAMBRIDGE UNIVERSITY PRESS

CAMBRIDGE
UNIVERSITY PRESS & ASSESSMENT

Shaftesbury Road, Cambridge CB2 8EA, United Kingdom

One Liberty Plaza, 20th Floor, New York, NY 10006, USA

477 Williamstown Road, Port Melbourne, VIC 3207, Australia

314–321, 3rd Floor, Plot 3, Splendor Forum, Jasola District Centre, New Delhi – 110025, India

103 Penang Road, #05–06/07, Visioncrest Commercial, Singapore 238467

Avenida Paulista, 807 conjunto 2315, 01311–915, São Paulo, Brazil

Torre de los Parques, Colonia Tlacoquemécatl del Valle, Mexico City C.P. 03200, Mexico

Cambridge University Press & Assessment is a department of the University of Cambridge.

We share the University's mission to contribute to society through the pursuit of education, learning and research at the highest international levels of excellence.

www.cambridge.org
Information on this title: www.cambridge.org/9781108923453

First published 2020

20 19 18 17 16 15 14 13 12 11 10 9 8 7

Printed in Malaysia by Vivar Printing

A catalog record for this publication is available from the British Library

ISBN 978-1-108-92345-3 Shape It! Teacher's Book & Project Book with Digital Pack Level 2
ISBN 978-1-108-72658-0 Own it! Teacher's Book with Digital Pack Level 2

Additional resources for this publication at www.cambridge.org/shapeit

Contents

Welcome to *Shape It!*

"It's your world, so SHAPE IT!"

Welcome to *Shape It!*, the course that ensures your students are confident and future-ready through a combination of global topics, collaborative projects, and strategies to develop learner independence.

While developing *Shape It!* we spoke with teachers and students around the world to identify their top priorities in the secondary classroom ...

I'd like to do project work with my students, but it can be too time-consuming to plan.
Merve, Turkey

Project Work

Collaboration is a key strand of this course. *Shape It!* includes a *CLIL project* in every even-numbered unit of the Student's Book and a *Culture Project* for every odd-numbered unit, available in the *Teacher's Resource Bank* online. These are accompanied by a Project Book with step-by-step guides and practical tips for teachers.

For more information: pages vi, vii, and xxv

I want my students to become more independent learners.
Maria, Spain

Learn to Learn

The *Learn to Learn* feature of the course is designed to introduce students to vital learning strategies and techniques that will help them become more independent learners, all aligned to the *Cambridge Life Competencies Framework*.

For more information: pages vi, vii, and xxiv

İleri Bilim Koleji, Turkey

4

What do you value most?

LEARNING OUTCOMES

I can ...

- understand texts about money and caring jobs
- make and respond to requests
- write an opinion essay
- understand how to use *could*, comparative and superlative adjectives, *too*, *too much*, *too many*, and (*not*) *enough* + noun
- talk about money and caring jobs
- remember similar words, identify key information, and organize my homework
- reach agreement as a group and make a poster

Start It!

1 Look at the photo. How does the boy feel?
2 Before you watch, how do you help other people?
3 How can helping others be good for you? Watch and check.
4 Which of the ways to help in the video do you like best?

Watch video 4.1

Grammar in Action 4.2 p49

Grammar in Action 4.3 p51

Everyday English 4.4 p52

46 WHAT DO YOU VALUE MOST? | UNIT 4

> I want my students to feel that they belong to the world; that they are global citizens.
> *Itana, Brazil*

Global Topics

Shape It! has a global, cultural focus, with topics from traditional dress to unique festivals. The documentaries and the *Around the World* pages bring these global topics to life, exposing students to different countries and asking questions that encourage students to think about the differences between their culture and other cultures.

For more information: page xxii

> I want a variety of videos that will help me to engage my students with the topic and see the language being used in a meaningful way.
> *Antonio, Mexico*

Teen-Friendly Videos

Shape It! includes four to five videos per unit made especially for this course. As well as documentaries, there are *Grammar in Action* and *Everyday English* videos designed to appeal to the teenage learner.

For more information: page xxvi

> I need resources and support to manage students of different levels in the same class.
> *Andrés, Ecuador*

Mixed-Ability Support

In *Shape It!* there is extensive support for teachers with mixed-ability classes, including:

- graded Workbook activities
- suggestions for differentiated activities
- an entire Project Book guiding teachers through each project
- graded grammar and vocabulary worksheets

For more information: page xxvii

Cambridge Life Competencies Framework

How can we prepare our students to succeed in a world that is rapidly changing? We need to help students develop transferable skills that allow them to work with people from around the world, think creatively, analyze sources critically, and communicate their views effectively. How can we teach these skills alongside language?

In response to these questions, we have developed the *Cambridge Life Competencies Framework*. This Framework underpins the syllabus for the *Learn to Learn* pages and the collaborative project work in *Shape It!*, helping teachers recognize and assess the many transferable skills that the course develops.

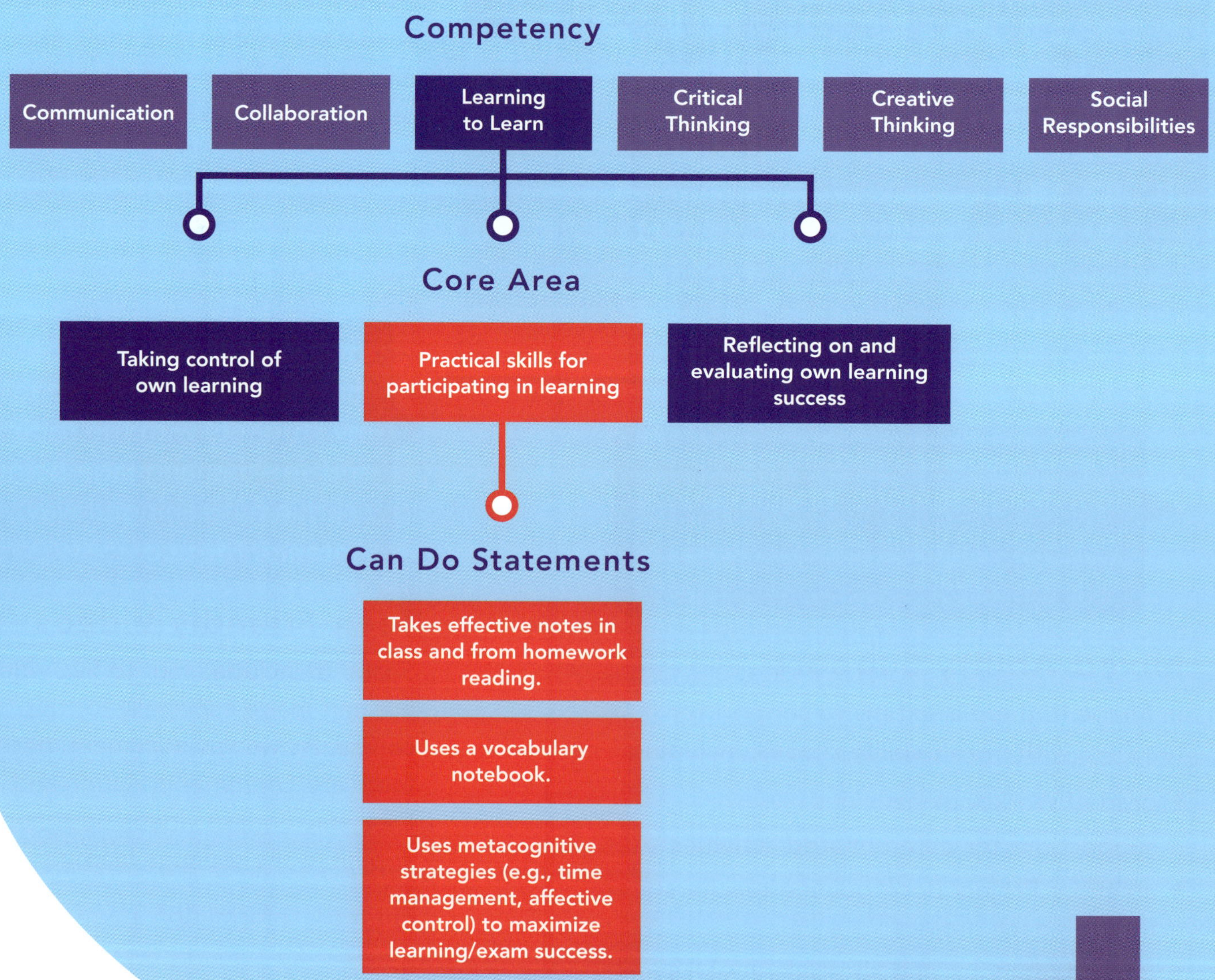

Learn to Learn

These core areas are developed in the *Learn to Learn* feature, which appears throughout the unit and on the *Learn to Learn* page at the end of each unit.

This page from Level 2 Unit 1 helps students organize their notebook by encouraging them to look at an example of a notebook, notice its features, and finally, plan their own notebook organization.

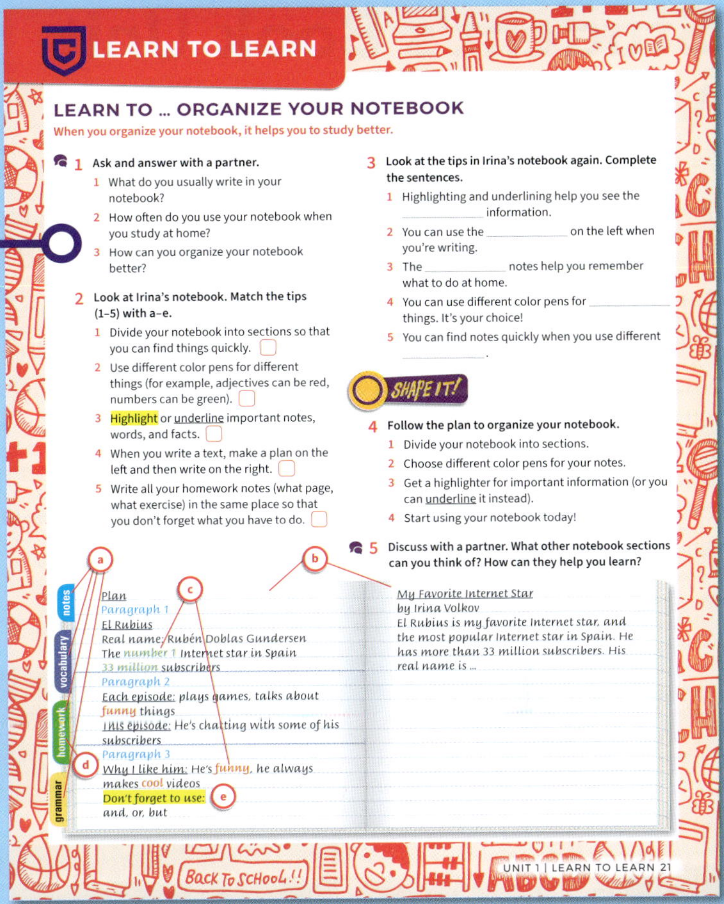

LEARN TO LEARN

LEARN TO ... ORGANIZE YOUR NOTEBOOK

When you organize your notebook, it helps you to study better.

1 Ask and answer with a partner.
1 What do you usually write in your notebook?
2 How often do you use your notebook when you study at home?
3 How can you organize your notebook better?

2 Look at Irina's notebook. Match the tips (1–5) with a–e.
1 Divide your notebook into sections so that you can find things quickly. ☐
2 Use different color pens for different things (for example, adjectives can be red, numbers can be green). ☐
3 Highlight or underline important notes, words, and facts. ☐
4 When you write a text, make a plan on the left and then write on the right. ☐
5 Write all your homework notes (what page, what exercise) in the same place so that you don't forget what you have to do. ☐

3 Look at the tips in Irina's notebook again. Complete the sentences.
1 Highlighting and underlining help you see the ________ information.
2 You can use the ________ on the left when you're writing.
3 The ________ notes help you remember what to do at home.
4 You can use different color pens for ________ things. It's your choice!
5 You can find notes quickly when you use different ________.

SHAPE IT!

4 Follow the plan to organize your notebook.
1 Divide your notebook into sections.
2 Choose different color pens for your notes.
3 Get a highlighter for important information (or you can underline it instead).
4 Start using your notebook today!

5 Discuss with a partner. What other notebook sections can you think of? How can they help you learn?

UNIT 1 | LEARN TO LEARN 21

Project Work

The *Collaboration* competency of the *Cambridge Life Competencies Framework* also plays a huge part in the course through CLIL projects included in the Student's Book and Culture Projects available in the *Teacher's Resource Bank* online – all of which have extensive support and guidance in the Project Book.

This project from Level 2 Unit 4 asks students to analyze some of the key features of a model project before planning and creating their own. Finally, they can evaluate other groups' tasks.

SOCIAL STUDIES PROJECT

A Poster

1 What is the purpose of the poster? Read and check (✓).
a to encourage more people to use a local park ☐
b to ask for more volunteers to clean the park ☐
c to tell people about a charity event ☐

2 Read the poster again. Under which heading can you find this information?
1 the place for the activity *Where?*
2 the type of activity
3 the people organizing the activity
4 the reasons it is a useful thing to do
5 the time and place to meet
6 why volunteers enjoy the activity

How to Agree as a Group

3 Read the tips on how to agree as a group. Put them in the best order.
a ☐ Ask other people for their opinions.
b ☐ Make a decision as a group. Check that everyone agrees.
c ☐ Introduce the decision you need to make.
d ☐ Give your own opinion politely.
e ☐ Interrupt politely if you want to comment.
f ☐ Summarize all the opinions.

4 Listen to the students. Write *Y* (Yusuf), *L* (Lara), or *T* (Thiago). Who ...
1 suggests ideas (two people)?
2 interrupts politely?
3 asks other people for their opinion and summarizes the opinions?

SHAPE IT!

PLAN

5 Work in groups. Plan a poster for a volunteer project. Follow the steps below.
• Choose one of these ideas for a volunteer project, or use your own idea.

Teaching older people how to use the latest gadgets.
Helping at an after-school or local sports club for younger students.
Working in an animal shelter.

• Think of what you can say to inform and attract volunteers.
• Organize your material under headings.
• Add photos to create an attractive design.

PRESENT

6 Display your poster on your classroom wall. Remember to include photos and useful information for volunteers, and to follow the tips in *How to Agree as a Group*.

CHECK

7 Look at your classmates' posters. Would you like to work on their projects? Discuss in your group and then vote on the best poster.

54 WHAT DO YOU VALUE MOST? | UNIT 4 UNIT 4 | WHAT DO YOU VALUE MOST? 55

For more information about how *Shape It!* correlates to the *Cambridge Life Competencies Framework*, go to pages xxviii and xxix.

Student's Book Unit Visual Guide

Every unit in *Shape It!* takes students on a journey from "starting it" to "shaping it"! Students are gradually introduced to the topic and target language through a variety of scaffolded activities that build their confidence and encourage independent learning. Vibrant videos, readings, and listening texts show language in context, allowing students to respond personally and work collaboratively. The *Shape It!* projects or *Around the World* pages at the end of the unit give students the opportunity to consolidate and demonstrate all their learning in a fun, personalized way.

Unit Questions encourage students to talk about the opening photo, as well as critically think about the unit story.

Start It! → Activate prior knowledge. Get interested in the topic. Provoke critical thinking.

Explore It! → Develop research skills. Extend learning beyond the classroom.

Use It! → Practice target language in a personalized, controlled activity.

Voice It! → Express a personal opinion on the topic.

SHAPE IT! → Demonstrate topic knowledge and language learning in a collaborative project on the *Around the World* pages.

The unit journey is underpinned by the *Learn to Learn* strand, which supports the development of vital learning skills, and the *How to …* feature, which provides useful tips for completing project work successfully. These features support students on their journey from *Start It!* to *Shape It!*

Learning Outcomes clearly show unit aims at a glance.

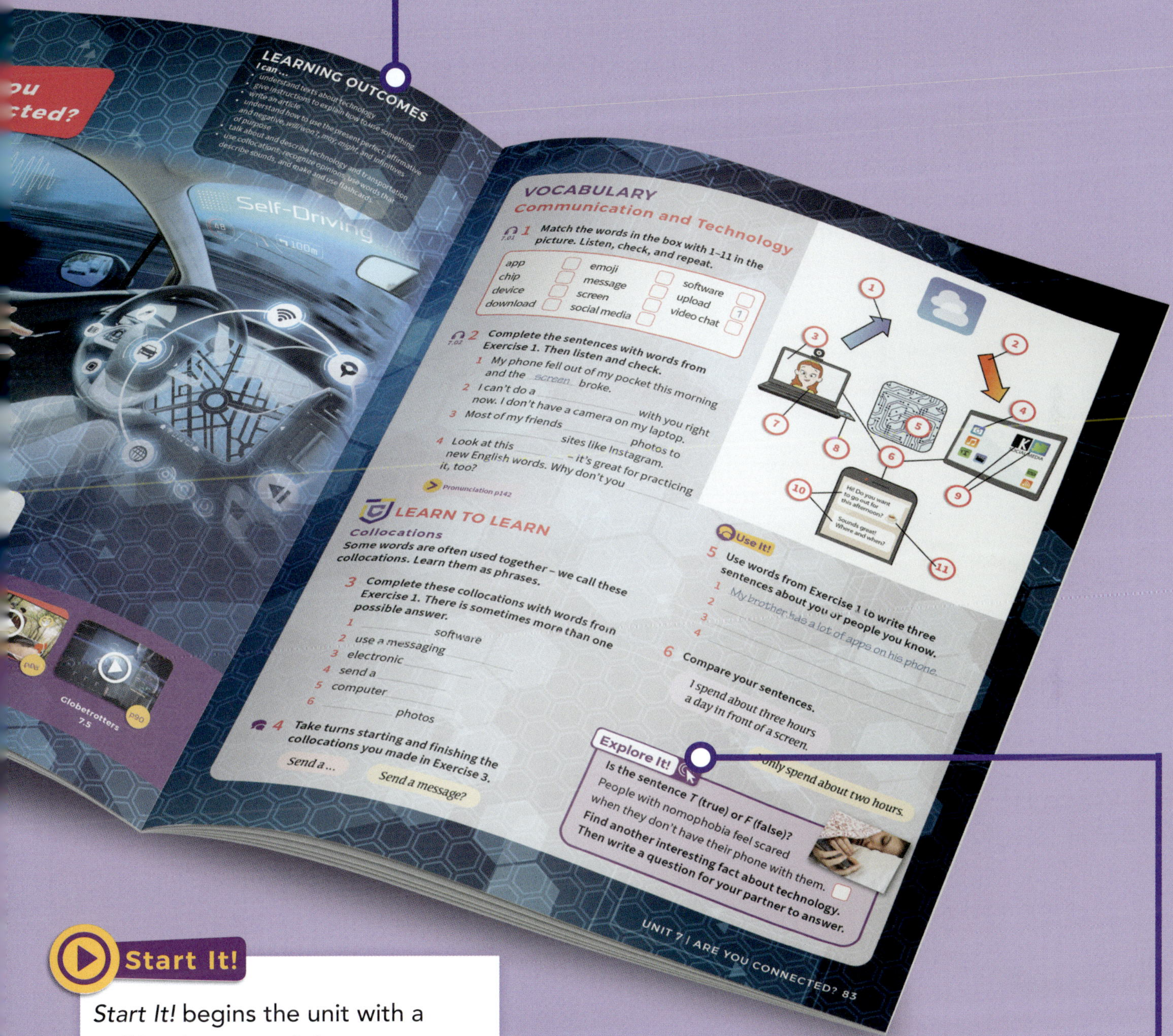

Start It!

Start It! begins the unit with a striking image and documentary video. The questions provoke curiosity, activate prior knowledge, and get students thinking critically.

Explore It!

Explore It! is a fun quiz-type activity to help students develop research skills and extend their learning beyond English.

Use It!

Use It! gets students practicing and producing the target language, often in a personalized way. The activity builds students' confidence by giving them the opportunity to prepare what they want to say before speaking.

EXAM

Exam questions help students practice for international exams.

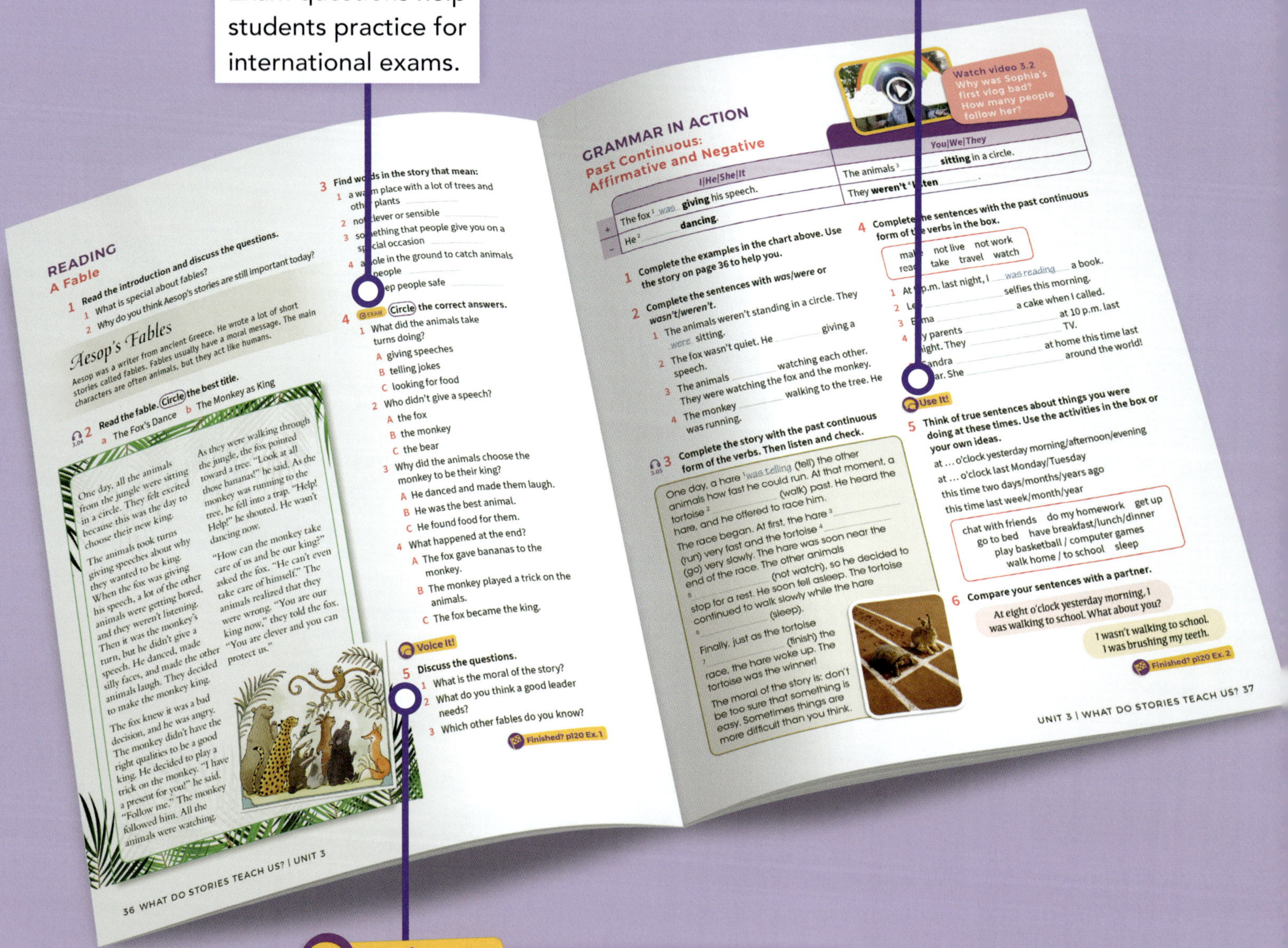

Voice It!

Voice It! is a thought-provoking speaking activity that asks students to give their personal response to a reading or listening text, encouraging critical thinking.

GRAMMAR IN ACTION VIDEOS

These videos show teenagers using the target language in context, in a teen-friendly vlog style, and include an interactive grammar presentation, perfect for flipped classrooms.

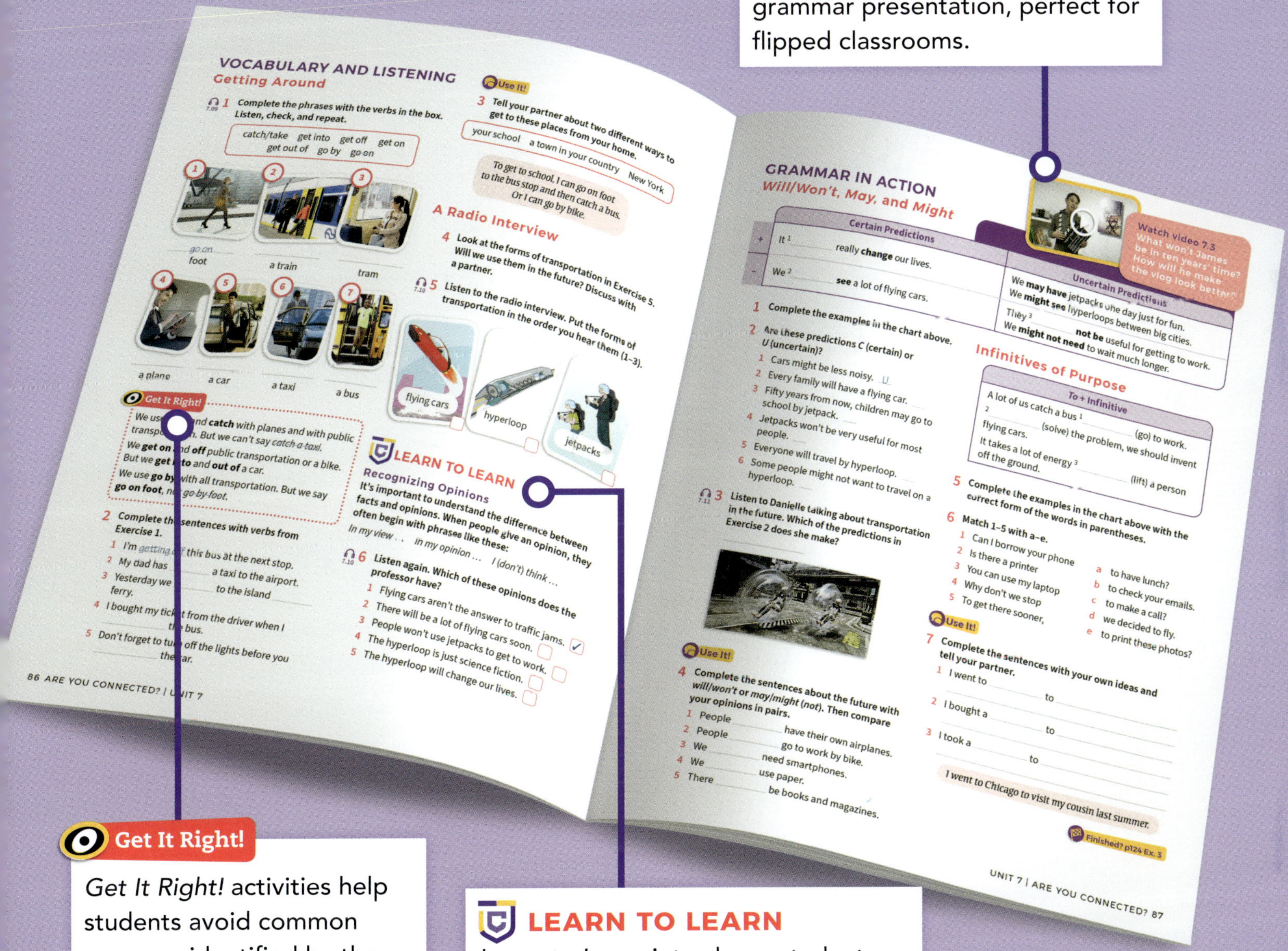

Get It Right!

Get It Right! activities help students avoid common errors as identified by the *Cambridge Learner Corpus.*

LEARN TO LEARN

Learn to Learn introduces students to vital learning strategies and techniques, which will help them become more independent learners, all aligned to the *Cambridge Life Competencies Framework.*

Everyday English

In every unit there's a fun vlog-style video to teach students the meaning, form, and use of the *Everyday English* used in the conversation on the speaking page.

Plan, Write, and Check

The scaffolded approach of the speaking and writing pages builds students' confidence by giving them time to prepare before they speak and write. The *Check* stage encourages self-assessment, a key step toward learner independence.

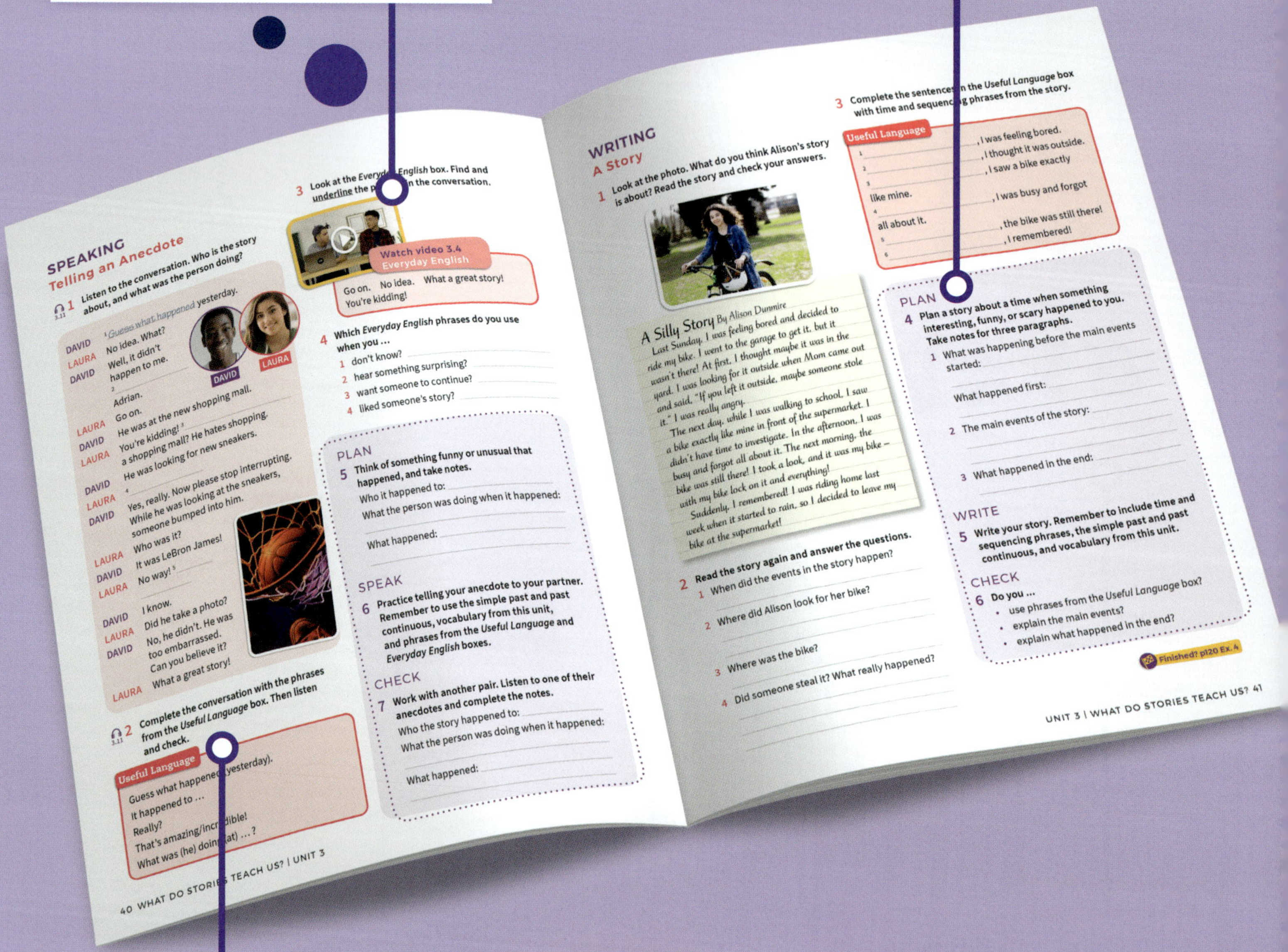

Useful Language

Useful Language boxes appear throughout the unit, highlighting topic-specific target language.

AROUND THE WORLD

The *Around the World* pages, which appear in Units 1, 3, 5, 7, and 9, introduce students to different people and cultures from around the world, encouraging critical thinking and raising cross-cultural awareness.

Globetrotters

These documentaries are thematically linked to either the topic of the unit or the *Around the World* pages. They contextualize the grammar and/or vocabulary of the unit and engage students' interest in the topic.

SHAPE IT!

CULTURE PROJECT

Optional *Culture Projects*, introduced on this page and available to download from the *Teacher's Resource Bank* online, encourage students to use their language skills and topic knowledge in a collaborative way. Extensive teacher's notes for these project are provided in the Project Book.

CLIL PROJECT

The *CLIL Project* pages appear in Units 2, 4, 6, and 8. They encourage students to apply the language and topic knowledge they have gained throughout the unit in an individual or collaborative project.

Plan, Present, and Check

The step-by-step guide helps students work through the project without the need for constant supervision by the teacher, promoting peer-learning and student autonomy.

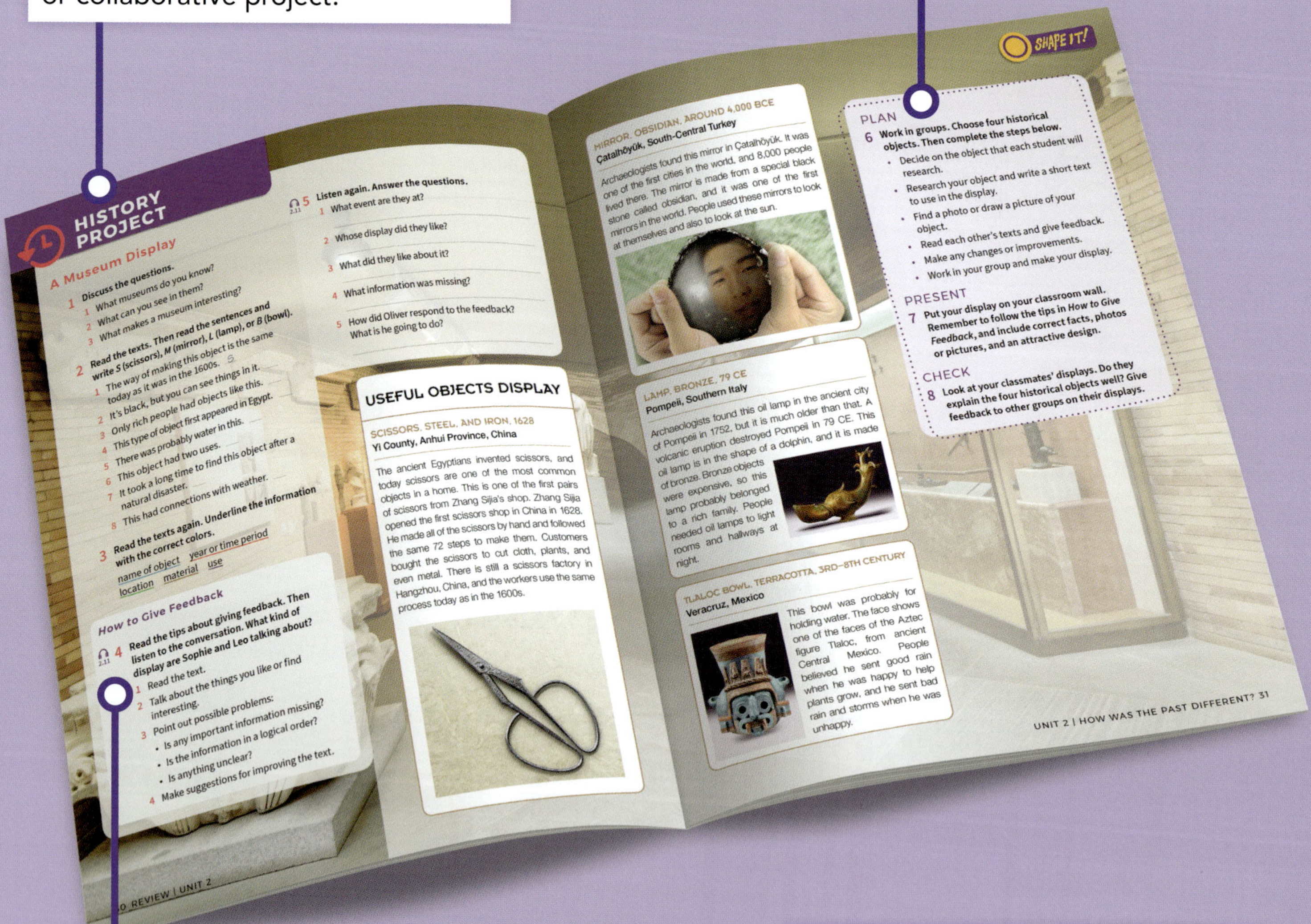

HISTORY PROJECT

A Museum Display

1 Discuss the questions.
1 What museums do you know?
2 What can you see in them?
3 What makes a museum interesting?

2 Read the texts. Then read the sentences and write S (scissors), M (mirror), L (lamp), or B (bowl).
1 The way of making this object is the same today as it was in the 1600s. S
2 It's black, but you can see things in it.
3 Only rich people had objects like this.
4 This type of object first appeared in Egypt.
5 There was probably water in this.
6 This object had two uses.
7 It took a long time to find this object after a natural disaster.
8 This had connections with weather.

3 Read the texts again. Underline the information with the correct colors.
name of object year or time period use location material

How to Give Feedback

4 Read the tips about giving feedback. Then listen to the conversation. What kind of display are Sophie and Leo talking about?
1 Read the text.
2 Talk about the things you like or find interesting.
3 Point out possible problems:
• Is any important information missing?
• Is the information in a logical order?
• Is anything unclear?
4 Make suggestions for improving the text.

5 Listen again. Answer the questions.
1 What event are they at?
2 Whose display did they like?
3 What did they like about it?
4 What information was missing?
5 How did Oliver respond to the feedback? What is he going to do?

USEFUL OBJECTS DISPLAY

SCISSORS, STEEL, AND IRON, 1628
Yi County, Anhui Province, China

The ancient Egyptians invented scissors, and today scissors are one of the most common objects in a home. This is one of the first pairs of scissors from Zhang Sijia's shop. Zhang Sijia opened the first scissors shop in China in 1628. He made all of the scissors by hand and followed the same 72 steps to make them. Customers bought the scissors to cut cloth, plants, and even metal. There is still a scissors factory in Hangzhou, China, and the workers use the same process today as in the 1600s.

MIRROR, OBSIDIAN, AROUND 4,000 BCE
Çatalhöyük, South-Central Turkey

Archaeologists found this mirror in Çatalhöyük. It was one of the first cities in the world, and 8,000 people lived there. The mirror is made from a special black stone called obsidian, and it was one of the first mirrors in the world. People used these mirrors to look at themselves and also to look at the sun.

LAMP, BRONZE, 79 CE
Pompeii, Southern Italy

Archaeologists found this oil lamp in the ancient city of Pompeii in 1752, but it is much older than that. A volcanic eruption destroyed Pompeii in 79 CE. This oil lamp is in the shape of a dolphin, and it is made of bronze. Bronze objects were expensive, so this lamp probably belonged to a rich family. People needed oil lamps to light rooms and hallways at night.

TLALOC BOWL, TERRACOTTA, 3RD–8TH CENTURY
Veracruz, Mexico

This bowl was probably for holding water. The face shows one of the faces of the Aztec figure Tlaloc, from ancient Central Mexico. People believed he sent good rain when he was happy to help plants grow, and he sent bad rain and storms when he was unhappy.

SHAPE IT!

PLAN
6 Work in groups. Choose four historical objects. Then complete the steps below.
• Decide on the object that each student will research.
• Research your object and write a short text to use in the display.
• Find a photo or draw a picture of your object.
• Read each other's texts and give feedback.
• Make any changes or improvements.
• Work in your group and make your display.

PRESENT
7 Put your display on your classroom wall. Remember to follow the tips in *How to Give Feedback*, and include correct facts, photos or pictures, and an attractive design.

CHECK
8 Look at your classmates' displays. Do they explain the four historical objects well? Give feedback to other groups on their displays.

30 REVIEW | UNIT 2

UNIT 2 | HOW WAS THE PAST DIFFERENT? 31

How to ...

These practical tips help students complete the project by raising their awareness of the particular skills required to carry it out.

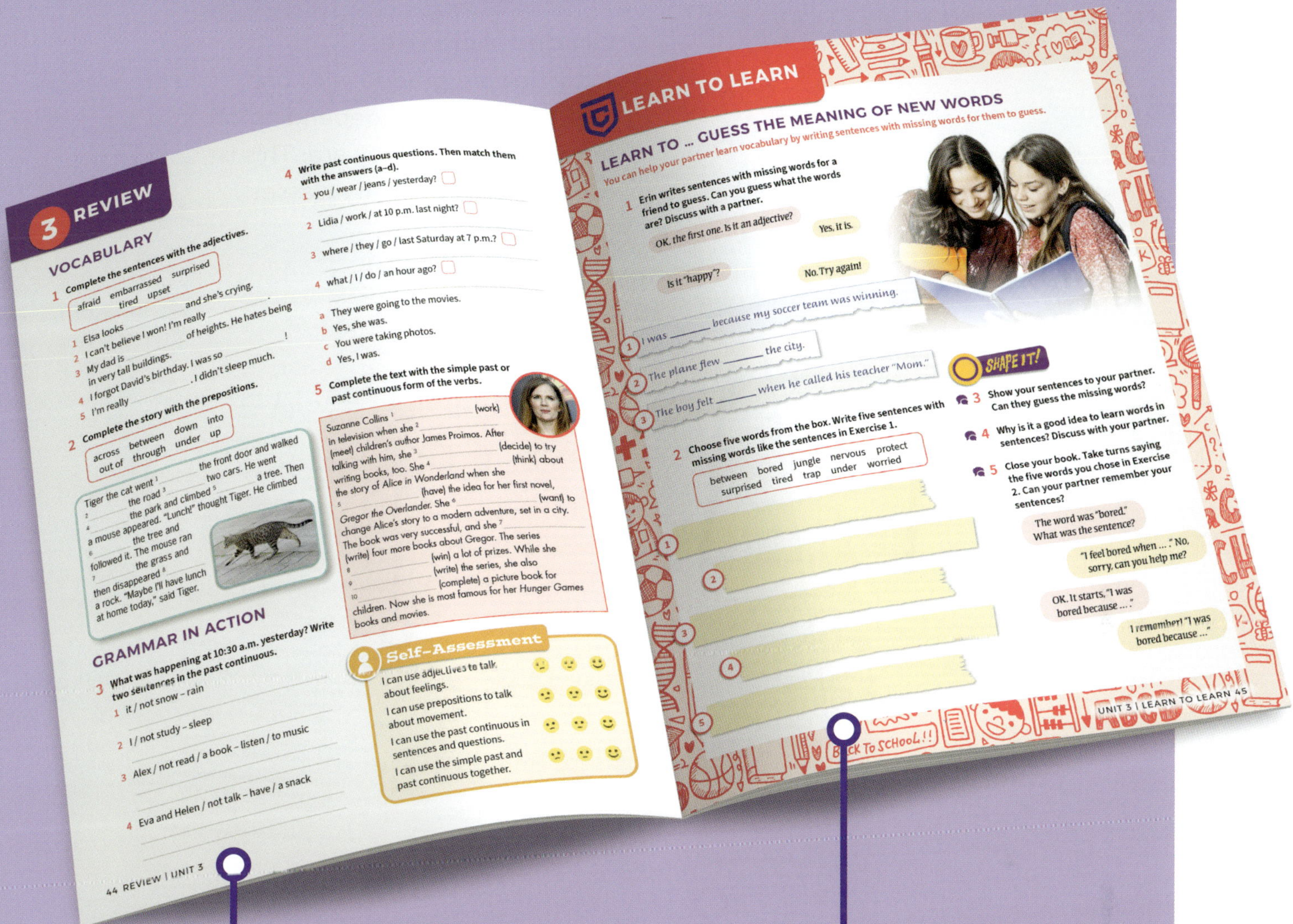

REVIEW

These useful pages review the language from the unit and include a self-assessment task, encouraging students' self-awareness.

LEARN TO LEARN

The *Learn to Learn* pages focus on developing core areas from the *Cambridge Life Competencies Framework*. Students have the opportunity to "shape" their learning by putting the new skill into practice.

Course Components

Workbook

The Workbook offers extra practice of the language and skills covered in the Student's Book. It also includes a special exam preparation feature and a *Language Bank*.

Graded Activities

Activities are graded with one, two, or three stars depending on how challenging they are. This is great for mixed-ability classes.

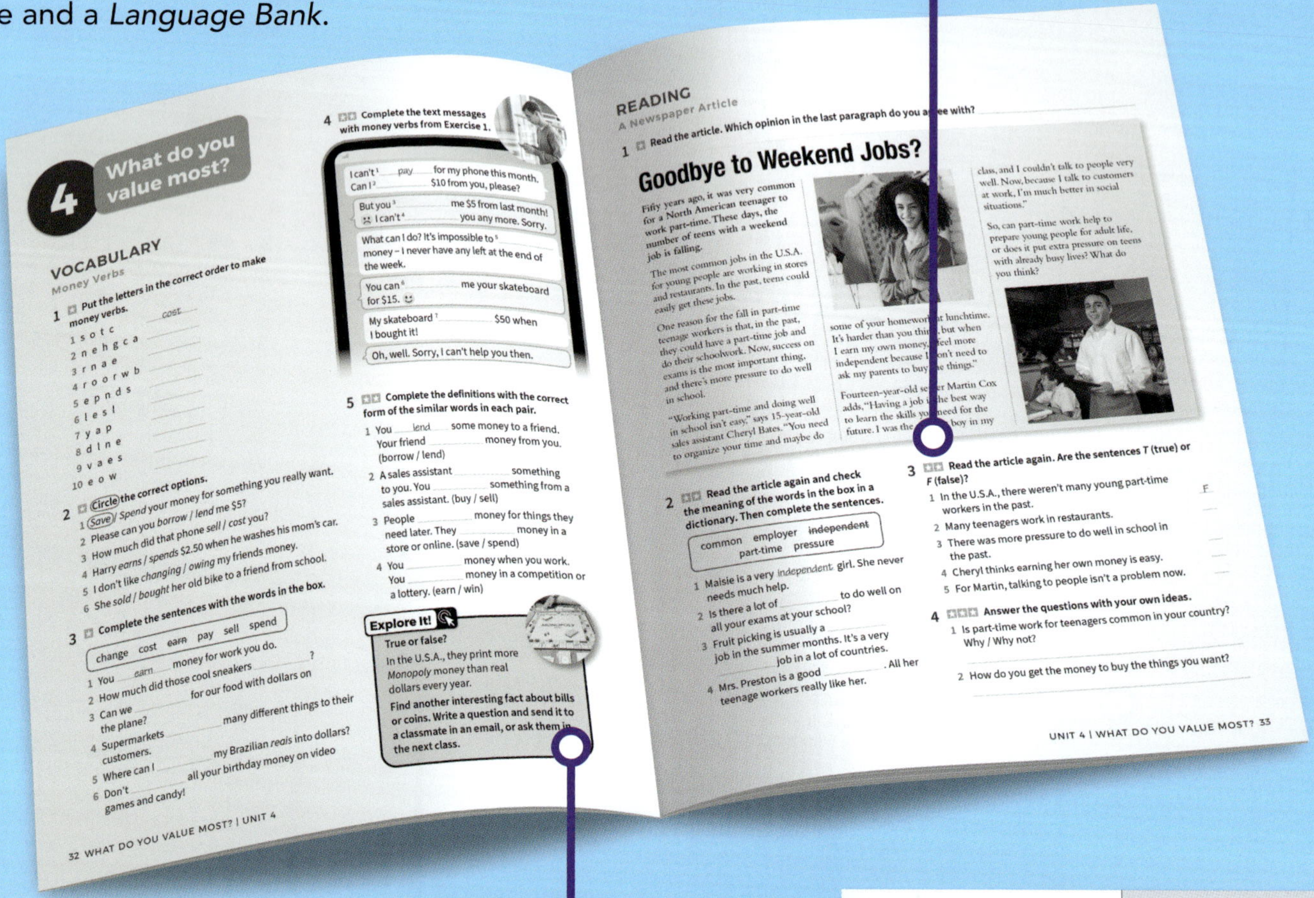

4 What do you value most?

VOCABULARY
Money Verbs

1 ☐ Put the letters in the correct order to make money verbs.
1 s o t c ___cost___
2 n e h g c a ______
3 r n a e ______
4 r o o r w b ______
5 e p n d s ______
6 l e s l ______
7 y a p ______
8 d l n e ______
9 v a e s ______
10 e o w ______

2 ☐ Circle the correct options.
1 (Save) / Spend your money for something you really want.
2 Please can you *borrow / lend* me $5?
3 How much did that phone *sell / cost* you?
4 Harry *earns / spends* $2.50 when he washes his mom's car.
5 I don't like *changing / owing* my friends money.
6 She *sold / bought* her old bike to a friend from school.

3 ☐ Complete the sentences with the words in the box.

change cost ~~earn~~ pay sell spend

1 You ___earn___ money for work you do.
2 How much did those cool sneakers ______?
3 Can we ______ for our food with dollars on the plane?
4 Supermarkets ______ many different things to their customers.
5 Where can I ______ my Brazilian *reais* into dollars?
6 Don't ______ all your birthday money on video games and candy!

4 ☐☐ Complete the text messages with money verbs from Exercise 1.

I can't [1] ___pay___ for my phone this month. Can I [2] ______ $10 from you, please?
But you [3] ______ me $5 from last month! I can't [4] ______ you any more. Sorry.
What can I do? It's impossible to [5] ______ money – I never have any left at the end of the week.
You can [6] ______ me your skateboard for $15.
My skateboard [7] ______ $50 when I bought it!
Oh, well. Sorry, I can't help you then.

5 ☐☐ Complete the definitions with the correct form of the similar words in each pair.
1 You ___lend___ some money to a friend. Your friend ______ money from you. (borrow / lend)
2 A sales assistant ______ something to you. You ______ something from a sales assistant. (buy / sell)
3 People ______ money for things they need later. They ______ money in a store or online. (save / spend)
4 You ______ money when you work. You ______ money in a competition or a lottery. (earn / win)

Explore It!
True or false?
In the U.S.A., they print more *Monopoly* money than real dollars every year.
Find another interesting fact about bills or coins. Write a question and send it to a classmate in an email, or ask them in the next class.

32 WHAT DO YOU VALUE MOST? | UNIT 4

READING
A Newspaper Article

1 ☐ Read the article. Which opinion in the last paragraph do you agree with? ______

Goodbye to Weekend Jobs?

Fifty years ago, it was very common for a North American teenager to work part-time. These days, the number of teens with a weekend job is falling.

The most common jobs in the U.S.A. for young people are working in stores and restaurants. In the past, teens could easily get these jobs.

One reason for the fall in part-time teenage workers is that, in the past, they could have a part-time job and do their schoolwork. Now, success on exams is the most important thing, and there's more pressure to do well in school.

"Working part-time and doing well in school isn't easy," says 15-year-old sales assistant Cheryl Bates. "You need to organize your time and maybe do some of your homework at lunchtime. It's harder than you think, but when I earn my own money, I feel more independent because I don't need to ask my parents to buy the things."

Fourteen-year-old server Martin Cox adds, "Having a job is the best way to learn the skills you need for the future. I was the ... boy in my class, and I couldn't talk to people very well. Now, because I talk to customers at work, I'm much better in social situations."

So, can part-time work help to prepare young people for adult life, or does it put extra pressure on teens with already busy lives? What do you think?

2 ☐☐ Read the article again and check the meaning of the words in the box in a dictionary. Then complete the sentences.

common employer ~~independent~~ part-time pressure

1 Maisie is a very ___independent___ girl. She never needs much help.
2 Is there a lot of ______ to do well on all your exams at your school?
3 Fruit picking is usually a ______ job in the summer months. It's a very ______ job in a lot of countries.
4 Mrs. Preston is a good ______. All her teenage workers really like her.

3 ☐☐ Read the article again. Are the sentences *T* (true) or *F* (false)?
1 In the U.S.A., there weren't many young part-time workers in the past. ___F___
2 Many teenagers work in restaurants. ______
3 There was more pressure to do well in school in the past. ______
4 Cheryl thinks earning her own money is easy. ______
5 For Martin, talking to people isn't a problem now. ______

4 ☐☐☐ Answer the questions with your own ideas.
1 Is part-time work for teenagers common in your country? Why / Why not?
2 How do you get the money to buy the things you want?

UNIT 4 | WHAT DO YOU VALUE MOST? 33

Explore It!

The *Explore It!* feature extends learning beyond the classroom and helps students develop research skills that are vital for learner independence.

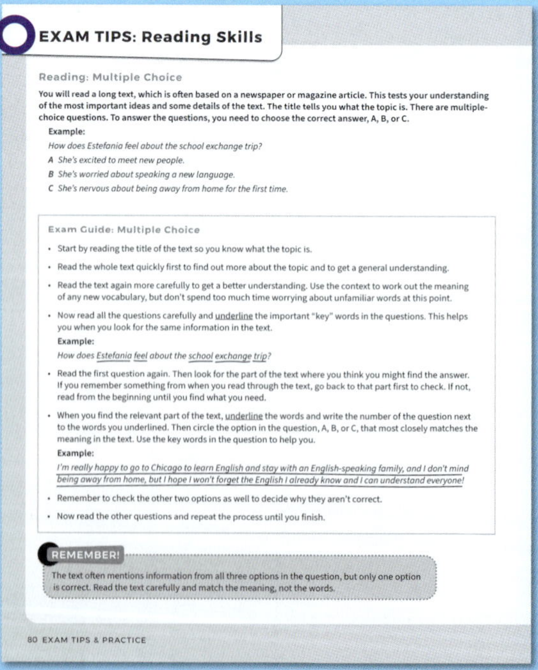

EXAM TIPS: Reading Skills

Reading: Multiple Choice

You will read a long text, which is often based on a newspaper or magazine article. This tests your understanding of the most important ideas and some details of the text. The title tells you what the topic is. There are multiple-choice questions. To answer the questions, you need to choose the correct answer, A, B, or C.

Example:
How does Estefania feel about the school exchange trip?
A She's excited to meet new people.
B She's worried about speaking a new language.
C She's nervous about being away from home for the first time.

Exam Guide: Multiple Choice

- Start by reading the title of the text so you know what the topic is.
- Read the whole text quickly first to find out more about the topic and to get a general understanding.
- Read the text again more carefully to get a better understanding. Use the context to work out the meaning of any new vocabulary, but don't spend too much time worrying about unfamiliar words at this point.
- Now read all the questions carefully and underline the important "key" words in the questions. This helps you when you look for the same information in the text.
  Example:
  How does Estefania feel about the school exchange trip?
- Read the first question again. Then look for the part of the text where you think you might find the answer. If you remember something from when you read through the text, go back to that part first to check. If not, read from the beginning until you find what you need.
- When you find the relevant part of the text, underline the words and write the number of the question next to the words you underlined. Then circle the option in the question, A, B, or C, that most closely matches the meaning in the text. Use the key words in the question to help you.
  Example:
  I'm really happy to go to Chicago to learn English and stay with an English-speaking family, and I don't mind being away from home, but I hope I won't forget the English I already know and I can understand everyone!
- Remember to check the other two options as well to decide why they aren't correct.
- Now read the other questions and repeat the process until you finish.

REMEMBER!
The text often mentions information from all three options in the question, but only one option is correct. Read the text carefully and match the meaning, not the words.

80 EXAM TIPS & PRACTICE

EXAM TIPS

The exam preparation pages at the end of the Workbook provide useful tips and practice to help students prepare for international exams.

SHAPE IT! Digital Resource Pack

All your digital tools together in one place!

With *Shape It!* everything you need is at your fingertips, including *Presentation Plus*, audio and video, additional practice, games, *Test Generator*, and an innovative digital collaboration space for students.

Presentation Plus

- Student's Book and Workbook with interactive exercises
- games
- accessible online and offline

Teacher's Resource Bank

- The online *Teacher's Resource Bank* has culture projects, graded grammar and vocabulary practice worksheets, video worksheets, communication worksheets, writing template worksheets, extra speaking activities, and more!
- *The Test Generator* includes unit tests, progress tests, and end-of-year tests, and more.

Digital Collaboration Space

- Students can collaborate digitally through *Collaboration Plus*, where teachers can assign, track, and assess students' work.
- Students can also archive and share their work inside and outside the classroom.

Practice Extra

- mobile-friendly content on Cambridge One
- bite-sized learning activities
- skills-based video tasks
- motivational performance tracking

For the most up-to-date information on *Shape It!'s* Digital Resource Pack, visit www.cambridge.org/shapeit or scan the QR code to the right.

How to Use the Teacher's Book

Class Challenge
Get students interested in the topic and extend their learning beyond language by using this quiz-style question.

Unit Aims
Unit aims are clearly shown at the start of every unit.

Unit 5 What is your dream house?
Lesson Aim: I can talk about unusual homes.

Teacher Support Hub ppxxxiv–xxxv

Start It!

Unit Quiz

1 In pairs, Student A opens the book, looks at the photo, and describes it to their partner. They look at the photo together and discuss if they would like to live there and why.

2 Describe your home to students. Say if it's an apartment, how big it is, how many rooms it has, if it's new or old, and if you like it and why. Invite questions. Then ask students to describe their own home in pairs.

3 & 4 Allow students to check in pairs after watching **video 5.1** the first time, and then play it again. Elicit the answers. Then show the video a third time without volume, and elicit vocabulary to describe the houses that it shows.

Video Comprehension Questions

Class Challenge
The most isolated home in the world is on an island in the UK / **Iceland** / Japan.

Flipped Class
Prepare for **Explore It!** (p59). Students research an interesting fact about furniture.

Unit Aims
Skills
I can …
- understand a text about different homes p60
- describe a photograph p64
- write a description of a house p65
- understand a text about living in igloos pp66–67

Language
I can …
- talk about furniture p59
- understand how to use (not) as + adjective + as and (not) + adjective + enough p61
- talk about household chores p62
- understand how to use have to and don't have to p63

Learn to Learn
I can …
- use spidergrams p59
- answer multiple-choice questions p62
- understand word families p67
- use a memory journey p69

Extra Resources
- Finished? Student's Book p122
- Vocabulary Bank, Student's Book p132
- Workbook pp40–47
- Grammar Reference and Practice, Workbook pp96–97
- Teacher Support Hub, Teacher's Book ppxxxiv–xl

Digital Resource Pack
(on Cambridge One)
- Teacher's Resource Bank for word lists, differentiated worksheets, Culture Projects, and many other extra resources
- Practice Extra, Presentation Plus, Test Generator, and Digital Collaboration Space

T58 What is your dream house? | Unit 5

5 What is your dream house?

Start It!
1 Look at the photo. Would you like to live in this house?
2 Before you watch, where do you live?
3 Why did people build homes in mountains? Watch and check.
4 What other unusual homes are there?

They felt safe. The caves stayed dry in the winter and cold in the summer.

Watch video 5.1 · Grammar in Action 5.2 · Grammar in Action 5.3 · Everyday English 5.4 · Globetrotters 5.5

58 WHAT IS YOUR DREAM HOUSE? | UNIT 5

Flipped Class
Discover useful ideas for activities that students could do at home to consolidate in-class learning and encourage independent study.

Extra Resources
See at a glance all the extra resources available for teachers to use with this unit.

Digital Resource Pack
The digital icon indicates when extra support or resources are available online.

Warmer
Use these engaging ideas to introduce students to the topic of the unit and activate their prior knowledge.

Pronunciation
Find the pronunciation for all target vocabulary easily.

Graded Activities
Some activities are graded with one or three stars. One-star activities show ideas for providing more support to students, and three-star activities show ideas for providing extra challenge – great for mixed-ability classes!

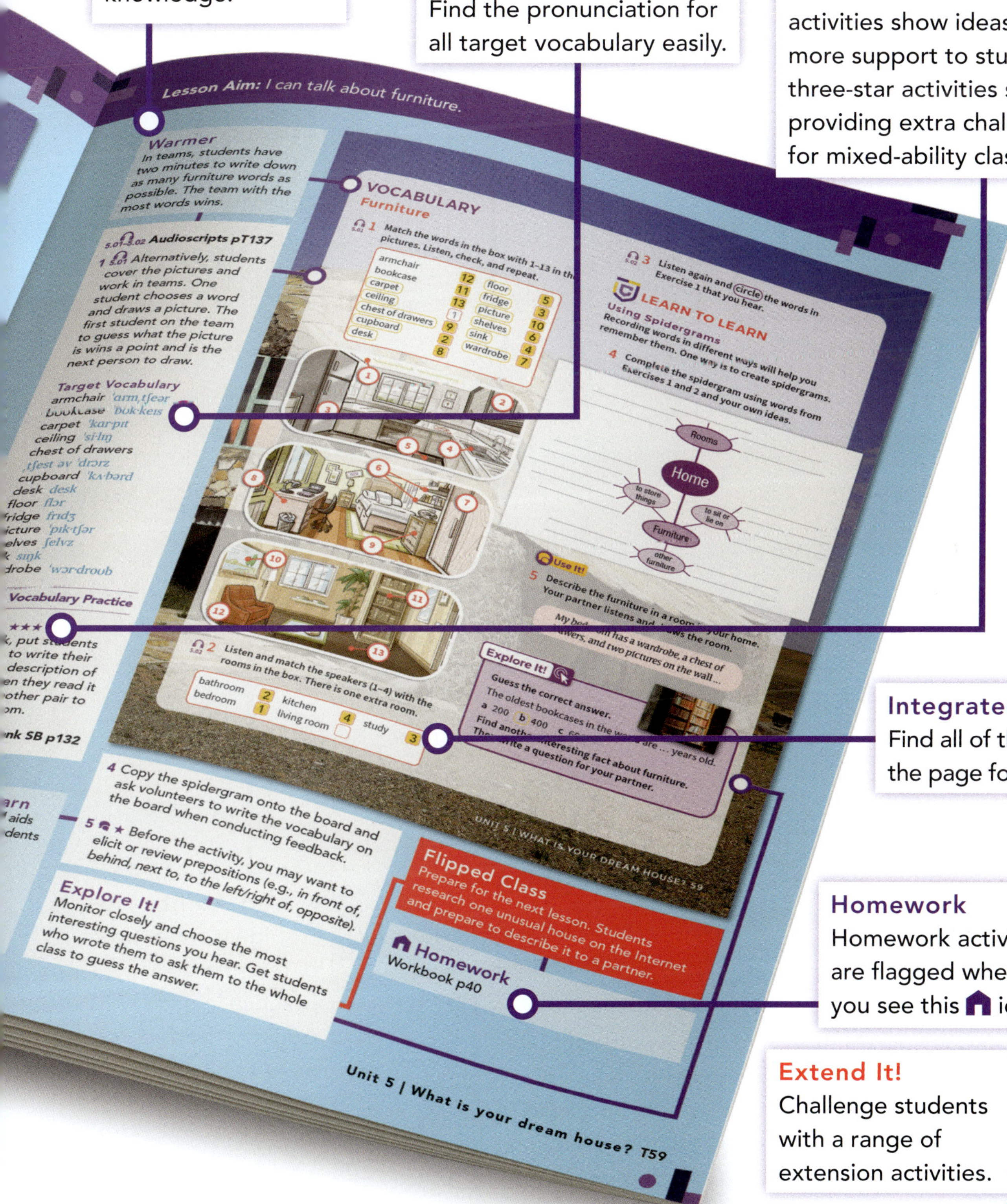

Integrated Answers
Find all of the answers on the page for quick access.

Homework
Homework activities are flagged wherever you see this icon.

Extend It!
Challenge students with a range of extension activities.

How to Use The Project Book

Project Pages
See where you can find the projects. The *CLIL Projects* are in the Student's Book. The *Culture Projects* are briefly introduced in the Student's Book and available as downloadable PDFs in the *Teacher's Resource Bank*.

Learning Outcomes
Refer to learning outcomes at a glance, as well as the skills students will develop, and the resources and evaluation tools you may wish to use.

Student Roles
Manage student roles and responsibilities.

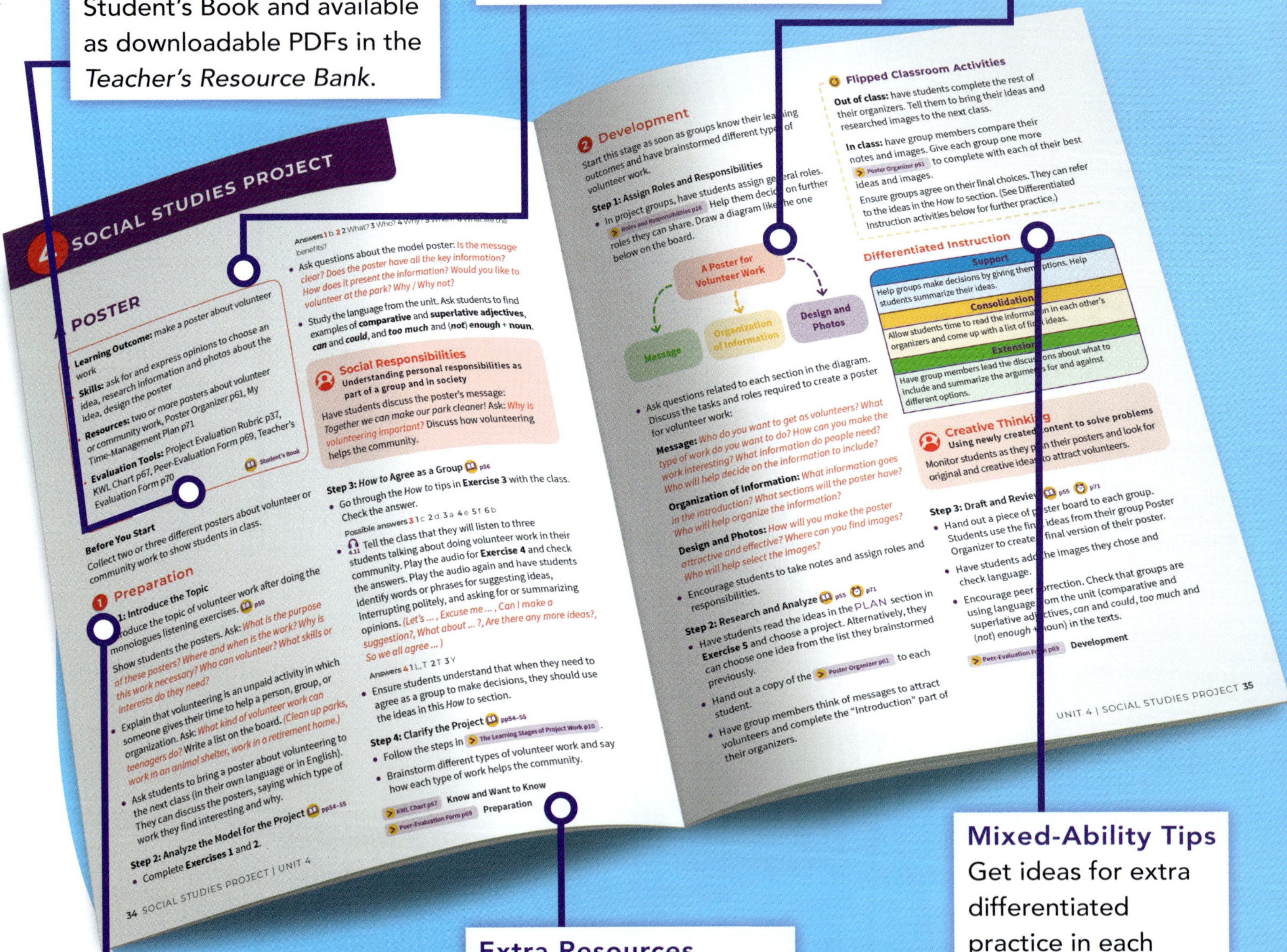

Mixed-Ability Tips
Get ideas for extra differentiated practice in each project – perfect for mixed abilities.

Extra Resources
Find useful photocopiable resources, such as easy-to-use graphic organizers, peer evaluation forms, and a learning diary.

Project Work Stages
Navigate the three stages of project work using this step-by-step guide.

Presentation Ideas
A bank of ideas for the last stage of project work.

Evaluation Guidelines
See clear guidelines for identifying and assessing student performance.

Competency Development
Extensive support for developing students' life competencies, aligned to the *Cambridge Life Competencies Framework*.

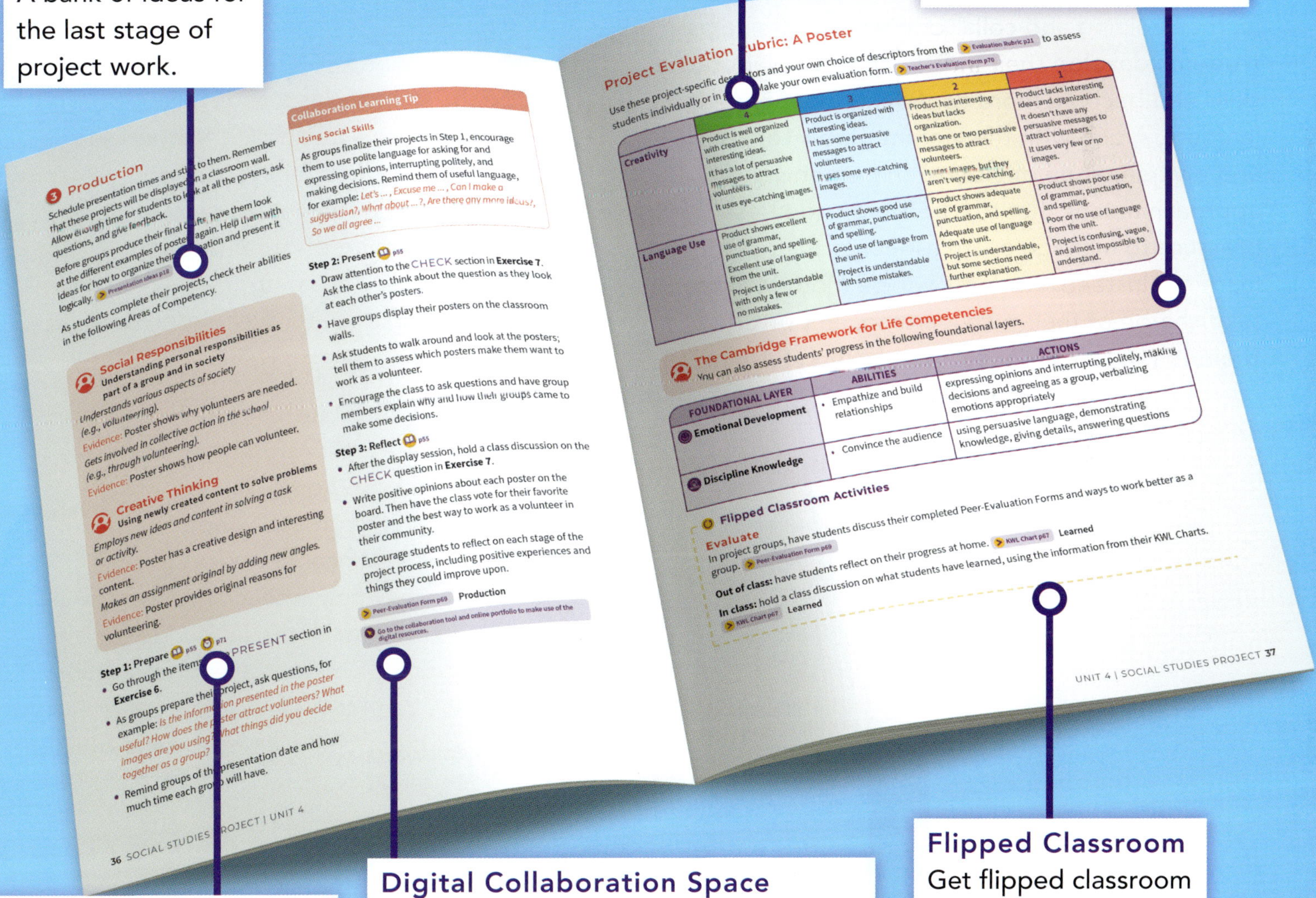

My Time Management Plan
This photocopiable template, which can be found at the back of the Project Book, helps you organize projects efficiently.

Digital Collaboration Space
Students can work together on their projects in the digital collaboration space, and teachers can track and assess their work. Students can also share and comment on each other's work via their digital portfolio.

Flipped Classroom
Get flipped classroom ideas for carrying out the activities both in and out of class.

Course Research and Rationale

We at Cambridge University Press have an unparalleled reputation for English Language courses underpinned by the latest language and pedagogical research. Here are some insights into how *Shape It!* is informed by this, and by feedback from teachers and learners from around the world.

Shape It! is designed to help students take ownership of their learning. The combination of learner training and collaborative projects helps students develop their individual and collaborative skills and become more confident, independent learners. Along with the vibrant global topics and diverse range of videos, this empowering approach means that teachers are under less pressure to manage every aspect of their students' learning. Instead, students will be motivated to take charge of their own learning, empowering them to prepare for their own exciting future.

You spoke. We listened.

I want my students to feel that they belong to the world; that they are global citizens.
Itana, Brazil

Global Cultural Topics

Shape It! includes a variety of global topics, with a dedicated *Around the World* page in every other unit. This helps students broaden their understanding of other people and places, preparing them for life in a diverse, multicultural environment.

Learners of English now outnumber speakers of English as a first language. Students are therefore far more likely to use English to communicate with people whose first language is not English. This has significant implications for traditional English teaching because an understanding of the language is now only part of successful communication, and we cannot underestimate the role of cross-cultural understanding in communication.

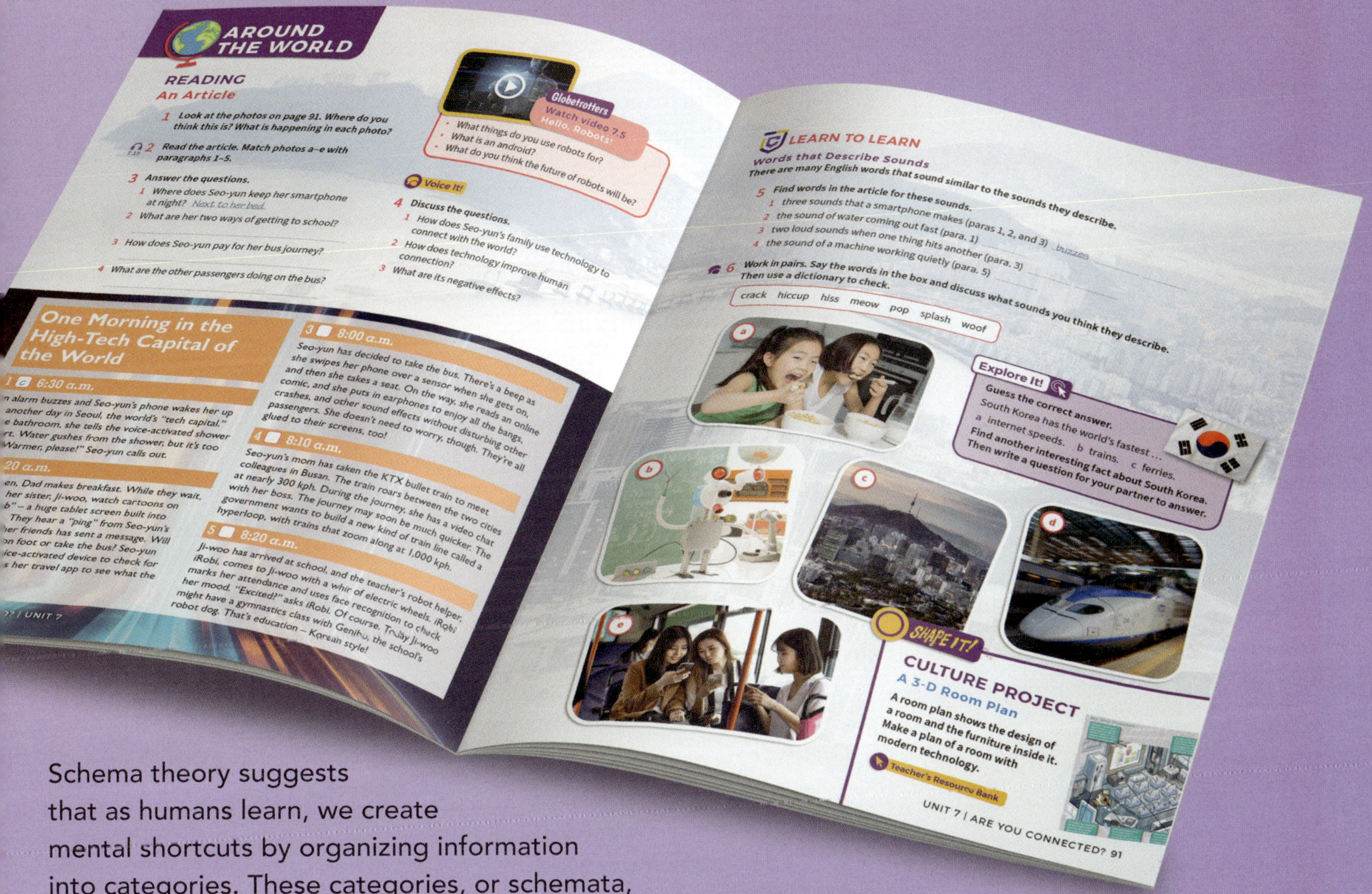

Schema theory suggests that as humans learn, we create mental shortcuts by organizing information into categories. These categories, or schemata, enable our brains to deal with most "typical" scenarios without too much effort, since we can base our responses on our expectations. Students who are told they are going to hear a conversation at an airport can reasonably expect to hear certain language: flight numbers, boarding times, and ticket types. Their expectations about these scenarios help them listen more effectively.

However, schemata can also work against a student's ability to understand. Their expectations are heavily influenced by their culture.

Teachers will be aware that their students are already interacting with globalized media. From watching international TV shows to playing online video games, teenagers are already encountering English being used by both native and non-native speakers from different cultural and social backgrounds. This interconnectedness is only going to increase, so it is vital that students develop the skills they need to communicate effectively.

That's why *Shape It!* has a global, cultural focus, supported by documentaries in every unit, all of which encourage students to think about the differences between their culture and other cultures.

You spoke. We listened.

I want my students to become more independent learners.
Maria, Spain

Learn to Learn

When students reach secondary school, they are expected to start taking more and more responsibility for their own learning, and once they complete secondary school, they should have acquired the ability to learn independently. The rapid rate of technological advance means that many jobs in the near future may become automated. To give the next generation the best chance in life, they need to be able to acquire new skills and knowledge throughout their lives, making them adaptable to whatever the future holds.

Yet teachers often find that their students do not know how to learn and lack basic learning techniques like taking notes, categorizing information, and assessing their strengths and weaknesses, particularly in the first year of secondary school. To address this, the *Learn to Learn* feature appears throughout each unit, extended by a dedicated full page at the end of every unit.

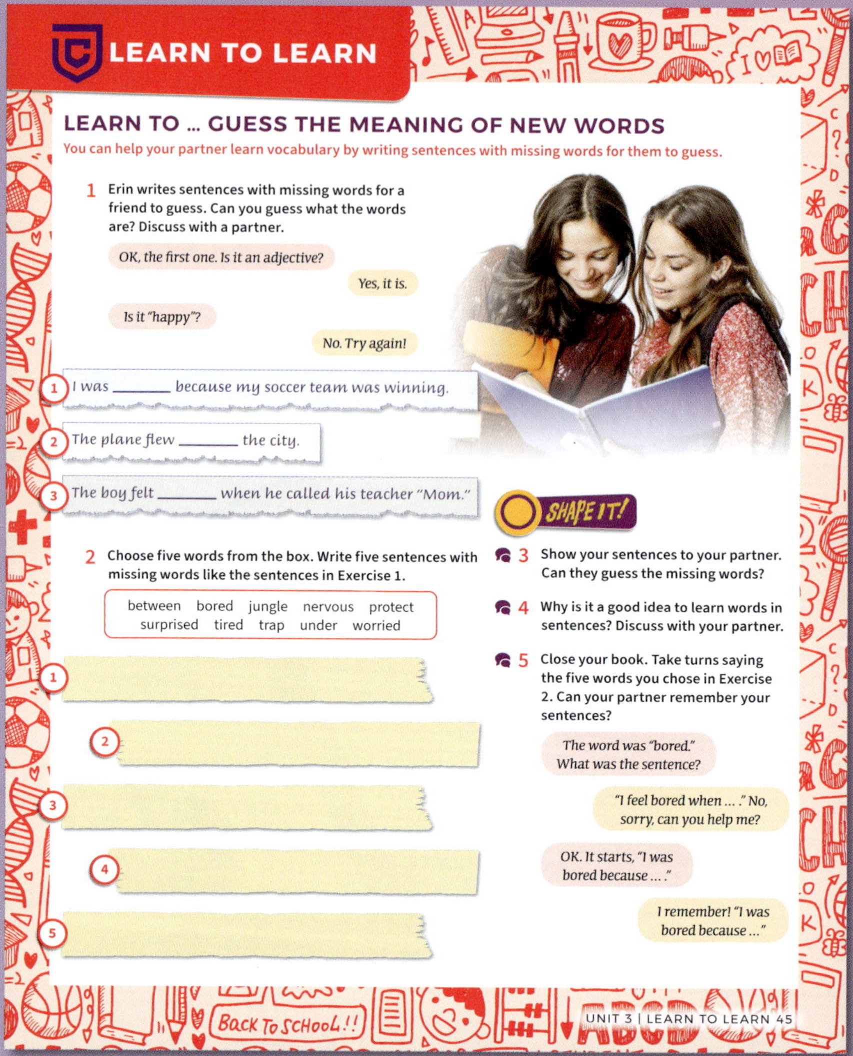

LEARN TO LEARN

LEARN TO ... GUESS THE MEANING OF NEW WORDS

You can help your partner learn vocabulary by writing sentences with missing words for them to guess.

1 Erin writes sentences with missing words for a friend to guess. Can you guess what the words are? Discuss with a partner.

OK, the first one. Is it an adjective?

Yes, it is.

Is it "happy"?

No. Try again!

1 I was ______ because my soccer team was winning.

2 The plane flew ______ the city.

3 The boy felt ______ when he called his teacher "Mom."

2 Choose five words from the box. Write five sentences with missing words like the sentences in Exercise 1.

between bored jungle nervous protect surprised tired trap under worried

1

2

3

4

5

SHAPE IT!

3 Show your sentences to your partner. Can they guess the missing words?

4 Why is it a good idea to learn words in sentences? Discuss with your partner.

5 Close your book. Take turns saying the five words you chose in Exercise 2. Can your partner remember your sentences?

The word was "bored." What was the sentence?

"I feel bored when ... ." No, sorry, can you help me?

OK. It starts, "I was bored because ... ."

I remember! "I was bored because ..."

BACK TO SCHOOL!!

UNIT 3 | LEARN TO LEARN 45

The *Learn to Learn* sections cover three broad areas of learner training:

1 practical skills for participating in learning
2 taking control of own learning
3 reflecting on and evaluating own learning success

After each *Learn to Learn* tip, students practice the techniques immediately in an activity. This helps students incorporate these into their learning routine.

You spoke. We listened.

> I'd like to do project work with my students, but it can be too time-consuming to plan.
> *Merve, Turkey*

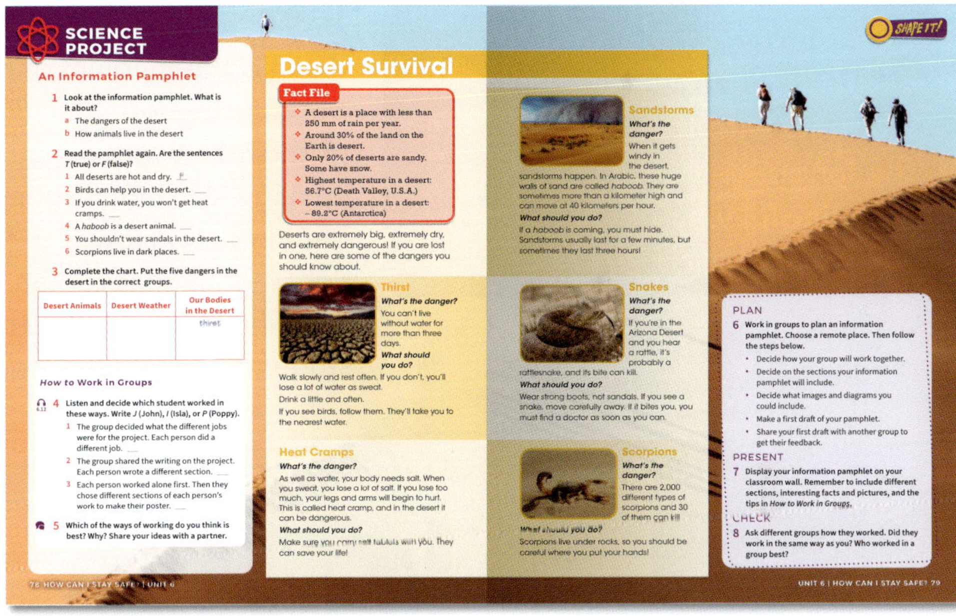

Project Work

Collaboration is an effective way of empowering students. *Shape It!* includes a project in every other unit of the Student's Book with more available in the online *Teacher's Resource Bank*, as well as an accompanying Project Book, which offers extra support and practical tips for teachers. In addition, students can work together on their projects in the digital collaboration space, and teachers can track and assess their work there.

Project work allows students to …

- build collaborative skills, such as communication, teamwork, and leadership.
- acquire practical, transferable skills associated with different types of projects, like doing research and making presentations.
- choose and explore areas that they are interested in, thereby increasing their motivation.
- engage with real-world issues, as projects are often interdisciplinary and based on real-world scenarios.

However, preparing project work can be very time-consuming for teachers. That's why *Shape It!*'s projects are aligned to the topic of the unit, with a step-by step guide and practical tips for students, plus a full teacher's guide in the Project Book. This is project work made simple!

In response to teacher feedback, the projects in the Student's Book have a cross-curricular approach, covering topic areas like science, history, social studies, and technology, giving students the opportunity to improve their subject knowledge while exploring a wide variety of topics in English. The *Around the World* pages also have an optional double-page project available online, which allows students to further explore the cultural theme of the unit.

All of the projects students will encounter develop competencies from the *Cambridge Life Competencies Framework*.

You spoke. We listened.

> I want a variety of videos that will help me to engage my students with the topic and see the language being used in a meaningful way.
> *Antonio, Mexico*

Teen-Friendly Videos

Video is the medium of communication in the modern world, with more than 300 hours of video being uploaded to YouTube every minute! So it is not surprising that teenage learners respond well to video content being used in class. However, finding appropriate videos at the right language level can be difficult for teachers. That's why *Shape It!* includes four to five videos per unit so that students can see the language in action.

Documentary Videos

Documentaries appear at the beginning of every unit. They get students thinking about the unit topic and activate any prior knowledge and language.

Globetrotters documentaries also appear on the *Around the World* pages in every other unit. These contextualize the grammar and vocabulary of the unit and are linked to the topic of the reading.

Teachers can use the video lesson in the downloadable video worksheets in the *Teacher's Resource Bank.*

Grammar in Action Videos

Grammar in Action videos appear on every grammar page of the unit. These fun vlogs feature teenagers using the target language in context and an animated presentation of the grammar. They are designed to make teaching and learning grammar more meaningful, and they give the teacher the option of using a flipped classroom model by getting students to watch the video before class.

Teachers can also use the downloadable video worksheets in the *Teacher's Resource Bank.*

Everyday English Videos

Everyday English videos appear on the speaking pages. Teachers often find that students love learning the latest colloquial words and phrases in English, and these videos are a great way of presenting them. They feature teenagers using authentic English from the speaking dialogue and give students the chance to try out these phrases for themselves.

You spoke. We listened.

I need resources and support to manage students of different levels in the same class.
Andrés, Ecuador

Mixed-Ability Support

The average English class will have students with a variety of different language abilities, not to mention different interests, levels of motivation, and learning preferences. In *Shape It!* there is extensive support for teachers with mixed-ability classes, including the following:

- On the Student's Book page, *Finished?* icons direct fast finishers to fun extra practice at the back of the book to ensure all students are challenged.

3 ★★ **Read the text again. Are the sentences *T* (true) or *F* (false)?**

1 Forrest Fenn hid expensive jewelry and gold in a box. T
2 He hid the box because he doesn't want people to find it. ___
3 The boys' parents didn't go with them. ___
4 Fenn's clues are on the Internet. ___
5 The boys can't get home because of the weather. ___
6 Jack enjoyed hunting for treasure. ___

4 ★★★ **Answer the questions with your own ideas.**

1 What outdoor activities do you do?
____
2 Do you like the idea of this treasure hunt? Why / Why not?
____

- Workbook activities are graded one, two, or three stars to indicate their difficulty level. This means that students can start at the easiest level and move onto more difficult activities when ready. Alternatively, teachers can assign different activities for different students according to their abilities.
- *Teacher's Book* notes provide suggestions for grading activities to different students' abilities.
- *Project Book* teacher's notes provide specific suggestions for differentiated instruction. These cater to students who need more support, as well as students who would benefit from more of a challenge.

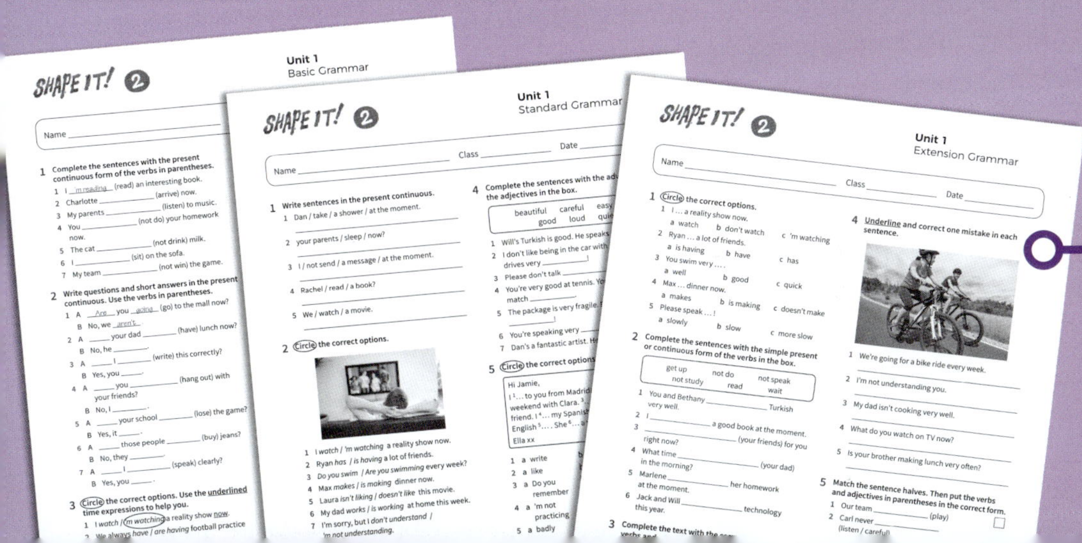

- Graded grammar and vocabulary worksheets at three different levels can be found in the online *Teacher's Resource Bank.*

SHAPE IT! and the Cambridge Life Competencies Framework

Although *Shape It!* focuses on both the *Learning to Learn* and the *Collaboration* competencies in the *Cambridge Life Competencies Framework*, all of the six Life Competencies are explored throughout the course.

The chart on the following page shows, at a glance, where you can find an activity that concentrates on a particular Core Area. There is also a link below that chart where you can download the comprehensive guide to how each level of *Shape It!* correlates to the *Framework*.

Here are a few examples of how activities can help your students develop particular Can Do Statements.

Competency: Collaboration
Core Area: Managing the sharing of tasks in a project
Can Do Statement: Works with others to plan and execute class projects.
In this exercise, students need to follow steps together to plan, present, and reflect on their project.

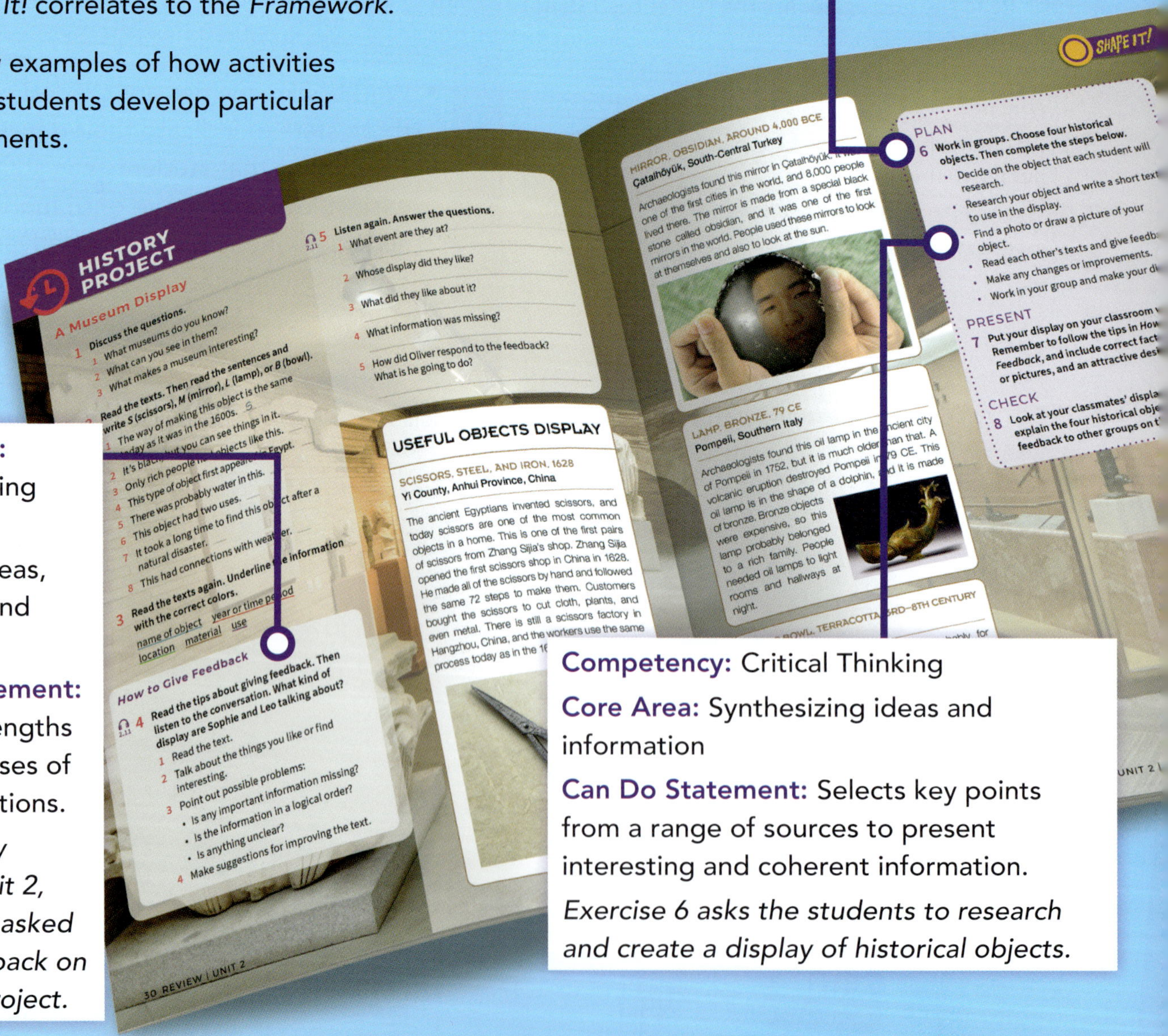

Competency: Critical Thinking
Core Area: Evaluating ideas, arguments, and options
Can Do Statement: Assesses strengths and weaknesses of possible solutions.
In the History Project in Unit 2, students are asked to give feedback on the model project.

Competency: Critical Thinking
Core Area: Synthesizing ideas and information
Can Do Statement: Selects key points from a range of sources to present interesting and coherent information.
Exercise 6 asks the students to research and create a display of historical objects.

The following chart shows which competencies are developed in this level.

Competency Area	Competency	U0	U1	U2	U3	U4	U5	U6	U7	U8	U9
Creative Thinking	Participating in creative activities		✓	✓	✓	✓					
	Creating new content from own ideas and other resources		✓		✓		✓				✓
	Using new content to solve problems and make decisions						✓				
Critical Thinking	Understanding and analyzing links between ideas	✓	✓	✓	✓			✓			
	Evaluating ideas, arguments, and options		✓	✓	✓	✓	✓		✓	✓	✓
	Synthesizing ideas and information		✓	✓	✓	✓		✓		✓	
Learning to Learn	Practical skills for participating in learning	✓	✓	✓	✓	✓	✓	✓	✓	✓	✓
	Taking control of own learning	✓	✓		✓					✓	✓
	Reflecting on and evaluating own learning success		✓	✓	✓	✓	✓	✓	✓	✓	✓
Communication	Using appropriate language/register for context					✓		✓		✓	
	Managing conversations		✓	✓				✓	✓		
	Participating with appropriate confidence and clarity		✓	✓		✓		✓	✓	✓	✓
Collaboration	Taking personal responsibility for own contributions to a group task									✓	
	Listening respectfully and responding constructively to others' contributions		✓	✓			✓	✓			✓
	Managing the sharing of tasks in a project			✓	✓	✓		✓		✓	
	Working toward a resolution for a task			✓		✓		✓		✓	
Social Responsibilities	Understanding personal responsibilities as part of a group and in society, including citizenship		✓	✓		✓	✓			✓	
	Taking active roles, including leadership			✓	✓	✓		✓		✓	
	Understanding and describing own and others' cultures		✓		✓		✓		✓		✓
	Understanding and discussing global issues – environmental, political, financial, and social		✓		✓		✓		✓		✓

For a comprehensive guide to the *Cambridge Life Competencies Framework*, please go to www.cambridge.org/shapeit or scan the QR code to the right.

SHAPE IT! Level 2

For a more comprehensive guide to the CEFR, please visit www.cambridge.org/shapeit or scan the QR code below.

The Common European Framework of Reference for Languages (CEFR) is a description of language ability. It is divided into six main levels, ranging from A1 (beginner) to C2 (advanced). The *Shape It!* course covers A1+ to B1+.

Skills Overview

Skill	Learners will be able to:
Listening	understand phrases and very high-frequency vocabulary related to areas of the most immediate personal relevance; catch the main point in short, clear, simple messages.
Reading	read short simple texts, personal letters, and emails; find specific information in simple everyday material, such as advertisements, menus, and timetables.
Speaking	communicate in simple and routine tasks requiring a simple exchange of information on familiar topics; handle very short social exchanges; use a series of phrases to describe in simple terms people, living conditions, their educational background, and their jobs.
Writing	write short simple notes, messages, and emails relating to matters in areas of immediate need; write a simple personal letter, for example, thanking someone.

Skills in Detail

How the goals of the CEFR are realized in *Shape It!* Level 2:

LISTENING

At A2, learners are expected to be able to understand speech that is clearly and slowly articulated and concerns predictable everyday matters.

OVERALL LISTENING COMPREHENSION
Can understand phrases and expressions related to very familiar topics (e.g., very basic personal and family information, shopping, local geography, employment).

Starter	Unit 1	Unit 2	Unit 3	Unit 4	Unit 5	Unit 6	Unit 7	Unit 8	Unit 9
6 (video)	10 (video)	22 (video)	34 (video)	46 (video)	58 (video)	70 (video)	82 (video)	94 (video)	106 (video)
7	13 (video)	25 (video)	37 (video)	49 (video)	61 (video)	73 (video)	85 (video)	97 (video)	109 (video)
8 (video)	14	26	38	50	62	74	86	98	110
	15 (video)	27 (video)	39 (video)	51 (video)	63 (video)	75 (video)	87 (video)	99 (video)	111 (video)
	16	28	40	52	64	76	88	100	112
	16 (video)	28 (video)	40 (video)	52 (video)	64 (video)	76 (video)	88 (video)		112 (video)
	18 (video)	30	42 (video)	54	66 (video)	79	90 (video)		114 (video)

UNDERSTANDING INTERACTION Can generally identify the topic of discussion around them that is conducted slowly and clearly.									
Starter	**Unit 1**	**Unit 2**	**Unit 3**	**Unit 4**	**Unit 5**	**Unit 6**	**Unit 7**	**Unit 8**	**Unit 9**
7	16	28	40	52	64	76	86	100	110
		30	40 (video)	52 (video)	64 (video)	76 (video)	88		112
				54		79	88 (video)		112 (video)

LISTENING TO ANNOUNCEMENTS AND INSTRUCTIONS Can catch the main point in short, clear, simple messages and announcements. Can understand simple directions relating to how to get from X to Y, on foot or by public transportation.									
Starter	**Unit 1**	**Unit 2**	**Unit 3**	**Unit 4**	**Unit 5**	**Unit 6**	**Unit 7**	**Unit 8**	**Unit 9**
	15 (video)					73 (video)			
						75 (video)			

LISTENING TO MEDIA AND RECORDINGS Can understand and extract the essential information from short recorded passages. Can identify the main point of TV news items reporting events, accidents, etc., where the visual supports the commentary.									
Starter	**Unit 1**	**Unit 2**	**Unit 3**	**Unit 4**	**Unit 5**	**Unit 6**	**Unit 7**	**Unit 8**	**Unit 9**
6 (video)	13 (video)	25 (video)	37 (video)	49 (video)	61 (video)	73 (video)	85 (video)	97 (video)	109 (video)
8 (video)	10 (video)	22 (video)	34 (video)	46 (video)	58 (video)	70 (video)	82 (video)	94 (video)	106 (video)
	15 (video)	26	39 (video)	51 (video)	63 (video)	74	86	98	111 (video)
	16 (video)	27 (video)	40 (video)	52 (video)	64 (video)	75 (video)	87 (video)	99 (video)	112 (video)
	18 (video)	28 (video)	42 (video)		66 (video)	76 (video)	88 (video)		114 (video)
							90 (video)		

READING

At A2, learners can understand short, simple texts on familiar topics that use high-frequency vocabulary.

READING CORRESPONDENCE Can understand basic types of standard routine letters, emails, short simple personal letters, etc.									
Starter	**Unit 1**	**Unit 2**	**Unit 3**	**Unit 4**	**Unit 5**	**Unit 6**	**Unit 7**	**Unit 8**	**Unit 9**
5	12					77		96	

READING FOR ORIENTATION Can find specific, predictable information in simple everyday material such as advertisements, websites, prospectuses, menus, reference lists, and timetables. Can understand everyday signs and notices in public places.									
Starter	**Unit 1**	**Unit 2**	**Unit 3**	**Unit 4**	**Unit 5**	**Unit 6**	**Unit 7**	**Unit 8**	**Unit 9**
		30		54					108

READING FOR INFORMATION AND ARGUMENT Can identify specific information in simple written material such as letters, brochures, and short newspaper or online articles.									
Starter	**Unit 1**	**Unit 2**	**Unit 3**	**Unit 4**	**Unit 5**	**Unit 6**	**Unit 7**	**Unit 8**	**Unit 9**
5	12	24	36	48	60	72	84	96	108
9	17	29	41	53	65	77	89	101	113
	18	30	42	57	66	78	90	102	114
						81		105	117

SPEAKING

OVERALL SPOKEN INTERACTION

At A2, learners can manage simple, routine exchanges fairly easily but would struggle with an extended conversation and often need help with understanding.

CONVERSATION
Can use simple, everyday, polite forms of greeting, address, farewells, introductions, giving thanks.
Can participate in short conversations in routine contexts on topics of interest.
Can express how they feel in simple terms.
Can make and respond to invitations and apologies.
Can say what they like and dislike.

Starter	Unit 1	Unit 2	Unit 3	Unit 4	Unit 5	Unit 6	Unit 7	Unit 8	Unit 9
4	10	22	34	46	58	70	82	94	106
5	11	23	35	49	60	76	84	95	107
7	14	24	36	50	64		87	96	109
	16	28	40	52			91	100	110
	19		43	57			93	105	112
									115

INFORMAL DISCUSSION (WITH FRIENDS)
Can participate in a discussion about everyday practical issues in a simple way.
Can make and respond to suggestions.
Can agree and disagree with others.
Can discuss what to do, where to go, and make arrangements to meet.

Starter	Unit 1	Unit 2	Unit 3	Unit 4	Unit 5	Unit 6	Unit 7	Unit 8	Unit 9
	16					76			117
						81			

GOAL-ORIENTED COOPERATION (e.g., Repairing a car, discussing a document, organizing an event)
Can manage simple, routine tasks, e.g.,
- asking for and providing things.
- getting simple information.
- discussing what to do next.
- making and responding to suggestions.
- asking for and giving directions.

Starter	Unit 1	Unit 2	Unit 3	Unit 4	Unit 5	Unit 6	Unit 7	Unit 8	Unit 9
		30		54		79		102	
		31		55		80		103	

INFORMATION EXCHANGE
Can ask for and provide personal information (e.g., about habits, routines, pastimes, and past activities).
Can give and follow simple directions and instructions (e.g., explain how to get somewhere).
Can communicate in simple and routine tasks requiring a simple and direct exchange of information.
Can exchange limited information on familiar and routine operational matters.

Starter	Unit 1	Unit 2	Unit 3	Unit 4	Unit 5	Unit 6	Unit 7	Unit 8	Unit 9
6	11	22	35	47	61	71	83	97	109
8	13	25	37	49	62	73	85	98	111
	14	27	38	51	63		86	99	
	15	28					87		
	21						88		

INTERVIEWING AND BEING INTERVIEWED
Can answer simple questions and respond to simple statements in an interview.

Starter	Unit 1	Unit 2	Unit 3	Unit 4	Unit 5	Unit 6	Unit 7	Unit 8	Unit 9
		25		48				100	

OVERALL SPOKEN PRODUCTION

At A2, learners can give simple descriptions or presentations about everyday things as a short series of simple phrases.

SUSTAINED MONOLOGUE: Describing Experience
Can tell a story as a simple list of points.
Can give short, basic descriptions of
- events and activities.
- plans and arrangements, habits and routines, past activities, and personal experiences.
- their family, living conditions, educational background, present or most recent job.
- people, places, and possessions.

Can use simple descriptive language to make brief statements about and compare objects and possessions.
Can explain what they like or dislike about something.

Starter	Unit 1	Unit 2	Unit 3	Unit 4	Unit 5	Unit 6	Unit 7	Unit 8	Unit 9
7	12	28	38		59	74		98	
			39		64	81			
			40		69				

WRITING

At A2 learners can write a series of simple phrases and sentences linked with simple connectors like *and*, *but*, and *because*.

CORRESPONDENCE
Can write very simple personal letters or emails, etc.

Starter	Unit 1	Unit 2	Unit 3	Unit 4	Unit 5	Unit 6	Unit 7	Unit 8	Unit 9
						77			

CREATIVE WRITING
Can write very short, basic descriptions of events, past activities, and personal experiences.
Can write a series of simple phrases and sentences about everyday/personal matters (e.g., family, people, places, a job or study experience, living conditions, educational background, present or most recent job).

Starter	Unit 1	Unit 2	Unit 3	Unit 4	Unit 5	Unit 6	Unit 7	Unit 8	Unit 9
9	17	29	41	53	65	77	89	101	113
		31		55		79		103	

COHERENCE
Can use the most frequently occurring connectors to link simple sentences and phrases in order to tell a story or describe something as a simple list of points.

Starter	Unit 1	Unit 2	Unit 3	Unit 4	Unit 5	Unit 6	Unit 7	Unit 8	Unit 9
	17	29	41		65		89		113
									115

Teacher Support Hub

Visual Literacy: What Are Visual Texts?

Visual media is an essential tool for communicating and exchanging ideas, and the *Shape It!* unit openers provide images as a starting point for exploring each topic.

In today's world, we are surrounded by a huge variety of images that communicate meaning, also known as "visual texts." These include billboards, photographs, TV, video, maps, memes, digital stories, video games, movies, and more.

Since students are constantly accessing and "reading" this type of content, it makes sense to use still and moving images in learning.

Using Our Brains

More than 50 percent of the cortex, the surface of the brain, is devoted to processing visual information.

Helping Us Learn

Adding illustrations to text, researchers have concluded, aids comprehension and learning.

Connecting People

We currently upload and share 1.8 billion photos every single day.

Visual Literacy Across the Curriculum

Visual literacy is an integral part of the digital age and has implications outside the language classroom. Images can help simplify difficult-to-understand or text-heavy topics in any subject. For example, in math, tables and graphs help students to interpret and compare data, maps allow a geography student to see the size and location of countries, and musical notes let a piano player know which keys to play. By practicing visual literacy in the ELT classroom, students get the opportunity to develop an essential skill that we use in all walks of life.

Unit Openers: Extra Activities

1 Circle of Viewpoints

Students can look at what the images represent from different perspectives: from their own point of view or by imagining themselves in the place of different people in the picture. Encourage them to ask questions.

I am thinking about (the topic) *from the point of view of …*

I think this person might be feeling …

You can wrap up by having students share different ideas about the image that they didn't have before.

2 Think-Pair-Share

This is a simple idea for using the questions on the unit openers or other questions you might want to ask students.

Give students a few minutes of "thinking time" on their own.

Students form pairs to share their ideas.

You can extend this activity to have pairs share their ideas in groups or as a class.

3 Going Beyond the Picture

Here are three ideas for using pictures with one or more person in them. Put students in pairs or groups to share ideas for these activities.

Dialogue Bubbles
Have students create a dialogue between the people in the picture.

Picture Profile
Build a profile of one of the people from the picture: name, profession, likes/dislikes, character, etc.

Compare and Contrast
Identify similarities and differences between people or things in a picture.

Reading Strategies

Before Reading

AROUND THE WORLD

READING
A Turkish Fairy Tale

1 Look at the pictures. What is happening in each picture? What do you think the story is about?

2 Read the fairy tale. Put the pictures in the order of the story.

a b c

3 Read the fairy tale again. Answer the questions in your notebook.
1 Why did the boy start his journey?
2 How did he feel when he started the journey?
3 What did the ogre try to do?
4 What did the boy do when he heard the people on the ship?

Globetrotters
Watch video 3.5
A Bee's Story
- Where are bees very busy?
- What is honey used for?
- Who did artists in the 18th century paint?

Voice It!

4 Discuss the questions.
1 How does the boy face fear in the story?
2 What causes fear? How can it affect your life?
3 How can fear be good?

The Boy Who Found Fear

Once upon a time, a woman and her son lived in a small house in a forest. They didn't have any neighbors, and the lonely boy stayed at home with his mother every day.

One winter's evening, they were having dinner when a storm started. The wind blew the door open and the mother said, "Close the door. I feel fear."

"What is fear?" asked the boy.

"Fear is when you feel afraid," she replied.

"I don't understand. I want to find fear."

So the next morning, the boy set off confidently. While he was looking for fear, he met a lot of different people and he faced a lot of challenges. First, there was a group of robbers. They made him do dangerous and difficult things, but he wasn't afraid. He continued his journey.

42 WHAT DO STORIES TEACH US? | UNIT 3

Previewing the Text: Topic Sentences

Have students preview the text by reading the first sentence in each paragraph before reading it completely. Can they guess *who* or *what* the text is going to be about? Elicit ideas.

Brainstorming

Students can help each other by sharing what they know about a topic. For example, if a student already knows the story they are about to read, they can share details about the characters, plot, and setting.

Asking Questions

When students look at a text for the first time and have identified the text type and topic, ask them what they want to know about the subject. Write a list of students' questions on the board.

While Reading

AROUND THE WORLD

READING
An Encyclopedia Entry

1 Look at the photos of homes on page 67. Where are these homes? What do you know about them?

2 Read the entry. Check your answers.

3 Read the entry again. Match headings a–e with paragraphs 1–5.
a Why Use Igloos?
b Keeping Warm
c Who Are the Inuit?
d Life Inside an Igloo
e How to Build an Igloo

Globetrotters
Watch video 5.5
Living in a Ger
- What does "ger" mean in Mongolian?
- Would you like to live in a *ger*?

Voice It!

4 Discuss the questions.
1 Nomadic people have temporary houses, so "home" isn't a permanent building in a place. How else can people define "home"?
2 Besides your house, how do you define "home"?
3 How can you appreciate and celebrate your home?

LIFE IN AN INUIT IGLOO

1 The Inuit are the native people of the Arctic Circle. Today, they usually live in modern houses in small villages. Until recently, however, they still used their famous houses made of snow – igloos.

2 The Arctic isn't warm enough to farm, so the Inuit had a nomadic life. This means they traveled during the year to find food. Every winter and summer, the Inuit traveled thousands of kilometers across the frozen Arctic ocean. All nomads have to make temporary homes while they travel, and in summer, the Inuit lived in tents made from animal skins, called *tupiqs*. Igloos were their traditional winter homes.

3 Snow is a perfect material for building. It's as light as wood and easy to cut. The snow has to be dry and hard enough to make good blocks because wet snow doesn't have the strength an igloo needs. The Inuit make a dome shape by putting the snow blocks in a spiral. This is quick to build and creates a very strong structure.

4 The heat inside an igloo comes from people's bodies only, but this is warm enough to keep the igloo comfortable. This is because snow is a good insulator. In other words, it keeps the cold out and the warmth in. The entrance is a tunnel that goes under the walls. The heavy, cold air always stays in the tunnel and the light, warm air stays in the igloo.

5 Igloos don't have windows, but there are small holes in the walls. These let in clean air and let out dangerous smoke from the small oil lamps. Traditionally, the Inuit didn't have any furniture, but a platform of snow just below the ceiling provided a simple sofa and bed in the warmest part of the igloo. Inuit families spent all winter in small igloos with no furniture, no bathroom … and no Internet. Just imagine that!

66 WHAT IS YOUR DREAM HOUSE? | UNIT 5

Checking Predictions

Encourage students to stop and think as they read a text. If they made predictions before reading, they could make a chart that shows their original predictions in one column and evidence they find for them in another. If their predictions were incorrect, a third column could show new information.

Rereading

Working in pairs, students can use a "Pause-Think-Retell" technique after each section or paragraph of a text. If they can't remember much about a section they have just read, have them reread and retell again. Ask questions to aid and check understanding.

Comparing and Contrasting

Have students take notes of similarities and differences they find between people, places, or opinions presented in texts as they read them. Give them specific categories or topics relevant to the text to focus on.

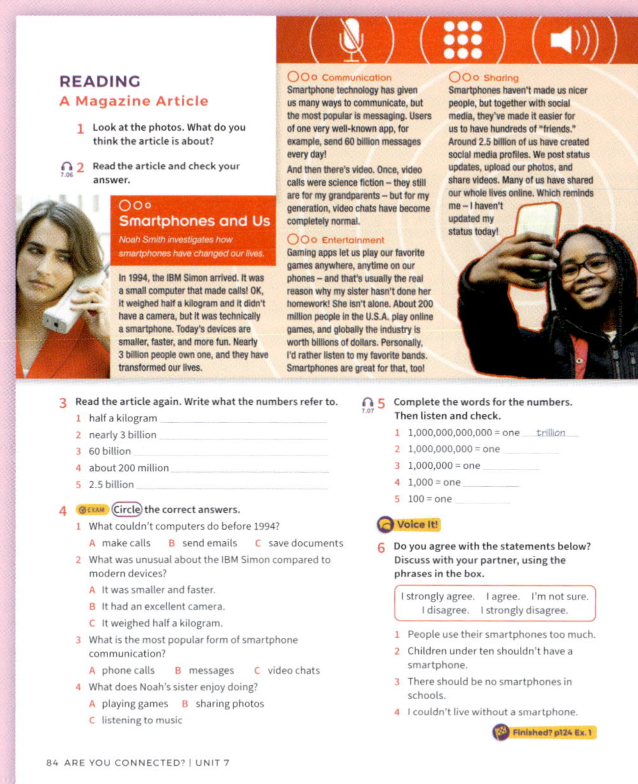

READING
A Magazine Article

1 Look at the photos. What do you think the article is about?

7.06 2 Read the article and check your answer.

Smartphones and Us

Noah Smith investigates how smartphones have changed our lives.

In 1994, the IBM Simon arrived. It was a small computer that made calls! OK, it weighed half a kilogram and it didn't have a camera, but it was technically a smartphone. Today's devices are smaller, faster, and more fun. Nearly 3 billion people own one, and they have transformed our lives.

Communication

Smartphone technology has given us many ways to communicate, but the most popular is messaging. Users of one very well-known app, for example, send 60 billion messages every day!

And then there's video. Once, video calls were science fiction – they still are for my grandparents – but for my generation, video chats have become completely normal.

Entertainment

Gaming apps let us play our favorite games anywhere, anytime on our phones – and that's usually the real reason why my sister hasn't done her homework! She isn't alone. About 200 million people in the U.S.A. play online games, and globally the industry is worth billions of dollars. Personally, I'd rather listen to my favorite bands. Smartphones are great for that, too!

Sharing

Smartphones haven't made us nicer people, but together with social media, they've made it easier for us to have hundreds of "friends." Around 2.5 billion of us have created social media profiles. We post status updates, upload our photos, and share videos. Many of us have shared our whole lives online. Which reminds me – I haven't updated my status today!

3 Read the article again. Write what the numbers refer to.
1 half a kilogram ______
2 nearly 3 billion ______
3 60 billion ______
4 about 200 million ______
5 2.5 billion ______

4 EXAM Circle the correct answers.
1 What couldn't computers do before 1994?
A make calls B send emails C save documents
2 What was unusual about the IBM Simon compared to modern devices?
A It was smaller and faster.
B It had an excellent camera.
C It weighed half a kilogram.
3 What is the most popular form of smartphone communication?
A phone calls B messages C video chats
4 What does Noah's sister enjoy doing?
A playing games B sharing photos
C listening to music

7.07 5 Complete the words for the numbers. Then listen and check.
1 1,000,000,000,000 = one trillion
2 1,000,000,000 = one ______
3 1,000,000 = one ______
4 1,000 = one ______
5 100 = one ______

Voice It!

6 Do you agree with the statements below? Discuss with your partner, using the phrases in the box.

I strongly agree. I agree. I'm not sure. I disagree. I strongly disagree.

1 People use their smartphones too much.
2 Children under ten shouldn't have a smartphone.
3 There should be no smartphones in schools.
4 I couldn't live without a smartphone.

Finished? p124 Ex. 1

84 ARE YOU CONNECTED? | UNIT 7

After Reading

Summarizing

Encourage students to find the main ideas of a text and summarize it. They can practice by giving one-sentence summaries of each paragraph and section, and finally give a one-sentence summary of the whole text. Help them to identify and ignore non-essential information.

Drawing Conclusions

You can provide students with a statement about a text and have them find reasons to support it (e.g., *Smartphones have had a positive effect on our lives.*). Then have students draw their own conclusions.

Finding Out More

Encourage students to find out more about topics they are interested in. They can research extra information or carry out a fact-finding task. Have them share new details in groups.

At Home

- Ask: *Where and when do you read at home? Are you comfortable?* Encourage students to establish a routine (ten minutes a day, at night, before dinner, etc.) and to make sure they have a comfortable reading environment (e.g., cushions, lamps, silence, etc.). Discuss what is most comfortable for them.
- Suggest students incorporate "fast-and-fun" reads into their daily lives. For example, if there is game, movie, or other product they are interested in, have them find advertisements or short reviews online in English. They can also read song lyrics, billboards, posters, and other material.
- Give students opportunities to talk about things they are reading at home and make recommendations to their classmates.

Listening Strategies

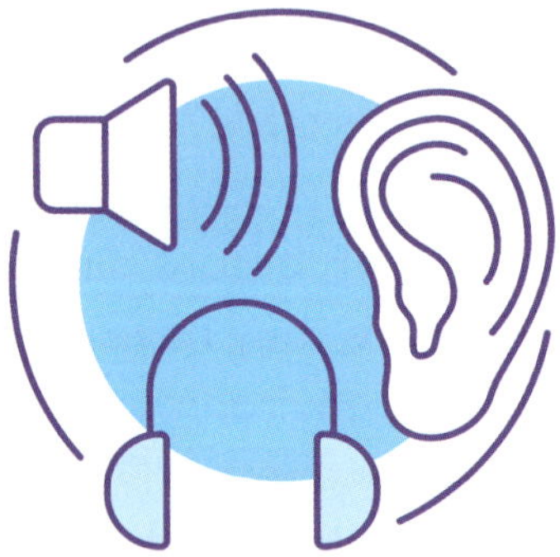

How can I understand the order of events?

Listening for Sequence

Students often have to identify the sequence of events or instructions when listening - for example, when finding out how something works or the sequence of a story. It is essential they get the order right. You can cut up steps or key information from the story for students to place in order as they listen, or have them identify sequencing words (*first, then, next, finally*, etc.) if they appear.

A Talk p98

Tell students to find and watch *How to* videos online. Tell them to play the video a number of times, but only listen to it, not watch it. Challenge them to take notes of the steps in the video. Then they can watch and check.

Which words help me form an overall picture?

Listening for Details

Give students fill-in-the-blank texts with essential information like names, places, and important objects missing. Ask students to identify what type of information they need to listen for before playing the recording. At higher levels, you can move on to more difficult specifics, such as how people feel or what they are doing.

A Guided Tour p14

Suggest students listen to a news item that interests them (they can find news sites in English online). Tell them to take notes of details related to *what, when, where, who*, etc. or prepare a list of questions for them. You can discuss interesting stories in class.

What is the most important information?

Listening for Gist

Remind students that the information they hear will be related to a specific topic and that key words will help them form a complete picture. For example, when they listen to a radio show or interview, they can identify place names, key objects, and actions that help them identify locations, objects, and events.

Students can watch short videos with subtitles in English on a topic that interests them. Tell them to use the title to predict content and then listen for key words. Then they should watch the video again with subtitles and see how much they understood. Tell them to repeat a week or two later to see if they understand more.

Radio Shows and Interviews pp74, 78

What is the speaker's message?

Listening for Functional Language

Remind students of language they have learned for expressing different functions, such as talking about plans and experiences, making suggestions, accepting or declining invitations, and so on. Have them identify how this language is used naturally in conversation. Have them repeat sentences or phrases that convey different ideas and write new expressions on the board before listening to check.

A Discussion p110

Tell students to find a short scene from a TV show or movie they like. They can make a note of words and expressions the characters use to convey different messages (e.g., *say you're sorry, offer help, give advice*, etc.). Encourage students to practice using these expressions in class.

Speaking Strategies

How can we collaborate in groups?

Communicate

Group members share ideas and pay attention to others. They should speak and listen and keep communication open.

Show Emotional Intelligence

They recognize and understand each other's needs. For example, if someone is tired or frustrated, they might need a break.

Respect Opinions

They accept others' ideas and do not try to force their opinions. Stress that they all have the right to express themselves respectfully.

Warmers: Get the class motivated!

Just a Minute!

Divide the class into groups of four and tell them to number themselves 1-2-3-4. Number ones go first. Call out a unit-related discussion topic (e.g., *your favorite movie*). All the number ones must talk to their group for a minute about that topic. You can reduce the amount of time for lower levels. If students stop or have a long pause, they lose the challenge. Repeat with numbers 2-3-4.

The Hot Seat

One student sits on a chair at the front of the room with their back to the board. Write a topic-related word on the board. The class helps the student to guess the word by describing it without actually saying the word. It is likely that everyone will shout at once, so this is a good opportunity for students to practice taking turns! For large groups, you could make this a team game, with two students at the front trying to guess a word being described by their team.

Level 2 Functions and Strategies

Function	Strategy	Teaching Tip
Asking for and Giving Opinions p16	Showing Interest	Have students use the phrases in *Useful Language* and *Everyday English* to respond appropriately and ask questions.
Talking About Your Weekend p28	Describing Events	Encourage students to use adjectives to describe places, activities, and feelings.
Telling an Anecdote p40	Sequencing	Ensure students relate events in a logical order and use appropriate connectors (e.g., *and, next, then, while*, etc.).
Making Requests p52	Practicing Question Intonation	Model the correct intonation for making requests. Have students repeat chorally and individually.
Discussing a Photo p64	Using Prepositions of Place	Ask students where things are in the picture. Have them describe the location using the phrases in *Useful Language*.
Making Suggestions p76	Showing Enthusiasm	Model phrases in an enthusiastic and unenthusiastic way. Encourage students to respond with enthusiasm to good suggestions.
Giving Instructions p88	Checking Understanding	Have students check the listener understands each step using the *Everyday English* phrases.
Conducting an Interview p100	Using Appropriate Body Language	Have students role-play their interviews and check their body posture, gestures, and eye contact in formal situations.
Making Polite Refusals p112	Expressing Emotion	Encourage students to change their tone to express interest and disappointment. Model where necessary.

Writing Strategies

Prewriting

Providing a Reason to Write

Motivate students by giving them a real reason to write, not only that you are going to grade it! They can brainstorm ideas for how to present their writing, such as class blogs for sharing ideas and advice, informative posters, text messages, and so on.

Asking Questions

If there is a broad topic to write about, such as technology, it can help when students ask defining questions that focus on specific areas. Have students use these questions to develop their main idea.

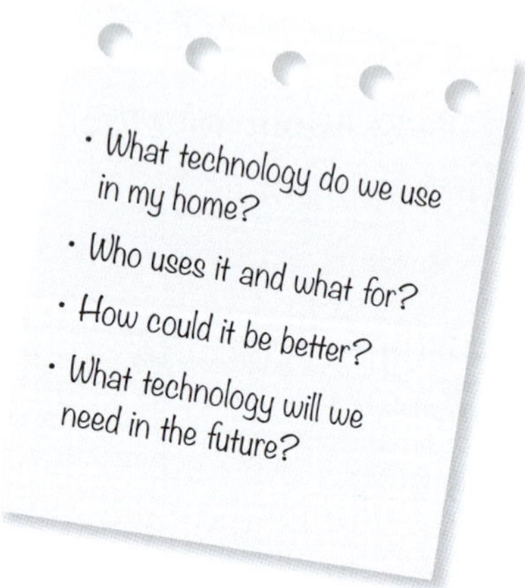

Organizing

Outlining

Students can use pre-reading strategies such as mind-mapping to organize their information into an outline. Help them arrange their ideas into a logical format that corresponds to the text type and encourage them to cut unnecessary ideas.

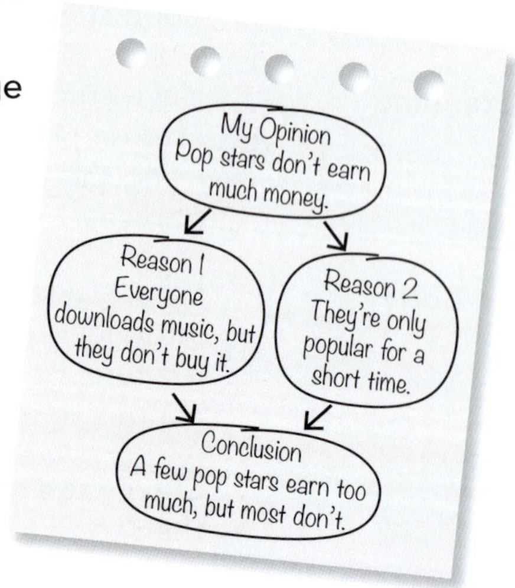

Identifying Audience

Have students think about the tone or format of the text. Make sure they understand the type of text they are writing and who it is for.

Writing

Making It Creative

While writing tasks are often intended as an opportunity for students to produce previously learned language, students can still write interesting and creative texts. Students can write poems, imagine they are characters in pictures, think of different endings for stories, make comic strips, and so on. Give students opportunities to express their creativity and produce texts in different ways.

Referring to the Model

Every writing task has a model text. As students write, encourage them to go back to the model whenever necessary. Elicit how the model works and what they need to reproduce in their own texts (e.g., *What information does it contain? How is it organised?*). Have students focus on language and structure.

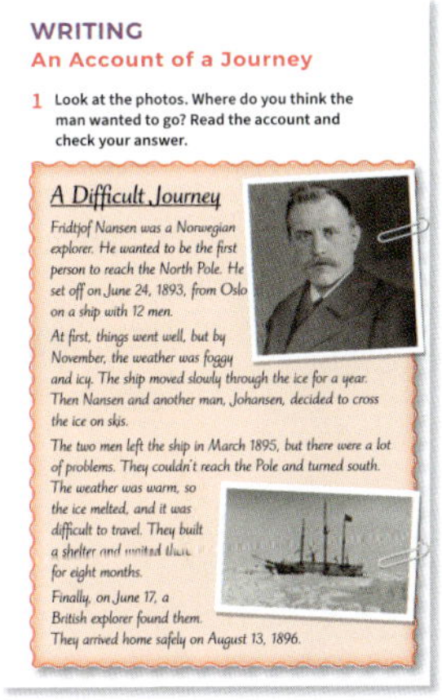

WRITING

An Account of a Journey

1 Look at the photos. Where do you think the man wanted to go? Read the account and check your answer.

A Difficult Journey

Fridtjof Nansen was a Norwegian explorer. He wanted to be the first person to reach the North Pole. He set off on June 24, 1893, from Oslo on a ship with 12 men.

At first, things went well, but by November, the weather was foggy and icy. The ship moved slowly through the ice for a year. Then Nansen and another man, Johansen, decided to cross the ice on skis.

The two men left the ship in March 1895, but there were a lot of problems. They couldn't reach the Pole and turned south. The weather was warm, so the ice melted, and it was difficult to travel. They built a shelter and [illegible] for eight months.

Finally, on June 17, a British explorer found them. They arrived home safely on August 13, 1896.

Editing/Rewriting

Focusing on Fluency

Give writing tasks that encourage students to express their ideas and what vocabulary they know. Emails and text messages are a good way for students to talk about things that are going on in their lives. Have other students respond to the message of these texts, without correcting them.

Using Dictionaries

Encourage students to use online or print dictionaries when they check their work. These can be bilingual for lower levels and then English-only. You can have students focus on different aspects of their work, such as spelling mistakes and misuse of words or word forms.

Mark positively!

Try using the "sandwich technique"

1 Give positive feedback
2 Give constructive feedback
3 Give positive feedback again

International Values

Voice It!

Voice It! activities on the *Around the World* pages give students an opportunity to explore an international value.

Working in Teams

p18

Further Discussion

Elicit examples of other activities where teamwork is essential (e.g., *doing a group project, playing team sports, volunteering to clean up a park,* etc.). Make a list on the board. Ask *Do you do any of these activities? What jobs or roles do you have? How do you help the team?*

Values Task

Have groups of four or five choose one of the ideas from the list on the board. Ask them how they can work together as a team to complete the activity they chose. Encourage them to assign roles within their groups according to each other's skills. Ask them to share their ideas with the class.

Facing Our Fears

p42

Further Discussion

Elicit a list of common fears people have (e.g., *spiders, heights,* etc.) and write them on the board. Go down the list one by one and ask *Why do people feel afraid of...?* Encourage discussion and remember to empathize with students who feel any of these fears themselves. Ask *Is it good to be afraid of any of these things?* Remind students that in some situations it can be good to feel fear.

Values Task

Divide the class into groups. Students choose one of the categories and create a spidergram of associated words or topics. Have them research facts about each topic (e.g., number of speakers of a language, origin of a type of dress, and so on). Students display or present their spidergrams with pictures.

Appreciating Home

p66

Further Discussion

Ask students about the similarities and differences between the Inuits' home life in the past and their own. Take notes in a comparative chart on the board. Ask *Which home life do you prefer? Why? What are the advantages and disadvantages of each one?* Have students discuss ideas.

Values Task

Have students draw a square with a roof (a house). Tell them to divide the square into four quarters. In each quarter, have them take notes about a place they call home. They can use these ideas for each quarter:
What objects make you feel at home?
Who makes you feel at home?
What activities do you do at home?
How does home make you feel?

Using Technology Responsibly

p90

Further Discussion

Make a spidergram of all the things Seo-yun uses her phone for each day. Ask *What other things do people do on phones?* Add them to the spidergram. Ask *Do you have a smartphone?* and ask for a show of hands.

Values Task

Have students work in groups and find out the following information from their classmates: (1) The average amount of time they use phones; and (2) what their favorite activity is. Based on their results, ask them to make suggestions for good use of technology. Elicit examples, such as not using phones at dinner, etc. Have them write ideas as signs and display them around the classroom.

Respecting Cultural Expression

p115

Further Discussion

Remind students that folk dance is a form of cultural expression. Ask *What other forms of cultural expression are there?* Write a list on the board (e.g., *music, food, language, clothes*, etc.). Ask for examples of each category in their culture. Ask *When and where do people celebrate or use these forms of cultural expression?* Share ideas.

Values Task

Have groups make an advertisement for a folk dance or other cultural event in their country. Tell them to include details about when, where, what the event is, and why people enjoy it. Ask groups to present their advertisements and talk about why the events are important for their culture.

Wrap-Up Ideas

Each unit ends with a review. This is a chance for students to reflect on the unit topic. Use the review questions provided in the teacher notes to support and consolidate students' learning.

Unit 1

What are you watching?

Support	Consolidation	Extension
Write a tweet to a friend about a series you are watching.	Write a description of your dream tour of a movie set.	Write a summary of your favorite TV show.

Unit 2

How was the past different?

Support	Consolidation	Extension
Describe a place you visited in the past.	Ask a partner questions about the journey they planned on p29.	Keep a diary to record what you do each day.

Unit 3

What do stories teach us?

Support	Consolidation	Extension
Choose a story from the unit and retell it.	Choose a story from the unit and describe how the characters feel.	Make a story map for one of the stories. Include setting, characters, and plot.

Unit 4

What do you value most?

Support	Consolidation	Extension
Create a spidergram of things that you value.	Make two lists: things you have too much/ many of and things you don't have enough of.	Write an ad for your dream job. Give five reasons why it is so special.

Unit 5

What is your dream house?

Support

Conduct a quick survey to find out who helps with chores in your class.

Consolidation

Categorize chores according to who does them, in which rooms, etc.

Extension

Copy the word family charts from p67 into your notebook and add more words.

Unit 6

How can I stay safe?

Support

Make a poster with labels for parts of the body.

Consolidation

Write a list of rules for staying safe in your town.

Extension

Write an online description of dangers in your country (see p72).

Unit 7

Are you connected?

Support

Make a picture dictionary of communication words. You can use illustrations, magazine cut-outs, photos, or symbols to represent each word.

Consolidation

Make a poster of personal predictions for home, school, work, etc.

Extension

Write a list of things you haven't done but want to do. Then predict when, where, and how you will do them.

Unit 8

What is success?

Support

Write three *Have you ever...?* questions and find someone who has done each thing.

Consolidation

Brainstorm more nouns for jobs and make a spidergram with categories for different suffixes.

Extension

Make a phrasal verb dictionary in your notebook with definitions.

Unit 9

How do you express yourself?

Support

Act out and guess music and dance words. Be as creative as you can!

Consolidation

Talk about your intentions and predictions for the summer vacation.

Extension

Write and present a schedule for a school festival (see p111).

Warmer

Books closed. Ask students to write down as many hobbies and sports as they can in one minute. Check answers and write new or unusual words on the board.

Teacher Support Hub ppxxxiv–xxxv

S.01–S.03 Audioscripts T129

1 S.01 Before doing the activity, point out that some verbs go with more than one item in the box.

Target Vocabulary

chat online tʃæt ˈɑnˈlaɪn
download songs ˈdaʊnˌloʊd sɔŋz
go shopping goʊ ˈʃɑ·pɪŋ
go for a bike ride goʊ fɔr ə baɪk raɪd
hang out with friends hæŋ aʊt wɪθ frendz
listen to music ˈlɪ·sən tə ˈmju·zɪk
make cookies/videos meɪk ˈkʊ·kiz / ˈvɪ·di·oʊz
play an instrument pleɪ ən ˈɪn·strə·mənt
read books rid bʊks
take photos teɪk ˈfoʊ·ṭoʊz
write a blog raɪt ə blɑg

2 S.02 ★ Pause the audio after each phrase to allow students to check their spelling in pairs.

Vocabulary Bank SB p127

3 S.03 After drilling the pronunciation, put students into small groups. Ask them to take turns miming and guessing sports.

Target Vocabulary

basketball ˈbæs·kɪtˌbɔl
gymnastics ˌdʒɪmˈnæs·tɪks
hockey ˈhɑ·ki
rugby ˈrʌg·bi
sailing ˈseɪ·lɪŋ
swimming ˈswɪ·mɪŋ
table tennis ˈteɪ·bəl ˌte·nɪs
track and field træk ən fild
volleyball ˈvɑ·liˌbɔl
windsurfing ˈwɪndˌsɜr·fɪŋ

STARTER WELCOME!

VOCABULARY

Free Time and Hobbies

S.01 **1 Match verbs 1–10 with the words in the box to make phrases. Listen, check, and repeat.**

a bike ride	cookies/videos	online
a blog	friends	photos
an instrument	music	shopping
~~books/magazines~~		

1 read *books/magazines*
2 chat online
3 go shopping
4 go for a bike ride
5 hang out with friends
6 listen to music
7 make cookies/videos
8 play an instrument
9 take photos
10 write a blog

S.02 **2 Listen and write the activities from Exercise 1.**

1 *play an instrument*
2 take photos
3 listen to music
4 go for a bike ride
5 go shopping
6 make cookies
7 read magazines

Sports

S.03 **3 Match the words with the pictures (1–8). Circle the two sports that aren't in the pictures. Listen, check, and repeat.**

basketball	6	swimming	5
gymnastics	*1*	table tennis	7
hockey	8	track and field	4
rugby	2	(volleyball)	
sailing	3	(windsurfing)	

LEARN TO LEARN

Verb and Noun Phrases

We often use verbs and nouns together to make different phrases. Learn them together.

4 Complete the list with nouns from Exercises 1 and 3.

Verb	Noun
play	*an instrument,* basketball, hockey, rugby, table tennis, volleyball
go	shopping, sailing, swimming, windsurfing
make	cookies, videos
write	a blog, books, magazines, music
read	a blog, books, magazines, music

Use It!

5 Discuss the questions.

1 What is your favorite sport to watch on TV?
2 What is your favorite sport to do?
3 What isn't a good sport to do on your own?

Explore It!

Is the sentence *T* (true) or *F* (false)?

Rugby is popular in many countries, but it is the only sport in Exercise 3 that isn't played at the Summer Olympic Games. F

Find another interesting fact about sports and write a question for your partner to answer.

Vocabulary Bank SB p127

Extra Vocabulary Practice

Learn to Learn

Encourage students to keep a vocabulary notebook where they can record any verb–noun phrases they notice.

4 Encourage students to copy the chart into their notebooks after feedback.

5 Students take notes on their answers to 1–3 before speaking.

Explore It!

Point out that all the sports in Exercise 3 are played at the Summer Olympics. If appropriate, allow students to use their smartphones to research a fact about sports.

Homework

Workbook p4, Exercises 1–2

Warmer

Talk with students about the types of content they watch and read online. Students discuss any blogs (or vlogs) they know about.

Teacher Support Hub ppxxxvi–xxxvii

1 Elicit the meaning of *blog post* and give students a few minutes of thinking time before discussing the question in pairs. Elicit questions on the board and leave them there, using this as an opportunity to gauge students' existing knowledge of question formation.

2 S.04 Set a three-minute time limit to encourage faster reading, and tell students not to worry about unknown vocabulary at this stage. Then elicit any information from the text that answers any of the questions on the board.

3 ★ Tell students where to find the vocabulary (2 Rosie; 3 Nora; 4 Nora; 5 comments section).

4 Encourage students to underline the key words in the text that helped them find the answers, and elicit these during feedback (e.g., *Rosie, I'm always busy!*).

Focus on Phrases

5 ★ Write phrases on the board for students to use in their discussion: (e.g., *I'm a lot like … because …*, *I'm nothing like … because …*, *I'm a bit like … because …*).

READING
A Blog Post

1 Look at the photos in the blog post. What do you want to know about the people?

2 (S.04) Listen as you read the blog post. Do you learn the information you wanted to know in Exercise 1?

3 Find words in the blog post that mean:

1. doing a lot of things busy
2. difficult tough
3. making you a little angry annoying
4. very bad terrible
5. very good awesome

4 Read the blog post again and write the names of the people. Who …

1. is a busy person? Rosie
2. are Rosie's brother and sister? Dan and Nora
3. likes computer magazines and computer games? Dan
4. is not a good singer? Nora
5. are Sara and Fatima? Rosie's best friends
6. thinks Rosie's blog is very good? Jody

Voice It!

5 Discuss the questions.

1. Are you like any of the people in Rosie's blog? If so, who and why?
2. Do you read blogs? Why / Why not?
3. What's your favorite blog? What's it about?

THOUGHTS FOR TODAY

Rosie Wilson

Hi everyone! Today, my blog is all about my hobbies, family, and friends. I'm always busy! So, what do I do?

I go swimming three mornings a week. I always get up at 5:30 a.m. 😴. It's tough, but swimming is my favorite thing (after my blog – obviously!).

My Big Brother, Dan

He plays computer games, and he sometimes reads magazines (computer game ones!). He plays soccer every day with his friends, but he doesn't leave the house! 🙄

My Annoying Little Sister, Nora

She often does her homework and listens to music at the same time. Does she sing, too? Yes, she does – but she's a terrible singer! 😱

Best Friends Forever: Sara and Fatima ❤❤❤

I don't see them during the week because we don't go to the same school. That isn't a problem because we usually hang out together on the weekend. They love taking selfies, and they post Snapchat stories every day!

What about you? Do you often read my blog? How do you spend your free time? **Let me know!**

COMMENTS:

Jody I read your blog in my free time. It's awesome!

STARTER UNIT 5

Extend It!

Ask students to work in pairs to write a comment for Rosie's blog post at the top of a letter-sized sheet of paper. Display the comments around the room, and allow students to read the comments, "like" them, and respond to them if they wish.

Flipped Class

▶ Ask students to watch **video S.1** and do **Video Worksheet S.1** in the *Teacher's Resource Bank* in preparation for the next lesson.

Homework

Workbook p4, Exercises 3–4

Lesson Aim: I can use the simple present and adverbs of frequency.

Warmer

▶ Play **video S.1**, if it wasn't assigned for homework, and ask students to raise their hands when Zara mentions an activity they also do. Elicit that Zara listens to music and Sophia, the vlogger, usually writes short stories. Students can then discuss their own summer routines.

S.05 Audioscript pT129

1 Give students two minutes to discuss what they remember from Rosie's blog before completing the chart.

2 Remind students that we use the simple present for actions that happen all the time or never happen.

3 S.05 ★★★ Ask students to underline the sentences in the blog post that are true for them. Then they can discuss in pairs, asking extra questions to find out more information.

4 ★★★ Challenge students to fill in the blanks before reading the chart. Elicit synonyms of *often* (e.g., *frequently*, *almost always*). Then write *5%* on the board and elicit adverbs like *rarely*, *hardly ever*, or *almost never*.

Extra Grammar Practice

5 & 6 Focus students' attention on the chart, and elicit that adverbs of frequency go before verbs (e.g., *go*, *read*, *buy*) but after the verb *to be*.

LANGUAGE IN ACTION

Simple Present

Watch video S.1
What does Zara do on the bus?
What does the vlogger do in the morning?

	I/You/We/They	He/She/It
+	I **read** your blog in my free time.	She [3] does her homework.
–	We [1] don't **go** to the same school.	He [4] doesn't **leave** the house.
?	[2] Do you **read** my blog? Yes, I **do**. / No, I **don't**.	[5] Does she **sing**, too? Yes, she [6] does. / No, she **doesn't**.

1 Complete the examples in the chart above. Use the blog post on page 5 to help you.

2 Write simple present sentences.

1 Rosie / get up / at 5:30 a.m. three mornings a week.
Rosie gets up at 5:30 a.m. three mornings a week.

2 Dan / play / computer games.
Dan plays computer games

3 Rosie / not listen / to music when she / do / her homework. Rosie doesn't listen to music when she does her homework.

4 Sara and Fatima / not see / Rosie during the week. Sara and Fatima don't see Rosie during the week.

3 S.05 Complete the blog post with the simple present form of the verbs. Then listen and check.

I [1] *like* (like) my new school. I [2] don't know (not know) all the students in my class yet, but I [3] sit (sit) next to a boy named Jorge in my English class. He [4] plays (play) basketball every day, but he [5] doesn't like (not like) other sports. [6] Do you get (get) a lot of homework? Our teachers [7] don't give (not give) us a lot. I [8] go (go) to homework club on Wednesdays. Some of the older students [9] help (help) us. They're nice. After homework club, I [10] don't get (not get) home until about 6:30 p.m.

Adverbs of Frequency

Rosie is **always** busy.
Dan **sometimes** reads magazines.
Nora **often** listens to music when she does her homework.
Rosie **usually** hangs out with friends on the weekend.

4 Complete the timeline with the adverbs of frequency in the chart above.

0% [1] sometimes [3] usually 100%
never [2] often [4] always

5 Rewrite the sentences with the words in parentheses.

1 I'm late for school. (never)
I'm never late for school.

2 I do my homework on the weekend. (always)
I always do my homework on the weekend.

3 Do you go shopping with friends? (sometimes)
Do you sometimes go shopping with friends?

4 I'm tired after school. (often)
I'm often tired after school.

5 Do you take photos with your phone? (usually)
Do you usually take photos with your phone?

Use it!

6 Discuss the sentences in Exercise 5. Are they true for you?

Are you always late for school?

No, I'm never late for school!

Grammar Game

Students write one extra true sentence about themselves using an adverb of frequency (e.g., *I always eat pizza on Friday.*). In groups, or with the whole class, students take turns reading their sentence aloud without saying the adverb of frequency. The other students must guess the adverb of frequency they think is missing.

Homework

Workbook p5, Exercises 1–3

Lesson Aim: I can talk about personal possessions.

Warmer

In pairs, students discuss who has the most things in their school bag.

Teacher Support Hub ppxxxviii–xxxix

S.06–S.07 Audioscripts ppT129–130

1 S.06 Alternatively, students can cover the pictures and play a game in small groups. Student A chooses an object from the box and draws it. The first student to guess what it is wins a point and takes the next turn.

Target Vocabulary

bus pass ˈbʌsˌpæs
camera ˈkæm·rə
headphones ˈhedˌfoʊnz
keys kiz
laptop ˈlæpˌtɑp
money ˈmʌ·ni
passport ˈpæsˌpɔrt
phone foʊn
portable charger ˈpɔr·t̬ə·bəl ˈtʃɑr·dʒər
tablet ˈtæb·lɪt

2 Encourage students to do the activity without looking at the box.

Extra Vocabulary Practice

Learn to Learn

Using vocabulary cards has some advantages over writing lists of words: cards can be easier to use when testing yourself and others, and you can shuffle them.

3 & 4 Tell students that the drawings do not need to be perfect.

5 ★ Allow students two minutes to think and take notes before attempting the activity.

Vocabulary Bank SB p127

VOCABULARY AND LISTENING

Personal Possessions

1 
2 
3 
4 

5 
6 
7 
8 
9 
10 

S.06 **1** **Match the words with the photos. Listen, check, and repeat.**

bus pass	4	money	3
camera	9	passport	8
headphones	2	phone	7
keys	6	portable charger	5
laptop	10	tablet	1

2 **Complete the sentences with words from Exercise 1.**

1 Where are my *keys*? I can't open the door.
2 Martin is always late. Can I borrow your **phone** to text him?
3 You can't go to France without your **passport**.
4 I want to take good photos. I need a nice **camera**.
5 That music is very loud. Use your **headphones**.

LEARN TO LEARN

Making Vocabulary Cards

Make vocabulary cards to help you learn new words. Draw a picture on one side and write the word on the other.

3 **Make your own vocabulary cards for the words in Exercise 1.**

4 **Test a partner. Show your cards. Can your partner say the words in English?**

Use It!

5 **Describe a possession from Exercise 1 for your partner to guess. Think about:**

- when and where you use it
- what you use it for

I use it every day. I always keep it in my bag. I use it to get to school.

Is it your bus pass?

A Conversation

S.07 **6** **Listen to the conversation. Circle the club Alex wants to go to.**

a (the coding club) b the photography club

S.07 **7** **Listen again and circle the correct answers.**

1 Emma goes to the … club.
a coding (b) photography
2 Alex … taking photos.
a likes (b) doesn't like
3 Alex has a …
(a) tablet. b laptop.
4 Mr. Adams …
(a) is a good teacher. b knows Bill Gates.
5 In her free time, Libby writes …
a a blog. (b) computer programs.

Voice It!

8 **Do you go to any school clubs? Which ones? What school club would you like to go to?**

STARTER UNIT 7

6 S.07 Write *coding club* and *photography club* on the board and ask students what vocabulary they might expect to hear relating to each club (e.g., *computer, programming, pictures, camera*).

7 S.07 Before playing the audio again, ask students, in pairs, to discuss the questions, based on what they remember from the first listening. Support weaker students by asking stronger ones to raise their hand when they hear an answer in the audio.

8 Elicit different school clubs and write a list on the board before students discuss the questions.

Flipped Class

▶ Ask students to watch **video S.2** and do **Video Worksheet S.2** in the *Teacher's Resource Bank* in preparation for the next lesson.

Homework

Workbook p5, Exercise 4

Lesson Aim: I can talk about likes and dislikes and use the verb *to have.*

Warmer

▶ Play **video S.2** and elicit that James hates using his phone and going shopping, but he loves using his computer, hanging out with friends, and watching a sci-fi series. Give students a few minutes, in groups, to discuss the things that they love or hate.

S.08 Audioscript pT130

1 & 2 After feedback, say *I love* … and then mime a number of activities (skiing, reading, playing tennis, etc.) to elicit the -*ing* form of the verbs.

3 ★ Elicit that *don't mind* means that you don't have any strong feelings about something.

4 Tell students that they can tell the truth or a lie. Their partner can ask extra questions to guess if they are lying.

Extra Grammar Speaking Practice

5 Elicit extra personalized examples (e.g., *I … glasses. You … an English book. Sara … a smartphone.*).

6 Fast finishers can write down the questions that statements 1–5 answer (e.g., *Does Alex have his own laptop?*).

7 S.08 Explain that we use *any* in negative sentences and questions.

8 Alternatively, students can write questions in pairs and carry out a class survey, speaking to as many students as possible.

GRAMMAR IN ACTION

Love, Like, Don't Mind, Hate + -ing

Watch video S.2 What two things does James hate? What four things does he love?

I **love** [1]**help**_ing_ people.
Emma **likes** [2]**us**_ing_ the new cameras.
Alex and Libby **like** [3]**writ**_ing_ computer programs.

1 Complete the words in the chart above.

2 Write the sentences with the correct form of the verbs in parentheses.

1. Emma likes _meeting_ (meet) new people.
2. Alex doesn't like _taking_ (take) photos.
3. Libby doesn't mind _helping_ (help) Alex.
4. Mr. Adams loves _telling_ (tell) stories.

3 Complete the blog post with the correct form of the verbs in the boxes.

love 😊😊😊 ~~like~~ 😊 not mind 😐 not like ☹ hate ☹☹☹

do get up help ~~listen~~ speak

Jack 😊 [1]_likes listening_ to music. Mic Lowry is his favorite band. He ☹☹☹ [2]_hates getting up_ early. He 😊😊😊 [3]_loves speaking_ English, even in our French class! I ☹ [4]_don't like doing_ my math homework, but Jack 😐 [5]_doesn't mind helping_ me.

Use It!

4 Think of five sentences using *love*, *like*, *don't mind*, and *hate*. Does your partner agree with you?

I don't mind cleaning the kitchen. *I hate doing it!*

To Have

	I/You/We/They	*He/She/It*
+	We [1]_have_ two new cameras.	She **has** a new camera.
–	I **don't have** a map of the school.	Alex **doesn't** [3]_have_ a map of the school.
?	**Do** you **have** your own laptop? Yes, I **do**. / No, I [2]_don't_.	[4]_Does_ he **have** his own laptop? Yes, he [5]_does_. / No, he **doesn't**.

5 Complete the examples in the chart above.

6 Complete the sentences with the correct form of *to have*.

1. Alex _doesn't have_ his own laptop. ✗
2. Alex _has_ a tablet. ✓
3. They _have_ a lot of laptops at the club. ✓
4. Libby _has_ her own computer. ✓
5. She _doesn't have_ much free time. ✗

7 S.08 Complete the text with the correct form of *to have*. Then listen and check.

We [1]_have_ a new student in our class. Her name's Paola. What [2]_do_ we _have_ in common? A lot! She [3]_has_ brown hair and blue eyes – just like me! [4]_Does_ she _have_ any brothers and sisters? Yes, she [5]_does_. She [6]_has_ two little sisters, just like me. She [7]_doesn't have_ any brothers. We [8]_have_ the same phones and headphones! We [9]_don't have_ school today because it's a holiday. I'd like to call Paola – but I [10]_don't have_ her phone number. It's annoying!

Use It!

8 Ask and answer questions using *to have*.

Do you have any brothers or sisters?

Grammar Game

Ask students to think about objects they have in their bags (they can look up any unknown words in a dictionary). In pairs, they take turns asking each other "Do you have a/any … (sunglasses/keys/phone/journal)?" When the answer is *yes*, the student takes the object out of their bag. After three minutes, the student whose partner has the most items out of their bag wins.

Homework

Workbook p6

Lesson Aim: I can write a personal profile.

Warmer

Students discuss free-time activities they enjoy. Encourage them to mention activities other students might not expect or be aware of.

Teacher Support Hub ppxlii–xliii

1 To recycle the vocabulary from p4, elicit the word *gymnastics* /ˌdʒɪmˈnæs·tɪks/ from the photo. Elicit that Ernesto likes gymnastics and going for bike rides. Then ask students to mark the parts where the text mentions what Ernesto likes.

2 ★ Guide students to find in the text the key words (or their synonyms) from the questions (2 *early* = *6 a.m.*; 3 *on his own* = *on my own*; 4 *weekend* = *weekend*).

3 ★★★ On the board, write *My cat's name's Dora and she is small, black, and cute.* Elicit the functions of the two apostrophes and the commas before students attempt the task.

4 After feedback, elicit the different functions of the apostrophes in sentences 1, 2, 3, and 5.

Useful Language Practice

5 Allow students to share their plans after completing them. Encourage them to ask each other questions to generate extra interesting ideas and information that they could include in their profile.

WRITING
A Personal Profile

1 **Look at the photo. What does Ernesto like doing? Read his profile and check.**

1 Hi! My name's Ernesto Mendes and I'm 14 years old. I'm from Vancouver in Canada. I live with my mom and dad, my grandma, and my cat. My cat's name is Tiger. My best friends are Joel and Ruby.

2 My favorite free-time activity is gymnastics. I train every day. Training starts at 6:00 a.m. It's tough because I hate getting up early, but I love practicing.

3 I also like going for bike rides on my own. I have a new bike, and I usually go for a bike ride after school. I don't have much free time, but I always hang out with my friends on the weekend. We often go to Joel's place because he has a swimming pool.

2 **Read the profile again. Answer the questions.**

1 Where is Ernesto from?
He's from Vancouver in Canada.

2 Why does Ernesto get up early?
because he does gymnastics training / because gymnastics training starts at 6 a.m.

3 What does he like doing on his own?
He likes going for bike rides.

4 What does he do on the weekend?
He hangs out with his friends.

3 **Look at the *Useful Language* box. Find and underline examples of apostrophes and commas in the profile. Match them with the correct use and write them in the box.**

Useful Language

We use apostrophes:
- for contractions / short forms: *name's*
  I'm, It's, don't
- to show possession: *My cat's name*
  Joel's place

We use commas to indicate a pause:
my mom and dad, my grandma, and my cat
I hate getting up early, but ... ; I have a new bike, and ... ; I don't have much free time, but ...

4 **Rewrite the sentences with commas and apostrophes in the correct places.**

1 Were from South Africa.
We're from South Africa.

2 Whats your history teachers name?
What's your history teacher's name?

3 That isnt my tablet.
That isn't my tablet.

4 I have a cat three horses and a parrot!
I have a cat, three horses, and a parrot!

5 My sisters friends very noisy!
My sister's friend's very noisy!

PLAN

5 **Plan your own personal profile. Take notes for each paragraph.**

1 You, your family, and friends:

2 Your favorite free-time activity:
- what it is, where and how often you do it

3 Other free-time activities:
- what you like doing on your own or with friends
- when and where you do the activities

WRITE

6 **Write your profile. Remember to include three paragraphs, the information in Exercise 5, the simple present, adverbs of frequency, *love*, etc. + *-ing*, and *to have*.**

CHECK

7 **Do you ...**
- describe you, your family, and friends?
- describe your favorite free-time activity?
- describe other things you like doing?
- use apostrophes and commas correctly?

STARTER UNIT 9

6 Write the things that students need to include on the board. Ask students to copy these in their notebooks with a box next to each that they can check as they are writing their profile.

7 After checking their work using the information in Exercise 5 and the items in Exercise 6, students display their profiles around the room and read as many of them as possible. Ask: *Which is the most interesting profile? Why?*

Homework

Workbook p7

Students can also write a new profile, this time about their best friend.

Lesson Aim: I can talk about TV shows.

Warmer

Give students three minutes to think of a famous TV show and write down a few sentences about it. In groups, they take turns reading their sentences one at a time. The first student to guess correctly wins a point.

Teacher Support Hub ppxxxiv–xxxv

▶ Start It!

Unit Quiz

1 & 2 Elicit that the boy is watching something on his tablet, and then ask students to name a few other ways that people can watch TV shows.

3 Elicit possible answers from the class. Play **video 1.1** and elicit that he built the first television (or "televisor," as he called it).

4 Give students three minutes, in groups, to discuss the question. Get feedback from the whole class.

Video Comprehension Questions

Flipped Class

In preparation for **Explore It!** (p11), students research interesting facts about TV.

1 What are you watching?

LEARNING OUTCOMES

I can ...

- understand Tweets, a guided tour, and a text about Japanese manga and anime
- talk about TV shows and making movies
- write a description of my favorite Internet or TV personality
- understand how to use the present continuous and simple present, and adverbs of manner
- ask for and give opinions
- use real examples, listen for specific information, understand new words, and organize your notebook

Start It!

1 Look at the photo. What is the boy doing?
2 Before you watch, where do you watch TV shows?
3 What did John Logie Baird build? Watch and check. television or "televisor," as he called it
4 How do you think TV changed the world?

Watch video 1.1

Grammar in Action 1.2 p13

Grammar in Action 1.3 p15

Everyday English 1.4 p16

Globetrotters 1.5 p18

10 WHAT ARE YOU WATCHING? | UNIT 1

Unit Aims

Skills

I can ...

- understand Tweets p12
- ask for and give opinions p16
- write a description of my favorite Internet or TV personality p17
- understand a text about Japanese manga and anime p18

Language

I can ...

- talk about TV shows p11
- understand how to use the present continuous p13
- talk about making movies p14
- understand how to use the simple present, present continuous, and adverbs of manner p15

Learn to Learn

I can ...

- use real examples to help learn vocabulary p11
- listen for specific information p14
- understand new words p19
- organize a notebook p21

Extra Resources

- Finished? Student's Book p118
- Vocabulary Bank, Student's Book p128
- Workbook pp8–15
- Grammar Reference and Practice, Workbook pp88–89
- Teacher Support Hub, Teacher's Book ppxxxiv–xlvii

Digital Resource Pack

(on Cambridge One)

- *Teacher's Resource Bank* for word lists, differentiated worksheets, *Culture Projects*, and many other extra resources
- *Practice Extra, Presentation Plus, Test Generator*, and *Digital Collaboration Space*

Lesson Aim: I can talk about TV shows.

Warmer

Give students two minutes to think of as many different types of TV shows as they can, and elicit ideas.

1.01–1.02 Audioscripts pT130

1 1.01 Pause after each word to drill the pronunciation. You can also write the words on the board and have the students come up and mark where the stress is in each word.

Target Vocabulary

cartoon kɑrˈtun
comedy ˈkɑ·mɪ·di
cooking show ˈkʊ·kɪŋ ˌʃoʊ
documentary ˌdɑk·jəˈmen·tə·ri
drama ˈdrɑ·mə
game show ˈgeɪm ˌʃoʊ
reality show riˈæ·lɪ·t̬i ˌʃoʊ
soap opera ˈsoʊp ˌɑ·pə·rə
sports show ˈspɔrts ˌʃoʊ
streaming series ˈstri·mɪŋ ˈsɪə·riz
talk show ˈtɔk ˌʃoʊ
the news ðə nuz

Extra Vocabulary Practice

2 Alternatively, act out a sentence with appropriate intonation and body language (e.g., excitedly, *Can they score in the last minute?!*), and ask the class to guess the type of TV show (e.g., *sports show*). Students can then work in groups to do the same and guess each other's types of shows.

3 1.02 ★ Play the audio once, and to support weaker students, ask volunteers to come to the board and write the key words they heard. Then play the audio again.

Vocabulary Bank SB p128

VOCABULARY
TV Shows

1 1.01 Match eight of the TV shows in the box with the photos. (Circle) the four shows that aren't in the photos. Listen, check, and repeat.

cartoon	6	reality show	3
(comedy)		soap opera	1
(cooking show)		(sports show)	
documentary	5	streaming series	7
drama	2	talk show	4
game show	8	(the news)	

2 Match the sentences with TV shows from Exercise 1.

1 "Put your potatoes in a pan and add some salt." *cooking show*
2 "They're coming! We need to get out of here." drama
3 "Giant pandas are in danger. There are only about 1,800 left." documentary
4 "We have some really interesting guests on tonight's show." talk show
5 "Can they score in the last minute?" sports show
6 "Today: A hurricane hits the the news

3 1.02 Listen. Write the shows the people talk about.

1 *comedy*
2 game show
3 streaming series
4 soap opera
5 reality show
6 cartoon

LEARN TO LEARN
Using Real Examples

When you learn vocabulary, think of examples to help you remember it.

4 Think of an example of each type of TV show in Exercise 1.

5 Ask about your partner's TV shows. Can you guess what they are?

What type of show is it? — *A sports show.*

Use It!

6 Complete the sentences so they are true for you. Tell your partner.

1 I love watching ______
2 My family often watches ______
3 My favorite TV show is ______
4 I hate ______

Explore It!

Guess the correct answer.

Which country in the world watches the most TV?

a Poland (b) U.S.A. c Japan

Find an interesting fact about TV. Then write a question for your partner to answer.

Learn to Learn

Examples can create memorable associations, especially if they are personalized (e.g., students could think of their favorite cartoon, soap opera).

4 & 5 Students could do Exercise 4 in pairs and Exercise 5 in a group with another pair so as to generate more ideas.

TV Shows Quiz

6 If there is time, ask students to walk around the class and talk to as many other people as possible until they find someone they have something in common with.

Explore It!

Students ask each other their questions in groups. After the answers are revealed, they vote on the most interesting fact, which they read to the whole class.

Homework

Workbook p8

Warmer

Elicit that a Tweet /twit/ is a short text posted on Twitter /ˈtwɪ·tər/. Elicit that Twitter is used to share ideas and content online, that the @ (at) symbol is used to reply or publicly message someone, and the # (hashtag) symbol is used to explain the topic of the Tweet.

Teacher Support Hub ppxxxvi-xxxvii

1 & 2 1.03 Ask students to skim the text quickly to check their guess to the question in Exercise 1. Then allow the students to read more slowly to answer the questions in Exercise 2.

3 EXAM Encourage students to underline the sections of the text where they found the answers.

4 Ask students to find the words from the box in the text and read the whole sentence around them to guess the meaning from context.

Extra Vocabulary Practice

5 Elicit a few historical events to generate ideas, and then allow a few minutes of thinking time before asking students to speak in pairs.

READING

Tweets

1 Look at the pictures and titles. What do you think the Tweets are about?

1.03 **2** Read the Tweets. Match the people with the TV shows. Then listen and check.

1 Jack — a a comedy
2 Holly — b the news
3 Rory — c a streaming series

3 EXAM Check (✓) the correct column.

	Jack	Holly	Rory
1 likes different TV shows from their friend			✓
2 does media studies	✓		
3 is with a friend now		✓	
4 talks about a friend in a different place			✓

4 Match the words with the definitions.

average episode season subscribe

1 one individual show in a series **episode**
2 typical, normal **average**
3 arrange to pay and receive something regularly **subscribe**
4 a period in which a show appears regularly on TV **season**

Voice It!

5 Imagine you are watching a famous event from history on the news. Discuss the questions.

1 Where are you?
2 Who or what can you see?
3 How many people are there?
4 How do you feel?

Crazy about TV @crazyabouttv
Apart from sleeping, the average teenager spends more time in front of a television than doing any other free-time activity! So … are you watching TV right now? Where are you watching it and who with? We want to know! Tweet us and send us your photos. #crazyaboutTV

JackLong @JLo-o-o-ng
I'm learning about the history of TV in media studies this week. So for homework, I'm traveling back to 1969 to watch the news about Neil Armstrong, the first person on the moon.

Crazy about TV @crazyabouttv
@JLo-o-o-ng Amazing! Neil Armstrong and Buzz Aldrin are walking on the moon. Around 530 million people are watching them with you. We're over the moon, too! #crazyaboutTV

Holly Bardsley @HBards
At the moment, I'm sitting in my bedroom with my best friend @superfanz. We're watching our favorite streaming series, *Stranger Things*, on my new tablet. We're super fans and this episode is so scary!

Crazy about TV @crazyabouttv
@HBards Here's a cool fact for you. More than 100 million people around the world subscribe to Netflix, and you're one of them. Do you want to know about the next season of *Stranger Things*? Just ask us! Spoiler alert! #crazyaboutTV

Rory Green @RoryG
I'm waiting for my favorite comedy to start, so I'm taking a selfie and I'm messaging my friend @laughingboi at the same time! He isn't watching TV – he's listening to music. He doesn't like comedies.

Crazy about TV @crazyabouttv
@RoryG Believe it or not, if you're an average American teenager, you probably send about 128 instant messages a day! #crazyaboutTV

Finished? p118 Ex. 1

Class Challenge

The person with the most Twitter followers is Rihanna / Taylor Swift / **Barack Obama**.

Extend It!

In pairs, students choose the most interesting idea from Exercise 5 and write a Tweet about it in reply to @crazyaboutTV. The Tweet should be a maximum of 280 characters (including spaces and punctuation).

Finished?

Students turn to p118 and do Exercise 1.

Flipped Class

Ask students to watch **video 1.2** and do **Video Worksheet 1.2** in the *Teacher's Resource Bank* in preparation for the next lesson.

Homework

Workbook p9

Lesson Aim: I can understand how to use the present continuous.

Warmer

Ask students to talk about a TV show they are watching at the moment and discuss if they like it or not, and why.

▶ Play **video 1.2**. Elicit that Ben and Nick are playing a video game and watching a vlog, and that the vlogger is chatting and vlogging.

1.05–1.06 Audioscripts pT130

1 Encourage students to complete the chart and compare answers in pairs before looking at p12.

Pronunciation

1.04–1.05 Ask students to turn to SB p141 for pronunciation practice of contractions with *to be*.

Grammar Game

Refer students back to SB p4 and review the phrases for talking about hobbies and sports. Put students into teams. Ask one student to stand in front of the class and mime an action. The first team to guess the action, using the present continuous (e.g., *You are playing tennis.*), wins a point and sends a new student to mime another activity.

Get It Right!

Point out to students that these verbs usually describe states (or situations), not actions.

2 & 3 Ask students to check their own work by circling all the *to be* verbs in their answers in one color and underlining the *-ing* in another color to promote self-correction.

Watch video 1.2
What are Ben and Nick doing?
What two things is the vlogger doing?

GRAMMAR IN ACTION

Present Continuous

	I	He/She/It	We/You/They
+	**I'm sitting** in my bedroom.	He [1] 's **listening** to music.	Neil Armstrong and Buzz Aldrin [3] are **walking** on the moon.
–	**I'm not sitting** in class.	He [2] isn't **watching** TV.	We **aren't watching** the news.
?	**Am** I **listening** to music? Yes, I **am**. / No, **I'm not**.	**Is** Rory's friend **listening** to music? Yes, he **is**. / No, he **isn't**.	[4] Are you **watching** TV right now? Where [5] are you **watching** it?

Pronunciation p141

Get It Right!

We don't usually use some verbs with the present continuous. For example, **know**, **understand**, **like**, **love**, **prefer**, **remember**.

Do you understand me? **NOT** ~~*Are you understanding me?*~~

1 Complete the examples in the chart above. Use the Tweets on page 12 to help you.

2 Write sentences with the present continuous.

1. Jack / watch TV / with 530 million other people.
   Jack is watching TV with 530 million other people.
2. Holly and her friend / not sit / in the library.
   Holly and her friend aren't sitting in the library.
3. Holly and her friend / watch / a streaming series now.
   Holly and her friend are watching a streaming series now.
4. Rory / not watch / his favorite comedy at the moment.
   Rory isn't watching his favorite comedy at the moment.

3 Complete the blog with present continuous verbs.

This week I [1] *'m researching* (research) my favorite subject – TV! I'm very happy because I [2] 'm not doing (not do) it on my own. I [3] 'm preparing (prepare) a presentation with my friend Saul. At the moment, Saul [4] isn't talking (not talk) to me. He [5] 's watching (watch) a new online series, and he [6] 's taking (take) notes. I'm tired right now, so I [7] 'm taking (take) a break. But we [8] 're really enjoying (enjoy) this project.

1.06 4 Complete the conversation with the present continuous form of the verbs. Then listen and check.

call ~~do~~ give interview study talk watch

ROSA What [1] *are* you *doing* right now, Toni?
TONI I [2] 'm talking to you.
ROSA Ha, ha. Very funny. [3] Are you studying for the math test?
TONI No, I [4] 'm watching a talk show. Why [5] are you calling me?
ROSA Well, this math homework [6] is giving me a headache. Can you help me?
TONI Sorry, Rosa. I can't talk now. They [7] 're interviewing Ed Sheeran. I'll call you back, OK? Bye.
ROSA Great. Thanks a lot, Toni.

Use it!

5 Write questions. Then ask and answer with a partner.

1. what / you / wear?
   What are you wearing?
2. what / your teacher / do / right now?
   What is your teacher doing right now?
3. where / your best friend / sit / today?
   Where is your best friend sitting today?

What are you wearing? *I'm wearing ...*

Finished? p118 Ex. 2

4 1.06 To support any weaker students, ask fast finishers to write the verbs in the box in the correct order on the board. Play the audio to check answers.

5 ★★★ Encourage students, in pairs, to write two extra questions for another pair to answer.

Extra Grammar Practice Speaking Game

Finished?

Students turn to p118 and do Exercise 2.

Homework

Workbook p10

Lesson Aim: I can talk about making movies.

Teacher Support Hub
ppxxxviii–xxxix

1.07–1.08 **Audioscripts pT131**

1 1.07 ★★★ Students cover the box and work in pairs to describe the picture using the present continuous. After feedback, the students repeat the task with a new partner, using the new vocabulary.

Target Vocabulary
actor ˈæk·tər
camera operator ˈkæm·rə ˈɑ·pəˌreɪ·t̬ər
costume ˈkɑs·tum
(digital) camera (ˈdɪ·dʒɪ·t̬əl) ˈkæm·rə
director dəˈrek·tər
lights laɪts
makeup artist ˈmeɪkˌʌp ˈɑr·t̬ɪst
script skrɪpt
set set
sound engineer saʊnd ˌen·dʒəˈnɪər

2 ★★★ After feedback, students choose one of the words they haven't selected and make a sentence with it.

Extra Vocabulary Practice

3 ★ Allow students to write their descriptions before speaking.

4 Elicit ideas on the board, but don't give answers at this stage: *They're used in movies. The castle is part of a set.*

5 1.08 Elicit the exact phrase in the audio: *Avatar's my favorite movie!*

Vocabulary Bank SB p128

VOCABULARY AND LISTENING
Making Movies

1.07 **1** Match the words with the people and things in the picture. Listen, check, and repeat.

actor	3	lights	2
camera operator	7	makeup artist	6
costume	9	script	8
(digital) camera	4	set	1
director	10	sound engineer	5

2 Circle the correct word in each sentence.
1 It's too dark. We need extra *lights* / *cameras*.
2 They're building the *director* / *set* this week.
3 We can't start filming – the main *operator* / *actor* isn't here.
4 Who is writing the *script* / *lights*?
5 I'm not wearing that *costume* / *camera*. No way!
6 We can't hear the voices very well. Where's the *makeup artist* / *sound engineer*?

Use It!

3 Choose a job from Exercise 1 and describe what you're doing. Can your partner guess the job?

I'm sitting in my chair. I'm talking to the actors, and I'm looking at the set.

A Guided Tour

4 Look at the photos. Where do you think you can see these things? What are they?

1.08 **5** Listen and circle Matt's favorite movie.
a *Thor* b *Avatar* c *The Lord of the Rings*

LEARN TO LEARN
Listening for Specific Information

Check what type of answer you need (a number, a name, a place, a job, etc.) before you listen.

6 Read the questions in Exercise 7. Write the type of answer you think you need to listen for.
1 a place
2 a number
3 a job
4 a place
5 a number
6 a job

1.08 **7** Listen again and answer the questions.
1 Where does Matt live? Wellington
2 How many people visit movie locations in New Zealand each year? more than 3 million
3 What is Clara's job? She's a guide.
4 Where do the students go first? to the costumes section
5 How tall are some of the bigatures? 9 metres
6 What is Martin's job? He's a camera operator.

Voice It!

8 What is on your dream movie studio tour?

6 ★ Do this as a whole-class activity and guide students to the correct answers.

7 1.08 Before they listen again, allow students to discuss the questions in pairs based on what they remember from the first listening.

8 Students work in small groups to invent their dream tour, thinking about:
1 a movie or TV series
2 what they might see on the tour
3 who they might meet.
They then present their ideas to the class and vote for the best tour they heard about.

Learn to Learn
Reflecting on the type of information they need before listening will help students cope better with longer texts and realize they don't need to understand every word.

Flipped Class
Ask students to watch **video 1.3** and do **Video Worksheet 1.3** in the *Teacher's Resource Bank* in preparation for the next lesson.

Homework
Workbook p11

Lesson Aim: I can understand how to use the simple present, present continuous, and adverbs of manner.

Warmer

Students discuss in pairs whether they would like to start a vlog in English and what they would talk about.

▶ Play **video 1.3** if it was not assigned for homework. Elicit that the boy is doing a vlog for media studies. He gives the following tips:

- You can use a camera that has a microphone or your phone.
- Check sound and lights.
- Outline what you want to say (take notes).
- Be yourself – don't speak too quickly.
- Have fun!

1.09 Audioscript pT131

1 Point out that we use the simple present for things that always happen. We use the present continuous for things that are happening now but will finish.

2 & 3 1.09 ★Allow students to compare answers in pairs before conducting feedback with the whole class.

Extra Grammar Practice
Speaking Game

4 Tell students that we don't use frequency adverbs like *always* or *sometimes* with the present continuous.

5 Explain that adverbs of manner give extra information about *how* someone does something.

6 Point out that *fast* is both an adjective and an adverb and that we need to change a final *-y* to *-ily*.

GRAMMAR IN ACTION

Simple Present and Present Continuous

Watch video 1.3
What is he doing? Describe two tips he gives.

Simple Present	Present Continuous
More than 3 million people [1] visit locations for movies here every year.	Today, I [2] 'm visiting / am visiting a movie workshop with my media studies class.
Time expressions: *always, sometimes, never, every day/week*, etc.	Time expressions: (*right*) *now, at the moment, today, this morning*, etc.

1 Complete the examples in the chart above with the correct form of *visit*.

2 Circle the correct verbs.

1. Matt (lives) / *is living* in Wellington.
2. They *wait* / (*are waiting*) for their tour guide.
3. Martin *works* / (*is working*) hard today.
4. Martin always (*uses*) / *is using* a digital camera.

3 1.09 Complete the text with the correct form of the verbs in parentheses. Then listen and check.

Media studies [1] is (be) my favorite subject at school. I [2] love (love) it! This week, we [3] 're studying (study) the history of film. We [4] 're learning (learn) all about talkies, CGI, and lots more! I [5] don't know (not know) much about it. It [6] takes (take) a long time and a lot of people to make a movie. Sorry! Time to go! My little brother [7] is making (make) a lot of noise downstairs. I think he [8] 's watching (watch) his favorite comedy with my mom and dad. They all [9] love (love) it, and they always [10] laugh (laugh) a lot! 😂 What [11] are you doing (do) at school this week?

Use It!

4 Write sentences with the verbs and time expressions. Use the correct tense.

do / sometimes drive / now ~~watch / always~~

1. We / sports shows on the weekend.
   We always watch sports shows on the weekend.
2. They / their homework together.
   They sometimes do their homework together.
3. My parents / me to the gym.
   My parents are driving me to the gym now.

Adverbs of Manner

If I'm not explaining [1] *clearly* (clear), let me know!
Talk [2] quietly (quiet), please.
He's working [3] hard (hard) today.

5 Complete the examples in the chart above with the correct form of the words in parentheses.

6 Write the adverbs for adjectives 1–6. Circle the ones that don't use *-ly*.

1. nice *nicely*
2. fast fast
3. beautiful beautifully
4. loud loudly
5. happy happily
6. good well

Use It!

7 Write questions. Use the simple present or present continuous and the adverb form of the adjectives.

1. you / always / make / new friends? (easy)
   Do you always make friends easily?
2. you / speak / English / today? (good)
   Are you speaking English well today?
3. your math teacher / explain / everything? (clear)
   Does your math teacher explain everything clearly?
4. you / work / this term? (hard)
   Are you working hard this term?

8 Ask and answer the questions in Exercise 7.

Finished? p118 Ex. 3

7 ★★★ Students write two extra questions about TV shows or movies, one with the simple present and one with the present continuous.

8 Monitor and take note of any common mistakes, writing them on the board for the class to correct.

Grammar Game

Students make three sentences about themselves using the present continuous, one of which is false. In groups, their classmates ask extra questions to guess which sentence is false.

Finished?

Students turn to p118 and do Exercise 3.

Homework

Workbook p12

Lesson Aim: I can ask for and give opinions.

Warmer

Tell students you don't know what TV show to watch at the moment. Elicit a few recommendations from them, drilling the phrase *You should watch … because it's …*

Teacher Support Hub ppxl–xli

1.10 Audioscript pT131

1 1.10 ★★★ Students listen and answer the question with their books closed. Elicit that Eva does like the show.

2 1.10 Clarify the meaning of *I'm not really into* (= I'm not very interested in) and the pronunciation of *awful* /ˈɔ·fəl/.

Useful Language Practice

3 Play **video 1.4** and drill the pronunciation of the phrases, dealing with any difficulties with meaning.

4 After feedback, encourage students to rehearse the conversations in pairs using appropriate intonation. Ask volunteers to perform the conversations for the whole class.

5 Give students plenty of thinking time and allow them to use dictionaries if needed. Students share their ideas with a partner, who should ask extra questions to generate more ideas to write about.

6 During rehearsal, encourage one student in each pair to check for correct grammar and one to check for appropriate vocabulary.

7 If appropriate, students can record their conversations on their phones, deleting the recording and trying again if they did not like their performance. They then pass their phone to another pair, who listens and answers the relevant questions.

Flipped Class

In preparation for the **Writing** lesson (p17), ask students to research facts about their favorite TV or Internet celebrity.

SPEAKING
Asking for and Giving Opinions

1.10 **1** Listen to the conversation. Does Eva like the show? Yes, she does.

EVA	What are you doing?
ALEX	I'm watching the second episode of this new comedy series.
EVA	But it's lunchtime.
ALEX	I'm not having lunch today. Lunch can wait.
EVA	So, what [1] do you think of the show?
ALEX	I love it! Do you like comedies?
EVA	No, I don't. I'm not [2] really into them. I [3] prefer watching documentaries and dramas.
ALEX	Everyone's watching this one. It's really cool! Why don't you watch it with me?
EVA	I'm not sure.
ALEX	I think you'll really like it.
EVA	OK. Let's see.
ALEX	Well? What do you think of it?
EVA	Actually, it's [4] not bad !

1.10 **2** Complete the conversation with the phrases from the *Useful Language* box. Then listen and check.

Useful Language

I prefer watching …
I'm not really into it/them.
It's great / good / not bad / awful.
What do you think of … ?

3 Look at the *Everyday English* box. Find and underline the phrases in the conversation.

Watch video 1.4
Everyday English

Actually … It's really cool!
Let's see. Well?

4 Complete the conversations with the *Everyday English* phrases.

1 A This actor is great, isn't he?
B Actually , I don't really like him.
2 A Well ? Do you like the show?
B Yes, I do. It's really cool !
3 A Come with us to the gym on Saturday.
B Maybe, but I'm not sure. Let's see .

PLAN

5 With your partner, choose two TV shows to talk about. Take notes about them.

Which shows? ______

What do you think of them? ______

Why? ______

SPEAK

6 Practice a conversation with your partner, asking for and giving opinions about TV shows. Remember to use the simple present and present continuous, vocabulary from this unit, and phrases from the *Useful Language* and *Everyday English* boxes.

CHECK

7 Work with another pair. Listen to their conversation and complete the notes.

Which shows? ______

What do they think of them? ______

Why? ______

Lesson Aim: I can write a description of my favorite Internet or TV personality.

Warmer

Students share what they learned about a TV or Internet celebrity for homework, asking each other extra questions.

Teacher Support Hub ppxlii–xliii

1 & 2 Set a time limit of one minute for the first gist task to encourage faster reading, and then allow more time for Exercise 2, encouraging students to underline key words in the text that helped them select the correct answers.

3 Ask students to discuss the statements and guess the answers in pairs, based on what they remember from the text, before reading again.

4 ★★★ Ask students to cover the *Useful Language* box and find all the instances of *and*, *but*, and *or*. In pairs, they discuss how these words are used before checking the *Useful Language* box.

5 ★★★ After feedback, ask students to write three extra sentences, one for each useful language word, using the vocabulary on p7 (e.g., *I have a phone, but I don't have a tablet. Do you take pictures with your phone or with your camera?*).

Useful Language Practice

6 Students write notes about the celebrity they researched for homework and show them to a new partner. Then they can use the notes to discuss what they will write about.

WRITING

A Description of a Celebrity

1 **Look at the photo. What is the woman holding? Read the description and find the answer.** She's holding a cake.

2 **Match topics a–c with paragraphs 1–3.**

a Why I like this person

b An introduction to the person and her show

c Typical episodes in the show

3 **Read Lidia's description again. Are the sentences *T* (true) or *F* (false)?**

Rosanna Pansino …

1 is from the U.S.A. T

2 has a game show on the Internet. F

3 likes trying other people's recipes. F

4 makes unusual cakes. T

4 **Find and underline examples of *and*, *but*, and *or* in Lidia's description. Complete the *Useful Language* box.**

Useful Language

We use [1] and to add similar information.
We use [2] but to show different information.
We use [3] or when there is a choice of two or more things.

5 **Circle the correct word.**

1 I don't like making cakes, *or* / *but* I love eating them! (but)

2 Ryan Higa is my favorite Internet star, *and* / *but* I often watch his videos. (and)

3 Do you prefer watching comedies *and* / *or* soap operas? (or)

4 Lots of people love talk shows, *and* / *but* I think they're boring. (but)

My Favorite Internet Star

By Lidia Suarez

1 b Rosanna Pansino is my favorite Internet star. She's an American actor, but she also has a cooking show – *Nerdy Nummies*. She bakes fantastic cakes. I love the show and trying her recipes. She has more than 10 million subscribers, and every month her show gets 75 million views.

2 c In each episode, she explains how to make her cakes. But they aren't normal cakes! They look like characters or objects from TV shows, video games, movies, or books. This week, she's making Batman cakes.

3 a I like her because she's a great cook and because she makes the videos herself, too. She uses her own computer, camera, and lights. She always explains her recipes clearly. They're easy to follow and the cakes taste great!

PLAN

6 **Plan a description of your favorite Internet or TV personality. Take notes for three paragraphs.**

1 Who the person is: ______
What they do: ______

2 What they do in each episode: ______
______
What they are doing in this week's episode: ______
______

3 Why I like this person and the show: ______
______

WRITE

7 **Write your description. Remember to include three paragraphs, the correct present tenses, adverbs, and *and*, *but*, and *or*.**

CHECK

8 **Do you …**

- use sentences with *and*, *but*, and *or*?
- give information about what the person usually does and is doing now?
- explain why you like the person?

Finished? p118 Ex. 4

7 & 8 After writing, ask students to highlight the simple present and present continuous forms, adverbs, and words from the *Useful Language* box in a bright color. This will help them with self-assessment. Students can swap texts with a partner to get feedback, and then write a new draft if needed.

Finished?

Students turn to p118 and do Exercise 4.

Flipped Class

Prepare for **Explore It!** (p19). Students research an interesting fact about animated movies.

Homework

Workbook p13

Lesson Aim: I can understand a text about Japanese manga and anime.

Background Information

Studio Ghibli is a Japanese studio that makes animated movies. The word *Ghibli* means "hot desert wind." The studio's movies include *Spirited Away* and *Princess Mononoke*, among many others.

Warmer

In groups, students brainstorm any animated movies they have seen. Then ask each group to choose the best and the worst ones. Elicit contrasting ideas from the class and encourage students to justify their answers.

Video 1.5 develops the theme of movies around the world. Before you play it, make sure students understand the questions. Put students into small groups to discuss them. Elicit that India produces almost 2,000 movies each year, that *Bollywood* comes from a mixture of "Bombay" and "Hollywood," and that actors can film scenes for four movies at the same time.

Video Comprehension Questions

AROUND THE WORLD

READING
An Online Article

1 Look at the photos. What kinds of movies can you see? What country are the movies from?

animated movies / anime, action movies. They're from Japan.

2 Read the article and check your answers.

3 Read the article again. Answer the questions in your notebook.

1 What is the difference between anime and manga?
2 How are manga comics different outside of Japan?
3 Why does the article mention *Howl's Moving Castle* and *Ponyo*?
4 Who is Hayao Miyazaki?
5 What does the number 170,000 refer to?

1 Anime are animated cartoons. Manga are comic books.
2 People read the books from left to right outside of Japan.
3 They are examples of anime movies from Studio Ghibli.
4 He's a director at Studio Ghibli.
5 the number of frames in the movie *Ponyo*

Globetrotters

Watch video 1.5 Bollywood

- How many movies does India produce a year?
- Where does the name Bollywood come from?
- How many different movies can actors be in at the same time?

Voice It!

4 Discuss the questions.

1 Teamwork is an important part of making a movie. Why?
2 What skills do you need to work as a team?
3 What teamwork skills do you have?

Magical Pictures – from Manga to Anime

Are you familiar with *anime*? *Anime* usually refers to Japanese animated cartoons. They often use *manga* (comic book) characters and stories. Manga and anime have a style that is popular around the world, with series such as *Naruto* and *Dragon Ball Z*.

People read Japanese manga comics from right to left. Outside of Japan, some printers change the direction of reading on the page so people can read the stories from left to right.

You may already like anime! Do you like *Howl's Moving Castle* (2004) or *Ponyo* (2008)? Studio Ghibli, an animation studio in Tokyo, Japan, produced these movies. The director, Hayao Miyazaki, is famous for beautiful anime movies. A single movie can take up to eight years and thousands of hours to produce! But what is the process like?

First, screenwriters develop a script for the story. Then they think about the characters. What do they look like? What are their personalities like? What do we learn about the characters in the story? What do they learn about themselves?

Hayao Miyazaki

After this, concept artists draw the characters, their expressions, and their clothes. Next, storyboard artists use the script to **sketch** a **storyboard**. A storyboard shows all the important **scenes** in the movie. Voice actors read the characters' lines in a recording studio, and animators draw the characters and the **backgrounds**. To animate a scene, they make tiny changes to each picture. When they play the **frames** as a video, the characters come alive. It requires a lot of pictures. The movie *Ponyo* has 170,000 frames, and artists animated every scene by hand, not with a computer. The final result is a movie that people everywhere can experience and enjoy.

1 Elicit guesses and write relevant vocabulary on the board, such as *drawing*, *characters*, and *actor*.

2 1.11 After checking the answers, ask students if they have ever seen a Studio Ghibli movie, and invite those who have to try to explain the story, helping them with unknown language.

3 Have students underline key words in the questions and use them to find the information in the text.

4 Write *teamwork* on the board. In groups of four, students brainstorm what it means to demonstrate teamwork (e.g., *We listen to others' ideas. We divide up tasks.*). Elicit a few ideas on the board before letting students discuss the questions.

Teacher Support Hub pxliv

Class Challenge

The first ever animated film was made in 1917 in Japan / the USA / **Argentina**.

Lesson Aim: I can understand a text about Japanese manga and anime.

Learn to Learn

Looking up every unknown word in a dictionary makes reading hard work, so students will be less likely to read in English for pleasure, which is very important. They should instead choose which words are needed for comprehension and which words can be ignored.

5 After feedback, encourage students, in pairs, to find one more difficult word in the text and use the strategies to guess its meaning before checking in a dictionary.

6 After the activity, ask students to choose the best sentences they produced and repeat the exercise in a bigger group so as to expose each other to as many examples as possible.

Extra Vocabulary Practice

Explore It!

Students write their questions based on the facts researched for homework and, in groups, prepare a quiz for the whole class.

Culture Project

See Project Book p22 for further information and activities.

LEARN TO LEARN

Understanding New Words

Don't worry if you don't understand some words. First, try to get a general understanding of the article. Then guess the meaning of the new words.

5 Look at the words in bold in the article. Try to guess their meaning. Then check in a dictionary.

- Look at the words before and after the word.
- Think of similar words in your language.
- Look at any pictures to help you understand.
- Look for other examples of the word in the article.

6 Think of your own sentences with the new words. Say each sentence, but don't say the new word. Can your partner guess it?

Explore It!

Guess the correct answer.

Spirited Away is a famous Studio Ghibli film. The location for the movie is in …

a Taiwan. b Tokyo. c Seoul.

Find three more interesting facts about animated movies. Choose your favorite fact and write a question for your partner.

SHAPE IT!

CULTURE PROJECT

An Infographic

An infographic has illustrations to present information in a clear and memorable way. Make an infographic about a movie-making job.

Teacher's Resource Bank

UNIT 1 | WHAT ARE YOU WATCHING? 19

Lesson Aim: I can review what I have learned and reflect on my progress.

The aim of this page is for students to review the grammar and vocabulary from the unit. You can either do it in class, as a timed progress test, or assign it for homework.

Vocabulary

1 Divide the class into four or five teams. Ask them to close their books. Read the sentences out loud. The first team to shout *Buzz!* and then correct the sentence wins a point.

2 In groups, students brainstorm vocabulary related to making movies. Write appropriate words and phrases on the board before the students attempt the task.

Grammar in Action

3 After feedback, pairs rehearse the conversation using appropriate intonation. Ask for volunteers to act out the conversation for the class.

4 ★★★ After feedback, ask students, in pairs, to write three more sentences, each with a missing word, and give them to another pair to complete.

5 Before the activity, students have three minutes, in groups, to brainstorm as many adverbs that end in *-ly* as possible. The team with the most correct adverbs wins.

6 Ask students to check their answers in pairs before feedback. If students have different answers, encourage them to discuss their reasons.

Unit Quiz Review

1 REVIEW

VOCABULARY

1 The TV shows are wrong. Write the correct ones.

1. My little sister loves **soap operas**. Her favorite character is Sponge Bob. **cartoons**
2. That new **documentary** is so exciting, and it's only the second episode! **streaming series**
3. This **sports show** is about dolphins. **documentary**
4. Which guests are on the **soap opera** tonight? **talk show**
5. Only one person can win the car and the money on this **drama**. **game show**

2 Write the TV and movie words for the definitions.

1. clothes that actors wear in movies **costumes**
2. a person who changes the actors' appearance **makeup artist**
3. the words for a movie **script**
4. the place where they film a TV show **set**
5. the person who tells actors what to do **director**

GRAMMAR IN ACTION

3 Complete the conversation with the present continuous form of the verbs.

HASAN Hey, Yusuf. Are you at home?
YUSUF Yes, I [1] **'m watching** (watch) last night's music show. Where [2] **are** you **calling** (call) from?
HASAN I [3] **'m standing** (stand) outside the house. I don't have my keys.
YUSUF Call Mom.
HASAN I [4] **'m calling** (call) you because Mom [5] **isn't answering** (not answer) her phone. Where are you?
YUSUF I [6] **'m sitting** (sit) in the backyard. The sun [7] **is shining** (shine), the birds [8] **are singing** (sing).
HASAN Yusuf, can you let me in, please? NOW!

4 Complete the sentences with the simple present or present continuous.

1. The actor **isn't reading** the script at the moment. (not read)
2. **Do** you usually **meet** your friends after school? (meet)
3. The students **are studying** for their drama exam this week. (study)
4. Simon always **watches** TV after school. (watch)

5 Rewrite the sentences with adverbs of manner.

1. The children are talking in the library. (quiet)
   The children are talking quietly in the library.
2. Are you writing in your notebooks? (careful)
   Are you writing carefully in your notebooks?
3. The teacher is explaining the activity. (clear)
   The teacher is explaining the activity clearly.
4. We're studying for our exams. (hard)
   We're working hard for our exams.

6 Complete Kim's blog with the simple present, present continuous, and adverbs of manner.

My friend Ava often [1] **comes** (come) to my place on Saturday afternoons, and we [2] **listen** (listen) to music together. This Saturday is different. My dad [3] **is driving** (drive) us to a movie premiere. There's a lot of traffic, so we [4] **aren't moving** (not move) [5] **quickly** (quick). I usually [6] **write** (write) my blog on Saturday evening in my bedroom, but today I [7] **'m typing** (type) it [8] **slowly** (slow) on my phone in the car!

Self-Assessment

I can talk about TV shows.
I can talk about making movies.
I can use the simple present and present continuous.
I can use adverbs of manner.

20 REVIEW | UNIT 1

Review the Unit Theme

Remind students of the unit title: *What are you watching?* Put students into pairs. Have them discuss the following questions: *What kinds of TV shows do you like? Do you prefer watching TV shows, movies, or short videos? What don't you like watching? Why?* Share answers as a class.

Teacher Support Hub ppxlvi

Self-Assessment

Ask students to look at the exercises on p20 and in the rest of the unit to help them decide how confident they are with each language point. Encourage them to discuss their opinions in pairs before deciding which face to circle. You can then give students additional practice exercises from the Workbook.

Homework

Workbook pp14–15

Encourage students to keep their own language notebooks. The notebooks can be paper-based or digital, but they should be organized in a way that is clear and easy to use.

1 Put students into small groups. Ask them to compare notebooks and discuss which they think are the best organized and why. Then they answer the questions. Elicit a few contrasting ideas, as there are no real correct or incorrect answers at this stage.

2 After feedback, students discuss which of these things they already do and why. Encourage volunteers to show the class their notebooks, if appropriate.

3 After feedback, students work in pairs to rank the tips from most to least useful and then compare with a new pair.

SHAPE IT!

4 Supply students with the necessary tools, or ask them to share pens with other students.

5 Encourage students to write a "contract", in which they explain how they will keep their vocabulary organized. Put aside time every week for students to check their partner's notebooks and make sure they are not breaking their contract!

LEARN TO LEARN

LEARN TO ... ORGANIZE YOUR NOTEBOOK

When you organize your notebook, it helps you to study better.

1 Ask and answer with a partner.

1. What do you usually write in your notebook?
2. How often do you use your notebook when you study at home?
3. How can you organize your notebook better?

2 Look at Irina's notebook. Match the tips (1–5) with a–e.

1. Divide your notebook into sections so that you can find things quickly. **a**
2. Use different color pens for different things (for example, adjectives can be red, numbers can be green). **c**
3. Highlight or underline important notes, words, and facts. **e**
4. When you write a text, make a plan on the left and then write on the right. **b**
5. Write all your homework notes (what page, what exercise) in the same place so that you don't forget what you have to do. **d**

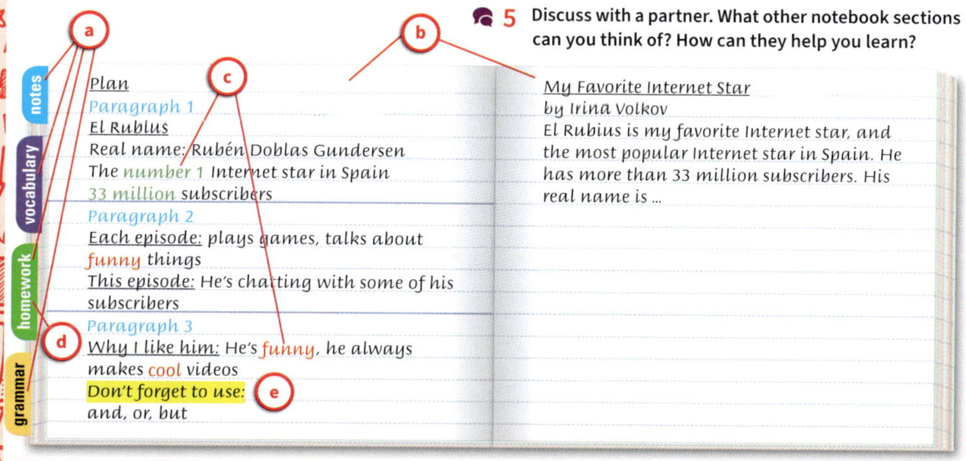

3 Look at the tips in Irina's notebook again. Complete the sentences.

1. Highlighting and underlining help you see the **important** information.
2. You can use the **plan** on the left when you're writing.
3. The **homework** notes help you remember what to do at home.
4. You can use different color pens for **different** things. It's your choice!
5. You can find notes quickly when you use different **sections**.

SHAPE IT!

4 Follow the plan to organize your notebook.

1. Divide your notebook into sections.
2. Choose different color pens for your notes.
3. Get a highlighter for important information (or you can underline it instead).
4. Start using your notebook today!

5 Discuss with a partner. What other notebook sections can you think of? How can they help you learn?

UNIT 1 | LEARN TO LEARN 21

Extend It!

Establish a notebook competition that takes place each month. In the first lesson of each month, ask students to show you their notebooks in order to find the "best notebook" and the "most improved" notebook.

Lesson Aim: I can talk about history.

Warmer

Write *ancient civilizations* on the board. Ask students, in small groups, to brainstorm places and people that come to mind. Elicit ancient civilizations they know about or have studied.

Teacher Support Hub ppxxxiv–xxxv

Start It!

Unit Quiz

1 Elicit that the photo shows an ancient Egyptian carving. Elicit students' ideas about the age of the artwork (between 3200 BCE and 40 CE).

2 & 3 Ask students to discuss the questions in pairs, and then play **video 2.1**.

4 In small groups, students agree on a list of three things. Elicit the things on the board and discuss them with the whole class.

Video Comprehension Questions

Flipped Class

Prepare for **Explore It!** (p23). Students research an interesting fact about the weather.

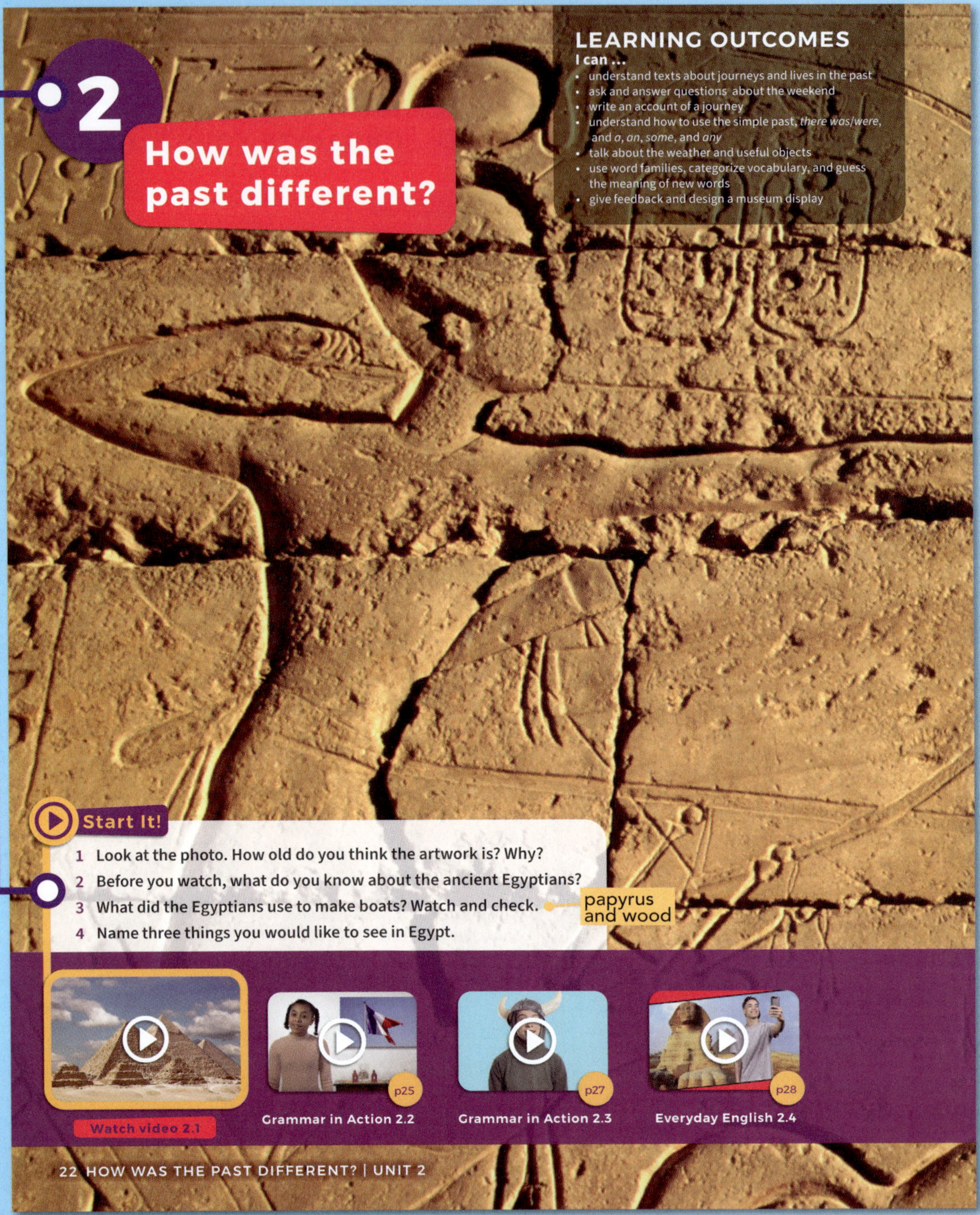

2 How was the past different?

LEARNING OUTCOMES

I can ...

- understand texts about journeys and lives in the past
- ask and answer questions about the weekend
- write an account of a journey
- understand how to use the simple past, *there was/were*, and *a*, *an*, *some*, and *any*
- talk about the weather and useful objects
- use word families, categorize vocabulary, and guess the meaning of new words
- give feedback and design a museum display

Start It!

1 Look at the photo. How old do you think the artwork is? Why?
2 Before you watch, what do you know about the ancient Egyptians?
3 What did the Egyptians use to make boats? Watch and check. papyrus and wood
4 Name three things you would like to see in Egypt.

Watch video 2.1 | Grammar in Action 2.2 p25 | Grammar in Action 2.3 p27 | Everyday English 2.4 p28

22 HOW WAS THE PAST DIFFERENT? | UNIT 2

Unit Aims

Skills

I can ...

- understand a text about lives in the past p24
- talk about my weekend p28
- write an account of a journey p29
- give feedback and design a museum display pp30–31

Language

I can ...

- talk about the weather p23
- understand how to use the simple past p25
- talk about useful objects p26
- understand how to use *there was/were* and *a*, *an*, *some*, and *any* p27

Learn to Learn

I can ...

- recognize word families p23
- categorize vocabulary p26
- guess the meaning of new words p33

Extra Resources

- Finished? Student's Book p119
- Vocabulary Bank, Student's Book p129
- Workbook pp16–23
- Grammar Reference and Practice, Workbook pp90–91
- Teacher Support Hub, Teacher's Book ppxxxiv–xlvii

Digital Resource Pack

(on Cambridge One)

- *Teacher's Resource Bank* for word lists, differentiated worksheets, *Culture Projects*, and many other extra resources.
- *Practice Extra*, *Presentation Plus*, *Test Generator*, and *Digital Collaboration Space*

Warmer

Give students two minutes to write down as many weather words as possible. The ones with the most correct words win.

2.01 Audioscript pT131

1 2.01 Point out that all the pictures, apart from one, show two or more types of weather at the same time.

Target Vocabulary

cloudy ˈklaʊ·di
cold koʊld
dry draɪ
foggy ˈfɔ·gi
hot hɑt
icy ˈaɪ·si
rainy ˈreɪ·ni
snowy ˈsnoʊ·i
stormy ˈstɔr·mi
sunny ˈsʌ·ni
warm wɔrm
wet wet
windy ˈwɪn·di

2 ★★★ Challenge students to complete the exercise without looking at the box.

Vocabulary Bank SB p129

Extra Vocabulary Practice

Learn to Learn

At this level, students should start developing their understanding of word forms, and be able to recognize and produce different parts of speech coming from the same root word.

3 During feedback, elicit that *ice* loses the *e* before the *y* when it becomes an adjective, and the *g* and *n* in *fog* and *sun* are doubled because there is a vowel before them.

Extra Vocabulary Practice

VOCABULARY

The Weather

2.01 **1** **What is the weather like in the photos? (Circle) the weather words that aren't in the photos. Listen, check, and repeat.**

cloudy cold ~~dry~~ foggy ~~hot~~ (icy) rainy snowy (stormy) ~~sunny~~ warm wet windy

1 *dry, hot, and sunny*
2 cold and snowy
3 cloudy and windy
4 foggy
5 rainy, warm, and wet

2 **Complete the sentences with adjectives from Exercise 1.**

1 It's [cloud] today. *cloudy*
2 Is it [thermometer] all year? cold
3 August is usually [rain]. rainy
4 We love [snow] weather! snowy
5 It isn't [storm]. It's [wind]. stormy windy

LEARN TO LEARN

Word Families (1)

Build your vocabulary by learning words from the same family. Many adjectives ending in *-y* come from a noun.

3 **Write the adjective forms.**

1 cloud *cloudy*
2 fog foggy
3 ice icy
4 rain rainy
5 snow snowy
6 storm stormy
7 sun sunny
8 wind windy

Use It!

4 **Complete the sentences with your own ideas. Tell your partner.**

1 When it's foggy, it's difficult to ______________.
2 In hot, sunny weather, I always wear ______________.
3 On wet days, I hate ______________.
4 I think cold, snowy weather is ______________.

Explore It!

Is the sentence *T* (true) or *F* (false)?

Snow isn't always white – sometimes there is pink snow in the Sierra Nevada mountains in the U.S.A. T

Find another interesting fact about the weather. Then write a question for your partner to answer.

UNIT 2 | HOW WAS THE PAST DIFFERENT? 23

4 Challenge pairs to come up with as many options as possible, and elicit these on the board together with any contrasting opinions.

Explore It!

For an extra challenge, ask students to create questions instead of true/false statements and use this as an opportunity to consolidate question formation.

Extend It!

If appropriate, ask students to use smartphones to find the weather forecast for a destination of their choice over the next few days. In pairs, they write a brief weather forecast using the vocabulary from the lesson and then present it to another pair.

Homework

Workbook p16

Lesson Aim: I can understand a text about lives in the past.

Warmer

Ask students to discuss the following questions in small groups. Then elicit answers and relevant vocabulary on the board.

1. *Do you like walking? Why / why not?*
2. *When you travel long distances, what is your favorite means of transportation?*
3. *How many kilometers do you think you could walk in a day?*

Teacher Support Hub ppxxxvi–xxxvii

READING
Diary Extracts

She is writing about her journey as a pioneer on the Oregon Trail.

1 Look at the photos. What do you think the girl is writing about?

2.02 **2** Read the text. Check your answer to Exercise 1.

3 Read the text again and find these things:

1. two American states Oregon, California
2. two types of furniture tables, chairs
3. five weather adjectives warm, dry, cold, rainy, wet
4. two musical instruments piano, violin
5. two animals oxen, horses

4 Match the highlighted words with the definitions.

1. a long trip to another place journey
2. wet and dirty after rain muddy
3. a difficult task challenge
4. not deep shallow
5. vehicles with four wheels to transport heavy things wagons
6. large animals like cows that can pull heavy things oxen

5 Complete the sentences with words from the text.

1. People on the Oregon Trail were called pioneers.
2. Oregon is on the west coast of the U.S.A.
3. The adults and children didn't usually travel in the wagons.
4. Louisa traveled across the country with her parents and two brothers.
5. One of Louisa's brothers played the violin.

Voice It!

6 Discuss the questions.

1. Do you think diaries are important?
2. What challenges do you face each day?

Finished? p119 Ex. 1

The Oregon Trail

Between 1843 and 1869, more than 500,000 pioneers left their homes in the east of the U.S.A. to travel more than 3,000 km west to Oregon and California. Some people wanted to find gold and others wanted to start a new life.

The pioneers used wagons to cross the country. They took things like tables, chairs, tents, and food – and also things they loved, like pianos! Oxen pulled the heavy wagons, but the adults and children usually walked or rode horses. The journey took between four and six months.

Louisa, age 14

Louisa Evans made the journey with her parents and two brothers, Samuel and Jesse. These are extracts from her diary.

April 8, 1850

I got up at 5:30 a.m. with Mother, and we made johnnycakes for breakfast. Then we cleaned up the wagon and we left at 7 a.m. We didn't stop until 5 p.m. After dinner, Samuel played his violin, and we sang songs and danced. It was a warm, dry day.

May 1, 1850

Last night it was cold and rainy, and my clothes got wet. I didn't sleep well, and I felt tired all day. It wasn't easy to walk on the muddy ground. We didn't travel far today, and we faced a new challenge: a river. It was high because of the rain and it looked dangerous. Did we cross it? Yes, we did. We found a shallow part and walked across. We were lucky, but other people weren't.

1 & 2 2.02 After feedback, allow students in groups to share their reactions to the text. Elicit a few opinions about someone walking several kilometers a day for months.

3 Set this activity up as a challenge, with the fastest five students being the winners, to encourage fast scanning.

4 Refer students back to p19 to review strategies for guessing meaning from context. During feedback, ask students to justify their answers.

5 ★ Give students two options for each sentence: 1 explorers / pioneers; 2 west / east; 3 wagons / horses; 4 parents and sisters / parents and two brothers; 5 violin / piano.

Reading Comprehension Questions

6 To demonstrate how personal you expect their answers to be, tell students about a challenge you face every day. Then allow a few minutes of thinking time before they discuss in pairs or groups.

Class Challenge

The first train line to cross from the east of the U.S.A. to the west opened in 1843 / **1869** / 1910.

Finished?

Students turn to p119 and do Exercise 1.

Flipped Class

Ask students to watch **video 2.2** and do **Video Worksheet 2.2** in the *Teacher's Resource Bank* in preparation for the next lesson.

Homework

Workbook p17

Lesson aim: I can understand how to use the simple past.

Warmer

▶ Play **video 2.2**, if it was not assigned for homework, and ask students to raise their hands when the vlogger mentions an activity they like the sound of. Elicit that she traveled by ferry (a type of ship) and that the weather was stormy and she didn't feel very well.

2.04–2.05 Audioscripts pT132

1 Encourage students to complete the chart and compare answers in pairs before looking at p24.

Pronunciation

2.03–2.04 Ask students to turn to SB p141 for pronunciation practice of the sounds /t/, /d/, and /ɪd/.

2 ★ Encourage students to use the irregular verbs list on SB p143 for support.

3 2.05 Before students attempt the task, elicit what they know about the ship called the *Mayflower*, or have them guess, as this will help their reading comprehension.

4 ★★★ Books closed. Increase the difficulty of this task by dictating the words and leaving out all the instances of *did*.

Extra Speaking Practice

5 & 6 Students rehearse their interviews in pairs and then perform them for the rest of the class or a bigger group. The class can vote for the most interesting interview.

GRAMMAR IN ACTION

Simple Past

Watch video 2.2
How did she travel?
What happened on the way back?

	Other Verbs	To Be	
	I/You/He/She/It/We/They	I/He/She/It	You/We/They
+	I **got up** at 5:30 a.m.	It **was** cold and rainy.	We [4] were lucky.
–	We **didn't stop** until 5 p.m.	It [2] wasn't easy to walk.	Other people **weren't** lucky.
?	**Did** we cross it? Yes, we [1] did. / No, we **didn't**.	**Was it** a hot day? Yes, it [3] was. / No, it **wasn't**.	**Were** all the people lucky? Yes, they **were**. / No, they [5] weren't.

Pronunciation p141

What did you do after school yesterday / yesterday after school?

1 Complete the examples in the chart above. Use the text on page 24 to help you.

2 Rewrite the sentences in the simple past.

1. More than 500,000 people leave the east coast.
   More than 500,000 people left the east coast.
2. The journey takes between four and six months.
   The journey took between four and six months.
3. April 8 is a warm, dry day.
   April 8 was a warm, dry day.
4. They don't stop until 5 p.m.
   They didn't stop until 5 p.m.

3 2.05 Complete the text with the simple past form of the verbs. Then listen and check.

On September 6, 1620, 102 people [1] left (leave) England to travel 4,500 km to North America. They [2] didn't agree (not agree) with some of the religious views in Europe at that time, so they [3] decided (decide) to start a new life.

They [4] traveled (travel) on a ship called the *Mayflower*, and the journey [5] took (take) 66 days. The first half of the journey [6] went (go) well. Then the weather [7] changed (change), and it [8] was (be) very cold and stormy. People got sick and some of them [9] didn't survive (not survive).

In December, they [10] arrived (arrive) in Plymouth Bay. They [11] didn't know (not know) anything about this new land, but the local Wampanoag people [12] helped (help) them find food and build houses.

4 Put the words in the correct order to make questions. Then ask and answer.

1. last / your friends / you / see / Did / weekend / ?
   Did you see your friends last weekend?
2. you / did / after school / What / yesterday / do / ?
3. night / Were / asleep / at 10:30 p.m. / last / you / ?
   Were you asleep at 10:30 p.m. last night?
4. any homework / your English teacher / Did / last week / give / you / ?
   Did your English teacher give you any homework last week?
5. Was / hot / yesterday / the weather / ?
   Was the weather hot yesterday?

Use It!

5 Think of questions to interview Louisa or a person from the *Mayflower* about their journey. Use the ideas below or your own ideas.

new friends | the challenges | the date
the food | the other people | the weather

6 Take turns asking and answering your questions.

When did you leave?

I left on April 2 with my family.

Finished? p119 Ex. 2

Grammar Game

Allow students to review the simple past forms of the irregular verbs on SB p143 for a few minutes and then divide the class into teams. Read one simple present verb aloud. The first team to call out the correct simple past form wins a point.

Finished?

Students turn to p119 and do Exercise 2.

Extend It!

Give students a few minutes to think about the last time they traveled somewhere. Then ask them to share their information with a partner.

Homework

Workbook p18

Lesson Aim: I can talk about useful objects.

Teacher Support Hub ppxxxviii–xxxix

2.06–2.08 **Audioscripts pT132**

1 2.06 After feedback, play a game. Divide the class into teams. The teams should each form a line, with one student in front of the board. Read aloud one word from the box. The student closest to the board in each team runs to the board and draws the item they just heard. The fastest student wins a point for their team. Teams then change so new students are in front of the board.

Target Vocabulary

blanket ˈblæŋ·kɪt
bowl boʊl
comb koʊm
cup kʌp
fork fɔrk
hairbrush ˈheərˌbrʌʃ
knife naɪf
lamp læmp
mirror ˈmɪ·rər
pillow ˈpɪ·loʊ
plate pleɪt
scissors ˈsɪ·zərz
spoon spun
toothbrush ˈtuθˌbrʌʃ

2 2.07 Challenge students to cover the box in Exercise 1 while doing the activity.

Vocabulary Bank SB p129

Extra Vocabulary Practice

VOCABULARY AND LISTENING

Useful Objects

2.06 **1** **Match the words with the pictures. Listen, check, and repeat.**

blanket	4	hairbrush	11	plate	8
bowl	9	knife	3	scissors	2
comb	6	lamp	13	spoon	12
cup	14	mirror	7	toothbrush	5
fork	1	pillow	10		

2.07 **2** **Listen. Write the objects the people are using.**

1 toothbrush
2 scissors
3 pillow
4 hairbrush
5 spoon and bowl
6 knife

LEARN TO LEARN

Categorizing

Recording new words in groups in your notebook can help you remember them.

3 **Write the words in Exercise 1 in the chart. Can you add any more words?**

Appearance	comb, hairbrush, mirror
Bedtime	blanket, lamp, pillow, toothbrush
Meals	bowl, cup, fork, knife, plate, spoon

Use It!

4 **Choose an object in Exercise 1. Ask questions to guess your partner's object.**

Do you use it every day? *Yes, I do.*

A Radio Show

2.08 **5** **Listen to an interview about a discovery from the Bronze Age. What can you see in the photo?**

2.08 **6** **Listen again and complete the text.**

This is the Egtved Girl. She's [1] 3,000 years old. Archaeologists found her body in [2] 1921, in Egtved, a small village in southern [3] Denmark. … We know she died in [4] 1370 BCE when she was between 16 and [5] 18 years old. And we know she died in the [6] summer because there were some summer flowers with her body.

26 HOW WAS THE PAST DIFFERENT? | UNIT 2

Learn to Learn

Instead of using the same methods, encourage students to try different ways of organizing new vocabulary in their notebook.

3 Elicit extra words and, if time allows, extra possible categories generated by the students.

4 Students win five points if they guess after one question, four if they guess after two, three after three, and so on.

5 2.08 After listening, elicit that the photo shows a body of a girl from the Bronze Age.

6 2.08 Allow students, in pairs, to discuss the sentences before playing the audio again.

Flipped Class

▶ Ask students to watch **video 2.3** and do **Video Worksheet 2.3** in the *Teacher's Resource Bank* in preparation for the next lesson.

Homework

Workbook p19

Lesson Aim: I can understand how to use *there was/were.*

Warmer

▶ Before playing **video 2.3**, if it was not assigned for homework, ask students in groups to brainstorm what they know about Vikings. After playing the video, elicit that the Viking Age wasn't peaceful, and that there were coins in the exhibition.

2.08–2.09 Audioscripts ppT132–133

1 Ask students to check their answers in pairs before conducting feedback with the whole class.

Get It Right!

Quickly review uncountable nouns. Write *weather*, *homework*, *information* on the board, and elicit that we can't say *weathers*, *homeworks*, *informations.*

2 2.08 Play the audio from Exercise 5 in the previous lesson again for students to check their answers.

3 ★ Give students time to write questions before they ask and answer them in pairs.

4 ★ Ask students to underline the nouns after the two options. Guide them to decide if they are countable or uncountable and if the sentence is positive, negative, or a question.

Extra Grammar Practice

5 & 6 2.09 After feedback, challenge students, in small groups, to come up with one extra quiz question. Elicit these and ask the class to guess the answers.

GRAMMAR IN ACTION

There Was/Were

Watch video 2.3
Was the Viking Age peaceful?
Were there any coins in the exhibition?

	Singular	Plural
+	**There was an** exhibition in Copenhagen.	**There** [3] were **some** summer flowers.
–	There [1] wasn't **any** information about clothes.	**There weren't any** plates.
?	**Was there a** blanket? Yes, **there** [2] was. / No, **there wasn't**.	**Were there any** other things? Yes, **there were**. / No, **there** [4] weren't.

1 Complete the examples in the chart above with *was*, *wasn't*, *were*, or *weren't*.

Get It Right!

We use **some** and **any** with plural countable nouns and uncountable nouns.

some/any plates **NOT** ~~*some/any plate*~~

some/any information **NOT** ~~*an information*~~

2 Correct the sentences about the Egtved girl.

1. There wasn't an exhibition about the Egtved girl.
   There was an exhibition about the Egtved girl.
2. There weren't any flowers with her body.
   There were some flowers with her body.
3. There weren't any useful objects with her body.
   There were some useful objects with her body.
4. There was a hairbrush.
   There wasn't a hairbrush.
5. There weren't a lot of travelers in northern Europe.
   There were a lot of travelers in northern Europe.

3 Ask and answer about the information in Exercise 2.

Was there was an exhibition about the Egtved girl?

Yes, there was.

4 (Circle) the correct words.

1. There were (*some*) / *any* students at the talk.
2. There was (*an*) / *some* interesting exhibition last week.
3. There weren't *some* / (*any*) audio guides.
4. Was there *some* / (*any*) snow in the mountains?
5. There wasn't (*a*) / *any* documentary on TV last night.

5 Write and (circle) to complete the sentences. Then answer the quiz.

DID YOU KNOW ... ?

1. There *were* ✓ (*some*) / *any* humans in ... 250,000 years ago.
   a Portugal (**b**) Africa
2. There wasn't ✗ *a* / (*an*) alphabet with letters in ... society.
   (**a**) Aztec **b** Roman
3. There were ✓ (*some*) / *any* university courses for students in ... in 1095.
   a Paris (**b**) Oxford
4. There weren't ✗ *some* / (*any*) ... for eating food in ancient Greece.
   (**a**) forks **b** knives
5. There was ✓ (*a*) / *some* famous Roman ... named Apicius.
   a emperor (**b**) cook

6 2.09 Discuss your answers to the quiz. Then listen and check.

Use It!

7 In pairs, choose a photo from Units 1 and 2 and look at it for one minute. Close your books. What can you remember?

Were there any clouds in the sky?

Yes, there were. There were some white clouds.

Finished? p119 Ex. 3

7 If appropriate, students can choose pictures on their smartphones and briefly show them to their partner, who has to remember as many details as possible.

Grammar Game

Students write three sentences about their last vacation using *there was/were.* One sentence must be false. Students ask each other questions to find out the lie.

Finished?

Students turn to p119 and do Exercise 3.

Homework

Workbook p20

Lesson Aim: I can talk about my weekend.

Warmer

Students write down three things they did over the weekend and then move around the room looking for another student who did at least two of the things on their list.

Teacher Support Hub ppxl–xli

2.10 Audioscript pT133

1 2.10 ★★★ Challenge students to listen and answer the question with their books closed. Elicit that Andy was in the country for his grandpa's 70th birthday.

2 2.10 After feedback, encourage students to read the conversation aloud along with the audio, and then to practice it in pairs.

Useful Language Practice

3 ▶ Play **video 2.4** and drill the pronunciation of the target phrases.

4 After feedback, say the following and ask students to react with *Everyday English* phrases: *The school is closed tomorrow. It will rain the whole weekend. Did you know Egyptian men used to wear makeup?*

5 To help generate ideas, elicit possible topics that students could write about, such as "my last birthday" or "my last vacation."

6 If appropriate, ask students to record their conversations with their phones and listen to the recordings, giving them time to repeat the task if they wish. This will help with their self-correction skills.

You learn something new every day!

SPEAKING

Talking About Your Weekend

2.10 **1** Listen to the conversation. Why was Andy in the country?

CARLA Hi Andy. [1]How was your weekend?
ANDY [2] It was OK, thanks.
CARLA What [3] did you do ?
ANDY I went to the country for my grandpa's 70th birthday.
CARLA Cool! What [4] was the weather like?
ANDY It was cold, wet, and windy.
CARLA That's a shame. [5] Where did you stay ?
ANDY We stayed on my grandpa's farm.
CARLA What was it like?
ANDY Well, there wasn't any Wi-Fi, and there were a lot of noisy sheep outside.
CARLA Really?
ANDY Yes, really. That region has more sheep than people.
CARLA Wow. You learn something new every day!
ANDY What [6] about you ? What did you do?
CARLA Nothing much. I watched TV and made some cupcakes.
ANDY Sounds good!

2.10 **2** Complete the conversation with the phrases from the *Useful Language* box. Then listen and check.

Useful Language

How was your weekend?
It was (OK/good/great/amazing/awful), thanks.
What about you?
What did you do?
What was the weather like?
Where did you stay?

3 Look at the *Everyday English* box. Find and underline the phrases in the conversation.

Watch video 2.4
Everyday English

Nothing much. Sounds good!
That's a shame.
You learn something new every day!

4 Which *Everyday English* phrase do we use to respond to …

1 negative news? That's a shame.
2 interesting facts? ________
3 positive news? Sounds good.
4 a question? Nothing much.

PLAN

5 Think about something you did in the past, and take notes.

Where you went: ________
What you did: ________
The weather: ________
Any problems you had: ________

SPEAK

6 Practice a conversation with your partner about what you did. Remember to use the simple past and *there was/were*, vocabulary from this unit, and phrases from the *Useful Language* and *Everyday English* boxes.

CHECK

7 Work with another pair. Listen to their conversation and take notes.

Where they went: ________
What they did: ________
The weather: ________
Any problems they had: ________

7 Put pairs together in groups of four. While each pair performs their conversation, one student from the other pair takes notes on content and the other student is responsible for correcting any grammar mistakes.

Flipped Class

Prepare for the **Writing** lesson. Students research a famous journey, real or fictional.

Lesson Aim: I can write an account of a journey.

Warmer

Students brainstorm things they associate with difficult journeys (e.g., traveling by ship, the North/South Pole, mountains, space travel).

Teacher Support Hub ppxlii–xliii

1 Focus students' attention on the ship in the second photo and elicit relevant vocabulary (e.g., *ice*, *icy*, *iceberg*). Elicit a few difficulties that explorers could encounter.

2 ★★★ Challenge students to correct each false statement (e.g., *2 He didn't start the journey on his own because he was with 12 men.*). Elicit these during feedback.

3 Turn this into a brief competition to encourage quick scanning. The first five students to circle all the phrases in the text win.

4 Ensure students understand *set off* (to start a journey) by asking a concept-checking question (e.g., *What time did you set off from home this morning?*).

Choose the Correct Word

5 Allow students to work in pairs, as this will help generate ideas. They can share any information they researched for homework and then choose the most exciting journey to write about.

6 You may want to allow students to write in pairs. This might be more time-consuming but can help students focus on form.

WRITING
An Account of a Journey

1 Look at the photos. Where do you think the man wanted to go? Read the account and check your answer. to the North Pole

A Difficult Journey

Fridtjof Nansen was a Norwegian explorer. He wanted to be the first person to reach the North Pole. He set off on June 24, 1893, from Oslo on a ship with 12 men.

At first, things went well, but by November, the weather was foggy and icy. The ship moved slowly through the ice for a year. Then Nansen and another man, Johansen, decided to cross the ice on skis.

The two men left the ship in March 1895, but there were a lot of problems. They couldn't reach the Pole and turned south. The weather was warm, so the ice melted, and it was difficult to travel. They built a shelter and waited there for eight months.

Finally, on June 17, a British explorer found them. They arrived home safely on August 13, 1896.

2 Read the account again. Are the sentences *T* (true) or *F* (false)?

1 Nansen left Norway in June 1893. T
2 He started the journey on his own. F
3 The weather was bad in November. T
4 Nansen and Johansen didn't have any problems. F
5 Nansen was the first person to reach the North Pole. F
6 Nansen returned to Norway one year after he left. F

3 Read the phrases in the *Useful Language* box. In what order do they appear in the account?

Useful Language

2 At first, …	1 (He) set off on …
4 Finally, …	3 There were a lot of problems.

4 Put the sentences in the correct order (1–4).

a 4 Finally, we arrived back safely at 9 p.m.
b 1 We set off from home early one morning.
c 2 At first, we made good progress.
d 3 There were a lot of problems.

PLAN

5 **Plan an account of a journey. Take notes for four paragraphs.**

1 Who made the journey: ______
When it started: ______
2 The first part of the journey: ______
The weather: ______
3 How the journey continued: ______
Any problems: ______
4 The end of the journey: ______

WRITE

6 **Write your account. Remember to include the simple past, *there was/were*, and phrases from the *Useful Language* box.**

CHECK

7 **Do you ...**

- use the simple past to talk about the past?
- explain what the journey was like?
- put the events in the correct order?

Finished? p119 Ex. 4

7 Students display their texts around the room and read as many as possible. Then they vote for the most exciting journey.

Finished?

Students turn to p119 and do Exercise 4.

Flipped Class

Prepare for the **History Project** (pp30–31). Students research a local museum (or any museum) and find out about three interesting artifacts there.

Homework

Workbook p21

Lesson Aim: I can give feedback and design a museum display.

Project Book

For more information and activities, see the Project Book, p26.

2.11 Audioscript pT133

1 In small groups, students discuss the museum they researched for homework. Elicit contrasting ideas about question 3. Ask: *Do you think museums should be interactive or only display artifacts? Should there be guides or only texts?*

2 Ask students to underline key words in the sentences and elicit these before students read the texts (e.g., 2 *black, see things*).

3 Getting students used to typical features in each text genre will help them to predict content. This can help them when reading new texts.

How to Give Feedback

At this stage, students should be improving their skills in giving constructive feedback to each other, pointing out both the positives and the negatives of each other's work in a way that offers opportunities for improvement.

4 2.11 Tell students that they will hear a conversation between three students, Sophie, Leo, and Oliver. Elicit that Sophie and Leo are talking about a display about Viking ships. Oliver created this display, and Sophie and Leo give him feedback on his work.

HISTORY PROJECT

A Museum Display

1 Discuss the questions.

1 What museums do you know?
2 What can you see in them?
3 What makes a museum interesting? *It had colorful pictures and surprising/cool facts.*

2 Read the texts. Then read the sentences and write *S* (scissors), *M* (mirror), *L* (lamp), or *B* (bowl).

1 The way of making this object is the same today as it was in the 1600s. S
2 It's black, but you can see things in it. M
3 Only rich people had objects like this. L
4 This type of object first appeared in Egypt. S
5 There was probably water in this. B
6 This object had two uses. M
7 It took a long time to find this object after a natural disaster. L
8 This had connections with weather. B

3 Read the texts again. Underline the information with the correct colors.

name of object year or time period location material use

How to Give Feedback

2.11 4 Read the tips about giving feedback. Then listen to the conversation. What kind of display are Sophie and Leo talking about?

1 Read the text.
2 Talk about the things you like or find interesting.
3 Point out possible problems:
- Is any important information missing?
- Is the information in a logical order?
- Is anything unclear?

4 Make suggestions for improving the text.

2.11 5 Listen again. Answer the questions.

1 What event are they at? *a school history festival*
2 Whose display did they like? *Oliver's*
3 What did they like about it?
4 What information was missing? *when the Vikings sailed to Canada*
5 How did Oliver respond to the feedback? What is he going to do? *He responded well. He's going to add the missing information.*

USEFUL OBJECTS DISPLAY

SCISSORS, STEEL, AND IRON, 1628
Yi County, Anhui Province, China

The ancient Egyptians invented scissors, and today scissors are one of the most common objects in a home. This is one of the first pairs of scissors from Zhang Sijia's shop. Zhang Sijia opened the first scissors shop in China in 1628. He made all of the scissors by hand and followed the same 72 steps to make them. Customers bought the scissors to cut cloth, plants, and even metal. There is still a scissors factory in Hangzhou, China, and the workers use the same process today as in the 1600s.

30 REVIEW | UNIT 2

5 2.11 Ask students to answer 1–4 in pairs before getting feedback. Then give students a few minutes to work on question 5 and elicit ideas from the whole class.

Class Challenge

The largest museum in the world is the **Louvre in Paris** / British Museum in London / Uffizi in Florence.

Lesson Aim: I can give feedback and design a museum display.

6 Students work in small groups and choose as many historical objects as there are students in the group. Students share information they researched about artifacts in their local museum, or any other museum, and then choose the most interesting ones. Ask them to brainstorm extra questions about each of the artifacts (e.g., *Where was it found? Whose was it?*). Students then research the objects individually and work on their display. They give each other feedback on their texts, using the steps in Exercise 4. Then they can make any changes to their displays and find or draw pictures.

7 & 8 Ensure that students plan their feedback before giving it. If possible, provide them with cards with two columns, one headed with a ☺ face and one with a ☹ face. After reading all the displays, ask students to go back to their group and take notes on each display, focusing on things they liked and things that need improvement. Groups then split up and form new ones containing a mixture of students from the original groups. They give each other feedback following the steps in Exercise 4.

Students can collaborate digitally through *Collaboration Plus*, where you can assign, track, and assess their work. Students can also share and showcase their work and comment on each other's projects.

SHAPE IT!

MIRROR, OBSIDIAN, AROUND 4,000 BCE
Çatalhöyük, South-Central Turkey

Archaeologists found this mirror in Çatalhöyük. It was one of the first cities in the world, and 8,000 people lived there. The mirror is made from a special black stone called obsidian, and it was one of the first mirrors in the world. People used these mirrors to look at themselves and also to look at the sun.

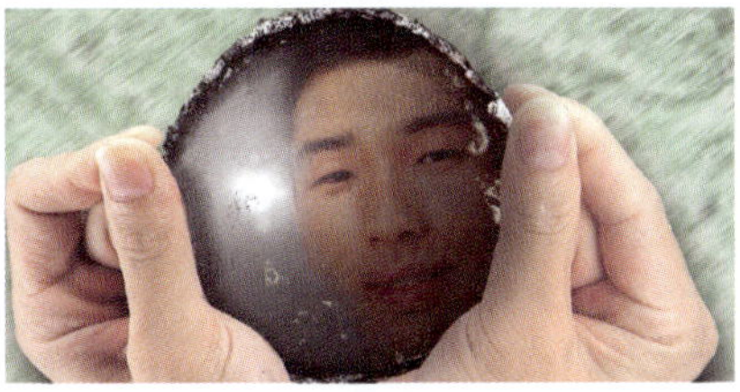

LAMP, BRONZE, 79 CE
Pompeii, Southern Italy

Archaeologists found this oil lamp in the ancient city of Pompeii in 1752, but it is much older than that. A volcanic eruption destroyed Pompeii in 79 CE. This oil lamp is in the shape of a dolphin, and it is made of bronze. Bronze objects were expensive, so this lamp probably belonged to a rich family. People needed oil lamps to light rooms and hallways at night.

TLALOC BOWL, TERRACOTTA, 3RD–8TH CENTURY
Veracruz, Mexico

This bowl was probably for holding water. The face shows one of the faces of the Aztec figure Tlaloc, from ancient Central Mexico. People believed he sent good rain when he was happy to help plants grow, and he sent bad rain and storms when he was unhappy.

PLAN

6 Work in groups. Choose four historical objects. Then complete the steps below.

- Decide on the object that each student will research.
- Research your object and write a short text to use in the display.
- Find a photo or draw a picture of your object.
- Read each other's texts and give feedback.
- Make any changes or improvements.
- Work in your group and make your display.

PRESENT

7 Put your display on your classroom wall. Remember to follow the tips in *How to Give Feedback*, and include correct facts, photos or pictures, and an attractive design.

CHECK

8 Look at your classmates' displays. Do they explain the four historical objects well? Give feedback to other groups on their displays.

UNIT 2 | HOW WAS THE PAST DIFFERENT? 31

For more work on history, students can turn to SB p137. See pT123 for teaching notes.

Extend It!

Ask students to pretend they are archaeologists from the year 2100 and to create a humorous museum display full of deliberately wrong information about our modern objects today. This could be, for example, a display of curling irons that says that in the past, people used these to make pancakes (e.g., *Archaeologists found them in a store called a "salon," which was the old word for a bakery*). Collect and correct language mistakes in the students' work. Then display their work for the whole class to read.

Lesson Aim: I can review what I have learned and reflect on my progress.

The aim of this page is for students to review the grammar and vocabulary from the unit. You can either do it in class, as a timed progress test, or assign it for homework.

Vocabulary

1 & 2 Put students into small groups, with two teams in each group. Team A reads out the sentences in Exercise 1 and team B has five seconds to guess the missing word and win a point. Then team B does the same with Exercise 2.

Grammar in Action

3 Ask students to check their answers in pairs and discuss any differing answers before feedback.

4 Refer students back to p27 to review this language point before they attempt the task in pairs.

5 After feedback, students can work in pairs to continue the conversation, with Max asking Chloe about her weekend.

Unit Quiz

Review the Unit Theme

Remind students of the unit title: *How was the past different?* Put students into pairs. Have them discuss the following questions: *What was the weather like yesterday? What ancient culture interests you? What was it like? How was your city or neighborhood different 50 years ago?* Share answers as a class.

Teacher Support Hub pxlvi

2 REVIEW

VOCABULARY

1 Complete the sentences with the adjective form of the nouns in the box.

cloud fog ice rain storm wind

1 I don't like it when it's **stormy** because it's dark and noisy.
2 It's dangerous to drive when it's **foggy** and you can't see well.
3 Take an umbrella. It's **rainy** today.
4 It's **windy** outside. The trees are moving.
5 It's **cloudy** today, so we can't sunbathe.
6 Watch out! It's **icy** outside. Don't slip.

2 Complete the sentences.

1 I need a **spoon** to stir my drink.
2 I have a **lamp**, so I can read in bed.
3 You can use a **hairbrush** or a **comb** to make your hair look better.
4 Do you have any **scissors** to cut this paper?
5 I slept on my friend's sofa last night without a **blanket** or a **pillow**!

GRAMMAR IN ACTION

3 Complete the text with the simple past.

Meriwether Lewis [1] **wanted** (want) to explore more of North America in the early 1800s. He and William Clark [2] **left** (leave) on May 14, 1804, to go to the west of Mississippi. It [3] **wasn't** (not be) an easy journey. They [4] **met** (meet) a lot of people, but they [5] **didn't speak** (not speak) their language. At times, they [6] **didn't have** (not have) enough food, and it [7] **was** (be) difficult to survive. After two years and more than 13,000 km, the men finally [8] **completed** (complete) their journey in September 1806.

4 Complete the review with *there was(n't)* or *there were(n't)* and *a, an, some,* or *any.*

I went to my local museum last week.
✓ [1] **There was an** amazing exhibition about Egypt.
✓ [2] **There were some** amazing things to see, like bronze mirrors and beautiful necklaces.
✓ [3] **There was a** board game called Senet. It was so much fun to play.
✗ [4] **There weren't any** Egyptian mummies!
✗ [5] **There wasn't a** café. I was hungry.
? [6] **Were there any** good exhibitions in your town last week?

5 Complete the conversation with simple past verbs or *there was(n't)/were(n't)*. (Circle) *a, an, some,* or *any*.

CHLOE What [1] **did** you **do** (do) on the weekend?
MAX I [2] **went** (go) to my grandma's town. [3] **There was** [4] *a* / (*an*) outdoor film festival.
CHLOE Cool! [5] **Did** you **watch** (watch) [6] *some* / (*any*) movies?
MAX Yes, I [7] **did**. [8] **There were** [9] (*some*) / *any* excellent movies, but the weather [10] **was** (be) rainy.
CHLOE Oh, no. When [11] **did** you **get** (get) home?
MAX This morning.
CHLOE You [12] **didn't text** (not text) me.
MAX I know. [13] **There was** [14] (*a*) / *any* problem with my phone.

Self-Assessment

I can talk about the weather.
I can talk about useful objects.
I can use the simple past.
I can use *there was/were.*

Homework

Workbook pp22–23

Self-Assessment

Ask students to write five weather words, five words about objects, five simple past verbs, and five sentences with *there was/ were.* Students check each other's work in groups, calling for help when needed. They then reflect on their performance and use this to complete the self-assessment box.

Lesson Aim: I can guess the meaning of new words.

Understanding word formation (how word beginnings and endings can change the meaning and grammar of a word) will help students guess the meaning of any unknown words in a text, as will clues in the context.

1 Encourage students to start reflecting on their own practices. Ask them to say *because* when they discuss their answers in pairs, and elicit justifications during feedback.

2 To encourage faster reading and prevent students from checking vocabulary with dictionaries or translation software, set a time limit of two minutes.

SHAPE IT!

3 & 4 Go through the example discussion of what *unusual* means (different from others of the same type). Elicit the meanings of the other words/phrases (*enjoyable* = something you like doing; *ran away* = left a bad situation quickly by running; *tent* = something you can sleep in and carry with you; *unforgettable* = something that you can't forget). Point out that sometimes words or phrases (e.g., *set off* at the beginning of paragraph 3) can have more than one meaning listed in a dictionary. Students need to look at the context that the vocabulary appears in to figure out the correct meaning (here, "to start a journey").

LEARN TO LEARN

LEARN TO ... GUESS THE MEANING OF NEW WORDS

When you don't know a word, the beginning of the word, the end of the word, and the rest of the sentence can help you guess the meaning.

1 **Circle the answer that is true for you. Compare and discuss your answer with a partner.**

When I see a word I don't know, I usually ...

1. guess the meaning from the rest of the sentence.
2. see if I can understand part of the word.
3. ask the teacher what it means.
4. look in a dictionary.
5. write it in my notebook.

2 **Read the text. Then tell your partner three things that surprise you.**

Our Incredible School Trip!

By David North

Last February, I went on a field trip to Oregon.

The weather was very **unusual** for that time of year. Normally, it's wet and windy, but it didn't rain once! It was a little cold, so we wore jackets or sweaters every day.

Our bus set off very early on the first day, at about 5:15 a.m. The campground was over 320 km away, and it took almost four hours. We couldn't take phones or tablets with us, so we chatted and played games instead.

When we saw the campground for the first time, we were really happy. There was a small store, and a room with table tennis and a TV. We hung out there in the evenings.

We did a lot of **enjoyable** activities. We went hiking and sailing, and I tried windsurfing for the first time. My favorite activity was survival skills. We collected wood in the forest, and then we built a small shelter. Clara and Ben saw some spiders and **ran away** – they hate things like spiders and bugs. In the evening, we cooked over a campfire. That night, we didn't sleep in a cabin. We slept in tents, and I shared a **tent** with my best friends.

It was an **unforgettable** experience, and I was very sad to leave.

SHAPE IT!

unusual: adjective
enjoyable: adjective
ran away: verb
tent: noun
unforgettable: adjective

3 **Read the text again. Discuss the questions about each of the words in bold with a partner. Take notes in your notebook.**

1. Is the word a noun, verb, or adjective?
2. What clues about the meaning can you find in the text?
3. Do any parts of the word give you clues to the meaning?
4. What do you think the word means?

I think "unusual" is an adjective.

"Unusual" describes the weather. The text says "Normally it's wet and windy, but it didn't rain once!"

Yes. It starts with "un-" which means "not."

I think "unusual" means "not usual."

4 **Check the meanings of the words in a dictionary or with your teacher. Did the questions in Exercise 3 help you guess correctly?**

Extend It!

Ask students to find another word or phrase from a text in the unit and use the steps they have learned to figure out what it means. Then ask them to explain the word to the rest of the class.

Lesson Aim: I can talk about stories.

Warmer

Ask the class to make a list of famous stories and find out if students know what they are called in English. Elicit these on the board.

Teacher Support Hub ppxxxiv–xxxv

Start It!

Unit Quiz

1 Elicit relevant vocabulary on the board (e.g., *reading*, *story*, *illustration*, etc.).

2 & 3 Elicit a list of verbs on the board (e.g., *act*, *travel*, *sing*, *dance*). Play **video 3.1** and ask students to raise their hands if they hear any of the verbs on the board in the documentary.

4 Allow students a few minutes of thinking time to form an opinion and a reason for it.

Video Comprehension Questions

Flipped Class

Prepare for **Explore It!** (p35). Students research an interesting fact about unusual phobias, i.e., things some people are scared of (e.g., *arachnophobia* – the fear of spiders).

3 What do stories teach us?

LEARNING OUTCOMES

I can ...

- understand a fable and a traditional fairy tale
- tell an anecdote and express interest
- write a story
- understand how to use the past continuous and simple past
- talk about feelings and use prepositions of movement
- personalize sentences to remember new words, use my knowledge, use phrasal verbs, and guess the meaning of new words

Start It!

1 Look at the photo. What is the boy doing?
2 Before you watch, what do you think people did in their free time in the past?
3 What did storytellers do? Watch and check.
4 What's your favorite story? Do you know where it came from?

They traveled around, shared stories, and brought new ones back with them.

Watch video 3.1 | Grammar in Action 3.2 (p37) | Grammar in Action 3.3 (p39) | Everyday English 3.4 (p40) | Globetrotters 3.5 (p42)

34 WHAT DO STORIES TEACH US? | UNIT 3

Unit Aims

Skills

I can ...

- understand a fable p36
- tell an anecdote p40
- write a story p41
- understand a fairy tale p42

Language

I can ...

- talk about feelings p35
- understand how to use the past continuous p37
- use prepositions of movement p38
- understand how to use the simple past and past continuous p39

Learn to Learn

I can ...

- personalize sentences to remember new words p35
- use my knowledge to understand a text better p38
- use phrasal verbs p43
- guess the meaning of new words p45

Extra Resources

- Finished? Student's Book p120
- Vocabulary Bank, Student's Book p130
- Workbook pp24–31
- Grammar Reference and Practice, Workbook pp92–93
- Teacher Support Hub, Teacher's Book ppxxxiv–xlvii

Digital Resource Pack

(on Cambridge One)

- *Teacher's Resource Bank* for word lists, differentiated worksheets, *Culture Projects*, and many other extra resources.
- *Practice Extra*, *Presentation Plus*, *Test Generator*, and *Digital Collaboration Space*

Lesson Aim: I can talk about feelings.

Warmer

In groups, students brainstorm adjectives to describe feelings (e.g., *happy*). They then play against another team. Team A mimes one adjective from their list, and team B must guess the word to win a point.

3.01 Audioscript pT133

1 3.01 Alternatively, read the words aloud and ask students to mime them using facial expressions.

Pronunciation

3.02–3.03 Ask students to turn to SB p141 for pronunciation practice of word stress in adjectives.

Target Vocabulary

afraid əˈfreɪd
angry ˈæŋ·ɡri
bored bɔrd
embarrassed ɪmˈbær·əst
excited ɪkˈsaɪ·t̬ɪd
lonely ˈloʊn·li
nervous ˈnɜr·vəs
surprised sərˈpraɪzd
tired taɪərd
upset ˌʌpˈset
worried ˈwɜ·rid

2 ★★★ After feedback, put students into pairs to make one extra sentence with a missing word and give it to another pair to complete.

Vocabulary Bank SB p130

Vocabulary Game

Extra Vocabulary Practice

Learn to Learn

Personalizing new vocabulary is a strategy that students should be continuing to use in order to maximize their chance of remembering it.

VOCABULARY
Adjectives of Feeling

3.01 **1** **Circle** the adjectives to describe the people in the photos. Listen, check, and repeat.

1 
(angry) / bored

2 
embarrassed / tired

3 
surprised / worried

4 
lonely / tired

5 
afraid / upset

6 
excited / nervous

Pronunciation p141

2 Complete the sentences with adjectives from Exercise 1.

1 Sam's ___afraid___ of dogs, so he doesn't want to walk through the park.
2 I felt so ___embarrassed___ when I dropped the glasses. My face went red.
3 I'm ___worried___ about my exams. What should I do?
4 It's Ana's birthday! She's very ___excited___.
5 I'm ___bored___. This documentary isn't very interesting.

LEARN TO LEARN
Personalizing

You can write a sentence that is true for you to help you remember new words.

I often feel tired in the evening.

3 Write a personal sentence for six of the adjectives from Exercise 1.

1 ______
2 ______
3 ______
4 ______
5 ______
6 ______

4 Read your sentences aloud, but don't say the adjectives. Can your partner guess the adjectives?

I feel … when I forget someone's name.

Embarrassed?

Use It!

5 Choose an adjective from Exercise 1 and tell your partner about a time when you felt like that. Ask questions to find out more.

I felt angry when my brother took my bike because he didn't ask me.

When did that happen?

Explore It!

Guess the correct answer.

If you have didaskaleinophobia, you are afraid of …

a cheese. b spiders. (c) school.

Find another unusual thing people are afraid of. Then write a question for your partner to answer.

---

3 & 4 Before the activity, ask students to circle the adjectives in Exercise 1 that were new for them. Then ask students to include those adjectives in their sentences.

5 Allow plenty of thinking time for this activity, as it is an opportunity for students to associate the language with a real event and make it personal.

Explore It!

In groups, students make questions about the phobias they researched for homework. Elicit the most interesting from each group.

Homework

Workbook p24

Lesson Aim: I can understand a fable.

Background Information

Aesop's Fables is a collection of fables credited to Aesop, a slave and storyteller believed to have lived in ancient Greece between 620 and 564 BCE. These stories are still told in modern times. The fables were originally kept alive orally and were not written down until about three centuries after Aesop's death. The fables covered ethical, religious, social, and political themes.

Teacher Support Hub ppxxxvi–xxxvii

1 Explain that a *moral* is a lesson that the fable teaches about the way we should behave.

2 & 3 3.04 Instead of asking students to read the story, you could tell it to them, eliciting some of the vocabulary (e.g., *monkey*) through facial expressions and miming. Engage students by frequently asking them what they think will happen next. During the story, elicit the vocabulary in Exercise 3.

Reading Comprehension Questions

4 EXAM If you followed the alternative technique above, ask students to cover the text and answer the questions from memory. They can then check their answers by reading the text.

5 Allow students a few minutes of thinking time to form opinions and think of relevant vocabulary. Monitor and assist, and encourage students to agree or disagree with each other, if appropriate.

READING
A Fable

1 **Read the introduction and discuss the questions.**

1. What is special about fables?
2. Why do you think Aesop's stories are still important today?

Aesop's Fables

Aesop was a writer from ancient Greece. He wrote a lot of short stories called fables. Fables usually have a moral message. The main characters are often animals, but they act like humans.

3.04 **2** **Read the fable. Circle the best title.**

a The Fox's Dance b The Monkey as King

One day, all the animals from the jungle were sitting in a circle. They felt excited because this was the day to choose their new king.

The animals took turns giving speeches about why they wanted to be king. When the fox was giving his speech, a lot of the other animals were getting bored, and they weren't listening. Then it was the monkey's turn, but he didn't give a speech. He danced, made silly faces, and made the other animals laugh. They decided to make the monkey king.

The fox knew it was a bad decision, and he was angry. The monkey didn't have the right qualities to be a good king. He decided to play a trick on the monkey. "I have a present for you!" he said. "Follow me." The monkey followed him. All the animals were watching.

As they were walking through the jungle, the fox pointed toward a tree. "Look at all those bananas!" he said. As the monkey was running to the tree, he fell into a trap. "Help! Help!" he shouted. He wasn't dancing now.

"How can the monkey take care of us and be our king?" asked the fox. "He can't even take care of himself." The animals realized that they were wrong. "You are our king now," they told the fox. "You are clever and you can protect us."

3 **Find words in the story that mean:**

1. a warm place with a lot of trees and other plants jungle
2. not clever or sensible silly
3. something that people give you on a special occasion present
4. a hole in the ground to catch animals or people trap
5. to keep people safe protect

4 EXAM **Circle the correct answers.**

1. What did the animals take turns doing?
   - **A giving speeches**
   - B telling jokes
   - C looking for food
2. Who didn't give a speech?
   - A the fox
   - **B the monkey**
   - C the bear
3. Why did the animals choose the monkey to be their king?
   - **A He danced and made them laugh.**
   - B He was the best animal.
   - C He found food for them.
4. What happened at the end?
   - A The fox gave bananas to the monkey.
   - B The monkey played a trick on the animals.
   - **C The fox became the king.**

Voice It!

5 **Discuss the questions.**

1. What is the moral of the story?
2. What do you think a good leader needs?
3. Which other fables do you know?

Finished? p120 Ex. 1

Possible answer: Think carefully before you make an important decision. / Being popular and entertaining doesn't make someone a good leader.

Extend It!

Elicit more fables on the board and ask students to discuss, in groups, the morals of these stories for a few minutes. Monitor and assist where necessary. Encourage discussions during whole-class feedback.

Class Challenge

The Little Prince by Antoine de Saint-Exupéry is one of the most translated books. You can read it in 55 / 150 / **more than 300** languages.

Finished?

Students turn to p120 and do Exercise 1.

Flipped Class

Ask students to watch **video 3.2** and do **Video Worksheet 3.2** in the *Teacher's Resource Bank* in preparation for the next lesson.

Homework

Workbook p25

Lesson Aim: I can understand how to use the past continuous.

Warmer

▶ Play **video 3.2** if it was not assigned for homework. Elicit that in her first vlog, Sophia wasn't speaking clearly or looking at the camera. She has over 300 followers.

3.05 Audioscript ppT133–134

1 In groups, students help each other remember as much as possible about the fable on p36 and retell the story collaboratively. Then they complete the chart. Elicit that the past continuous is used to talk about past actions that happened for a period of time.

2 During feedback, drill the pronunciation of *was* /wəz/ and *were* /wɜr/, and point out that we don't normally stress these words in the past continuous – we stress the first syllable of the main verb instead (e.g., *We were dancing.*).

Extra Grammar Practice

3 & 4 3.05 After completing the activities, encourage students to circle each *was*/*were* and underline all the *-ing* verbs to help them self-correct. Then check the answers with the whole class

5 & 6 ★★★ Alternatively, students make two true sentences and one false one. Then they ask each other extra questions to find the lie.

GRAMMAR IN ACTION

Past Continuous: Affirmative and Negative

Watch video 3.2
Why was Sophia's first vlog bad?
How many people follow her?

	I/He/She/It	You/We/They
+	The fox [1] was **giving** his speech.	The animals [3] were **sitting** in a circle.
–	He [2] wasn't **dancing**.	They **weren't** [4] **listen**ing.

1 Complete the examples in the chart above. Use the story on page 36 to help you.

2 Complete the sentences with *was/were* or *wasn't/weren't*.

1 The animals weren't standing in a circle. They were sitting.
2 The fox wasn't quiet. He was giving a speech.
3 The animals weren't watching each other. They were watching the fox and the monkey.
4 The monkey wasn't walking to the tree. He was running.

3 3.05 Complete the story with the past continuous form of the verbs. Then listen and check.

One day, a hare [1] was telling (tell) the other animals how fast he could run. At that moment, a tortoise [2] was walking (walk) past. He heard the hare, and he offered to race him.

The race began. At first, the hare [3] was running (run) very fast and the tortoise [4] was going (go) very slowly. The hare was soon near the end of the race. The other animals [5] weren't watching (not watch), so he decided to stop for a rest. He soon fell asleep. The tortoise continued to walk slowly while the hare [6] was sleeping (sleep).

Finally, just as the tortoise [7] was finishing (finish) the race, the hare woke up. The tortoise was the winner!

The moral of the story is: don't be too sure that something is easy. Sometimes things are more difficult than you think.

4 Complete the sentences with the past continuous form of the verbs in the box.

make not live not work read take travel watch

1 At 9 p.m. last night, I was reading a book.
2 Leo was taking selfies this morning.
3 Esma was making a cake when I called.
4 My parents weren't working at 10 p.m. last night. They were watching TV.
5 Sandra wasn't living at home this time last year. She was traveling around the world!

Use It!

5 Think of true sentences about things you were doing at these times. Use the activities in the box or your own ideas.

at … o'clock yesterday morning/afternoon/evening
at … o'clock last Monday/Tuesday
this time two days/months/years ago
this time last week/month/year

chat with friends do my homework get up go to bed have breakfast/lunch/dinner play basketball / computer games walk home / to school sleep

6 Compare your sentences with a partner.

At eight o'clock yesterday morning, I was walking to school. What about you?

I wasn't walking to school. I was brushing my teeth.

Finished? p120 Ex. 2

Grammar Game

If possible, find a picture of a group of people doing different activities and display it for 30 seconds. In groups, students then write down sentences about it using the past continuous (e.g., *A girl was laughing.*). The team with the most correct sentences wins.

Finished?

Students turn to p120 and do Exercise 2.

Homework

Workbook p26

Lesson Aim: I can use prepositions of movement.

Teacher Support Hub ppxxxviii–xxxix

3.06–3.08 **Audioscripts pT134**

1 3.06 After feedback, students work in pairs to come up with gestures to correspond to each preposition.

Target Vocabulary

across əˈkrɔs
along əˈlɔŋ
between bɪˈtwin
down daʊn
into ˈɪn·tu
off ɔf
out of ˈaʊt əv
over ˈoʊ·vər
past pæst
through θru
under ˈʌn·dər
up ʌp

2 3.07 During feedback, encourage students to use the gestures they came up with in Exercise 1 to reinforce their understanding of the prepositions.

Extra Vocabulary Practice

3 Students then delete the prepositions from their description and give it to another student to complete.

Vocabulary Bank SB p130

VOCABULARY AND LISTENING

Prepositions of Movement

3.06 **1** **Match the prepositions with the pictures. Listen, check, and repeat.**

across	12	into	5	past	8
along	11	off	7	through	10
between	4	out of	2	under	6
down	1	over	3	up	9

3.07 **2** **Circle the correct prepositions. Then listen and check.**

1 Be careful! Don't fall *over* / *down* the stairs.
2 Who is that coming *out of* / *under* Bruno's house? Is it Carla?
3 Let's jump *into* / *up* the water together! Are you ready?
4 Don't cross the road *through* / *between* those cars. It's dangerous.
5 Why don't we swim *across* / *off* the lake to the other side? It isn't far.
6 Laura walked *along* / *past* me without saying hello.

Use It!

3 **In your notebook, write about your trip to school today using prepositions from Exercise 1. Compare with a partner.**

First, I went out of my house. Then I walked down the street and over the bridge.

A Radio Phone-in

LEARN TO LEARN

Using your Knowledge

Before you listen, think about what you already know about the topic and words you might hear.

4 **Look at the photos and think about words you might hear.**

3.08 **5** **Listen to Melissa's story. How many of your words from Exercise 4 do you hear?**

3.08 **6** **Listen again and put the events in the correct order.**

a 4 A boy fell into the lake in the park.
b 3 A photographer was taking a photo of Clayton's wife.
c 2 Clayton and his wife were in a park.
d 1 Clayton Cook got married.
e 6 Clayton jumped into the water and rescued the boy.
f 5 Some children started shouting.

7 **Close your book. Take turns telling the story. Can you remember the events in order?**

Learn to Learn

Students might already know about a topic even if they don't fully understand how to talk about it in English. Thinking about the type of things they might hear will help them guess what speakers are talking about.

4 Put students into teams and give them four minutes to brainstorm as many words as possible. Then elicit the words and write them on the board.

5 3.08 Ask students to raise their hand when they hear a word on the board.

6 3.08 Allow students to discuss the events in pairs and guess the order before listening again.

7 ★ Write some key vocabulary from the story on the board to support students.

Flipped Class

Ask students to watch **video 3.3** and do **Video Worksheet 3.3** in the *Teacher's Resource Bank* in preparation for the next lesson.

Homework

Workbook p27

Lesson Aim: I can understand how to use the simple past and past continuous.

Warmer

If appropriate, ask students to show one of their own photos on their smartphones and tell each other the story behind it.

▶ Play **video 3.3** if it was not assigned for homework. Elicit that the people were walking and that the sister was holding an apple.

3.09–3.10 Audioscripts ppT134–135

1 Point out that we pronounce *was* /wʌz/ and *were* /wɜr/ more fully in short answers.

2 3.09 ★★★ After feedback, challenge students to write one more short conversation using a past continuous question.

3 Explain that the simple past is one complete action in the past. We can use the past continuous to give background information about what was happening before and after the simple past action.

Get It Right!

Explain that clauses starting with *when* or *while* cannot stand on their own (e.g., *While I was doing my homework*) and always need a main clause (e.g., *She called me while I was doing my homework.*).

Extra Grammar Practice

4 3.10 ★ Before students attempt the task, go through the text with them, eliciting whether each action is one complete action or background information.

GRAMMAR IN ACTION

Past Continuous: Questions

Watch video 3.3
What were they doing in the country?
What was her sister holding?

I/He/She/It	You/We/They
Was he **wearing** his wedding clothes?	[3] Were the children **standing** close to the lake?
Yes, he [1] was. / No, he [2] wasn't.	Yes, they [4] were. / No, they **weren't**.

1 Complete the examples in the chart above.

3.09 **2** Write the conversations using the past continuous form of the verbs. Then listen and check.

1 A you / TV at 8 p.m. last night? (watch)
Were you watching TV at 8 p.m. last night?
B ✓
Yes, I was.

2 A What / you / yesterday? (wear)
What were you wearing yesterday?
B jeans and a hoodie
I was wearing jeans and a hoodie.

3 A your brother / at 5 p.m. yesterday? (chat online)
Was your brother chatting online at 5 p.m. yesterday?
B ✗ play basketball
No, he wasn't. He was playing basketball.

4 A Where / Alice and her family / in 2017? (live)
Where were Alice and her family living in 2017?
B in Mexico City
They were living in Mexico City.

Simple Past and Past Continuous

When Clayton jumped into the water, he [1] was wearing (wear) his wedding clothes.

While the photographer [2] was preparing (prepare) his camera, Clayton noticed three children.

3 Complete the examples in the chart above with the correct form of the verbs in parentheses.

Get It Right!

We can use **when**, **while**, and **as** + past continuous for a longer action in progress.
We use the simple past for a short action that interrupts a longer action in the past continuous.

simple past
past continuous

3.10 **4** Complete the text with the simple past or past continuous. Then listen and check.

I [1] was walking (walk) to the bus stop one afternoon when I [2] fell (fall) down on the icy street. I [3] was carrying (carry) a heavy bag with all my school things, and I [4] broke (break) my glasses. I [5] felt (feel) very embarrassed. Other people [6] were waiting (wait) for the bus, but they [7] didn't help (not help) me. However, one woman [8] picked up (pick up) my bag and glasses, and she [9] found (find) an empty seat for me. While I [10] was sitting (sit) there, she [11] cleaned (clean) my face and gave me some water. But when I [12] looked (look) for her a few minutes later, there was no one there.

Use It!

5 Work in pairs. Continue and finish the story below. Use the simple past and past continuous.

While I was walking to school this morning, I saw …

Finished? p120 Ex. 3

5 Allow students to first make up the story as they go, then work on retelling it properly, and finally, if there's time, write it down.

Grammar Game

Students show their photo from the warmer to a different partner. Encourage them to ask each other questions about what was happening. They win a point every time they can use a correct past continuous question.

Finished?

Students turn to p120 and do Exercise 3.

Homework

Workbook p28

Lesson Aim: I can tell an anecdote.

Warmer

Tell the students a funny story about your life (you can invent one if you want), and elicit reactions and follow-up questions. You could also have them guess if the anecdote is true or false. Explain that an *anecdote* is a short, often funny, story about something that happened to someone.

Teacher Support Hub ppxl–xli

3.11 Audioscript pT135

1 3.11 ★★★ Books closed. Students listen twice and then work in pairs to retell the story. Elicit the story on the board together with relevant vocabulary.

2 3.11 After feedback, play the audio again and ask students to read the text out loud with the audio.

3 Encourage students to use the context of the conversation to guess what the phrases mean.

4 Play **video 3.4** and drill the pronunciation of the phrases.

Everyday English Practice

5 Ask students to work in small groups to share any funny or unusual stories they have. If they can't think of a true one, they can invent one. Then they can choose the best ones to focus on.

6 If appropriate, encourage students to record their conversations on their phones and listen to the recording. Give them time to repeat the task if they wish.

SPEAKING
Telling an Anecdote

It's about Adrian. He was looking for new sneakers at the new shopping mall.

3.11 **1 Listen to the conversation. Who is the story about, and what was the person doing?**

DAVID LAURA

DAVID	[1] Guess what happened yesterday.
LAURA	No idea. What?
DAVID	Well, it didn't happen to me. [2] It happened to Adrian.
LAURA	Go on.
DAVID	He was at the new shopping mall.
LAURA	You're kidding! [3] What was he doing at a shopping mall? He hates shopping.
DAVID	He was looking for new sneakers.
LAURA	[4] Really?
DAVID	Yes, really. Now please stop interrupting. While he was looking at the sneakers, someone bumped into him.
LAURA	Who was it?
DAVID	It was LeBron James!
LAURA	No way! [5] That's amazing!
DAVID	I know.
LAURA	Did he take a photo?
DAVID	No, he didn't. He was too embarrassed. Can you believe it?
LAURA	What a great story!

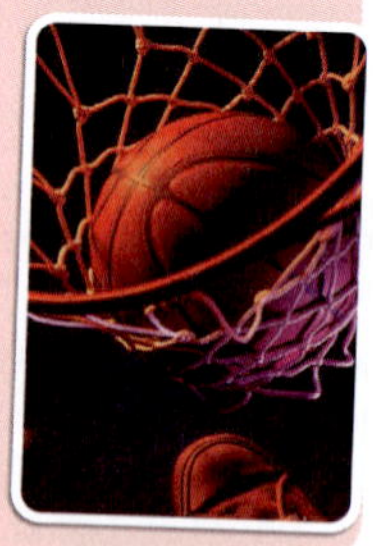

3.11 **2 Complete the conversation with the phrases from the *Useful Language* box. Then listen and check.**

Useful Language

Guess what happened (yesterday).
It happened to …
Really?
That's amazing/incredible!
What was (he) doing (at) … ?

3 Look at the *Everyday English* box. Find and underline the phrases in the conversation.

Watch video 3.4
Everyday English

Go on. No idea. What a great story!
You're kidding!

4 Which *Everyday English* phrases do you use when you …

1 don't know? No idea.
2 hear something surprising? You're kidding!
3 want someone to continue? Go on.
4 liked someone's story? What a great story!

PLAN

5 Think of something funny or unusual that happened, and take notes.

Who it happened to: ____________
What the person was doing when it happened: ____________
What happened: ____________

SPEAK

6 Practice telling your anecdote to your partner. Remember to use the simple past and past continuous, vocabulary from this unit, and phrases from the *Useful Language* and *Everyday English* boxes.

CHECK

7 Work with another pair. Listen to one of their anecdotes and complete the notes.

Who the story happened to: ____________
What the person was doing when it happened: ____________
What happened: ____________

40 WHAT DO STORIES TEACH US? | UNIT 3

7 Encourage students to use the *Everyday English* phrases to react to each others' stories. Then they swap pairs and tell their stories again. This task repetition will help improve students' fluency and confidence. Tell them to have fun with the phrases, exaggerating their reactions.

Extend It!

Students have a new conversation about a story that was not chosen in Exercise 5, ensuring that they use the phrases from the *Everyday English* box.

Lesson Aim: I can write a story.

Warmer

Ask students when people tell funny stories (e.g., with friends or family) and when people write stories down (e.g., sharing on social media, sharing in books or articles). Brainstorm situations in which students have read or heard stories before.

Teacher Support Hub ppxlii–xliii

1 ★ Elicit the girl's name: Alison Dunmire. Elicit the title: *A Silly Story*. Ask students if they know any silly stories about bikes.

2 Students discuss the questions in pairs before checking them against the text.

3 ★★★ Give students two minutes to read the story again and memorize useful phrases. They then cover the story and try to complete the exercise without checking the story.

Useful Language Practice

4 After planning, students share their ideas with a partner, who can ask follow-up questions to generate more ideas.

5 & 6 Ask students to highlight in different colors the simple past, the past continuous, vocabulary from the unit, and any *Useful Language* phrases. This will encourage self-assessment. Then students read each other's stories and vote for the most interesting ones.

WRITING
A Story

1 Look at the photo. What do you think Alison's story is about? Read the story and check your answers.

A Silly Story By Alison Dunmire

Last Sunday, I was feeling bored and decided to ride my bike. I went to the garage to get it, but it wasn't there! At first, I thought maybe it was in the yard. I was looking for it outside when Mom came out and said, "If you left it outside, maybe someone stole it." I was really angry.

The next day, while I was walking to school, I saw a bike exactly like mine in front of the supermarket. I didn't have time to investigate. In the afternoon, I was busy and forgot all about it. The next morning, the bike was still there! I took a look, and it was my bike – with my bike lock on it and everything!

Suddenly, I remembered! I was riding home last week when it started to rain, so I decided to leave my bike at the supermarket!

2 Read the story again and answer the questions.

1 When did the events in the story happen?
last Sunday, the next day, and the next morning

2 Where did Alison look for her bike?
She looked in the garage and outside / in the yard.

3 Where was the bike?
It was in front of the supermarket.

4 Did someone steal it? What really happened?
No, Alison left her bike at the supermarket last week when it started to rain.

3 Complete the sentences in the *Useful Language* box with time and sequencing phrases from the story.

Useful Language

1 Last Sunday, I was feeling bored.
2 At first, I thought it was outside.
3 The next day, I saw a bike exactly like mine.
4 In the afternoon, I was busy and forgot all about it.
5 The next morning, the bike was still there!
6 Suddenly, I remembered!

PLAN

4 Plan a story about a time when something interesting, funny, or scary happened to you. Take notes for three paragraphs.

1 What was happening before the main events started: ______

What happened first: ______

2 The main events of the story: ______

3 What happened in the end: ______

WRITE

5 Write your story. Remember to include time and sequencing phrases, the simple past and past continuous, and vocabulary from this unit.

CHECK

6 Do you ...
- use phrases from the *Useful Language* box?
- explain the main events?
- explain what happened in the end?

Finished? p120 Ex. 4

Finished?
Students turn to p120 and do Exercise 4.

Flipped Class
Prepare for **Explore It!** (p43). Students research an interesting fact about a fairy tale.

Homework
Workbook p29

Lesson Aim: I can understand a fairy tale.

Background Information

Fairy tales are traditional stories that involve magic. Many fairy tales were passed down through storytelling before they were recorded in books. Some popular fairy tales, such as *Beauty and the Beast* and *Jack and the Beanstalk*, may be 4,000 to 6,000 years old.

Warmer

▶ Play **video 3.5** and elicit the answers: bees are busy in Slovenia; honey is used to make drinks and food sweet, and for medicine; artists painted characters from folk tales and history.

Video Comprehension Questions

1 Focus students on the pictures, and elicit relevant vocabulary before students predict the story's plot (e.g., *path*, *clock tower*, *doves*, *storm*, *ship*, *danger*).

The story is about a boy's journey to understand what fear is.

2 3.12 Encourage students to circle key words in the text that relate to the pictures (e.g., *set off*, *ship*), and elicit these during feedback.

3 In pairs, students first answer the questions without looking at the text before checking the text to see if they are correct.

Matching Pictures to Sentences

AROUND THE WORLD

READING

A Turkish Fairy Tale

1 Look at the pictures. What is happening in each picture? What do you think the story is about?

3.12 2 Read the fairy tale. Put the pictures in the order of the story.

a 1

b 3

c 2

Globetrotters

Watch video 3.5 A Bee's Story

- Where are bees very busy?
- What is honey used for?
- Who did artists in the 18th century paint?

Voice It!

4 Discuss the questions.

1 How does the boy face fear in the story?
2 What causes fear? How can it affect your life?
3 How can fear be good?

3 Read the fairy tale again. Answer the questions in your notebook.

1 Why did the boy start his journey?
2 How did he feel when he started the journey?
3 What did the ogre try to do?
4 What did the boy do when he heard the people on the ship?

1 He wanted to find fear (because he didn't understand what it was).
2 He felt confident.
3 He tried to attack the boy.
4 He jumped into the water and saved them.

The Boy Who Found Fear

Once upon a time, a woman and her son lived in a small house in a forest. They didn't have any neighbors, and the lonely boy stayed at home with his mother every day.

One winter's evening, they were having dinner when a storm started. The wind blew the door open and the mother said, "Close the door. I feel fear."

"What is fear?" asked the boy.

"Fear is when you feel afraid," she replied.

"I don't understand. I want to find fear."

So the next morning, the boy set off confidently. While he was looking for fear, he met a lot of different people and he faced a lot of challenges. First, there was a group of robbers. They made him do dangerous and difficult things, but he wasn't afraid. He continued his journey.

4 Allow students a few minutes of thinking time to form opinions about questions 2 and 3. If appropriate, students can discuss these in their own language first and then work together to form their opinions in English, using a dictionary if available.

Teacher Support Hub pxliv

Class Challenge

There is a statue of the Little Mermaid, famous from Hans Christian Anderson's fairy tale, in London / New York / **Copenhagen**.

Learn to Learn

Remind students that they should record and learn groups of words and phrases, not just individual words (e.g., *set off on a journey*, *set off for school*, *set off late*). This is particularly true of phrasal verbs, as the word *set* has many meanings, none of which have the meaning of *set off*.

5 Make sure students are clear about the meaning of definitions 1–5 before they look in the text for synonyms.

6 ★ Elicit the answers using less complex vocabulary first (1 *go*; 2 *continue*; 3 *search for*; 4 *arrive at*; 5 *found*).

Students can collaborate digitally through *Collaboration Plus*, where you can assign, track, and assess their work. Students can also share and showcase their work and comment on each other's projects.

Explore It!

Turn this into a class quiz. Divide students into two groups. Students from different teams take turns reading a question aloud. The other team wins a point if they guess the correct answer.

Culture Project

See Project Book p30 for further information and activities.

LEARN TO LEARN

Phrasal Verbs

A phrasal verb is a verb + a small word like *for* or *on*. They have a special meaning that is different from the verb on its own.

5 Find phrasal verbs in the story that mean:

1. to start a journey __set off__
2. to try to find __look for__
3. to find by accident __come across__
4. to arrive or reach __get to__
5. to continue __go on__

6 Complete the sentences with the phrasal verbs in Exercise 5.

1. Are we all ready to go? Let's __set off__ now before it gets too hot.
2. A I don't think it's a good idea to __go on__ in the dark.
   B OK. Let's camp here for the night.
3. Can you help me __look for__ my phone? I don't know where it is.
4. A How long did it take you to __get to__ the beach?
   B Ages! It was really far away.
5. While I was doing some research, I __came across__ this photo of our street in 1885.

Next, he came across an angry ogre who tried to attack him, but the boy ran away. After that, he got to the ocean. There was a terrible storm, and he saw a ship in great danger. The people on the ship were terrified, and they were shouting for help, so he jumped into the water and saved them. He wasn't afraid at all.

He went on until finally he got to a city. There were people everywhere, and it was very busy. One man told the boy that the people were sad because their king was dead, but today they were choosing a new king. Just then, three beautiful doves flew down from a tower, and they sat on the boy's head. The people were excited. "This is the sign! You are our king!"

At that moment, he saw into the future: he was the king, he was trying to make everyone happy, but the people were angry. And he suddenly realized what fear was, and he was afraid.

Explore It!

Is the sentence *T* (true) or *F* (false)?

The story of *Cinderella* first appeared in a Chinese book around the year 850. __T__

Find another interesting fact about a fairy tale. Write a question for your partner to answer.

SHAPE IT!

CULTURE PROJECT

A Comic Strip

A comic strip uses words and pictures to tell a story. Make a comic strip using a traditional story from around the world.

Teacher's Resource Bank

UNIT 3 | WHAT DO STORIES TEACH US? 43

Lesson Aim: I can review what I have learned and reflect on my progress.

The aim of this page is for students to review the grammar and vocabulary from the unit. You can either do it in class, as a timed progress test, or assign it for homework.

Vocabulary

1 Before the activity, brainstorm vocabulary from SB p35 and elicit example sentences from students. After feedback, ask students, in pairs, to choose one more adjective and write a sentence with it. They then delete the adjective and give the sentence to another pair to complete.

2 After feedback, encourage students to read the story in pairs, using the gestures they associated with each preposition on SB p38.

Grammar in Action

3 Before the activity, elicit the form of the past continuous on the board and elicit examples with different verbs. After feedback, students make true sentences about what was happening (to them) two hours ago.

4 Ask fast finishers to write questions for sentences 1–4 in Exercise 3 (e.g., *Was it snowing this morning?*).

5 Before the activity, elicit the difference in meaning between the simple past and past continuous, drawing a timeline on the board and eliciting examples from students.

Unit Quiz

3 REVIEW

VOCABULARY

1 Complete the sentences with the adjectives.

afraid embarrassed surprised tired upset

1 Elsa looks upset and she's crying.
2 I can't believe I won! I'm really surprised.
3 My dad is afraid of heights. He hates being in very tall buildings.
4 I forgot David's birthday. I was so embarrassed!
5 I'm really tired. I didn't sleep much.

2 Complete the story with the prepositions.

across between down into out of through under up

Tiger the cat went [1] out of the front door and walked [2] across the road [3] between two cars. He went [4] into the park and climbed [5] up a tree. Then a mouse appeared. "Lunch!" thought Tiger. He climbed [6] down the tree and followed it. The mouse ran [7] through the grass and then disappeared [8] under a rock. "Maybe I'll have lunch at home today," said Tiger.

GRAMMAR IN ACTION

3 What was happening at 10:30 a.m. yesterday? Write two sentences in the past continuous.

1 it / not snow – rain
It wasn't snowing. It was raining.
2 I / not study – sleep
I wasn't studying. I was sleeping.
3 Alex / not read / a book – listen / to music
Alex wasn't reading a book. He/She was listening to music.
4 Eva and Helen / not talk – have / a snack
Eva and Helen weren't talking. They were having a snack.

4 Write past continuous questions. Then match them with the answers (a–d).

1 you / wear / jeans / yesterday? d
Were you wearing jeans yesterday?
2 Lidia / work / at 10 p.m. last night? b
Was Lidia working at 10 p.m. last night?
3 where / they / go / last Saturday at 7 p.m.? a
Where were they going last Saturday at 7 p.m.?
4 what / I / do / an hour ago? c
What was I doing an hour ago?

a They were going to the movies.
b Yes, she was.
c You were taking photos.
d Yes, I was.

5 Complete the text with the simple past or past continuous form of the verbs.

Suzanne Collins [1] was working (work) in television when she [2] met (meet) children's author James Proimos. After talking with him, she [3] decided (decide) to try writing books, too. She [4] was thinking (think) about the story of *Alice in Wonderland* when she [5] had (have) the idea for her first novel, *Gregor the Overlander*. She [6] wanted (want) to change Alice's story to a modern adventure, set in a city. The book was very successful, and she [7] wrote (write) four more books about Gregor. The series [8] won (win) a lot of prizes. While she [9] was writing (write) the series, she also [10] completed (complete) a picture book for children. Now she is most famous for her *Hunger Games* books and movies.

Self-Assessment

I can use adjectives to talk about feelings.
I can use prepositions to talk about movement.
I can use the past continuous in sentences and questions.
I can use the simple past and past continuous together.

Review the Unit Theme

Remind students of the unit title: *What do stories teach us?* Put students into pairs. Have them discuss the following questions: *What traditional stories do you know? What kinds of modern stories do you read, watch, or listen to? What kinds of stories are interesting to you? Why?* Share answers as a class.

Teacher Support Hub pxlvi

Self-Assessment

After students have completed the checklist, assign homework from the Workbook, depending on the areas students need to focus on.

Extend It!

In pairs, students write a conversation with as much language from the unit as possible. They can perform it in groups, with other students raising their hands every time they hear language from the unit.

Homework

Workbook pp30–31

Lesson Aim: I can guess the meaning of new words.

Asking students to write test questions is a useful way to get them to focus on creating accurate language that other people need to understand.

1 Encourage students to discuss what type of word it might be and the meaning of the whole sentence, rather than just saying what they think the missing word is.

SHAPE IT!

2 & 3 Allow plenty of time for this activity. Emphasize that the sentences should make the meaning of the vocabulary very clear. For example: *In the jungle, there are lots of trees and exotic animals* is a good sentence, but *We were in the jungle* isn't because the answer is not necessarily *jungle*.

4 Refer students back to SB p43, where they learned that it's better to learn words in context than in isolation.

5 This exercise will help students focus on how words are used in context.

Extend It!

Ask students to choose a few more vocabulary items from the previous units and create sentences with missing words for a partner to work with.

LEARN TO LEARN

LEARN TO ... GUESS THE MEANING OF NEW WORDS

You can help your partner learn vocabulary by writing sentences with missing words for them to guess.

1 Erin writes sentences with missing words for a friend to guess. Can you guess what the words are? Discuss with a partner.

OK, the first one. Is it an adjective?

Yes, it is.

Is it "happy"?

No. Try again!

1. *I was ______ because my soccer team was winning.*
2. *The plane flew ______ the city.*
3. *The boy felt ______ when he called his teacher "Mom."*

Possible answers:
1 excited
2 over
3 embarrassed

2 Choose five words from the box. Write five sentences with missing words like the sentences in Exercise 1.

between	bored	jungle	nervous	protect
surprised	tired	trap	under	worried

1.
2.
3.
4.
5.

SHAPE IT!

3 Show your sentences to your partner. Can they guess the missing words?

4 Why is it a good idea to learn words in sentences? Discuss with your partner.

5 Close your book. Take turns saying the five words you chose in Exercise 2. Can your partner remember your sentences?

The word was "bored." What was the sentence?

"I feel bored when ... ." No, sorry, can you help me?

OK. It starts, "I was bored because ... ."

I remember! "I was bored because ..."

Lesson Aim: I can talk about helping people.

Warmer

In groups, students brainstorm things that make people happy but that don't cost any money, such as friendship. Elicit the idea of helping others.

Teacher Support Hub ppxxxiv–xxxv

Start It!

Unit Quiz

1 Use this as an opportunity to review the adjectives to describe feelings from p35. Elicit ideas about how the boy probably feels and why.

2 & 3 Students discuss the questions in groups. Elicit ways of helping people on the board. Play **video 4.1** and ask students to raise their hands when they hear an idea that's on the board.

4 Allow students one minute of thinking time before discussing in pairs.

Video Comprehension Questions

Flipped Class

Prepare for **Explore It!** (p47). Students research an interesting fact about money.

4

What do you value most?

LEARNING OUTCOMES

I can ...

- understand texts about money and caring jobs
- make and respond to requests
- write an opinion essay
- understand how to use *could*, comparative and superlative adjectives, *too*, *too much*, *too many*, and (*not*) *enough* + noun
- talk about money and caring jobs
- remember similar words, identify key information, and organize my homework
- reach agreement as a group and make a poster

Start It!

1 Look at the photo. How does the boy feel?
2 Before you watch, how do you help other people?
3 How can helping others be good for you? Watch and check.
4 Which of the ways to help in the video do you like best?

You can learn new skills; it can make you healthier and keep you fit; it can be fun/rewarding.

Watch video 4.1

Grammar in Action 4.2 p49

Grammar in Action 4.3 p51

Everyday English 4.4 p52

46 WHAT DO YOU VALUE MOST? | UNIT 4

Unit Aims

Skills

I can ...

- understand a text about money p48
- understand a monologue about caring jobs p50
- make and respond to requests p52
- write an opinion essay p53
- reach agreement as a group and make a poster pp54–55

Language

I can ...

- talk about money p47
- understand how to use *could* and comparative and superlative adjectives p49
- talk about caring jobs p50
- understand how to use *too*, *too much*, *too many*, and (*not*) *enough* + noun p51

Learn to Learn

I can ...

- understand words with similar meanings p47
- identify key information before listening p50
- organize my homework p57

Extra Resources

- Finished? Student's Book p121
- Vocabulary Bank, Student's Book p131
- Workbook pp32–39
- Grammar Reference and Practice, Workbook pp94–95
- Teacher Support Hub, Teacher's Book ppxxxiv–xlvii

Digital Resource Pack

(on Cambridge One)

- *Teacher's Resource Bank* for word lists, differentiated worksheets, *Culture Projects*, and many other extra resources
- *Practice Extra*, *Presentation Plus*, *Test Generator*, and *Digital Collaboration Space*

Lesson Aim: I can talk about money.

Warmer

Put students into teams to brainstorm vocabulary related to money (e.g., *expensive*, *dollars*, *price*, etc.). The team with the most words wins.

4.01–4.02 **Audioscripts pT135**

1 ★★★ After feedback, challenge students to test each other in pairs. Student A reads one of the sentences, replacing the verb in bold with *Beep!* Student B repeats the sentence, adding the correct verb.

Target Vocabulary

borrow ˈbɑ·roʊ
change tʃeɪndʒ
cost kɔst
earn ɜrn
lend lend
owe oʊ
pay peɪ
save seɪv
sell sel
spend spend

2 4.01 ★★★ If students need practice with spelling, ask them to listen and write down the words they hear and then check their spelling with the words in the box.

Extra Vocabulary Practice

3 4.02 ★ After feedback, students write a new conversation in pairs and then perform it for another pair, who must guess the correct verb.

Vocabulary Bank SB p131

VOCABULARY
Money Verbs

1 **Look at the verbs in bold. Then match the sentences with the photos.**

1 Don't worry. I can **pay** for you, too. g
2 He **spends** all his money on video games. He should **save** it for something he needs. e
3 Friendships don't **cost** money. They're free! c
4 I want to **earn** money. Can I wash your car? b
5 I **owe** my friend $50. I can **sell** my bike. f
6 **A** Could you **lend** me some money?
B How much do you want to **borrow**? d
7 I want to **change** this money, please. a

a

b

c

d

e

f

g

2 4.01 **Listen to the verbs in Exercise 1 and repeat.**

3 4.02 **Listen and write the correct verb from Exercise 1 for each situation. Sometimes there is more than one possible answer.**

1 pay
2 borrow/lend
3 save
4 change
5 sell

LEARN TO LEARN
Similar Words

Many words have similar meanings. Think of ways to help you understand the differences.

You lend money to someone (it's yours).
You borrow money from someone (it isn't yours).

4 **Look at these pairs of verbs. Think of more ways to remember the different meanings.**

spend / buy   earn / win

5 **Compare with a partner. How does your partner remember the meanings?**

Use It!

6 **Complete the sentences in your notebook with your own ideas. Tell your partner.**

1 A good way to earn money is to …
2 The last time I borrowed money was …
3 I spend most of my money on …

Explore It!

Is the sentence *T* (true) or *F* (false)?

In Zimbabwe, there was a $100 trillion bill. At that time, bread cost $300 billion. T

Find another interesting fact about money. Then write a question for your partner.

Learn to Learn

Encourage students to record easily confused words in their vocabulary notebooks with full example sentences and an explanation of their differences. Point out that in these cases, translation may not always be appropriate.

4 & 5 Elicit that you *buy* something, but you *spend* money, and that you *earn* money by working but *win* money through luck. Elicit other ideas the students may have had.

Extra Vocabulary Practice

6 After feedback, elicit that writing personalized example sentences, when possible, is an important way to remember vocabulary.

Explore It!

After pair work, students choose the most interesting question they discussed and read it aloud for the rest of the class to answer.

Homework

Workbook p32

Lesson Aim: I can understand a text about money.

Warmer

In groups, students talk about what they bought or spent money on in the last 24 hours. Elicit full sentences, reviewing vocabulary from the previous lesson and the simple past.

Teacher Support Hub ppxxxvi–xxxvii

1 & 2 Students discuss the question in pairs, looking at the photos and predicting which of the two summaries might fit best. Elicit guesses and give students a time limit for the first reading to encourage faster skimming.

3 4.03 Allow students to discuss the questions in pairs before reading the article again. Students then read and underline the sentences in the text where they found the answers. They can check their answers with a partner.

Reading Comprehension Questions

4 Elicit a few questions to review simple past question formation. Then students write questions in pairs about what Mark Boyle did in the past. Monitor and correct mistakes with the simple past.

5 Monitor and take note of common mistakes with the simple past and question formation. Write these on the board for the whole class to correct. Then elicit the most interesting questions that were asked and discuss the possible answers.

READING
A Newspaper Article

1 Look at the photos. What do you think the man did?

2 Skim the article and choose the correct summary.

a A man sold his home and bought an RV to travel around the world for three years.

(b) A man lived without money for three years.

3 4.03 Read the article and answer the questions.

1 Where did Mark live after he sold his own home?
in an RV on a farm

2 How did he use his laptop without electricity?
He used solar power.

3 Which three things were difficult for him at first?
getting food, washing, and traveling

4 What did he buy after his time without money?
a pair of sneakers from a thrift store

A Different Life

Can you imagine living for a day without money? Mark Boyle, from Ireland, did that for three years.

Mark had a good job and he earned a lot of money. One day, a friend challenged him to live without money. Mark decided he could change his life and do it.

First, he sold his houseboat, and he went to live in an RV on a farm. He kept his laptop and cell phone – he knew he could use solar power to charge them. He couldn't make any calls, but he could receive them.

The first few months were the worst – simple things were more difficult than before. Mark couldn't buy food, take a shower, or travel easily. But he soon found his own food – usually vegetables, fruit, and other plants. He made a stove to cook outside, and he collected wood to use as fuel. He washed in a river, and he used plants to clean himself. He even made his own toothpaste! He walked or cycled everywhere, so he was fitter and healthier than he was before.

So, was life without money better for Mark than life with money? Yes, it was. He was happier than before, and the best thing was that he felt

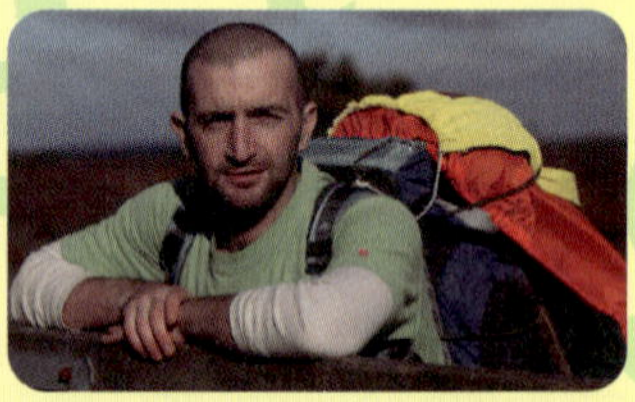

more alive. He also discovered that friendship is more important than money.

The biggest and most difficult decision for Mark was to return to a life with money. After three years without money, what was the first thing he bought? A pair of sneakers from a thrift store!

Voice It!

4 Imagine you can interview Mark Boyle after his three years without money. Write questions to ask him using the ideas below.

Family and friends: ______

Clothes: ______

Food: ______

Work: ______

Travel: ______

5 Take turns being Mark Boyle and the interviewer and do the interview.

How often did you see your family?

When did you see your friends?

Finished? p121 Ex. 1

Class Challenge

When he was younger, Mark Boyle studied **business** / farming / history in college.

Finished?

Students turn to p121 and do Exercise 1.

Flipped Class

Ask students to watch **video 4.2** and do **Video Worksheet 4.2** in the *Teacher's Resource Bank* in preparation for the next lesson.

Homework

Workbook p33

Lesson Aim: I can understand how to use *could* and comparative and superlative adjectives.

Warmer

▶ Play **video 4.2**, if it was not assigned for homework, and elicit the answers to the two questions: she couldn't buy a horse, but she could draw them. Elicit that *could* is the past of *can* and is used to talk about ability in the past.

4.04 Audioscript pT135

1 After feedback, drill the pronunciation of *could* /kʊd/ (or /kəd/ in faster speech) and elicit that there is no /l/ sound present.

2 After feedback, elicit that there is no *to* after *could*.

Extra Grammar Practice

3 & 4 ★★★ After feedback, ask students to repeat the task, this time using their own ideas.

5 ★ Point out that a "short" adjective has one syllable (or one syllable and another ending in *-y*). A "long" adjective has two or more syllables.

Get It Right!

Drill the pronunciation of *than* in the example sentence. When pronounced naturally as part of a sentence, it is /ðən/ rather than /ðæn/.

6 After feedback, students briefly discuss in pairs what was the most interesting fact about the text on p48. Elicit ideas and several uses of "more interesting" and "most interesting" during feedback.

7 4.04 ★ Remind students that they need to use *the* before superlative adjectives.

GRAMMAR IN ACTION
Could

Watch video 4.2
Could she buy a horse?
Could she draw horses?

+	He [1] could change his life.
–	He [2] couldn't make any calls.
?	Could he live without money? Yes, he [3] could . / No, he [4] couldn't .

1 Complete the examples in the chart. Use the article on page 48 to help you.

2 Complete the sentences with *could* or *couldn't* and the verbs in parentheses. Check your answers in the article.

1 Mark could receive calls on his phone. (receive)
2 He couldn't buy food. (buy)
3 He could charge his laptop with solar power. (charge)
4 He couldn't take a shower. (take)

Use It!

3 Complete the sentences. Use *could* or *couldn't* and the ideas in the box.

buy my own clothes
make my own lunch
ride a bike use a laptop

1 When I was five, I ______

2 When my grandparents were young, they ______

3 A year ago, I ______

4 Ask and answer with a partner.

Could you buy your own clothes when you were five?

Comparative and Superlative Adjectives

more important	Adjective	Comparative	Superlative
Short Adjective	fit happy	[1] fitter [2] happier	the fittest the happiest
Long Adjective	important difficult	[3] ______ [4] more difficult	the most important the most difficult
Irregular Adjective	good bad	[5] better worse	the best [6] the worst

5 Complete the examples in the chart above. Use the article on page 48 to help you.

Get It Right!

We use **than**, not **that**, to compare two things.
My sister is fitter than me. **NOT** ~~*My sister is fitter that me.*~~

6 Complete the sentences with the comparative or superlative form of the adjectives.

1 Life for Mark without money was better (good) than before.
2 The best (good) thing was that he felt more alive.
3 The most difficult (difficult) decision was to return to a life with money.

7 4.04 Complete the text with the comparative or superlative form of the adjectives. Then listen and check.

It's the fourth Friday in November and it's Black Friday. It's [1] the busiest (busy) shopping day of the year. Things are [2] cheaper (cheap) than usual today. Shoppers can get [3] the best (good) prices for [4] the latest (late) gadgets or [5] the most stylish (stylish) sneakers. In my opinion, Black Friday is [6] the worst (bad) day of the year. People seem to be [7] more interested (interested) in shopping than anything else! I think we could all be [8] happier (happy) without spending money all the time.

Use It!

8 Choose a topic from the box or use your own. Discuss with a partner. Use comparatives and superlatives.

math / history / science
market / shopping mall / online shopping

History is more difficult than … but … is the most difficult.

Finished? p121 Ex. 2

8 Elicit some more adjectives on the board that students can use, such as *boring*, *easy*, *interesting*, *exciting*, *useful*, etc.

Grammar Game

Put students into groups. One student in each group thinks of another student in the class. The others must guess the student but can only ask questions with comparatives or superlatives (e.g., *Is he taller than you? No, he is shorter than me.*). The first student to guess wins and thinks of the next student.

Finished?

Students turn to p121 and do Exercise 2.

Homework

Workbook p34

Lesson Aim: I can talk about caring jobs.

Teacher Support Hub ppxxxviii–xxxix

4.05–4.08 **Audioscripts ppT135–136**

1 4.05 Before the activity, students cover the box and work in pairs to think of the names of the jobs in the pictures.

Target Vocabulary

caregiver ˈkerˌɡɪ·vər
firefighter ˈfaɪrˌfaɪ·t̬ər
garbage collector ˈɡɑr·bɪdʒ kəˌlek·tər
lawyer ˈlɔɪ·ər
lifeguard ˈlaɪf·ɡɑrd
nurse nɜrs
paramedic ˌper·əˈme·dɪk
police officer pəˈlis ˌɔ·fə·sər
preschool teacher ˈpri·skul ˈti·tʃər
surgeon ˈsɜr·dʒən
vet vet
volunteer ˌvɑ·lənˈtɪər

Pronunciation

4.06–4.07 Students turn to the pronunciation exercises on SB p141 for practice saying *-er* at the end of words.

2 ★★★ After feedback, students, in pairs, make one extra sentence and give it to another pair to guess the person.

Extra Vocabulary Practice

3 Allow a minute of thinking time, and then monitor closely and assist when needed.

4 & 5 4.08 EXAM Before listening, elicit ideas from Exercise 4 and write relevant vocabulary on the board to support students while they listen. Check to find out if they heard any of the ideas they discussed, and then play the audio again.

Vocabulary Bank SB p131

VOCABULARY AND LISTENING

Caring Jobs

4.05 **1** Match eight jobs with the photos. (Circle) the jobs that aren't in the photos. Listen, check, and repeat.

(caregiver)		(paramedic)	
firefighter	3	police officer	7
garbage collector	4	preschool teacher	5
lawyer	2	surgeon	8
(lifeguard)		vet	1
nurse	6	(volunteer)	

1
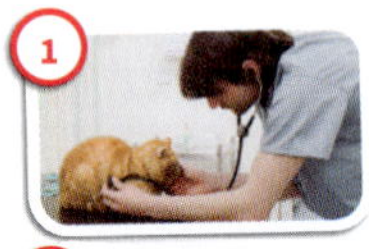
2

3

4

5

6
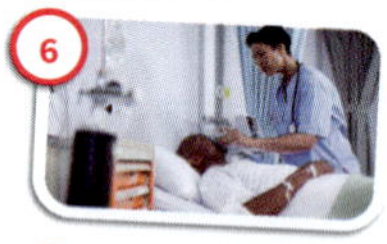
7

8
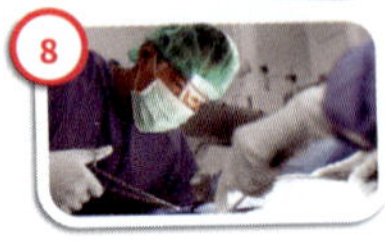

Pronunciation p141

2 Write which person you need in these situations.

1 You're at the swimming pool. Your friend has a problem. *lifeguard*
2 There's a fire at your school. firefighter
3 Your grandma needs help at home. caregiver
4 Your cat has a problem with its eye. vet
5 Your friend is in the hospital. This person is doing an operation on them. surgeon

Use It!

3 Work with a partner. Discuss the questions.

1 What do the jobs in Exercise 1 have in common?
2 Which people in these jobs do you see every week?
3 Which job would you like to do?

Job Profiles

4 What do you think are the best and worst things about doing a caring job? Discuss with a partner.

4.08 **5** EXAM Listen to the job profiles and match the speakers with their jobs. There are two extra jobs.

Speaker 1 c
Speaker 2 e
Speaker 3 a
Speaker 4 b

a lifeguard
b paramedic
c volunteer
d nurse
e vet
f lawyer

LEARN TO LEARN

Identifying Key Information

When you are matching people with information, check key words before you listen. This helps you to focus on the information you need.

6 Read the questions in Exercise 7. (Circle) the key words you need to listen for.

4.08 **7** Listen again. Write *1*, *2*, *3*, or *4*.

Who …

a usually (takes care) of (dogs) and (cats)? 2
b (wants people) to (follow rules)? 3
c (collects clothing) and (blankets)? 1
d (drives) an (ambulance)? 4
e only (works) during the (summer)? 3
f (serves meals) to people? 1

8 Imagine you have one of the jobs in Exercise 1. In your notebook, write five sentences about your day. Read your sentences aloud, but don't say the job. Can your partner guess?

I sometimes work all night.

Are you a nurse?

Learn to Learn

Listening is often a demanding skill, so it is important to make sure students know what information they need to listen for.

6 & 7 4.08 Point out that key words are often nouns, verbs, or adjectives. In pairs, students discuss the questions before listening again.

8 Monitor students' writing closely and take note of common mistakes. Before students read aloud, write the mistakes on the board and elicit corrections.

Extend It!

Students play the game in Exercise 8 again but this time choosing any profession they like.

Flipped Class

▶ Ask students to watch **video 4.3** and do **Video Worksheet 4.3** in the *Teacher's Resource Bank* in preparation for the next lesson.

Homework

Workbook p35

Lesson Aim: I can understand how to use *too, too much, too many, and (not) enough + noun.*

Warmer

▶ Play **video 4.3** and elicit the reasons why people don't volunteer: they are too busy; they have too much homework; they don't have enough time. Elicit that volunteering helps the vlogger with his IT class.

4.09 Audioscript pT136

1 Point out that we often use *too* (*many/much*) when we are complaining or not happy about something.

2 & 3 ★ Guide students to underline the words after the options or blanks and identify if they are adjectives, uncountable nouns, or plural nouns.

4 Challenge students to turn each question into a conversation with at least two follow-up questions.

5 Point out that *enough* goes before nouns, but after adjectives (e.g., *The chair is not comfortable enough.*).

6 4.09 Fast finishers can retell the story to their partner using only the phrases in the box as prompts.

Extra Grammar Practice

7 Encourage students to use *too* and *not enough* when they describe the worst thing about the job.

GRAMMAR IN ACTION

Too, Too Much, Too Many

Watch video 4.3
Say three reasons why some people don't volunteer. How does volunteering help the vlogger at school?

Too + Adjective	*Too Much* + Uncountable Noun	*Too Many* + Plural Countable Noun
I'm **too** [1] busy to have lunch.	Some kids make **too much** [2] noise.	I have **too many** [3] clothes.

1 Complete the examples in the chart above with the words in the box.

busy clothes noise

2 Read the sentences about the people you listened to on page 50. Circle the correct words.

1 The hours were (too) / *too much* / *too many* long in the paramedic's last job.
2 The volunteer thinks people own *too* / *too much* / (*too many*) books.
3 Sometimes the pool is (*too*) / *too much* / *too many* noisy for the lifeguard.
4 The vet spends *too* / (*too much*) / *too many* time at work.

3 Complete the questionnaire with *too*, *too much*, or *too many*.

All About You!

Do you have ...
1 *too much* homework this week?
2 too many clothes?

Do you ...
3 spend too much money on clothes?
4 buy too many snacks?

Are you ...
5 too busy to listen to your friends?
6 too young to drive a car?

Use It!

4 Work with a partner. Ask and answer the questions in Exercise 3.

(Not) Enough + Noun

I can't volunteer. I don't have [1] enough time (time).	He can invite 20 people. He has [2] enough chairs (chairs).

5 Complete the examples in the chart above with the words in parentheses and *enough*.

6 4.09 Complete the text with the words in the box. Then listen and check.

enough chairs enough space enough time too many animals too many people too much information too noisy ~~too young~~

I'm [1] *too young* to have a full-time job, but every Saturday I'm a volunteer with a local vet. I help the receptionist when she doesn't have [2] enough time to do everything. Last week, there were [3] too many people in the waiting room – we didn't have [4] enough chairs for them to sit on! Sometimes it gets [5] too noisy for me, especially when there are [6] too many animals and there isn't [7] enough space in the waiting room.

The best thing: I love animals and I can spend all day with them! 🙂

The worst thing: Sometimes there's [8] too much information for me, and I don't understand it all.

Use It!

7 Imagine a day doing your dream job. Take notes. Then compare with a partner.

- What the job is: ______
- The best thing: ______
- The worst thing: ______

My dream job is to be a firefighter. It's an exciting job, but it can be dangerous.

Finished? p121 Ex. 3

UNIT 4 | WHAT DO YOU VALUE MOST? 51

Grammar Game

Put students into groups. One student chooses something (e.g., a job, a TV show, a restaurant, a book) and talks about it (e.g., *I don't like it because there isn't enough action and there are too many characters, so I find it too boring.* – a TV show). The other students in the group guess what the student is talking about.

Finished?

Students turn to p121 and do Exercise 3.

Homework

Workbook p36

Lesson Aim: I can make and respond to requests.

Warmer

Elicit the difference between *lend* and *borrow*, and write on the board *You should never lend or borrow money*. Ask students if they agree and why.

Teacher Support Hub ppxl–xli

4.10 Audioscript pT136

1 4.10 ★★★ Challenge students to listen and answer the question with their books closed.

2 4.10 After feedback, students practice creating short conversations using the language in the box.

Useful Language Practice

3 Play **video 4.4** and drill the pronunciation of the target phrases, focusing students' attention on the stressed words.

4 After feedback, encourage students to read the conversation aloud along with the audio and then practice it in pairs.

5 & 6 Challenge students to take notes and rehearse the conversation as many times as needed to memorize it.

7 Encourage groups to give each other feedback on the language used in the conversations.

SPEAKING
Making Requests

4.10 **1** Listen to the conversation. Who lends Rita some money? Greg.

BILLY Hey, Rita. What's up? You look worried.
RITA I am. [1] Could you do me a favor?
BILLY [2] It depends. What do you need?
RITA [3] Would you mind lending me $20?
BILLY Oh. [4] I'm sorry, I can't. I spent too much money on the weekend.
RITA OK, no problem. What about you, Greg?
GREG Maybe. What's it for?
RITA I want to buy a bag for Maisie's birthday. There's a really cute one that I want to get her, but I don't have enough money.
GREG When's her birthday?
RITA Yesterday! Please, Greg.
GREG [5] Sure, since you asked so nicely. There you go.
RITA Thanks, Greg. You're the best! I owe you one.
GREG Actually, you owe me 20!

4.10 **2** Complete the conversation with the phrases from the *Useful Language* box. Then listen and check.

Useful Language

Could you do me a favor?
I'm sorry, I can't.
It depends.
Sure.
Would you mind …ing … ?

3 Look at the *Everyday English* box. Find and underline the phrases in the conversation.

Watch video 4.4 Everyday English

cute I owe you one.
There you go. What's up?

4 Complete the conversations with the *Everyday English* phrases.

1 A What's up, Kate?
B I need a favor.
2 A Thanks for paying. I owe you one.
B Any time.
3 A Can I borrow your phone for a second?
B Sure. There you go.
4 Look at that little dog! It's so cute.

PLAN

5 Work in groups of three. One person wants to borrow something. One friend can't lend it, but the other can. Take notes.

What the person wants to borrow and why: ______

Why one friend can't lend it: ______

SPEAK

6 Practice a conversation making requests in your group. Remember to use (*not*) *enough* and *too*, *too much*, *too many*, vocabulary from this unit, and phrases from the *Useful Language* and *Everyday English* boxes.

CHECK

7 Work with another group. Listen to their conversation and complete the notes.

What the person wanted to borrow and why: ______

Why one friend couldn't lend it: ______

Extend It!

Students improvise a new conversation using one of the useful objects on SB p26 but replacing the object with a *Beep!* The group listening must guess what the correct word is. For example:
– *Can you do me a favor?*
– *It depends.*
– *Can I borrow your Beep! (mirror)? I want to check my makeup.*
– *Sure.*

Flipped Class

Prepare for the **Writing** lesson. Students make a list of their ideas about one of the two essay topics in Exercise 5, p53.

Lesson Aim: I can write an opinion essay.

Warmer

In pairs or small groups, students share the ideas they brainstormed for homework about one of the two essay topics in Exercise 5.

Teacher Support Hub ppxlii–xliii

Class Challenge

In 2019, Lionel Messi, the Barcelona FC soccer player, was the highest paid athlete in the world. He earned 12.7 / **127** / 172 million dollars.

1 Before reading, ask students if they agree with the statement and allow one minute of thinking time before eliciting ideas.

2 Allow students to briefly discuss each statement in pairs before rereading the essay.

3 After feedback, elicit that a text without these types of phrases would feel strange because it would be more like a collection of separate sentences than a complete text.

4 ★★★ Books closed. Dictate the jumbled words in each sentence, as in the book, but don't say (1) *think*, (2) *my*, and (3) *of*. In pairs, students reorder the words and add the missing ones.

Useful Language Practice

5 Students can use the ideas they discussed in the warmer.

WRITING

An Opinion Essay

1 Read Min-Seo's essay. Does she agree with the statement? Yes, she does.

Professional sports stars earn too much money. Do you agree?

By Lim Min-Seo

1 *Nowadays, sports stars can earn a lot of money. Some basketball players earn more than $40 million every year. In my opinion, this is too much.*

2 *First of all, sports stars work less than other people. They only entertain people for a short time each week. Also, they have long vacations.*

3 *Personally, I think that other jobs are more important. For example, nurses, like my dad, save lives. I also think it's easier to live without sports or sports stars than to live without nurses and firefighters.*

4 *In conclusion, I believe that some sports stars earn too much money, and people with important life saving jobs don't earn enough. We need to find a better and fairer way to pay those people more.*

2 Circle the correct words.

1 According to Min-Seo, sports stars earn *enough* / *too much* money. (too much)

2 Min-Seo thinks sports stars *help* / *entertain* people. (entertain)

3 In Min-Seo's opinion, sports stars have *more* / *less* important jobs than firefighters. (less)

4 It is *easier* / *more difficult* to live without nurses than without sports stars. (more difficult)

5 People with life-saving jobs *don't earn enough* / *earn too much* money. (don't earn enough)

3 Complete the phrases in the *Useful Language* box.

Useful Language

1 In my opinion,
2 First of all,
3 Personally, I think (that)
4 In conclusion,
5 I believe (that)

4 Put the words in the correct order.

1 need / less / think / Personally, /we / homework / I / that — Personally, I think that we need less homework.

2 students / homework / In / too much / have / opinion, / my — In my opinion, students have too much homework.

3 work / all, / enough / in class / do / we / of / First — First of all, we do enough work in class.

PLAN

5 Plan your own opinion essay. Choose one of these topics and take notes for four paragraphs in your notebook.

- Pop stars earn too much money.
- Money can't buy happiness.

1 Introduce the topic and give your opinion.
2 Give a reason for your opinion.
3 Give a second reason.
4 Summarize your opinion.

WRITE

6 Write your opinion essay. Remember to include (*not*) *enough* and *too*, *too much*, *too many*, and phrases from the *Useful Language* box.

CHECK

7 Do you ...

- have four paragraphs?
- give reasons for your opinions?
- summarize your opinion at the end?

Finished? p121 Ex. 4

6 & 7 To encourage self-assessment, have students highlight the target grammar in their writing in different colors. Then they swap essays and discuss ways to improve each other's writing. Allow time for students to make any necessary corrections before collecting the essays.

Finished?

Students turn to p121 and do Exercise 4.

Homework

Workbook p37

Warmer

Write the following questions on the board and allow students to discuss them in groups before eliciting ideas.

1 *How can you encourage more people to go to your local park?*
2 *How clean do you think your local park is?*
3 *What type of charity events can you think of?*

Project Book

For more information and activities, see the Project Book p34.

4.11 Audioscript ppT136–137

1 Allow one minute for students to skim the text and find the answer.

2 Allow students to discuss ideas in pairs before checking the text.

How to Agree as a Group

At this stage, students should be able to work collaboratively in decision-making tasks, inviting others' opinions, expressing their own opinions respectfully, and interrupting and agreeing in appropriate ways.

3 Students check in pairs before feedback. Ask students to write ☺, 😐, or ☹ next to each tip, based on how confident they feel about carrying it out.

4 4.11 After feedback, show or hand students the audioscript if possible. In pairs, students underline each tip from Exercise 3 in the script and write down any useful phrases they want to practice, especially for tips they wrote ☹ next to.

SOCIAL STUDIES PROJECT

A Poster

1 What is the purpose of the poster? Read and check (✓).

a to encourage more people to use a local park ☐
b to ask for more volunteers to clean the park ☑
c to tell people about a charity event ☐

2 Read the poster again. Under which heading can you find this information?

1 the place for the activity *Where?*
2 the type of activity **What?**
3 the people organizing the activity **Who?**
4 the reasons it is a useful thing to do **Why?**
5 the time and place to meet **When?**
6 why volunteers enjoy the activity **What are the benefits?**

How to Agree as a Group

3 Read the tips on how to agree as a group. Put them in the best order.

a **3** Ask other people for their opinions.
b **6** Make a decision as a group. Check that everyone agrees.
c **1** Introduce the decision you need to make.
d **2** Give your own opinion politely.
e **4** Interrupt politely if you want to comment.
f **5** Summarize all the opinions.

4 4.11 **Listen to the students. Write *Y* (Yusuf), *L* (Lara), or *T* (Thiago).**

Who …

1 suggests ideas (two people)? **L** **T**
2 interrupts politely? **T**
3 asks other people for their opinion and summarizes the opinions? **Y**

Could you be a volunteer with us?

Do you have enough time to help us? All ages are welcome.

Don't give us your money – give us your time!

Together we can make our park better!

54 WHAT DO YOU VALUE MOST? | UNIT 4

5 Give students different roles. Suggested roles may be: a chairperson, who introduces the topic, asks for opinions, and summarizes; someone who writes down everyone's ideas; a graphic designer. Monitor closely and check that students are following the tips from Exercise 3, reminding them to do so if necessary. Encourage students to use English as much as possible. Take notes on common language problems and stop the class halfway through the activity to write these on the board and elicit corrections. Students then resume their work.

6 & 7 Alternatively, each group displays their poster in a corner of the room, four groups at a time. Other groups read the posters and ask follow-up questions. Students then swap and new groups display their poster in the corners of the room. At the end, students write on pieces of paper which volunteering activity they would like to sign up for and why. Collect the votes and reveal the winner. Then discuss the reasons given on the pieces of paper.

Students can collaborate digitally through *Collaboration Plus*, where you can assign, track, and assess their work. Students can also share and showcase their work and comment on each other's projects.

For more work on social studies, students can turn to SB p138. See pT124 for teaching notes.

SHAPE IT!

Your Community Needs You!

WHAT?

Help us to make the park a cleaner space for the whole community.

WHERE?

Greenhill Park

WHO?

We have a team of five volunteers, but there's too much work for us. We need more volunteers.

WHEN?

10 a.m. every Saturday. Meet at the park café.

WHY?

It helps your community! There aren't enough people using the park. We want more people to use it.

WHAT ARE THE BENEFITS?

We need only an hour of your time once a week. You can get fitter and have fun. It's one of the best ways to make new friends and make a difference!

PLAN

5 **Work in groups. Plan a poster for a volunteer project. Follow the steps below.**

- Choose one of these ideas for a volunteer project, or use your own idea.

> Teaching older people how to use the latest gadgets.
> Helping at an after-school or local sports club for younger students.
> Working in an animal shelter.

- Think of what you can say to inform and attract volunteers.
- Organize your material under headings.
- Add photos to create an attractive design.

PRESENT

6 **Display your poster on your classroom wall. Remember to include photos and useful information for volunteers, and to follow the tips in *How to Agree as a Group*.**

CHECK

7 **Look at your classmates' posters. Would you like to work on their projects? Discuss in your group and then vote on the best poster.**

Extend It!

You may want to provide more practice of group decision-making. In groups, students create a radio advertisement for their charity activity and record it using their smartphones, if appropriate. Play the recordings for the class and discuss which were the best and why.

Lesson Aim: I can review what I have learned and reflect on my progress.

The aim of this page is for students to review the grammar and vocabulary from the unit. You can either do it in class, as a timed progress test, or assign it for homework.

Vocabulary

1 Encourage students to refer back to the example sentences they wrote in *Learn to Learn* on SB p47 before attempting the task.

2 Before the activity, students work in groups to write a list of all the jobs from SB p50 they can remember. The group with the most jobs wins.

Grammar in Action

3 ★ Before the activity, ask students to identify the adjectives as short, long, or irregular, and review the formation of comparative and superlative adjectives with them.

4 & 5 Ask students to refer back to SB p51 to review how to use the target grammar before attempting the task.

Unit Review Quiz

Extend It!

Students write a brief text, similar to but shorter than the one in Exercise 5, about themselves or their best friend.

4 REVIEW

VOCABULARY

1 Complete the conversations with the pairs of verbs in the box.

borrow / owe | pay / lend | spend / save | sell / earn

1 A Can you **lend** me $5 for coffee?
B Don't worry. I can **pay** for yours.
2 A Those people **sell** hats at the market.
B Yes, but they don't **earn** much money.
3 A Should I **save** my money for the future?
B No! Why don't you **spend** it now? Let's go shopping.
4 A Could I **borrow** some money for the bus?
B Sure, but you now **owe** me $5!

2 Read the descriptions and write the correct job.

1 I give my free time to help people. I don't earn any money, but I love my job. **volunteer**
2 I have a difficult job in a hospital. I'm not a normal doctor or a nurse. **surgeon**
3 I keep our community safe. I can arrest people who are breaking the law. **police officer**
4 I treat very sick people at home and then take them to the hospital. **paramedic**

GRAMMAR IN ACTION

3 Complete the quiz with the comparative or superlative form of the adjectives. Then decide if the sentences are *T* (true) or *F* (false).

1 Basketball players are usually **taller** than soccer players. (tall) **T**
2 **The driest** place on Earth is in Antarctica. (dry) **T**
3 Chris Hemsworth is **older** than Chris Evans. (old) **F**
4 The Istanbul Cevahir shopping mall is **the biggest** in the world. (big) **F**
5 A hippo is **more dangerous** than a lion. (dangerous) **T**
6 New York is **the most expensive** city to live in. (expensive) **F**

4 Put the words in the correct order.

1 lifeguard / you're / too / be / young / to / a
You're too young to be a lifeguard.
2 a / money / I / soda / to / don't / have / enough / buy
I don't have enough money to buy a soda.
3 room / there / too / people / were / the / many / in
There were too many people in the room.
4 much / week / I / last / spent / too / money
I spent too much money last week.

5 Complete the blog with *too* + adjective, *too much* / *too many* or *enough*, or a comparative or superlative adjective.

All About Denise

Appearance She's [1] **taller** (tall) than me, and she has [2] **longer** (long) hair. So, I'm [3] **shorter** (short) than her in two ways!

Personality She always makes me laugh. She's the [4] **funniest** (funny) and [5] **happiest** (happy) person I know!

Sports Denise's favorite sport is basketball. Unfortunately, she can't get into the school team because there are [6] **too many** good players, so she only plays for fun.

Jobs She wants to be a firefighter. She's [7] **braver** (brave) than me – I think that job is [8] **too dangerous** (dangerous). There are a lot more things to say about Denise, but I don't have [9] **enough** time now. I have [10] **too much** homework.

Self-Assessment

I can talk about money.	☹	😐	☺
I can talk about caring jobs.	☹	😐	☺
I can use *could* and *couldn't*.	☹	😐	☺
I can use comparative and superlative adjectives.	☹	😐	☺
I can use *too*, *too much*, *too many*, and (*not*) *enough*.	☹	😐	☺

Review the Unit Theme

Remind students of the unit title: *What do you value most?* Put students into pairs. Have them discuss the following questions: *Do you save money? Why / Why not? What do you value that doesn't cost money? Is it possible to have too much money?* Share answers as a class.

Teacher Support Hub pxlvi

Self-Assessment

Encourage students to be honest when circling the appropriate emoji, thinking back to how hard they found each exercise on the page. Depending on what they need to focus on, encourage them to ask for extra homework from the Workbook.

Homework

Workbook pp38–39

At this stage, students should be starting to take more responsibility for their learning, organizing their work and out-of-class activities, and thinking about their learning preferences.

Warmer

If students have a planner where they write down their homework assignments, ask them to share this in small groups and discuss whose looks the most organized.

1 Put students into groups, and ask them to guess who among them is the biggest "homework superstar." Students then do the quiz and share their results. Elicit a few results from the class.

2 Allow students plenty of time to deal with this individually and then compare their answers with a partner's. After feedback, ask students to discuss Esma's homework planner in pairs and say what they like and don't like about it. Elicit ideas from the whole class.

SHAPE IT!

3 In pairs, students show each other their planners and explain their choices before making any necessary changes.

Extend It!

Challenge students to use this technique for one month. Quickly check their homework planners once a week. Praise students who keep it going for an entire month.

LEARN TO LEARN

LEARN TO ... ORGANIZE YOUR HOMEWORK

When you organize your homework, you study and use your time better.

1 Do the quiz. Find out your score. Do you agree with what it says about you? Discuss the results with a partner.

Homework Superstar?

Knowing What to Do

When your teacher gives you homework, do you ...

a write it in your notebook or homework planner?
b write it on your hand?
c listen but then forget?

Organizing Your Time

When do you do your homework?

a After school or on the weekend.
b Sometimes after school, sometimes before.
c Always while I'm having breakfast!

Deciding What Comes First

You have too much homework and not enough time. Do you ...

a do the most important things first?
b do the easiest things first?
c look at your books but never start?

Concentrating

While you're doing your homework, do you ...

a put your phone on silent?
b try not to look at your phone?
c spend a lot of time checking your phone?

Results

a = 2 points b = 1 point c = 0 points

6–8: You're a superstar! You organize your homework well.
3–5: Not bad! You try to organize your homework, but our advice can help.
0–2: Oh, no! You really need our advice!

2 Complete Esma's homework planner with the words in the box.

difficult | first | For when? | Homework | hours | Notes | Other things | Subject

Date	[1] Subject	[2] Homework	[3] For when?	[4] Notes
Mon Feb. 11	English	Page 27, Exercise 4	Mon Feb. 18	☺ Nice and easy!
Tues Feb. 12	Science	Label the parts of plants.	Thurs Feb. 14	It's [5] difficult – ask Jo for help.
Wed Feb. 13	History Math	Page 36 Study for the test.	Thurs Feb. 14 Fri Feb. 15	Do math [6] first – there's a LOT to study!
Thurs Feb. 14	English	Write story.	Tues Feb. 19	I need about two [7] hours.
Fri Feb. 15		No homework!		

[8] Other things: Remember Zoe's party on Saturday afternoon! ☺

SHAPE IT!

3 Copy Esma's design for a homework planner in your notebook , using the same headings. Then complete the planner with your homework for next week.

BACK TO SCHOOL!!

UNIT 4 | LEARN TO LEARN 57

Teacher Support Hub ppxxxiv–xxxv

▶ Start It!

Unit Quiz

1 In pairs, Student A opens the book, looks at the photo, and describes it to their partner. They look at the photo together and discuss if they would like to live there and why.

2 Describe your home to students. Say if it's an apartment, how big it is, how many rooms it has, if it's new or old, and if you like it and why. Invite questions. Then ask students to describe their own home in pairs.

3 & 4 Allow students to check in pairs after watching **video 5.1** the first time, and then play it again. Elicit the answers. Then show the video a third time without volume, and elicit vocabulary to describe the houses that it shows.

Video Comprehension Questions

5 What is your dream house?

LEARNING OUTCOMES

I can ...

- understand texts about different homes and doing household chores
- describe a photograph
- write a description of a house
- understand how to use (*not*) *as* + adjective + *as*, (*not*) + adjective + *enough*, and *have to* / *don't have to*
- talk about furniture and household chores
- make spidergrams to record vocabulary, use techniques to answer multiple-choice questions, use word families, and a memory journey

Start It!

1 Look at the photo. Would you like to live in this house?
2 Before you watch, where do you live?
3 Why did people build homes in mountains? Watch and check.
4 What other unusual homes are there?

They felt safe. The caves stayed dry in the winter and cold in the summer

Watch video 5.1 | Grammar in Action 5.2 p61 | Grammar in Action 5.3 p63 | Everyday English 5.4 p64 | Globetrotters 5.5 p66

58 WHAT IS YOUR DREAM HOUSE? | UNIT 5

Class Challenge

The most isolated home in the world is on an island in the UK / **Iceland** / Japan.

Flipped Class

Prepare for **Explore It!** (p59). Students research an interesting fact about furniture.

Unit Aims

Skills

I can ...

- understand a text about different homes p60
- describe a photograph p64
- write a description of a house p65
- understand a text about living in igloos pp66–67

Language

I can ...

- talk about furniture p59
- understand how to use (*not*) *as* + adjective + *as* and (*not*) + adjective + *enough* p61
- talk about household chores p62
- understand how to use *have to* and *don't have to* p63

Learn to Learn

I can ...

- use spidergrams p59
- answer multiple-choice questions p62
- understand word families p67
- use a memory journey p69

Extra Resources

- Finished? Student's Book p122
- Vocabulary Bank, Student's Book p132
- Workbook pp40–47
- Grammar Reference and Practice, Workbook pp96–97
- Teacher Support Hub, Teacher's Book ppxxxiv–xlvii

Digital Resource Pack

(on Cambridge One)

- *Teacher's Resource Bank* for word lists, differentiated worksheets, *Culture Projects*, and many other extra resources
- *Practice Extra, Presentation Plus, Test Generator,* and *Digital Collaboration Space*

Lesson Aim: I can talk about furniture.

Warmer
In teams, students have two minutes to write down as many furniture words as possible. The team with the most words wins.

5.01–5.02 Audioscripts pT137

1 5.01 Alternatively, students cover the pictures and work in teams. One student chooses a word and draws a picture. The first student on the team to guess what the picture is wins a point and is the next person to draw.

Target Vocabulary
armchair ˈɑrmˌtʃeər
bookcase ˈbʊk·keɪs
carpet ˈkɑr·pɪt
ceiling ˈsi·lɪŋ
chest of drawers ˌtʃest əv ˈdrɔrz
cupboard ˈkʌ·bərd
desk desk
floor flɔr
fridge frɪdʒ
picture ˈpɪk·tʃər
shelves ʃelvz
sink sɪŋk
wardrobe ˈwɔr·droʊb

Vocabulary Game
Extra Vocabulary Practice

2 & 3 5.02 ★★★ After feedback, put students into pairs to write their own short description of a room. Then they read it aloud for another pair to guess the room.

Vocabulary Bank SB p132

Learn to Learn
Spidergrams are visual aids that may help some students remember vocabulary related to one particular topic more efficiently. Students should try out different ways of recording vocabulary to find the ones best suited to them.

VOCABULARY
Furniture

5.01 **1** Match the words in the box with 1–13 in the pictures. Listen, check, and repeat.

armchair	12	floor	5
bookcase	11	fridge	3
carpet	13	picture	10
ceiling	1	shelves	6
chest of drawers	9	sink	4
cupboard	2	wardrobe	7
desk	8		

5.02 **2** Listen and match the speakers (1–4) with the rooms in the box. There is one extra room.

bathroom	2	kitchen	4	study	3
bedroom	1	living room			

5.02 **3** Listen again and (circle) the words in Exercise 1 that you hear.

LEARN TO LEARN
Using Spidergrams
Recording words in different ways will help you remember them. One way is to create spidergrams.

4 Complete the spidergram using words from Exercises 1 and 2 and your own ideas.

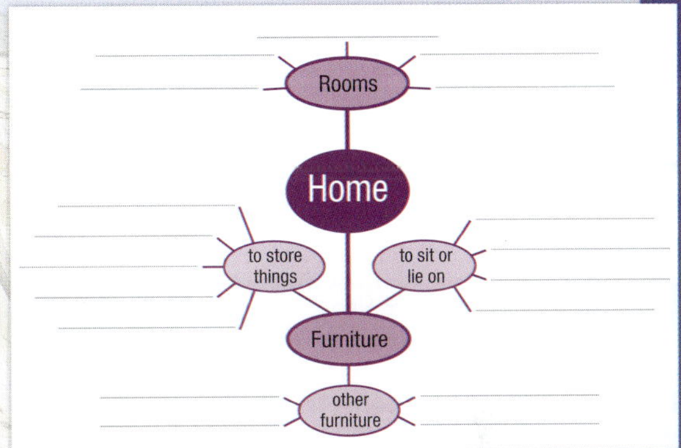

Use It!

5 Describe the furniture in a room in your home. Your partner listens and draws the room.

My bedroom has a wardrobe, a chest of drawers, and two pictures on the wall ...

Explore It!

Guess the correct answer.
The oldest bookcases in the world are ... years old.
a 200 (b) 400 c 600
Find another interesting fact about furniture. Then write a question for your partner.

4 Copy the spidergram onto the board and ask volunteers to write the vocabulary on the board when conducting feedback.

5 ★ Before the activity, you may want to elicit or review prepositions (e.g., *in front of, behind, next to, to the left/right of, opposite*).

Explore It!
Monitor closely and choose the most interesting questions you hear. Get students who wrote them to ask them to the whole class to guess the answer.

Flipped Class
Prepare for the next lesson. Students research one unusual house on the Internet and prepare to describe it to a partner.

Homework
Workbook p40

Lesson Aim: I can understand a text about different homes.

Warmer

In groups, students describe the unusual houses they have researched for homework, share images of them, and discuss which is the most unusual and why.

Teacher Support Hub ppxxxvi–xxxvii

1 Allow students one minute of thinking time and allow dictionaries and translation software before discussing ideas in pairs. Then elicit relevant vocabulary, such as *round*, *small*, *thin/narrow*, etc.

2 5.03 Allow two minutes to encourage faster reading.

3 After feedback, students write one more sentence with incorrect information and give it to their partner to correct.

4 ★★★ Ask students to cover the options in 1–5 and decide what the underlined pronouns refer to in the text. They then check the options and choose the correct ones.

5 Disallow dictionaries and translation software and encourage students to guess the meaning of words 1–6 only by looking at the context in the text.

Extra Vocabulary Practice

6 Encourage students to justify their answers, saying not only why they like one of the houses, but also what they dislike about the others. For question 3, students can talk about the unusual homes they researched for homework.

READING

A Magazine Article

1 Look at the pictures. Discuss the questions.

1 What's unusual about these homes?
2 Who do you think lives in them?

5.03 **2 Read the article. Match the pictures with the houses.**

Amazing Homes

Everyone's home is special, but some homes are really amazing…

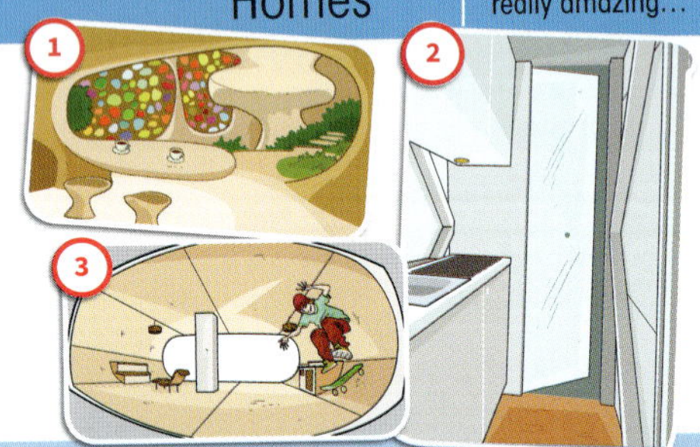

2 Keret House, Poland

A Polish architect designed this house for an Israeli author. [1]**It**'s in a space between two apartment buildings in Warsaw. To enter the house, you climb through a trap door in the floor of the living room. The living room is wide enough for a small sofa, but the back of the house is only as wide as a large armchair! There's a tiny bathroom upstairs and a tiny kitchen with a sink and a fridge … but you need to stand in another room to open [2]**it**!

1 Nautilus House, Mexico

Nautilus House isn't as tiny as Keret House, but it's also very strange. Its owners – a Mexican couple and their two children – thought ordinary houses weren't close enough to nature. [3]**They** wanted their home to feel like a beautiful, colorful shell. Everything in Nautilus House is curved: the floors, the ceilings, and, of course, all the furniture.

3 The PAS House, U.S.A.

Lots of kids love skateboarding, but not many kids are as crazy about [4]**it** as Pierre André Senizergues. Senizergues learned to skateboard at school in France and later became the world champion. He designed the PAS House as a dream home for skateboarders. You can skate in every room. You can even skate on the furniture [5]**there**, and your mom won't yell at you!

60 WHAT IS YOUR DREAM HOUSE? | UNIT 5

3 Read the article again and correct the sentences.

1 The entrance to Keret House is through the kitchen.
The entrance to Keret House is through the living room.
2 Five people live in Nautilus House.
Four people live in Nautilus House.
3 The rooms in Nautilus House have straight walls.
The rooms in Nautilus House have curved walls.
4 The PAS House is in France.
The PAS House is in the U.S.A.
5 An architect had the idea for the PAS House.
A skateboarder had the idea for the PAS House.

4 Look at the words highlighted in the text. What do they refer to? Circle the correct answers.

1 a Polish architect / Keret House
2 the fridge / the sink
3 ordinary houses / the owners
4 the PAS house / skateboarding
5 the PAS House / France

5 Match the words with the definitions.

1 architect	a a home for a sea animal
2 author	b a door in the floor
3 apartment building	c a writer
4 trap door	d not straight
5 shell	e a building with homes in it
6 curved	f a person who designs buildings

Voice It!

6 Discuss the questions.

1 Which house do you like most?
2 Why do you like it?
3 Do you know any other unusual houses? Describe them.

Finished? p122 Ex. 1

Class Challenge

The narrowest house in the world is in Poland and it is 52 / **152** / 552 cm wide.

Finished?

Students turn to p122 and do Exercise 1.

Flipped Class

Ask students to watch **video 5.2** and do **Video Worksheet 5.2** in the *Teacher's Resource Bank* in preparation for the next lesson.

Homework

Workbook p41

Lesson Aim: I can understand how to use (*not*) *as* … *as* and (*not*) … *enough*.

Warmer

▶ Play **video 5.2**, if it was not assigned for homework, and ask students to discuss which bedroom they prefer and why. Elicit that bedroom 1 isn't big enough, and the other bedrooms aren't as nice as bedroom 3.

5.04 Audioscript pT137

1 After feedback, point out that we normally pronounce *as* with a schwa /əz/ in full sentences.

2 ★ Point out that students have to read and understand the information on SB p60 in order to get the information they need.

Get It Right!

Remind students that nouns can come after *enough* (e.g., *I don't have enough time*), but not adjectives.

Extra Grammar Practice

3 & 4 After feedback, students make extra sentences with the target language about their own homes (e.g., *My house isn't large enough for a pool*.).

5 5.04 ★ Students check their answers in pairs and discuss any differences before whole-class feedback.

6 & 7 You may want to turn this into a group game, with students taking turns reading their sentences aloud and guessing the correct ones, winning points as they go.

GRAMMAR IN ACTION
(*Not*) *As* … *As*, (*Not*) … *Enough*

Watch video 5.2
What's wrong with bedroom 1? Why does the vlogger prefer bedroom 3?

	(*Not*) *As* + Adjective + *As*	(*Not*) Adjective + *Enough*
+	The back of the house is only [1] as wide as (wide) a large armchair.	The living room is [3] wide enough (wide) for a small sofa.
–	Nautilus House isn't / is not [2] as tiny as (tiny) Keret house.	They thought ordinary houses weren't / were not [4] close enough (close) to nature.

1 **Complete the examples in the chart above with *as* … *as* or *enough* and the words in parentheses. Use the article on page 60 to help you.**

2 **Circle the correct words. Check your answers in the article on page 60.**

1 Keret House *is* / *isn't* as wide as other houses in Warsaw.
2 *It's* / *It's not* large enough for a kitchen.
3 The owners of Nautilus House think that straight walls *are* / *are not* as interesting as curved walls.

Get It Right!

We never put adjectives after **enough**.
I'm not tall enough. **NOT** *~~I'm not enough tall.~~*

3 **Complete the sentences with *as* … *as* or *enough* and the adjective in parentheses.**

1 My bedroom isn't as big as my sister's. (big)
2 I'm not tall enough to reach the top shelf. (tall)
3 Is this sofa wide enough for three people? (wide)
4 That phone is as expensive as a laptop! (expensive)

4 **Complete the second sentence so that it has the same meaning as the first. Use (*not*) *as* … *as* or *enough* and the adjective in parentheses.**

1 We can't put a sofa in this small room.
This room isn't large enough for a sofa. (large)
2 My room is neater than my sister's room.
My sister's room isn't / is not as neat as mine. (neat)
3 A microwave is quicker than a stove.
A stove isn't / is not as quick as a microwave. (quick)
4 Enes is 18 now, so he can drive a car.
Enes is old enough to drive a car. (old)

5 5.04 **Complete the text using *as* … *as* or *enough* and the adjectives in parentheses. Then listen and check.**

Kids' toys aren't cheap these days, but not many toys are [1] as expensive as (expensive) the Astolat Dollhouse Castle. It's [2] as tall as (tall) a small Christmas tree and [3] as heavy as (heavy) a horse.

The castle was the idea of an American artist, Elaine Diehl, and it took 13 years to build. It isn't really a toy. It's a work of art, and it's [4] good enough (good) to be in a museum.

The furniture is [5] small enough (small) to fit in your hand, and it's [6] as beautiful as (beautiful) the furniture in a real palace. The tiny sofas and beds are [7] as soft as (soft) the real things. The books on the shelves aren't [8] large enough (large) to read, but they have real pages. One thing that isn't small is the price – over $8 million! Are you [9] rich enough (rich) to buy it?

Use It!

6 **In your notebook, write one true sentence and one false sentence about places in the world with (*not*) *as* … *as* or (*not*) … *enough*.**

The Amazon River is as long as the Nile River.

7 **Say your sentences. Can your partner guess which sentence is true?**

Finished? p122 Ex. 2

Grammar Game

In groups, students have three minutes to write as many true sentences about themselves as possible (e.g., *Sarah isn't as tall as James*.). The group with the most correct sentences wins.

Finished?

Students turn to p122 and do Exercise 2.

Homework

Workbook p42

Warmer

Elicit the meaning of *chore* /tʃɔr/ (a job or piece of work that is often boring or unpleasant but needs to be done regularly). Ask students to say a few chores that they do at home.

Teacher Support Hub ppxxxviii–xxxix

5.05–5.07 Audioscripts ppT137–138

1 5.05 After feedback, drill the pronunciation of the phrases.

Target Vocabulary

do the dishes du ðə ˈdɪʃ·əz
do the ironing du ðə ˈaɪ·ər·nɪŋ
do the laundry du ðə ˈlɔn·dri
dust (the furniture) dʌst (ðə ˈfɜr·nɪ·tʃər)
load/empty the dishwasher loʊd/ˈemp·ti ðə ˈdɪʃˌwɑʃ·ər
make the bed meɪk ðə bed
mop the floor mɑp ðə flɔr
sweep the floor swip ðə flɔr
vacuum (the carpet) ˈvæk·jum (ðə ˈkɑr·pɪt)

Extra Vocabulary Practice

2 5.06 ★★★ Challenge students to cover the box in Exercise 1 to complete the exercise, and then play the audio to check answers.

3 During feedback, find out what percentage of the class does chores a lot, a little, or not at all, and why.

4 Discuss any interesting differences between the percentages you got from the last activity and the statistics.

VOCABULARY AND LISTENING

Household Chores

5.05 1 Match the phrases in the box with the pictures. Listen, check, and repeat.

do the dishes	7	make the bed	1
do the ironing	3	mop the floor	5
do the laundry	2	sweep the floor	4
dust (the furniture)	9	vacuum (the carpet)	6
load/empty the dishwasher	8		

5.06 2 Complete the note with verbs from Exercise 1. Then listen and check.

Hi kids. Can you please help with some things around the house while I'm out?

Ollie: Please [1] mop the floor and [2] load the dishwasher with the plates and cups from breakfast. Can you also [3] dust the furniture in the living room, please, and [4] vacuum the carpet?

Mia: [5] Make your bed and [6] sweep the floor in your bedroom. Then can you please [7] do the ironing for me?

Thanks, kids. I'll see you this evening. Love, Dad

Use It!

3 How often do you do the chores in Exercise 1? Compare with your partner.

I do the dishes every day!

Street Interviews

4 Look at the results of a survey in the UK. Does the information surprise you?

Do teenagers help with household chores?

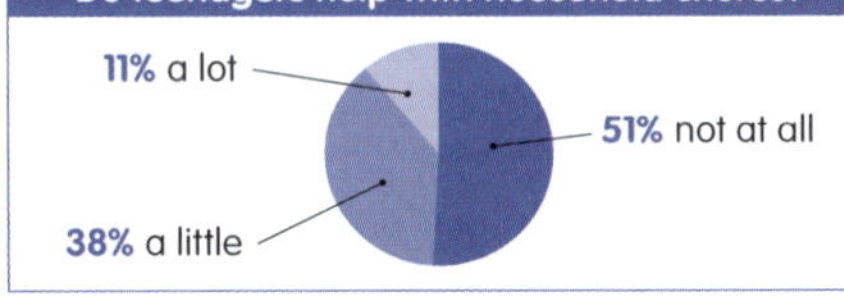

LEARN TO LEARN

Answering Multiple-Choice Questions

Before you listen, read the questions and options carefully, and try to guess the answers.

5 Read the questions in Exercise 6. Discuss with a partner which answers are probably wrong.

5.07 6 EXAM You will hear some people talk about doing chores. Listen and circle the correct answers.

1 What does Cindy do in the kitchen?
A She cooks dinner.
B She loads the dishwasher.
(C) She does the dishes.

2 When do Kim and her sister do household chores?
A every morning
(B) on the weekend
C during school vacations

3 What doesn't Kim like?
A cleaning the bathroom
(B) vacuuming the living room
C practicing the piano

4 When Adam does the ironing, what else does he like doing?
(A) listening to music
B moving around
C doing his homework

Learn to Learn

Trying to predict answers prepares students for both the vocabulary and the ideas that they might hear and can help make listening less stressful.

5 ★ Point out that all the people in the story are teenagers. Encourage students to justify their guesses during feedback.

6 5.07 EXAM Play the audio once and allow students to check ideas in pairs before listening again.

Vocabulary Bank SB p132

Flipped Class

Ask students to watch **video 5.3** and do **Video Worksheet 5.3** in the *Teacher's Resource Bank* in preparation for the next lesson.

Homework

Workbook p43

Lesson Aim: I can use *have to* and *don't have to.*

Warmer

▶ Play **video 5.3**, if it was not assigned for homework, and elicit the answers to the two questions. (Syd has to load the dishwasher, and Harumi has to clean her school.)

5.10 Audioscript pT138

1 Stress that *have to* means "must," but *don't have to* doesn't mean "must not." It means "don't need to."

Pronunciation

5.08–5.09 Ask students to turn to SB pp141–142 for pronunciation practice of *have:* /f/ and /v/.

2 After feedback, read 1–5 to the students and check their understanding, asking *Is it necessary?* (1, 2, 5 – yes; 3, 4 – no).

Extra Grammar and Vocabulary Practice

3 ★★★ Challenge stronger students to cover the options, fill in the blanks, and then check against the options.

4 After feedback, elicit extra example sentences from students, using the vocabulary on SB p62.

5 5.10 After feedback, put students into pairs to discuss whether they would like to live on a farm or not.

6 ★ Support weaker students by asking them to write down their questions before speaking.

GRAMMAR IN ACTION

Have To

Watch video 5.3
How does Syd from Brazil help in the restaurant? What does Harumi have to clean?

	I/You/We/They	*He/She/It*
+	I [1] have to **clean** the kitchen.	He **has to make** his bed.
–	I **don't have to load** the dishwasher.	He [3] doesn't have to **do** much.
?	[2] Do you have to **do** the dishes? Yes, I **do**. / No, I **don't**.	**Does** Jake **have to help**? Yes, he **does**. / No, he [4] doesn't.

Pronunciation p141–142

Complete the examples in the chart above with the correct form of *have to / don't have to*.

2 **Complete the sentences with the correct form of *have to*.**

1. Cindy has to (+) clean the kitchen.
2. Kim and Maisie have to (+) do a lot of homework.
3. They don't have to (–) do housework on school days.
4. Jake doesn't have to (–) help a lot.
5. Adam has to (+) do the ironing.

3 **Circle the correct answer.**

1. I ... do the gardening this weekend because my parents are on vacation.
   a has to b doesn't have to (c) have to
2. ... to do a lot of homework on weekends?
   a Does you have b Do you has (c) Do you have
3. We ... go to school on Monday because it's a national holiday.
   (a) don't have to b have to c doesn't have to
4. Dad ... do the cooking in the evenings because Mom works then.
   (a) has to b doesn't have to c have to

4 **Complete the sentences with the correct form of *have to* and a verb from the box.**

do help go work

1. The children don't have to go to school in summer.
2. Sam doesn't have to help with chores because he's only four.
3. I have to do the ironing on Saturdays, and it's so boring.
4. Does your mom have to work on weekends?

5 5.10 **Complete the text with the correct form of *have to* and the verbs in parentheses. Then listen and check.**

[1] Do you have to help (help) with the housework? [2] Do you have to make (make) your bed or clean the kitchen? Martha Pinter and her brother, Ben, [3] have to do (do) more than most young people their age. They live on a farm in Queensland, Australia, and the whole family [4] has to share (share) the work. Martha [5] has to get up (get up) early to milk the cows. In spring, she also [6] has to take (take) care of the new lambs – that's her favorite job. Ben [7] has to collect (collect) the hens' eggs before breakfast. But Martha and Ben [8] don't have to catch (not catch) the bus to school every day. There isn't a school near their farm, so they [9] have to have (have) all their lessons at home.

Use It!

6 **Think of questions to ask your partner using *have to*. Ask and answer your questions.**

Does your dad have to do the ironing on the weekend?

No, he doesn't. I have to do it!

Finished? p122 Ex. 3

Grammar Game

Say one of the actions below and get students to say if they *have to, don't have to,* or *must not* do this action at school. The first student to say a correct sentence wins a point.

- wear a tie
- clean the classroom
- wear shorts
- do homework
- arrive late
- raise their hand to speak
- bring a laptop

Finished?

Students turn to p122 and do Exercise 3.

Flipped Class

If appropriate, ask students to take a photo of their room at home. They will use it in the next lesson.

Homework

Workbook p44

Lesson Aim: I can discuss a photo.

Warmer

Put students into pairs. Ask them to describe their rooms at home and then to ask each other questions about them and discuss what they like and don't like about the rooms.

Teacher Support Hub ppxl–xli

1 5.11 ★★★ Challenge students to listen and answer the question with their books closed.

2 5.11 Use one of the pictures on SB p59 to check students' understanding of the phrases (e.g., *What's that at the bottom on the left? A trash can.*).

Useful Language Practice

3 Play **video 5.4** and drill the pronunciation of the target phrases, focusing students' attention on the stressed words.

4 After feedback, if appropriate, ask students to think of equivalent phrases in their language and test each other using the translations.

5 Encourage students to use photos of their own room, if appropriate. Alternatively, students could draw a simple sketch of their room to talk about.

6 Allow students to perform the conversation twice. The first time, they should focus only on content. The second time, they focus on language and (if possible) record their conversation to improve self-correcting skills.

SPEAKING
Discussing a Photo

5.11 **1 Listen to the conversation. Who likes the room more, Oscar or Nina?** Oscar

OSCAR Hey, Nina. Look at this photo – it's Liam's bedroom in his new house.
NINA Oh! It looks big enough for two people. Does he have to share it?
OSCAR No, it's all his. Actually, it isn't as big as it looks. There's a large mirror in the [1]background, so it looks bigger.
NINA Oh, yes, I see. [2] What's that thing on the wall?
OSCAR It's a clock. What do you think of the color of the walls?
NINA Hmm. I'm not convinced.
OSCAR Really? I think it looks awesome! I don't think much of those curtains, though.
NINA: Me neither. And what's that [3] at the bottom? Is it a carpet?
OSCAR Yes, I think so. I like it. And I love those pictures [4] on the left.
NINA Me too. They look great.

5.11 **2 Complete the conversation with phrases from the *Useful Language* box. Then listen and check.**

Useful Language

at the bottom/top	in the background
on the left/right	What's that ... ?

3 Look at the *Everyday English* box. Find and underline the phrases in the conversation.

Watch video 5.4
Everyday English

I'm not convinced.
It looks awesome!
Me neither.
Me too.

4 Match the phrases in the *Everyday English* box with the phrases that mean the same.

1 I feel the same way (after a positive statement). Me too.
2 I feel the same way (after a negative statement). Me neither.
3 I don't think I like it. I'm not convinced.
4 It looks great. It looks awesome!

PLAN

5 Write about a room. Take notes about the photo below or your own photo.

Who the room belongs to: ______
What is in it: ______

SPEAK

6 Practice discussing your room with your partner. Remember to use adjectives with (*not*) *as ... as* and *enough*, *have to* / *don't have to*, vocabulary from this unit, and phrases from the *Useful Language* and *Everyday English* boxes.

CHECK

7 Work with another pair. Listen to their conversation and complete the notes.

Who the room belongs to: ______
What is in it: ______

7 Students look at the other pair's photo for a minute before listening to the recorded conversation (or the pair performing it). Then pairs give each other feedback.

Flipped Class

In preparation for the **Writing** lesson, ask students to think about their dream house and take notes.

Lesson Aim: I can write a description of a house.

Warmer

In pairs, students share their ideas about their dream house, which they thought about for homework.

Teacher Support Hub ppxlii–xliii

1 Support students by eliciting guesses about the size, location, and style of the house, and elicit ideas about what might be inside that makes the house special.

2 Allow one minute to read the text to encourage faster reading.

3 You may want students to do this in pairs to improve collaboration skills. Students then compare drawings with other pairs. Choose the most accurate one to show the class during feedback.

4 Elicit more examples of the use of this language by eliciting sentences to describe the classroom from different students.

Useful Language Practice

5 Allow students to share their plans with a partner to generate more ideas.

6 & 7 After writing, students highlight (*not*) *as ... as*, (*not*) *enough*, and *have to* / *don't have to*, and expressions from the *Useful Language* box in a bright color. This will help them with their self-assessment.

WRITING

A Description of a House

1 **Look at the information about the competition and the photo. What can you guess about Olivia's dream house? Discuss with a partner.**

2 **Read Olivia's description of her dream house. Match the topics a–c with paragraphs 1–3.**

a What does the house have?
b Where is the house?
c What is the best thing about the house?

Describe Your Dream House and Win a Digital Camera!

1 b I'd like to tell you about my dream house. It's near the beach on a sunny island. It has to be near the ocean because I love swimming.

2 a The house has big windows and a fantastic view of the ocean. There's a lovely yard, too. It's large enough for people to play outdoor games, and it also has a swimming pool. As well as a pool, there's a skatepark. Inside the house, there's a huge fish tank. It's full of beautiful tropical fish.

3 c But the really special thing about my house is the technology. There are robots in every room. I think they're as intelligent as humans. They cook the meals and do the dishes. They make my bed, and they vacuum the living room as well. I don't have to do any chores.

Olivia Reed (13), Newcastle

3 **Read the description again. Draw Olivia's house and yard in your notebook.**

4 **Find and underline the *Useful Language* phrases in the description. Answer the questions.**

1 Which go at the end of a sentence? as well, too
2 Which goes before a noun? as well as
3 Which often goes before a verb? also

Useful Language

also as well as well as too

PLAN

5 **Plan a description of your own dream house. Take notes for three paragraphs.**

1 Where your house is: ______
2 What rooms, furniture, and other things it has: ______
3 What the best thing in the house is: ______

WRITE

6 **Write your description. Remember to include adjectives with (*not*) *as ... as*, *enough*, *have to* / *don't have to*, and phrases from the *Useful Language* box.**

CHECK

7 **Do you ...**

- have three paragraphs?
- describe what the house has?
- describe one special thing in the house?

Finished? p122 Ex. 4

Extend It!

Students display their descriptions around the room for other students to read. Then they vote for the most interesting dream home.

Finished?

Students turn to p122 and do Exercise 4.

Flipped Class

Ask students to watch **video 5.5** and do **Video Worksheet 5.5** in the *Teacher's Resource Bank* in preparation for the next lesson.

Prepare for **Explore It!** (p67). Students research an interesting fact about Inuits.

Homework

Workbook p45

Lesson Aim: I can understand a text about living in igloos.

Background Information

Students may have limited knowledge of the indigenous peoples living in remote communities of Alaska, Canada, Greenland, and parts of Russia. They may be familiar with the term "Eskimo" but surprised to learn that this is a general term that refers to many different groups living in these parts of the world. Many of the indigenous peoples do not like the term, so students should avoid using it.

Warmer

In pairs, students discuss how people can live in very cold places. Ask them to make a list of ideas (e.g., *wear warm clothes, have a fireplace, eat a lot of fat*).

▶ Play **video 5.5**, if it was not assigned for homework, and ask students to answer the questions in groups. Elicit that "ger" means "house" in Mongolian.

Video Comprehension Questions

1 Elicit relevant vocabulary, such as *snow, ice, igloo, tent, frozen, dome.*

2 5.12 ★★★ Ask students, in pairs, to write down an additional question they have about igloos and read the text to see if it mentions an answer.

3 Encourage students to underline language in the text that helped them match the headings with the paragraphs. Elicit this during feedback.

Reading Comprehension Questions

AROUND THE WORLD

Globetrotters

Watch video 5.5 Living in a *Ger*

- What does "ger" mean in Mongolian?
- Would you like to live in a *ger*?

READING

An Encyclopedia Entry

1 Look at the photos of homes on page 67. Where are these homes? What do you know about them?
The homes are in the Arctic Circle.

5.12 2 Read the entry. Check your answers.

3 Read the entry again. Match headings a–e with paragraphs 1–5.

a Why Use Igloos?
b Keeping Warm
c Who Are the Inuit?
d Life Inside an Igloo
e How to Build an Igloo

Voice It!

4 Discuss the questions.

1 Nomadic people have temporary houses, so "home" isn't a permanent building in a place. How else can people define "home"?
2 Besides your house, how do you define "home"?
3 How can you appreciate and celebrate your home?

LIFE IN AN INUIT IGLOO

1 c The Inuit are the native people of the Arctic Circle. Today, they usually live in modern houses in small villages. Until recently, however, they still used their famous houses made of snow – igloos.

2 a The Arctic isn't warm enough to farm, so the Inuit had a nomadic life. This means they traveled during the year to find food. Every winter and summer, the Inuit traveled thousands of kilometers across the frozen Arctic ocean. All nomads have to make temporary homes while they travel, and in summer, the Inuit lived in tents made from animal skins, called *tupiqs*. Igloos were their traditional winter homes.

3 e Snow is a perfect material for building. It's as light as wood and easy to cut. The snow has to be dry and hard enough to make good blocks because wet snow doesn't have the strength an igloo needs. The Inuit make a dome shape by putting the snow blocks in a spiral. This is quick to build and creates a very strong structure.

4 b The heat inside an igloo comes from people's bodies only, but this is warm enough to keep the igloo comfortable. This is because snow is a good insulator. In other words, it keeps the cold out and the warmth in. The entrance is a tunnel that goes under the walls. The heavy, cold air always stays in the tunnel and the light, warm air stays in the igloo.

5 d Igloos don't have windows, but there are small holes in the walls. These let in clean air and let out dangerous smoke from the small oil lamps. Traditionally, the Inuit didn't have any furniture, but a platform of snow just below the ceiling provided a simple sofa and bed in the warmest part of the igloo. Inuit families spent all winter in small igloos with no furniture, no bathroom … and no Internet. Just imagine that!

4 Write *home* on the board. In groups of four, students brainstorm what *home* means (e.g., *a house or apartment, a family, a neighborhood, a community, a country, a culture*). Elicit a few ideas on the board before letting students discuss the questions.

Teacher Support Hub pxlv

Lesson Aim: I can understand a text about living in igloos.

Learn to Learn

Understanding how word families work and how words are formed is an advantage in both comprehension and production skills because it is a way of quickly expanding vocabulary.

5 & 6 After feedback, challenge students to think of extra adjectives ending in *-ful*, *-ic*, and *-ous* and what nouns they come from. The team with the most words wins. Elicit as many as practical on the board.

Students can collaborate digitally through *Collaboration Plus*, where you can assign, track, and assess their work. Students can also share and showcase their work and comment on each other's projects.

Class Challenge

The temperature in Death Valley in the U.S.A, which is the hottest place on Earth, is usually 38 / **47** / 57 degrees.

Explore It!

Students write their questions on a piece of paper and give it to you. Put students into teams and read out all the questions, awarding points for each correct guess and encouraging the writer of the question to add extra information.

LEARN TO LEARN

Word Families (2)

Many nouns have a related adjective. We usually form the related adjective or noun by adding extra letters. We sometimes need to change other letters, too.

Noun	Adjective	Extra Letters
beauty	beauti**ful**	-ful
tru**th**	true	-th

5 Complete the chart. Use the encyclopedia entry to help you.

Noun	tradition	2 strength	comfort	4 warmth	danger
Adjective	1 traditional	strong	3 comfortable	warm	5 dangerous

6 Complete the sentences with the correct form of the words in parentheses. Use the extra letters in the box.

-ful -ic ~~-ly~~ -ous -th

1 My neighbor isn't very friendly. (friend)
2 Andy's room is full of photos of famous people. (fame)
3 Nadir found a helpful website for his homework. (help)
4 Ava's yard is the length of a soccer field! (long)
5 My sister runs a lot. She's really athletic. (athlete)

Explore It!

Guess the correct answer.

The Inuit live in Canada, Alaska, and …

a Iceland. **b** Greenland. c Norway.

Find three more interesting facts about the Inuit. Choose your favorite fact and write a question for your partner.

SHAPE IT!

CULTURE PROJECT

A Poster

A poster uses words and pictures to display information.

Teacher's Resource Bank

Culture Project

See Project Book p38 for further information and activities.

Lesson Aim: I can review what I have learned and reflect on my progress.

The aim of this page is for students to review the grammar and vocabulary from the unit. You can either do it in class, as a timed progress test, or assign it for homework.

Vocabulary

1 Before the task, students play a guessing game in groups. They take turns saying the names of furniture in a room. The first group member to guess the correct room wins a point.

2 Ask students to review the vocabulary to talk about chores on SB p62 before attempting the task.

Grammar in Action

3 ★ Guide students to identify which blanks are followed by nouns or noun phrases and elicit that these will require *as … as* because they will be comparisons.

4 Ask students to review the meaning of *have to* and *don't have to* on SB p63 before attempting the task. Elicit that *don't have to* means "it is not necessary."

Unit Quiz Review

Review the Unit Theme

Remind students of the unit title: *What is your dream house?* Put students into pairs. Have them discuss the following questions: *What is the most useful piece of furniture in your house? Do you do any household chores? What? What is the best location for a house?* Share answers as a class.

Teacher Support Hub pxlvii

5 REVIEW

VOCABULARY

1 Complete the sentences.

1 The **shelves** on my walls are full of books.
2 This room needs some nice **pictures** on the walls.
3 Can you put this milk back in the **fridge** please?
4 I do all my homework at the kitchen table because I don't have a **desk** in my room.
5 We painted the **ceiling** blue. Look up!
6 There's a lovely, soft **carpet** on the floor.

2 Complete the "to do" list from John's mom.

- *Please clean your bedroom and make your* [1] **bed**.
- *After breakfast, load the* [2] **dishwasher**.
- *Please do the* [3] **laundry**, *but don't do the* [4] **ironing**! *I'll do that when I get home.*

GRAMMAR IN ACTION

3 Complete Katy's email with *as … as* or *enough* and the adjective in parentheses.

Hi Lily,

I'm living in a new house. It isn't [1] **as large as** (large) our old one, but it's [2] **big enough** (big) for all of us, and we love it. We're in the middle of the country, but the nearest town is [3] **close enough** (close) to go shopping or to the movies. We have a big yard. It isn't [4] **as beautiful as** (beautiful) yours, but I like it! Anyway, it's [5] **good enough** (good) for our pet rabbit. He's [6] **as happy as** (happy) a baby, running around in the sunshine.

Write soon with your news.

Katy

4 Complete the conversation. Use the words in parentheses with *as … as*, *enough* or the correct form of *have to* / *don't have to*.

RENA Have you seen Bianca's new house? She told me it isn't [1] **as nice as** (nice) her old one.
MIKE Really? The yard's amazing. It's [2] **as large as** (large) a soccer field!
RENA Wow!
MIKE Well maybe it's not that big. But it's [3] **big enough** (big) to play soccer, anyway.
RENA So why isn't she [4] **as happy as** (happy) she was in her old house?
MIKE Because now she [5] **has to share** (share) her room with her little sister.
RENA I have a little sister, so I know how she feels! [6] **Does** she still **have to take** (take) the bus to school?
MIKE No, her new house is [7] **close enough** (close) for her to walk. She and her sister are pleased because they [8] **don't have to wake up** (wake up) as early as before.

Self-Assessment

I can talk about rooms and furniture in a home.
I can talk about household chores.
I can use (*not*) *as* + adjective + *as*.
I can use (*not*) adjective + *enough*.
I can use *have to* / *don't have to*.

Self-Assessment

Encourage the students to write one sentence with each piece of target language to help them decide which face to circle. Give students homework from the Workbook, depending on what they need to focus on.

Homework

Workbook pp46–47

Lesson Aim: I can use a memory journey.

Students should be encouraged to try out different methods of recording and remembering vocabulary so that they can find methods that are suitable for them.

1 ★ Check that students understand the words in the box before starting the activity. Then focus their attention on the word *those* in step a, which will help them recognize that this step follows step c.

2 Ask students to read the text and decide which steps (a–d) it shows.

3 Allow plenty of time for this task. If you think students may struggle with creativity, put them into pairs or small groups to generate more ideas.

4 Monitor closely and help where needed. During feedback, elicit the most interesting journeys you heard while monitoring.

SHAPE IT!

5 & 6 Encourage students to do the activity on their own this time and ask them to give feedback or suggestions after listening to their partner's story.

7 Elicit as many places as possible and write them on the board. Remind students that the places don't need to be real. They can come from fiction or from their own imagination.

LEARN TO ... USE A MEMORY JOURNEY

A memory journey connects images with words. It can help you remember lists of vocabulary.

1 **Imagine you're going to use a memory journey to learn the words in the box for a test. Put steps a–d in order.**

awesome	beautiful	dangerous
famous	traditional	warm

a 3 Imagine walking around your house, looking at those pieces of furniture.

b 4 Think of an image for each word you need to learn, and put it with one of the pieces of furniture. Be creative!

c 2 Think of six pieces of furniture in your house, for example, the shelves in your bedroom, the living room carpet, the kitchen sink.

d 1 Think of your house.

2 **Read the example memory journey below. Which steps are included from Exercise 1? Discuss with a partner.** steps a–c

First, I walk through the front door and into the living room. My dad and brother are having an awesome game of soccer on the carpet. Then I go into the kitchen. I see a famous singer cleaning the sink. After that, I go up to my bedroom. There's a dangerous snake on one of the shelves. Next ...

3 **Follow the steps in Exercise 1 to make your own memory journey for the words in the box.**

4 **Describe your memory journey to your partner. Who has the strangest or funniest images?**

SHAPE IT!

5 **Use rooms and objects in your school to make a memory journey for the words in the box.**

comfortable	curved	friendly
helpful	nervous	strong

6 **Close your book. Can you remember the words from Exercise 5? Describe your memory journey to your partner.**

7 **What other places could you use for memory journeys? Discuss with a partner.**

Extend It!
Students choose another six words from this unit that they want to learn and create a memory journey for.

Lesson Aim: I can talk about dangers.

Warmer

Write the word *danger* on the board and give students two minutes to brainstorm dangerous things, animals, and situations. Elicit these on the board. You could also do this as a game, splitting the students into teams. The team with the most words wins.

Teacher Support Hub ppxxxiv–xxxv

Start It!

Unit Quiz

1 After feedback, elicit more examples of dangerous things that students can find in the ocean.

2 & 3 Before playing **video 6.1**, elicit the meaning of *sidewalk* and encourage students, in pairs, to guess what *smartphone lanes* might be. Elicit a few ideas for the students to check in the video.

4 Encourage students to say why they do or don't do this.

Video Comprehension Questions

Flipped Class

Prepare for **Explore It!** (p71). Students research an interesting fact about an animal that bites or stings.

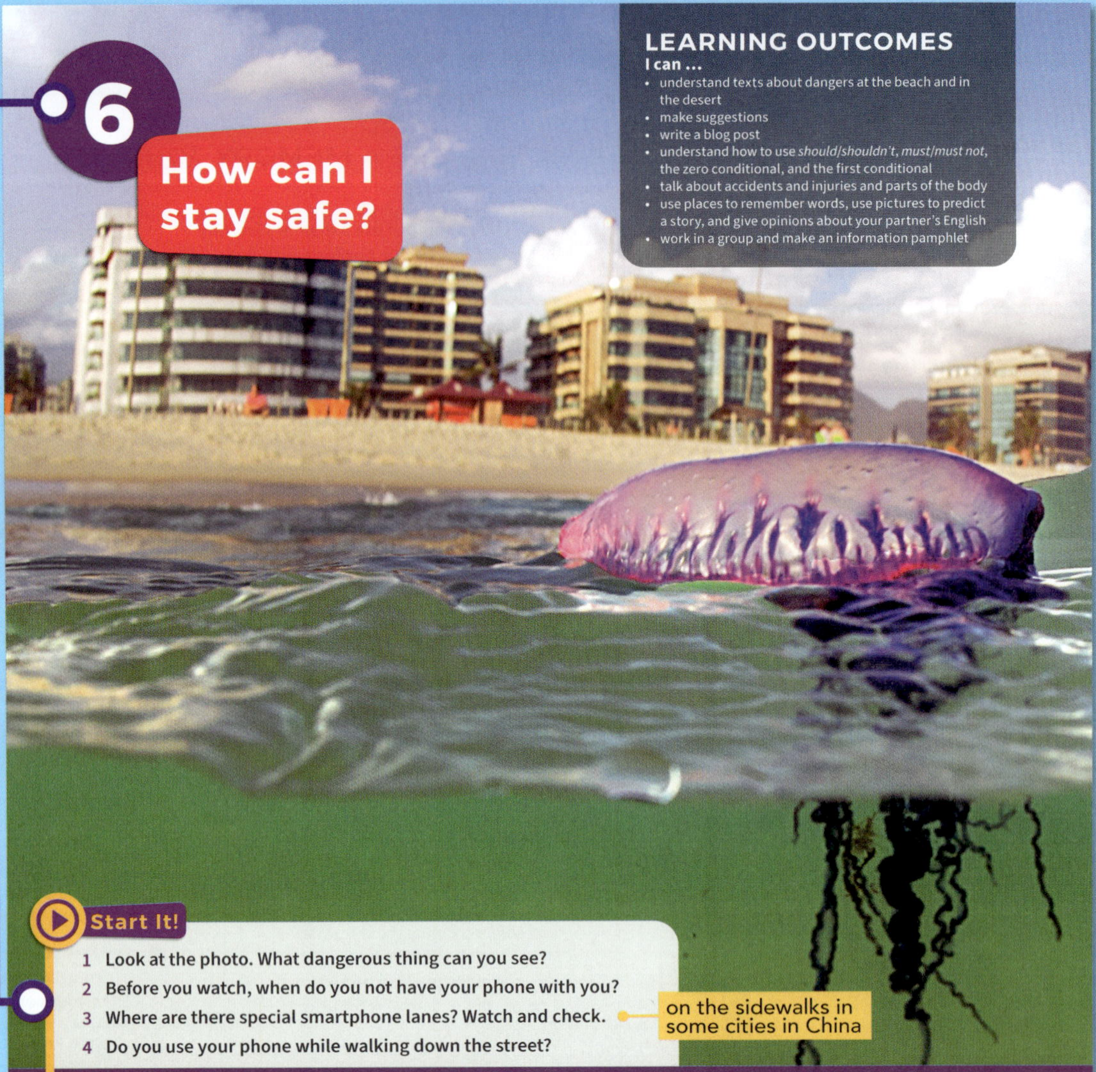

6 How can I stay safe?

LEARNING OUTCOMES

I can ...

- understand texts about dangers at the beach and in the desert
- make suggestions
- write a blog post
- understand how to use *should/shouldn't*, *must/must not*, the zero conditional, and the first conditional
- talk about accidents and injuries and parts of the body
- use places to remember words, use pictures to predict a story, and give opinions about your partner's English
- work in a group and make an information pamphlet

Start It!

1. Look at the photo. What dangerous thing can you see?
2. Before you watch, when do you not have your phone with you?
3. Where are there special smartphone lanes? Watch and check. — on the sidewalks in some cities in China
4. Do you use your phone while walking down the street?

Watch video 6.1 | Grammar in Action 6.2 (p73) | Grammar in Action 6.3 (p75) | Everyday English 6.4 (p76)

70 HOW CAN I STAY SAFE? | UNIT 6

Unit Aims

Skills

I can ...

- understand a text about dangers at the beach and in the desert p72
- make suggestions p76
- write a blog post p77
- work in a group and make an information pamphlet pp78–79

Language

I can ...

- talk about accidents and injuries p71
- understand how to use *should/shouldn't* and *must/must not* p73
- talk about parts of the body p74
- understand how to use zero and first conditionals p75

Learn to Learn

I can ...

- use places to remember words p71
- use pictures to predict a story p74
- give useful opinions about my partner's English p81

Extra Resources

- Finished? Student's Book p123
- Vocabulary Bank, Student's Book p133
- Grammar Reference and Practice, Workbook pp98–99
- Workbook pp48–55
- Teacher Support Hub, Teacher's Book ppxxxiv–xlvii

Digital Resource Pack

(on Cambridge One)

- *Teacher's Resource Bank* for word lists, differentiated worksheets, *Culture Projects*, and many other extra resources
- *Practice Extra*, *Presentation Plus*, *Test Generator*, and *Digital Collaboration Space*

Lesson Aim: I can talk about accidents and injuries.

6.01–6.02 **Audioscripts pT138**

1 6.01 ★★★ Students cover the box and look at the pictures. In pairs, they try to fill the blanks and then check with the box.

Target Vocabulary

break breɪk
bruise bruz
burn bɜrn
cut kʌt
fall off fɔl ɔf
get bitten get ˈbɪ·tən
get stung get stʌŋ
hit hɪt
scratch skrætʃ
slip slɪp
sprain spreɪn
trip over trɪp ˈoʊ·vər

Extra Vocabulary Practice

Get It Right!

Point out that we don't say *I hit **the** head* or *Lisa burned **the** hand*. Instead, we use possessive adjectives (e.g., *my*, *her*).

2 6.02 After feedback, students play a game in groups. Students take turns miming phrases from Exercise 1. The first student to guess the phrase wins a point and mimes the next word.

Vocabulary Bank SB p133

Extra Vocabulary Practice

VOCABULARY
Accidents and Injuries

6.01 **1** Complete the phrases with the words in the box. Listen, check, and repeat.

break	bruise	burn	~~cut~~	fall off	get bitten
get stung	hit	scratch	slip	sprain	trip over

1 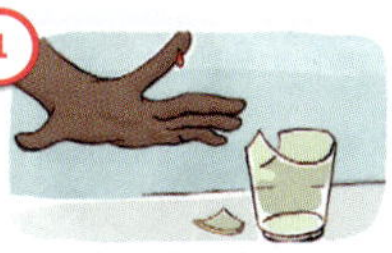
cut your finger

2 
slip

3 
get stung by a bee

4 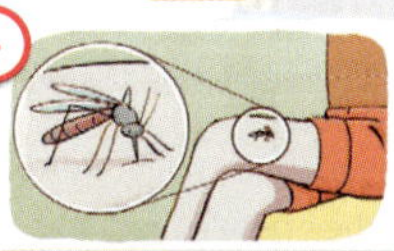
get bitten by a mosquito

5 
hit your head

6 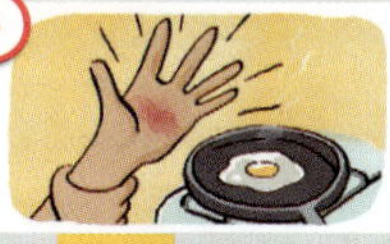
burn your hand

7 
scratch your arm

8 
break your leg

9 
trip over a chair

10 
fall off your horse

11 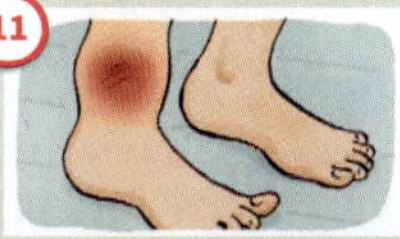
sprain your ankle

12 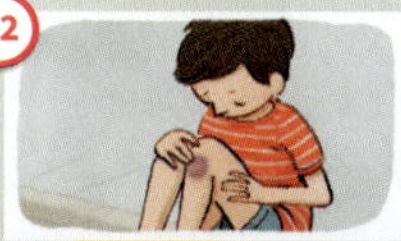
bruise your leg

Get It Right!

We usually use words like **my**, **your**, **his**, **her** when we talk about parts of the body.

*I hit **my** head. Did Lisa burn **her** hand?*

6.02 **2** Listen. Write the accidents and injuries from Exercise 1 that you can hear.

1 get stung by a bee
2 fall off your bike
3 trip over a cat
4 slip (on the ice)
5 burn your hand/finger

LEARN TO LEARN
Using Places to Remember Words

It can help you to remember new words if you think of where they might happen.

3 Think of a place where each accident in Exercise 1 might happen.

trip over a chair – in the classroom

4 Test your partner. Say a place that you thought of in Exercise 3. Your partner guesses the accident or injury you thought of.

The kitchen. *Cut your finger?*

Use It!

5 Think about a time when one of the accidents or injuries happened to you or someone you know. Tell your partner about it.

My sister sprained her ankle last month.

How did that happen?

Explore It!

Is the sentence *T* (true) or *F* (false)?

All bees can sting. F

Find another interesting fact about an animal that bites or stings. Then write a question for your partner to answer.

UNIT 6 | HOW CAN I STAY SAFE? 71

Learn to Learn

Associating new vocabulary with places, people, and times increases the chances that it will be remembered.

3 & 4 Encourage personalization. Students think of places where these things have happened to them.

5 Allow a few minutes of thinking time before asking students to discuss the questions in pairs. For an extra challenge, tell students they may lie, and their partner must ask questions to guess if the story is true or not.

Explore It!

Monitor and correct language mistakes before eliciting the questions for the whole class to answer.

Extend It!

In groups, students make up a story called "Fred's Unlucky Day" using the vocabulary from Exercise 1. The story begins with "Yesterday, Fred had a really bad day. In the morning, he was making breakfast and he …"

Homework

Workbook p48

Warmer

In groups, students brainstorm all the dangers at the beach they can think of. Elicit ideas and relevant vocabulary on the board.

Teacher Support Hub ppxxxvi–xxxvii

1 Allow dictionaries for this activity, and ask pairs to match the phrases with the pictures.

2 6.03 Disallow dictionaries and translation software, as it would preempt the following activity.

3 ★ Remind students that it is not necessary to be familiar with a word to understand its meaning in context. To check comprehension, ask students to think of more sentences containing the words from this activity. Have volunteers write their sentences on the board.

4 Fast finishers can write one more sentence about the text, true or false. Elicit these sentences during feedback and ask the class to decide if they are true or false.

Reading Comprehension Questions

5 Allow students a minute of thinking time before discussing the questions. Monitor closely and note useful vocabulary the students needed to express their opinions. Elicit this on the board during feedback and then ask students to discuss the questions again with a new partner.

READING

An Online Article

1 Check the meaning of the words in the box. Can you see some of these things in the photos?

animals that sting	broken glass	large waves
quicksand	rip currents	shark attack

2 6.03 **Read the article. Which danger in Exercise 1 is not in the article?** large waves

3 Find words in the article that mean …

1 difficult to find (para. 1) hidden
2 quickly (para. 2) swiftly
3 something dangerous from an animal (para. 4) venom
4 move your body to get free (para. 5) struggle
5 when the ocean goes in and out at different times of the day (para. 5) tide

4 Are the sentences *T* (true) or *F* (false)?

1 Some beaches are more dangerous than others. T
2 Rip currents move away from the beach. T
3 Crocodiles don't live near the ocean. F
4 The blue-ringed octopus is a large and ugly animal. F
5 One blue-ringed octopus can kill a lot of people. T
6 All British beaches are safe. F

Voice It!

5 Discuss the questions.

1 What other dangers at the beach can you think of?
2 What other dangerous places do some people like to visit? Why do they go there?

Finished? p123 Ex. 1

DANGERS AT THE BEACH

Beaches promise sun, sand, and fun and are usually safe places to go, but accidents can happen. You can slip and break your leg, or step on some glass and cut your foot. Ouch! Some beaches around the world have hidden dangers, however, and you should take extra care.

HAWAII

It's great for surfing, but beaches in Hawaii also have dangerous rip currents. Rip currents happen when water moves swiftly away from the beach. They are difficult to see and can move very fast. They can take people far out to sea, so swimmers must not try to swim against them. Instead, they should swim sideways along the beach until they get to safer waters.

AUSTRALIA

Everyone knows that huge sharks sometimes swim near Australian beaches, and crocodiles can also come very near. You must always be careful. Never swim when there isn't a lifeguard on the beach.

Sharks and crocodiles aren't the only danger on Australia's beaches. The beautiful Australian blue-ringed octopus, for example, is as small as your hand. But you must not go near them. They have enough venom to kill ten people!

UK

The sand can be as unsafe as the ocean, and on some British beaches it can kill! Dangerous quicksand is full of water, and it's very easy for people to sink in it. You shouldn't kick or struggle. You must move very slowly and carefully to get out … before the tide comes in!

Extend It!

Ask students, in pairs, to underline three or four other unknown vocabulary items in the text. Together they look up the meaning of the words or phrases and write a short exercise like the one in Exercise 3. Pairs swap their exercises and complete them. Monitor closely and elicit the most useful definitions with the whole class.

Class Challenge

The animal that is responsible for killing the most people is the shark / **mosquito** / crocodile.

Finished?

Students turn to p123 and do Exercise 1.

Homework

Workbook p49

Warmer

▶ Play **video 6.2** and elicit that you must not put anything on the burn and you should hold it under cold water for 20 minutes. For a sprained ankle, you should put some ice on it to stop the swelling.

6.05–6.07 **Audioscripts ppT138–139**

1 After feedback, point out that we don't use *to* after *must* or *should*. Then elicit that both *must* and *should* can be used to give advice, but *must* is used more for rules.

Pronunciation

6.04–6.06 Ask students to turn to SB p142 for pronunciation practice of /ʌ/ and /ʊ/.

2 Fast finishers can expand on the sentences (e.g., 1 *… because there might be some broken glass.*).

3 ★ Ask students to decide if each sentence is advice, strong advice, or a rule.

Extra Grammar Practice

4 6.07 Before the activity, allow students, in pairs, to discuss one piece of advice and one rule about cycling. Elicit a few examples on the board.

5 & 6 Encourage students to personalize the activity and write about other activities, especially ones that they do themselves.

GRAMMAR IN ACTION

Should/Shouldn't and *Must/Must not*

Watch video 6.2
What should you do if you get burnt?
What should you do with a sprained ankle?

	Should for Advice	*Must* for Strong Advice or a Rule
+	You [1] should **take** extra care.	You [3] must always **be** careful.
–	You [2] shouldn't **kick** or struggle.	Swimmers [4] must not **try** to swim against them.

Pronunciation p142

1 Complete the examples in the chart above with *should/shouldn't* or *must/must not*. Use the article on page 72 to help you.

2 Correct the sentences about the article on page 72.

1. You shouldn't wear sandals on the beach.
   You should wear sandals on the beach.
2. In a rip current, you must swim toward the beach.
   In a rip current, you must not swim toward the beach.
3. You should swim near the blue-ringed octopus.
   You must not swim near the blue-ringed octopus.
4. In quicksand, you should kick and jump to get out.
   In quicksand, you shouldn't kick and jump to get out.

3 Circle the correct words.

1. You *should* / *shouldn't* (circled: shouldn't) swim here. The water isn't clean.
2. You *must* / *must not* (circled: must not) speak while you're doing an exam.
3. I think everyone *should* / *must* (circled: should) play a sport. Exercise is good for you.
4. You *must* / *should* (circled: must) wear a seatbelt in the car. It's the law.
5. I think you *should* / *must* (circled: should) learn to speak another language.
6. You *shouldn't* / *must not* (circled: shouldn't) go outside in shorts. It's cold today.

4 6.07 Complete the teacher's message with *should/shouldn't* or *must/must not*. Then listen and check.

Mrs. Harrison <jharrison@WGhighschool.org>
To: All students
Subject: Cycling

Hi everyone,

Now that spring is here, I think you [1] should all think about walking or cycling to school if you can.

Cycling is fun and healthy, but you [2] must be careful. For example, you [3] shouldn't ride when the weather is bad, and you [4] must wear a helmet. That's extremely important. However, you also [5] must not forget that there are rules on the road for cyclists, and you [6] must learn these rules.

The school website has some good advice, such as which clothes you [7] should wear when riding your bike, and I think all cyclists [8] should read it carefully.

One more thing: we need to know which students are cycling to school, so you [9] must tell Mrs. Jones if you plan to ride your bike. That's a school rule, so you [10] must not forget!

Use It!

5 In your notebook, write rules and advice for staying safe while doing these activities.

ice skating | mountain biking | rock climbing | surfing

6 Read your rules and advice to your partner, but don't say the activities. Can your partner guess them?

You should wear a wetsuit to do this. But you must not do it in bad weather. What is it?

Surfing?

Finished? p123 Ex. 2

Grammar Game

Write one of these situations on the board: *at the beach, at school, at the gym, on a plane*. In groups, students have two minutes to write as many sentences with *should(n't)* or *must not* as possible. They swap ideas with another team, who can challenge the sentences if they seem inaccurate. Encourage discussions if possible (e.g., *You don't have to wear sunscreen at the beach all the time.*). Repeat with other situations.

Finished?

Students turn to p123 and do Exercise 2.

Homework

Workbook p50

Lesson Aim: I can talk about parts of the body.

Warmer

In groups, students have two minutes to brainstorm all the body vocabulary they know.

Teacher Support Hub ppxxxviii–xxxix

6.08–6.09 Audioscripts pT139

1 6.08 After feedback, play the audio again and ask students to point to their own body parts when they hear them.

Target Vocabulary

cheek tʃik
chest tʃest
chin tʃɪn
elbow ˈel·boʊ
forehead ˈfɔrˌhed
heel hil
knee ni
neck nek
shoulder ˈʃoʊl·dər
teeth tiθ
toe toʊ
wrist rɪst

2 Fast finishers can write one more fill-in-the-blank sentence using a different word from Exercise 1. Elicit these during feedback.

Extra Vocabulary Practice

3 Challenge students to name the body part within five seconds, before pointing to others.

Vocabulary Bank SB p133

Learn to Learn

Pictures are another way for students to predict what a reading or listening text might include. Guessing what a text contains may help students feel less anxious about it.

VOCABULARY AND LISTENING

Parts of the Body

6.08 **1** Match the words in the box with 1–12 in the photo. Listen, check, and repeat.

cheek	2	forehead	1	shoulder	6
chest	7	heel	11	teeth	3
chin	4	knee	10	toe	12
elbow	9	neck	5	wrist	8

2 Complete the sentences with words from Exercise 1.

1 Your _wrist_ is between your hand and your arm.
2 People have ten fingers and ten **toes**.
3 Children have 20 **teeth** and adults have 32.
4 Your **forehead** is just above your eyes.
5 Your **knee** is in the middle of your leg.
6 Your **shoulder** is at the top of your arm.

Use It!

3 Point to a part of the body from Exercise 1. Name the part your partner points to.

A Radio Interview

LEARN TO LEARN

Using Pictures to Predict a Story

Before you listen, look carefully at any pictures and use them to imagine a story.

4 Look at the pictures in Exercise 6. With your partner, choose one picture from each set of three and use them to make a story.

6.09 **5** Listen to the interview. What parts of your story were the same?

6.09 **6** Listen again. (Circle) the correct answers.

1 What job does Pam do?

2 What was Jamie doing before his accident?

3 What did Jamie do?

4 What injuries did Jamie get?

7 Work with your partner to tell Jamie's story. Use the pictures to help you.

8 EXAM Look again at the pictures in Exercise 6. Write Jamie's story in your notebook. Use 35 words or more.

4 After students discuss the pictures, elicit different versions of the story and write useful vocabulary on the board.

5 & 6 6.09 Students check their ideas in pairs.

7 Change pairs once or twice to allow students to repeat the story. This will help improve fluency and build confidence.

8 EXAM Remind students to use the pictures to help them.

Extend It!

In pairs, students invent a new short story and draw three simple pictures to go with it. They give the drawings to a different pair, who try to guess the story from the pictures.

Flipped Class

Ask students to watch **video 6.3** and do **Video Worksheet 6.3** in the *Teacher's Resource Bank* in preparation for the next lesson.

Homework

Workbook p51

Lesson Aim: I can understand how to use zero and first conditionals.

Warmer

▶ Play **video 6.3** if it was not assigned for homework. Elicit that you should not put out your hands. You should keep your hands and elbows in and roll onto your shoulder. If you do this, it won't hurt as badly, and rolling can protect you when you fall.

6.10 Audioscript pT139

1 Point out that the *if/when* clause can come either before or after the result clause, but if it comes before, the two clauses need to be separated by a comma.

Extra Grammar Practice

2 ★ Point out that each sentence has an *if/when* clause and a result clause. Suggest that students circle each *if* and *when* to help them match the sentence halves.

3 6.10 ★★★ Fast finishers work in pairs to discuss why the zero or first conditional is used in each case (i.e., Is it about a general truth or a specific situation?).

4 Support students by pointing out that snakes don't run. Remind them that the verb will change if the subject is third person singular (*jaguar*).

5 & 6 Monitor to make sure students are forming correct sentences. Write any errors on the board for the whole class to correct at the end of the activity.

GRAMMAR IN ACTION

Zero Conditional and First Conditional

Watch video 6.3
How can you fall off a skateboard safely?
Is this a good way to fall?

Zero Conditional		First Conditional	
Action/Situation	Result	3 Action/Situation	5 Result
When a crocodile gets you,	that's the end!	If you swim in safe places,	you won't be in any danger.
1 Result	2 Action/Situation	4 Result	6 Action/Situation
A croc sometimes opens its mouth	if you hit it in the eye.	You won't see any crocodiles	if you're on vacation in Spain.

1 Complete the headings in the chart above with *Action/Situation* or *Result*.

2 Match 1–5 with a–e. Then complete the results with the correct form of the verb in parentheses.

1. When people aren't careful, a
2. If you don't go near a crocodile, d
3. If a crocodile grabs you, b
4. When a crocodile wants to cool down, e
5. If a crocodile loses a tooth, c

a. accidents happen (happen).
b. it will try (try) to pull you under the water.
c. another one will grow (grow).
d. it will probably ignore (ignore) you.
e. it opens (open) its mouth.

3 6.10 Complete the email with the correct form of the verbs in parentheses. Then listen and check.

> So you're going to visit Queensland. Great idea! If you [1] like (like) beaches and forests, you [2] 'll / will love (love) Port Douglas. It's amazing. It usually [3] takes (take) about an hour to get there if you [4] take (take) a bus from the airport. Buses are frequent, so if you [5] miss (miss) one, you [6] won't have (not have) a long wait. Of course, if you [7] don't mind (not mind) spending more money, there [8] are (be) always taxis at the airport, too! If you [9] visit (visit) Four Mile Beach, you [10] 'll / will have (have) a great time surfing. But be careful! If you [11] don't see (not see) anyone else in the water, it probably [12] means (mean) there are sharks or jellyfish in the ocean!
> Have fun and take care!

4 Complete the information about the Amazon jungle. Use the words in the box.

go have hide run away

Snakes
Snakes [1] hide if they hear people coming. Most snake venom isn't fatal if you [2] go straight to the hospital.

Bigger Animals
You probably won't see any jaguars because they [3] run away when they feel threatened. However, if a jaguar [4] has young cubs, it is more dangerous.

5 Imagine you're planning a jungle vacation. Write what you will do if the following things happen.

1. If I see a snake on the path, I'll wait for it to go away.
2. If I'm very hot and I find a river, ______
3. If I get bitten by a spider, ______
4. If I get lost, ______

Use It!

6 Say the second half of your sentences from Exercise 5. Can your partner guess the first half?

I'll look for a river to follow. *If I get lost?*

Finished? p123 Ex. 3

Grammar Game

Put students into groups. On the board, write: *If school is closed next week, I …* One student finishes the sentence (e.g., *I'll stay home.*). The next student repeats this last idea and continues: *If I stay home, I'll watch TV.* The next student continues with *If I watch TV, … .* The group continues like this for three minutes. Elicit the final stories from teams and ask for the best ones to be repeated for the whole class.

Finished?

Students turn to p123 and do Exercise 3.

Homework

Workbook p52

Lesson Aim: I can make suggestions.

Warmer

Tell students you want to try a new sport but don't know which one yet. In pairs, students discuss which sport they'd recommend and why. Elicit a few ideas.

Teacher Support Hub ppxl–xli

6.11 Audioscript ppT139–140

1 6.11 ★★★ Play the audio without focusing students on the photo and ask them to discuss what they heard. Elicit that Hayley is giving Dan suggestions about buying a bike.

2 6.11 Books closed. In pairs, students try to remember the complete phrases in the text (e.g., *How about joining my bike club?*) and write them down.

Useful Language and Everyday English Practice

3 Play **video 6.4** and drill pronunciation of the phrases, especially of *awesome* /ˈɔːsəm/.

4 ★★★ Challenge students to create a short conversation using all the phrases, for example:
– *My buddies recommended an awesome beach for surfing, so I'll have a go at it.*
– *Good job!*

5 & 6 In pairs, students develop their ideas from the warmer. They then rehearse the conversation, repeating it again if necessary to make sure they include the language from the unit.

SPEAKING
Making Suggestions

6.11 **1** **Listen to the conversation. Who knows more about mountain bikes, Dan or Hayley?** Hayley

DAN Awesome mountain bike, Hayley.
HAYLEY Thanks, Dan.
DAN I'd like to get one, too. Do you think I should buy one online?
HAYLEY Not really. Some online stores aren't reliable. Their bikes aren't very safe. Anyway, [1] make sure you don't buy one without trying it first. [2] Why don't you try The Bike Shack in town? They're really good.
DAN OK. I'll have a go at it.
HAYLEY And [3] you should definitely buy a good helmet, too. You can really hurt yourself if you fall off, so you must not ride without one.
DAN Good idea. I think I should find some buddies to ride with, too. What do you think?
HAYLEY Sure. [4] How about joining my bike club? We go out every weekend.
DAN Yeah! Good job, Hayley. I'll do that.

6.11 **2** **Complete the conversation with the phrases from the** ***Useful Language*** **box. Then listen and check.**

Useful Language

How about …ing … ?	Why don't you … ?
Make sure you don't …	You should definitely …

3 **Look at the** ***Everyday English*** **box. Find and underline the phrases in the conversation.**

Watch video 6.4
Everyday English

Awesome	buddies
I'll have a go at it.	Good job

4 **Complete the sentences with the** ***Everyday English*** **phrases.**

1 Awesome snowboard, Maya!
2 Skateboarding? That sounds hard, but I'll have a go at it.
3 You remembered your camera! Good job, Beth!
4 That's Alfie. He's one of my surfing buddies.

PLAN

5 **Work in pairs. Choose a sport and think of advice for someone trying it for the first time. Take notes.**

What you should or must do: ______________

What you shouldn't or must not do: ______________

SPEAK

6 **Practice a conversation asking for and giving advice about the sport. Remember to use** ***should/shouldn't*** **and** ***must/must not*****, vocabulary from this unit, and phrases from the** ***Useful Language*** **and** ***Everyday English*** **boxes.**

CHECK

7 **Work with another pair. Listen to their conversation and complete the notes.**

What you should or must do: ______________

What you shouldn't or must not do: ______________

The best suggestion: ______________

7 After students have performed their conversation in pairs, ask them to change partners and repeat the conversations in order to promote fluency.

Homework

Ask students to write a paragraph of about 100 words giving advice about the sport they talked about in this lesson.

Lesson Aim: I can write a blog post.

Warmer

In small groups, students read each other's paragraphs they wrote for homework and ask each other follow-up questions about them.

Teacher Support Hub ppxlii–xliii

1 & 2 ★★★ Elicit that the blog post is about skateboarding, and ask students to think of two questions on this subject that they would like to find answers to. After students read the blog, ask if any of their questions were answered by the text and, if so, where the answers were found.

3 Encourage students to underline the sentences in the text where they found the answers. Elicit these during feedback, focusing students' attention on how the ideas in the questions are paraphrased in the text (e.g., *aren't very good – it's best to avoid them*).

4 & 5 Point out that in blogs we often use *I* and *you* to write in a more personal, friendly style.

Useful Language Practice

6 & 7 Brainstorm possible activities with the whole class, and allow students to choose one they want to write about.

8 Encourage students to read each other's texts and to say if they agree with the advice or not, giving reasons.

WRITING
A Blog Post

1 Look at the photo. What do you think the blog post is about? Read it and check.

MATT'S BLOG

Thanks for all your comments on my posts. Here are my answers to your questions.

1 b

There are cheap boards, but it's best to avoid them. If you want a good board, you need to spend more. I'd say at least $100. Also, make sure you get the right size deck. If you have small feet, you'll need a narrow deck. If it's too wide, you won't be able to control the board.

2 c

Yes! When you're a beginner, accidents happen. That's why you need a helmet. It must be a proper skateboarder's helmet, and it must be the right size. If it moves when you shake your head, it's too big.

3 a

If you ask me, the street is too dangerous. A skatepark is the best place, but if there isn't one near you, any park will be good.

That's all for now. Have fun, but stay safe!

2 Match questions a–c with paragraphs 1–3.

a Can I skate in the street?
b What board should I buy?
c Should I wear a helmet?

3 Read the blog post again. Which of these opinions does Matt have?

1 Cheap skateboards aren't very good. ✓
2 You won't get a good skateboard for less than $100. ✓
3 For some people, narrow skateboards are best. ✓
4 Your helmet shouldn't move when you wear it. ✓
5 The only safe place for skateboarding is a skatepark. ☐

4 Complete the phrases in the *Useful Language* box with words that Matt uses for giving advice.

Useful Language

[1] I'd say	[3] That's why
[2] make sure	If you [4] ask me

5 Complete the sentences with the *Useful Language* phrases.

1 If you fall off a board, you can really hurt your head. That's why skateboarders wear helmets.
2 If you ask me, all skateboarders should wear knee and elbow pads as well.
3 Make sure you keep your board in good condition.
4 Many people skate on their own, but I'd say it's more fun and safer to skate with friends.

PLAN

6 Plan a blog post to give safety advice. Choose an activity and think of three questions about doing it safely. Take notes for the answers.

1 ______
2 ______
3 ______

WRITE

7 Write your blog post. Remember to include an introduction, three questions and answers, an ending, and phrases from the *Useful Language* box.

CHECK

8 Do you ...

- answer each question?
- use *should/shouldn't* and *must/must not*?
- use vocabulary from this unit?

Finished? p123 Ex. 4

Finished?

Students turn to p123 and do Exercise 4.

Flipped Class

In preparation for the **Science Project** (pp78–79), ask students to research a remote and dangerous place, such as Death Valley in the U.S.A., and find out at least four dangerous things about it.

Homework

Workbook p53

Lesson Aim: I can work in a group and make an information pamphlet.

Warmer

In groups, students share information about the remote places they researched for homework.

Project Book

For more information and activities, see the Project Book p42.

6.12 Audioscript pT140

1 Encourage students to look quickly at the pamphlet, without reading it in detail, as they can predict a lot about the text from the visual information and how it is organized.

2 Display the text, if possible, and ask volunteers to come and underline or point to the parts of the text where the answers can be found.

3 After feedback, ask students to find and underline examples of conditional sentences in the text.

How to Work in Groups

At this stage, students should be able to reflect on how they wish to organize themselves while working in groups, making conscious decisions about the process and the allocation of responsibilities. You may want to elicit from students what the consequences are in real life when one or more people in a group don't do their fair share of work in a project.

SCIENCE PROJECT

An Information Pamphlet

1 **Look at the information pamphlet. What is it about?**

(a) The dangers of the desert

b How animals live in the desert

2 **Read the pamphlet again. Are the sentences *T* (true) or *F* (false)?**

1 All deserts are hot and dry. F

2 Birds can help you in the desert. T

3 If you drink water, you won't get heat cramps. F

4 A *haboob* is a desert animal. F

5 You shouldn't wear sandals in the desert. T

6 Scorpions live in dark places. T

3 **Complete the chart. Put the five dangers in the desert in the correct groups.**

Desert Animals	Desert Weather	Our Bodies in the Desert
snakes		thirst
scorpions	sandstorms	heat cramps

How to Work in Groups

6.12 **4** **Listen and decide which student worked in these ways. Write *J* (John), *I* (Isla), or *P* (Poppy).**

1 The group decided what the different jobs were for the project. Each person did a different job. I

2 The group shared the writing on the project. Each person wrote a different section. J

3 Each person worked alone first. Then they chose different sections of each person's work to make their poster. P

5 **Which of the ways of working do you think is best? Why? Share your ideas with a partner.**

Desert Survival

Fact File

- A desert is a place with less than 250 mm of rain per year.
- Around 30% of the land on the Earth is desert.
- Only 20% of deserts are sandy. Some have snow.
- Highest temperature in a desert: 56.7°C (Death Valley, U.S.A.)
- Lowest temperature in a desert: – 89.2°C (Antarctica)

Deserts are extremely big, extremely dry, and extremely dangerous! If you are lost in one, here are some of the dangers you should know about.

Thirst

What's the danger?

You can't live without water for more than three days.

What should you do?

Walk slowly and rest often. If you don't, you'll lose a lot of water as sweat.

Drink a little and often.

If you see birds, follow them. They'll take you to the nearest water.

Heat Cramps

What's the danger?

As well as water, your body needs salt. When you sweat, you lose a lot of salt. If you lose too much, your legs and arms will begin to hurt. This is called heat cramp, and in the desert it can be dangerous.

What should you do?

Make sure you carry salt tablets with you. They can save your life!

4 & 5 6.12 After doing Exercise 4, allow students two minutes of thinking time to form an opinion before they discuss the ways of working. If appropriate, divide the class into different groups according to which ways of working they liked best.

6 Ask students to share the information about a remote place that they researched for homework, and choose the most interesting. Stress that no matter which strategy from Exercise 4 students want to try, they still must make decisions together at the beginning regarding content, structure, and visuals.

7 One student in each group stands next to their pamphlet and answers questions about it while the others walk around looking at other posters and asking extra questions.

8 Before this activity, ask students individually to write a number from 1 to 5 on a piece of paper, where 1 means "We worked very well together" and 5 means "We didn't work well together at all." Each group puts all the pieces of paper together, shuffles them, and reveals the numbers so that everyone can get an idea of how the others felt about their collaboration.

Students can collaborate digitally through *Collaboration Plus*, where you can assign, track, and assess their work. Students can also share and showcase their work and comment on each other's projects.

SHAPE IT!

Sandstorms

What's the danger?

When it gets windy in the desert, sandstorms happen. In Arabic, these huge walls of sand are called *haboob*. They are sometimes more than a kilometer high and can move at 40 kilometers per hour.

What should you do?

If a *haboob* is coming, you must hide. Sandstorms usually last for a few minutes, but sometimes they last three hours!

Snakes

What's the danger?

If you're in the Arizona Desert and you hear a rattle, it's probably a rattlesnake, and its bite can kill.

What should you do?

Wear strong boots, not sandals. If you see a snake, move carefully away. If it bites you, you must find a doctor as soon as you can.

Scorpions

What's the danger?

There are 2,000 different types of scorpions and 30 of them can kill.

What should you do?

Scorpions live under rocks, so you should be careful where you put your hands!

PLAN

6 Work in groups to plan an information pamphlet. Choose a remote place. Then follow the steps below.

- Decide how your group will work together.
- Decide on the sections your information pamphlet will include.
- Decide what images and diagrams you could include.
- Make a first draft of your pamphlet.
- Share your first draft with another group to get their feedback.

PRESENT

7 Display your information pamphlet on your classroom wall. Remember to include different sections, interesting facts and pictures, and the tips in *How to Work in Groups*.

CHECK

8 Ask different groups how they worked. Did they work in the same way as you? Who worked in a group best?

UNIT 6 | HOW CAN I STAY SAFE? 79

For more work on science, students can turn to SB p139. See pT125 for teaching notes.

Class Challenge

The largest desert in the world is the Sahara desert / the Gobi desert / **Antarctica**.

Lesson Aim: I can review what I have learned and reflect on my progress.

The aim of this page is for students to review the grammar and vocabulary from the unit. You can either do it in class, as a timed progress test, or assign it for homework.

Vocabulary

1 You could turn this into a game in teams. Give students one minute to review the vocabulary on SB p71 and then close their books. Read each sentence aloud, replacing the options with a *Beep!* The first team to call out the correct answer wins a point.

2 Before the exercise, review the vocabulary. In small teams, students challenge each other in pairs. A student from one team points to a part of the body, and the other team wins a point if they can name it. Teams take turns. The team with the most points after three minutes wins.

Grammar in Action

3 During feedback, encourage students to say if they agree or disagree with the statements.

4 Ask students to review SB p75 before doing this exercise.

5 Students can work in pairs to compare answers. Allow them to discuss any answers that are different before checking as a class.

Unit Quiz Review

6 REVIEW

VOCABULARY

1 Circle the correct words.

1. Sue touched a hot pan and **burned** / *sprained* her fingers.
2. Juan **slipped** / *scratched* on some ice.
3. Jane *bruised* / **fell off** her bike.
4. Andy got *bitten* / **stung** by a bee.
5. Masha *fell off* / **tripped over** a plant in the garden.
6. I **cut** / *broke* my finger with a knife.

2 Match the words in the box with the descriptions. You can use the words more than once.

cheek	chin	elbow	forehead	
heel	knee	shoulder	toe	wrist

1. We have two or more of these. **cheek, elbow, heel, knee, shoulder, toe, wrist**
2. These are parts of your arm. **elbow, shoulder, wrist**
3. These are parts of your leg and foot. **knee, toe**
4. These are parts of your face. **cheek, chin, forehead**

GRAMMAR IN ACTION

3 Complete the sentences with *should*/*shouldn't* or *must*/*must not* and the verbs in the box.

sleep	stay	talk	wear

1. You **must wear** a seatbelt in the car.
2. You **shouldn't stay** in the sun too long.
3. You **should sleep** for eight hours at night.
4. You **must not talk** on your phone while you're riding a bike.

4 Complete the sentences with the zero or first conditional.

1. If you **aren't** (not be) more careful, you **'ll / will have** (have) an accident.
2. When Gina **goes** (go) skateboarding, she always **wears** (wear) a helmet.
3. If someone **breaks** (break) a leg, it **hurts** (hurt) a lot.
4. If the weather **gets** (get) worse, the climbers **will be** (be) stuck on the mountain.
5. Snakes **don't** usually **bite** (not bite) you if you **don't disturb** (not disturb) them.

5 Circle the best words to complete the notes.

Stay Safe in the Forest

Before you go, you [1]**should** / *shouldn't* tell someone where you're going. If you get lost, it [2]*is* / **will be** easier to find you.

You [3]**must** / *must not* take a map. If you [4]**don't** / *won't* follow a map, you'll probably get lost.

You [5]*shouldn't* / **must not** eat mushrooms. Some are very dangerous – if you [6]**eat** / *will eat* them, you can get extremely sick.

You [7]*should* / **shouldn't** run away from a bear. If you stay calm and walk away slowly, you [8]**will be** / *are* OK.

Self-Assessment

- I can talk about accidents and injuries.
- I can talk about parts of the body.
- I can use *should*/*shouldn't* and *must*/*must not*.
- I can use the zero conditional and first conditional.

80 REVIEW | UNIT 6

Review the Unit Theme

Remind students of the unit title: *How can I stay safe?* Put students into pairs. Have them discuss the following questions: *What parts of the body can you name? What are some common injuries? How can they happen? How can you stay safe at the beach?* Share answers as a class.

Teacher Support Hub pxlvii

Self-Assessment

Allow students a few minutes to look back at the page and the whole unit. On the board, write: *I need more practice with …* and encourage students to tell you what they need. Give them additional homework from the Workbook as necessary.

Homework

Workbook pp54–55

Lesson Aim: I can give useful opinions about my partner's English.

Peer-feedback is a useful classroom tool, and it strengthens students' self-assessment and self-correction skills, as well. At this stage, students should be able to give each other constructive feedback and see this as an opportunity to improve.

1 After feedback, elicit why options a–c are not advisable, guiding students to say what the consequences of these comments might be.

2 Point out that intonation is important when giving an opinion. If someone's intonation is very flat, the opinion could sound negative, even if the words are positive.

3 & 4 You may want to give students some things to think about when listening to their partner. For example:

- pronunciation (How well could you understand your partner?)
- language (Was their message clear? Was your partner's grammar full of mistakes?)
- vocabulary (Did your partner use interesting vocabulary?)

LEARN TO LEARN

LEARN TO ... GIVE USEFUL OPINIONS ABOUT YOUR PARTNER'S ENGLISH

Be polite when you give opinions about your partner's English. You can help each other improve.

1 **Read the advice about how to give useful opinions. Complete the advice with *should* or *shouldn't*.**

What you [1] should do to help your partner improve their English

You [2] shouldn't ...

a say what you think in a mean way.
b talk about your partner's personality.
c say that something is better or worse than it is.

You [3] should ...

d say what you think, but also be nice.
e say positive things.
f give ideas for how your partner can improve.

2 **Match 1–6 with the advice (a–f) in Exercise 1.**

1 b *Well done! You're a really interesting person.*
2 d *That wasn't your best English, but I know you can do better.*
3 c *That was the worst presentation ever!*
4 f *You made some mistakes with the first conditional. Why don't you study the grammar from the unit again?*
5 e *You used a lot of adjectives to describe things. That was really nice!*
6 a *Your English was awful!*

3 **Invent a story about an accident. Use one word or phrase from each box, and think about the answers to the questions below.**

crocodile	knife	mirror	scissors	snake

break	cut	get bitten	hit	slip

- What were you doing when the accident happened?
- What happened?
- How did you feel?
- Did anybody help you?
- What happened then?
- What should people do to avoid a similar accident?

4 **Take turns telling your stories. While your partner is speaking, think about what they do well and how they can improve.**

SHAPE IT!

5 **Give three helpful opinions about your partner's English. Use the phrases in the box.**

I liked the way you ...
Why don't you ... ?
You made some mistakes with ...
You used ... That was nice!

SHAPE IT!

5 Make sure that students have at least two minutes of thinking time to organize their ideas and plan how they are going to give each other feedback. Remind students that their feedback should be helpful and positive. Monitor and help, as needed, and take note of sentences you hear that you think might be too direct or impolite. Write these examples on the board, and during feedback, ask the class how to change them.

Unit 7 Are you connected?
Lesson Aim: I can talk about technology.

Warmer
In groups, students have two minutes to brainstorm all the technological devices they can think of. The group with the most wins.

Teacher Support Hub ppxxxiv–xxxv

Start It!
Unit Quiz

1 After eliciting that this a self-driving car, elicit students' opinions about whether they would like to ride in one.

2 Write on the board: *Today, I have used* … and invite students to discuss ways of finishing the sentence in groups. This will prepare them for the language focus on SB p85.

3 Ask students to guess the year when this happened, before playing **video 7.1**.

4 Allow students a minute of thinking time to choose one piece of technology they couldn't live without, and reasons why. Then students discuss in groups.

Video Comprehension Questions

7 Are you connected?

LEARNING OUTCOMES

I can …

- understand texts about technology
- give instructions to explain how to use something
- write an article
- understand how to use the present perfect: affirmative and negative, *will/won't*, *may*, *might*, and infinitives of purpose
- talk about and describe technology and transportation
- use collocations, recognize opinions, use words that describe sounds, and make and use flashcards.

Start It!

1 Look at the photo. What type of car is it? — a driverless car
2 Before you watch, what technology have you used today?
3 Who planned the first programmable computer? Watch and check. — Charles Babbage in 1837
4 Which technology would be most difficult to live without?

Watch video 7.1 | Grammar in Action 7.2 p85 | Grammar in Action 7.3 p87 | Everyday English 7.4 p88 | Globetrotters 7.5 p90

82 ARE YOU CONNECTED? | UNIT 7

Flipped Class
Prepare for **Explore It!** (p83). Students research an interesting fact about technology.

Unit Aims

Skills
I can …
- understand a text about technology p84
- give instructions to explain how to use something p88
- write an article p89
- understand a text about technology in Seoul pp90–91

Language
I can …
- talk about and describe technology p83
- understand how to use the present perfect: affirmative and negative p85
- talk about and describe transportation p86
- understand how to use *will/won't*, *may*, *might*, and infinitives of purpose p87

Learn to Learn
I can …
- use collocations p83
- recognize opinions p86
- use words that describe sounds p91
- make and use flashcards p93

Extra Resources
- Finished? Student's Book p124
- Vocabulary Bank, Student's Book p134
- Workbook pp56–63
- Grammar Reference and Practice, Workbook pp100–101
- Teacher Support Hub, Teacher's Book ppxxxiv–xlvii

Digital Resource Pack
(on Cambridge One)
- *Teacher's Resource Bank* for word lists, differentiated worksheets, *Culture Projects*, and many other extra resources
- *Practice Extra*, *Presentation Plus*, *Test Generator*, and *Digital Collaboration Space*

Lesson Aim: I can talk about and describe technology.

7.01–7.04 **Audioscripts pT140**

1 7.01 ★★★ Student A chooses one word and describes it as much as possible without saying the word, and Student B guesses the word.

Target Vocabulary

app æp
chip tʃɪp
device dɪˈvaɪs
download ˈdaʊnˌloʊd
emoji iˈmoʊ·dʒi
message ˈme·sɪdʒ
screen skrin
social media ˈsoʊ·ʃəl ˈmi·di·ə
software ˈsɔftˌweər
upload ʌpˈloʊd
video chat ˈvɪ·di·oʊ tʃæt

Extra Vocabulary Practice

2 7.02 Fast finishers can make one extra fill-in-the-blank sentence using another word from Exercise 1. Elicit this during feedback.

Vocabulary Bank SB p134

Pronunciation

7.03–7.05 Students can turn to SB p142 for pronunciation practice of the letter *i*.

Learn to Learn

Point out that it isn't only verbs and nouns that go together to make collocations. We can also have adjective–noun and noun–noun collocations.

3 & 4 During feedback, elicit all the possible answers together with extra collocations that students might know (e.g., *send an email*).

Extra Vocabulary Practice

VOCABULARY
Communication and Technology

1 7.01 **Match the words in the box with 1–11 in the picture. Listen, check, and repeat.**

app	4	emoji	11	software	8
chip	5	message	10	upload	1
device	6	screen	3	video chat	7
download	2	social media	9		

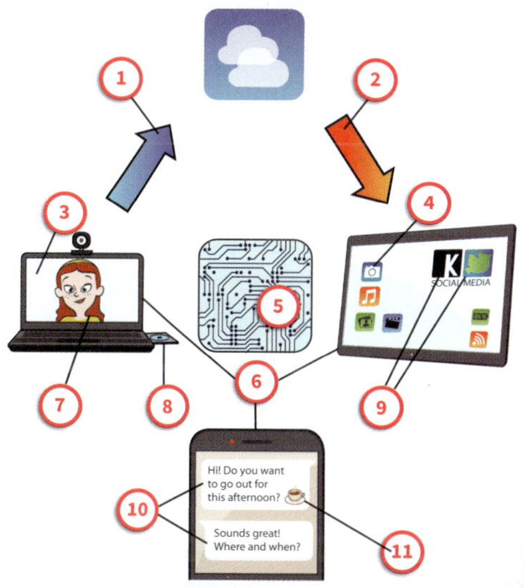

2 7.02 **Complete the sentences with words from Exercise 1. Then listen and check.**

1 My phone fell out of my pocket this morning and the *screen* broke.
2 I can't do a **video chat** with you right now. I don't have a camera on my laptop.
3 Most of my friends **upload** photos to **social media** sites like Instagram.
4 Look at this **app** – it's great for practicing new English words. Why don't you **download** it, too?

Pronunciation p142

LEARN TO LEARN
Collocations

Some words are often used together – we call these collocations. Learn them as phrases.

3 **Complete these collocations with words from Exercise 1. There is sometimes more than one possible answer.**

1 **download** software
2 use a messaging **app**
3 electronic **device**
4 send a **message**
5 computer **chip / screen / software**
6 **upload / download** photos

4 **Take turns starting and finishing the collocations you made in Exercise 3.**

Send a ... *Send a message?*

Use It!

5 **Use words from Exercise 1 to write three sentences about you or people you know.**

1 *My brother has a lot of apps on his phone.*
2 ______
3 ______
4 ______

6 **Compare your sentences.**

I spend about three hours a day in front of a screen.

I only spend about two hours.

Explore It!

Is the sentence *T* (true) or *F* (false)?
People with nomophobia feel scared when they don't have their phone with them. **T**
Find another interesting fact about technology. Then write a question for your partner to answer.

5 & 6 Remind students to personalize new vocabulary, when possible, to help them remember it more easily.

Explore It!

Monitor closely and elicit the most interesting questions for the whole class to answer.

Extend It!

In groups, students write five personal questions using the target vocabulary (e.g., *What app do you use every day?*) and carry out a class survey, walking around and interviewing as many students as possible in five minutes. They then organize and present their findings to the class.

Homework

Workbook p56

Lesson Aim: I can understand a text about technology.

Teacher Support Hub ppxxxvi–xxxvii

1 Elicit that the object in the photo on the left is an early cell phone. Take the opportunity to practice comparatives, eliciting that it was *bigger*, *slower*, *heavier*, etc., than modern smartphones.

2 7.06 Alternatively, students read the introduction and answer the question. Then Student A reads the *Communication*, paragraph, Student B *Entertainment*, and Student C *Sharing*. Students then tell each other what they read in their paragraph.

3 ★ Before students attempt the task, ask them to find and circle all the numbers in the text.

4 EXAM Inform students that, at this level, the answers to the questions won't always be clearly stated in the text but will sometimes have to be inferred from whole paragraphs.

Reading Comprehension Questions

5 7.07 Encourage students to check their spelling of *billion*, *million*, and *thousand*.

6 Allow students a few minutes of thinking time to form opinions and think of reasons. Then ask students to work in pairs or small groups. Elicit contrasting ideas during feedback if possible.

READING

A Magazine Article

1 Look at the photos. What do you think the article is about?

7.06 2 Read the article and check your answer. how technology has changed over the years

Smartphones and Us

Noah Smith investigates how smartphones have changed our lives.

In 1994, the IBM Simon arrived. It was a small computer that made calls! OK, it weighed half a kilogram and it didn't have a camera, but it was technically a smartphone. Today's devices are smaller, faster, and more fun. Nearly 3 billion people own one, and they have transformed our lives.

Communication

Smartphone technology has given us many ways to communicate, but the most popular is messaging. Users of one very well-known app, for example, send 60 billion messages every day!

And then there's video. Once, video calls were science fiction – they still are for my grandparents – but for my generation, video chats have become completely normal.

Entertainment

Gaming apps let us play our favorite games anywhere, anytime on our phones – and that's usually the real reason why my sister hasn't done her homework! She isn't alone. About 200 million people in the U.S.A. play online games, and globally the industry is worth billions of dollars. Personally, I'd rather listen to my favorite bands. Smartphones are great for that, too!

Sharing

Smartphones haven't made us nicer people, but together with social media, they've made it easier for us to have hundreds of "friends." Around 2.5 billion of us have created social media profiles. We post status updates, upload our photos, and share videos. Many of us have shared our whole lives online. Which reminds me – I haven't updated my status today!

3 Read the article again. Write what the numbers refer to.

1 half a kilogram the weight of the IBM Simon
2 nearly 3 billion people who own smartphones
3 60 billion messages sent every day
4 about 200 million people who play online games
5 2.5 billion people with social media profiles

4 EXAM Circle the correct answers.

1 What couldn't computers do before 1994?
(A) make calls B send emails C save documents

2 What was unusual about the IBM Simon compared to modern devices?
A It was smaller and faster.
B It had an excellent camera.
(C) It weighed half a kilogram.

3 What is the most popular form of smartphone communication?
A phone calls (B) messages C video chats

4 What does Noah's sister enjoy doing?
(A) playing games B sharing photos
C listening to music

7.07 5 Complete the words for the numbers. Then listen and check.

1 1,000,000,000,000 = one trillion
2 1,000,000,000 = one billion
3 1,000,000 = one million
4 1,000 = one thousand
5 100 = one hundred

Voice It!

6 Do you agree with the statements below? Discuss with your partner, using the phrases in the box.

I strongly agree. I agree. I'm not sure. I disagree. I strongly disagree.

1 People use their smartphones too much.
2 Children under ten shouldn't have a smartphone.
3 There should be no smartphones in schools.
4 I couldn't live without a smartphone.

Finished? p124 Ex. 1

Class Challenge

Ray Tomlinson sent the first email in history in 1971. The email read "Can you read this?" / "Hello." / "**qwertyuiop**."

Flipped Class

Ask students to watch **video 7.2** and do **Video Worksheet 7.2** in the *Teacher's Resource Bank* in preparation for the next lesson.

Finished?

Students turn to p124 and do Exercise 1.

Extend It!

In groups, students choose a technological device (e.g., a TV, tablet, or smart watch). Then they collaborate to think of three ways this device is useful to us and prepare to tell the class about it.

Homework

Workbook p57

Lesson Aim: I can understand how to use the present perfect: affirmative and negative.

Warmer

▶ Play **video 7.2**, if it was not assigned for homework, and elicit that Sophia has learned how to create a vlog, how to use a camera, how to do sound and lighting, and how to edit. The vlog has given her many friends.

7.08 Audioscript pT140

1 Elicit that the present perfect focuses on the present results of a past action, not the details of an event in the past. For example, in 1, the focus is on the fact that our lives are different now, not on when or how the transformation happened.

2 Ask students to think of how other technological devices have changed over the years, eliciting sentences with the present perfect.

3 7.08 Ask students to practice the conversation in pairs, using contractions. Monitor closely and ask for a volunteer pair to perform it for the class.

Extra Grammar Practice

4 Remind students that they can check the list of irregular verbs on SB p143 to find the past participles.

5 & 6 Encourage students to extend the activity using other activities (not only the ones in the box).

GRAMMAR IN ACTION

Present Perfect: Affirmative and Negative

Watch video 7.2
Name two things Sophia has learned.
What's the best thing that the vlog has given her?

	I/You/We/They	He/She/It
+	Smartphones [1] have **transformed** our lives.	Technology [3] has **given** us many ways to communicate.
–	Smartphones [2] haven't **made** us nicer people.	My sister [4] hasn't **done** her homework.

1 Complete the examples in the chart above with the correct form of *have* (*not*). Use the article on page 84 to help you.

2 Complete the sentences with the present perfect form of the verbs in parentheses.

1 Smartphones have changed our lives. (change)
2 They have become easier to carry. (become)
3 Smartphone technology has become more interesting. (become)
4 Smartphones have made it possible to communicate with more people. (make)
5 Noah hasn't updated his online status. (not update)

7.08 **3** Complete the conversation with the present perfect form of the verbs. Then listen and check.

ask find leave look ~~lose~~
not charge not hear not see put

JACK What's wrong, Kim?
KIM I [1] 've lost my phone. Do you know where it is?
JACK No, I don't. I [2] haven't heard it ring, either. Maybe it's in your coat pocket.
KIM I [3] 've looked in all my pockets. It's not there.
JACK Maybe you [4] 've left it in Mom's car.
KIM No, I don't think so. I used it this afternoon, but I can't remember where I left it.
JACK Maybe Mom [5] 's / has put it somewhere.
KIM No, I [6] 've asked her and she says she [7] hasn't seen it. Jack, can you call me?
JACK I think so. I [8] haven't charged my phone, but I think it has enough power left. Hang on … OK, I'm calling you …
KIM Here, look! I [9] 've found it. It was in my bag all the time.

4 Answer the questions with present perfect sentences. Use the words in the boxes.

break buy forget

password screen tablets

1 Why can't Orla use her laptop?
She's forgotten her password.
2 Why are Elena and Ruby so happy?
They've bought new tablets.
3 Why is Andrey upset?
He's broken the screen.

Use It!

5 Write three sentences about what you have or haven't done today. Use the ideas in the box.

chat / on social media check / my emails
upload / a photo watch / TV

1 I've watched TV.
2 ______
3 ______
4 ______

6 Tell your partner about the things you've done.

I haven't uploaded a photo, but I've played my favorite computer game.

Finished? p124 Ex. 2

Grammar Game

Write *Today Billy is feeling … because …* on the board, and then fill the first blank with a feeling (e.g., *angry*). Teams have two minutes to write down as many reasons as possible (e.g., *His mother has asked him to stop playing video games.*). The team with the most reasons wins. Repeat with other vocabulary.

Finished?

Students turn to p124 and do Exercise 2.

Homework

Workbook p58

Lesson Aim: I can talk about and describe transportation.

Warmer

Ask: *What is the longest trip you have ever been on?* Students discuss the question in pairs. Monitor closely to gauge what the students already know of the target vocabulary of the lesson.

Teacher Support Hub ppxxxviii–xxxix

7.09–7.10 Audioscripts ppT140–141

1 7.09 After feedback, students test each other. Student A says a noun, and Student B says the corresponding verb.

Target Vocabulary

catch / take kætʃ / teɪk
get into get ˈɪn·tu
get off get ɔf
get on get ɑn
get out of get aʊt əv
go by goʊ baɪ
go on goʊ ɑn

Get It Right!

Encourage students to create a spidergram in their notebooks using the target language and ask two volunteers to draw their diagrams on the board.

Extra Vocabulary Practice

2 ★★★ Fast finishers can write an extra fill-in-the-blank sentence for the whole class.

3 Monitor closely and collect mistakes to be corrected on the board.

4 & 5 7.10 Tell students that a *hyperloop* is a proposed idea for a network of underground tunnels where cars or pods can travel at very high speeds across huge distances, avoiding traffic.

Vocabulary Bank SB p134

VOCABULARY AND LISTENING

Getting Around

7.09 **1** Complete the phrases with the verbs in the box. Listen, check, and repeat.

catch/take get into get off get on
get out of go by ~~go on~~

1 *go on* foot
2 get on a train
3 go by tram

4 catch / take a plane
5 get out of a car
6 take / get into a taxi
7 get off a bus

Get It Right!

We use **take** and **catch** with planes and with public transportation. But we can't say ~~*catch a taxi*~~.

We **get on** and **off** public transportation or a bike. But we **get into** and **out of** a car.

We use **go by** with all transportation. But we say **go on foot**, not ~~*go by foot*~~.

2 Complete the sentences with verbs from Exercise 1.

1 I'm *getting off* this bus at the next stop.
2 My dad has taken a taxi to the airport.
3 Yesterday we went to the island by ferry.
4 I bought my ticket from the driver when I got on the bus.
5 Don't forget to turn off the lights before you get out of the car.

Use It!

3 Tell your partner about two different ways to get to these places from your home.

your school a town in your country New York

To get to school, I can go on foot to the bus stop and then catch a bus. Or I can go by bike.

A Radio Interview

4 Look at the forms of transportation in Exercise 5. Will we use them in the future? Discuss with a partner.

7.10 **5** Listen to the radio interview. Put the forms of transportation in the order you hear them (1–3).

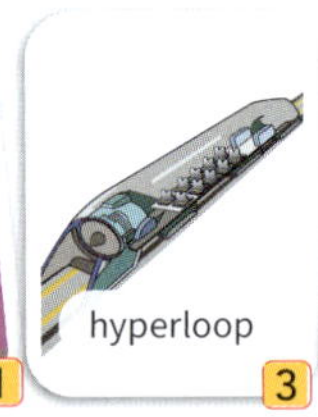

LEARN TO LEARN

Recognizing Opinions

It's important to understand the difference between facts and opinions. When people give an opinion, they often begin with phrases like these:

In my view …   In my opinion …   I (don't) think …

7.10 **6** Listen again. Which of these opinions does the professor have?

1 Flying cars aren't the answer to traffic jams. ✓
2 There will be a lot of flying cars soon. ☐
3 People won't use jetpacks to get to work. ✓
4 The hyperloop is just science fiction. ☐
5 The hyperloop will change our lives. ✓

Learn to Learn

Understanding the difference between facts and opinions is an important critical-thinking skill that enables students to make sense of what they hear or read in their everyday lives, on TV and in the news, for example.

6 7.10 In pairs, students discuss the statements before listening again. Challenge stronger students to write down phrases that indicate that the speakers are expressing an opinion (e.g., *I think*).

Extend It!

In groups, students discuss their opinions about the predictions in Exercise 6, using the phrases given to express opinions.

Flipped Class

Ask students to watch **video 7.3** and do **Video Worksheet 7.3** in the *Teacher's Resource Bank* in preparation for the next lesson.

Homework

Workbook p59

Lesson Aim: I can understand how to use *will/won't*, *may*, *might*, and infinitives of purpose.

Warmer

▶ Play **video 7.3** if it was not assigned for homework. Elicit that James won't be an actor. He'll learn about special effects and may interview people on the street.

7.11 Audioscript pT141

1 Point out that *may* and *might* have the same meaning, and we can use either when we are not sure.

2 ★ Before students attempt the task, consolidate the meaning of the verbs using facial expressions and gestures. Say *will* with a serious face and a gesture that means certainty in the students' culture. Then say *might* with an unsure face and a culturally appropriate gesture, such as a shrug.

Extra Grammar Practice

3 7.11 After feedback, play the audio again and ask students to use facial expressions and gestures when they hear *will/won't* and *might*.

4 During feedback, encourage students to justify their answers, and elicit contrasting ideas if possible.

5 & 6 Make sure students understand that we use *to* + a reason when we want to explain why something is happening.

7 Encourage students to make the sentences true for them and as memorable as possible.

GRAMMAR IN ACTION
Will/Won't, May, and Might

Watch video 7.3
What won't James be in ten years' time? How will he make the vlog look better?

	Certain Predictions	Uncertain Predictions
+	It [1] will really **change** our lives.	We **may have** jetpacks one day just for fun. We **might see** hyperloops between big cities.
-	We [2] won't **see** a lot of flying cars.	They [3] may **not be** useful for getting to work. We **might not need** to wait much longer.

1 Complete the examples in the chart above.

2 Are these predictions *C* (certain) or *U* (uncertain)?

1. Cars might be less noisy. U
2. Every family will have a flying car. C
3. Fifty years from now, children may go to school by jetpack. U
4. Jetpacks won't be very useful for most people. C
5. Everyone will travel by hyperloop. C
6. Some people might not want to travel on a hyperloop. U

3 7.11 Listen to Danielle talking about transportation in the future. Which of the predictions in Exercise 2 does she make?

1, 2, 4, 6

Use It!

4 Complete the sentences about the future with *will/won't* or *may/might* (*not*). Then compare your opinions in pairs.

1. People ________ have their own airplanes.
2. People ________ go to work by bike.
3. We ________ need smartphones.
4. We ________ use paper.
5. There ________ be books and magazines.

Infinitives of Purpose

***To* + Infinitive**

A lot of us catch a bus [1] to go (go) to work.

[2] To solve (solve) the problem, we should invent flying cars.

It takes a lot of energy [3] to lift (lift) a person off the ground.

5 Complete the examples in the chart above with the correct form of the words in parentheses.

6 Match 1–5 with a–e.

1. Can I borrow your phone
2. Is there a printer
3. You can use my laptop
4. Why don't we stop
5. To get there sooner,

a. to have lunch?
b. to check your emails.
c. to make a call?
d. we decided to fly.
e. to print these photos?

Use It!

7 Complete the sentences with your own ideas and tell your partner.

1. I went to ________ to ________
2. I bought a ________ to ________
3. I took a ________ to ________

I went to Chicago to visit my cousin last summer.

Finished? p124 Ex. 3

Grammar Game

Write on the board: *Today, I bought a newspaper to …* Students, in teams, have three minutes to brainstorm all the possible uses of a newspaper (e.g., *read it, make a paper plane, cover the floor while I paint my room*). Elicit the students' ideas using *to* + infinitive. The class votes for the most creative uses of the newspaper.

Finished?

Students turn to p124 and do Exercise 3.

Homework

Workbook p60

Lesson Aim: I can give instructions to explain how to use something.

Warmer

In groups, students discuss their experiences of trying to explain to their older relatives how to use technological devices. This might generate some funny stories. Monitor and elicit these from the whole class.

Teacher Support Hub ppxl–xli

7.12 Audioscript pT141

1 7.12 ★★★ Students listen and answer the question with their books closed.

2 7.12 Elicit that these phrases are used to soften the instructions. In some languages, including English, imperatives can be quite strong and direct, so we can use phrases like these instead.

3 Play **video 7.4** and drill the students' pronunciation.

4 If appropriate, encourage students to think of how these phrases translate into their own language.

Everyday English Practice

5 Brainstorm different types of technology, write them on the board, and invite students to choose one of them to write about. They should explain this to someone who has never used the technology before.

6 If possible, encourage students to have the type of technology with them, and demonstrate using it. Student A can give instructions while Student B follows the instructions.

SPEAKING

Giving Instructions

7.12 **1 Listen to the conversation. What is Tom explaining to his dad?**

a How to take a photo

(b) How to record a video

TOM So, Dad, before [1] you start, switch the camera to video mode. Have you done that?
DAD Like this?
TOM Yes, that's right. It needs to be in video mode to record a video. Now, look at this little screen.
DAD I can't see anything.
TOM Ah. Remember [2] not to put your hand in front of the camera!
DAD Is this better?
TOM Not quite. Look, you need to keep your fingers here. That's it. Now, do you see this button?
DAD This one?
TOM No, not that one. This one here. It's [3] really important that it's turned on if you want to record sound. Oh, and [4] make sure that the light is red. That means you're recording. Got it?
DAD Yes, I think so. Thanks, Tom!

7.12 **2 Complete the conversation with the phrases from the *Useful Language* box. Then listen and check.**

Useful Language

Before you start, …
It's really important that …
Make sure that …
Remember (not) to …

3 Look at the *Everyday English* box. Find and underline the phrases in the conversation.

Watch video 7.4 Everyday English

Got it? Like this?
Not quite. That's it.

4 Match the phrases in the *Everyday English* box with their meanings.

1 That's right. That's it.
2 Do you understand? Got it?
3 This way? Like this?
4 Not exactly. Not quite.

PLAN

5 Work in pairs. Plan some instructions for using an electronic device. Write your ideas below.

What you are teaching people to do: ______

The steps that are needed to use the device:

1 ______
2 ______
3 ______
4 ______

SPEAK

6 Work in pairs. Practice a conversation giving instructions for your device. Remember to use infinitives of purpose, vocabulary from this unit, and phrases from the *Useful Language* and *Everyday English* boxes.

CHECK

7 Work with another pair. Listen to their conversation and complete the notes.

What are the instructions for? ______

Are the instructions clear? ______

7 Pairs listen to each other's instructions, and then give each other feedback (e.g., *Were the instructions clear? Could you use the technology now? How can you make the instructions better?*).

Flipped Class

In preparation for the next lesson, ask students to look around their homes and take notes on what technology they use (e.g., for cooking, cleaning, and entertainment).

Lesson Aim: I can write an article.

Warmer
In groups, students compare the technology they use in their homes.

Teacher Support Hub ppxlii–xliii

1 Elicit that the students are using tablets and an electronic whiteboard in their classroom. If your school does not use much technology, ask students to brainstorm technology they'd like to see in the classroom.

2 Set a strict time limit to encourage skimming.

3 ★★★ After feedback, allow students a few minutes, in pairs, to discuss whether they think robots will ever replace teachers and why.

4 Elicit what is different about *such as*: it cannot be used at the beginning of a sentence like all the other phrases.

Useful Language Practice

5 Ask the class what times in the past and future they would like to write about (e.g., 30 years ago, 30 years in the future). Make sure that the whole class is focusing on the same time periods.

6 You may want students to use three different color pens, as in the text in Exercise 2, to focus their attention on text structure and tense usage. The green paragraph, for stronger students, could also feature the present perfect.

WRITING
An Article

1 What are the students in the photo doing? What technology do you use at school?

2 Read the article. Underline the modern technology words it mentions.

School Technology

1 Teaching has changed a lot. For instance, in the past, teachers used blackboards, and children wrote everything with pen and paper. What's more, the only technology in classrooms was a TV or perhaps a cassette player.

2 Today, in contrast, teachers use a lot of technology. For example, most classrooms have Wi-Fi. In addition, teachers use interactive whiteboards, and children use tablets to do exercises or play games. With technology such as video chat, classes can work with students in another country. This makes learning easier and more fun.

3 Some people think that robots might teach students one day. However, I don't think that will happen. Teachers help us learn things, but they take care of us, too. Robots can't do that. The technology may change over time, but the best teachers will always be real people.

3 Read the article again. Are the sentences *T* (true) or *F* (false)?

1 In the past, there was a lot of technology in the classroom. F
2 It's normal now for classrooms to be connected to the Internet. T
3 Today, students chat with their classmates using video chat. F
4 Robots will replace teachers. F

Useful Language

Giving examples:
For instance, For example, such as

Adding more information:
In addition, What's more,

4 Read the phrases in the *Useful Language* box. Then circle the correct words.

1 Tablets are often cheaper than laptops. *What's more,* / *For example,* they're easier to carry.
2 The first cell phones could only make calls. *In addition,* / *For instance,* they were huge.
3 In the future, schools might use technology *such as* / *what's more* 3-D printing.

PLAN

5 Plan an article about technology in the home. Think about cooking, cleaning, and entertainment. Take notes for three paragraphs.

1 Technology at home in the past: ____________
2 Technology at home today: ____________
3 Predictions for the future: ____________

WRITE

6 Write your article. Remember to include three paragraphs, past and present tenses, predictions with *will*/*won't* and *may*/*might* (*not*), and phrases from the *Useful Language* box.

CHECK

7 Do you ...
- describe technology in the past?
- describe technology in the present?
- make certain and uncertain predictions for the future?

Finished? p124 Ex. 4

7 After students have checked their own work, they give it to another student to read and comment on. Ask them to say what predictions they agree and disagree with, and why.

Finished?
Students turn to p124 and do Exercise 4.

Flipped Class
In preparation for **Explore It!** (p91), students research an interesting fact about South Korea.

Homework
Workbook p61

Lesson Aim: I can understand a text about technology in Seoul.

Background information

Help students find South Korea, an Asian country on a peninsula between China and Japan, on a map. South Korea is known for technology, shopping, pop music, the sport of taekwondo, and a dish called *kimchi*.

Warmer

In groups, students discuss types of voice-activated technology, whether they use it, and why they like it or dislike it.

▶ Play **video 7.5** and ask students to answer the questions. Robots do tasks such as building cars, answering questions, carrying luggage, and doing chores, and they also do dangerous jobs. Elict that an *android* is a type of robot that looks and behaves just like a person. Then ask the students, in pairs, to discuss which of the robot functions in the video they think is most important in society and why.

Video Comprehension Questions

AROUND THE WORLD

READING
An Article

1 Look at the photos on page 91. Where do you think this is? What is happening in each photo?

2 (7.13) Read the article. Match photos a–e with paragraphs 1–5.

3 Answer the questions.

1. Where does Seo-yun keep her smartphone at night? *Next to her bed.*
2. What are her two ways of getting to school? going on foot, taking the bus
3. How does Seo-yun pay for her bus journey? with her smartphone
4. What are the other passengers doing on the bus? They're using their smartphones and tablets.

Globetrotters
Watch video 7.5
Hello, Robots!

- What things do you use robots for?
- What is an android?
- What do you think the future of robots will be?

Voice It!

4 Discuss the questions.

1. How does Seo-yun's family use technology to connect with the world?
2. How does technology improve human connection?
3. What are its negative effects?

One Morning in the High-Tech Capital of the World

1 c 6:30 a.m.

An alarm buzzes and Seo-yun's phone wakes her up for another day in Seoul, the world's "tech capital." In the bathroom, she tells the voice-activated shower to start. Water gushes from the shower, but it's too cold. "Warmer, please!" Seo-yun calls out.

2 a 7:20 a.m.

In the kitchen, Dad makes breakfast. While they wait, Seo-yun and her sister, Ji-woo, watch cartoons on the "family hub" – a huge tablet screen built into the fridge door. They hear a "ping" from Seo-yun's phone – one of her friends has sent a message. Will she go to school on foot or take the bus? Seo-yun asks the family's voice-activated device to check for rain while she checks her travel app to see what the traffic is like.

3 e 8:00 a.m.

Seo-yun has decided to take the bus. There's a beep as she swipes her phone over a sensor when she gets on, and then she takes a seat. On the way, she reads an online comic, and she puts in earphones to enjoy all the bangs, crashes, and other sound effects without disturbing other passengers. She doesn't need to worry, though. They're all glued to their screens, too!

4 d 8:10 a.m.

Seo-yun's mom has taken the KTX bullet train to meet colleagues in Busan. The train roars between the two cities at nearly 300 kph. During the journey, she has a video chat with her boss. The journey may soon be much quicker. The government wants to build a new kind of train line called a hyperloop, with trains that zoom along at 1,000 kph.

5 b 8:20 a.m.

Ji-woo has arrived at school, and the teacher's robot helper, iRobi, comes to Ji-woo with a whir of electric wheels. iRobi marks her attendance and uses face recognition to check her mood. "Excited?" asks iRobi. Of course. Today Ji-woo might have a gymnastics class with Genibo, the school's robot dog. That's education – Korean style!

1 Ask students, in pairs, to guess how technology fits into each photo (e.g., *Maybe a robot prepared the children's food.*).

2 (7.13) Set a strict time limit to encourage faster skimming. During feedback, elicit the key words in the texts that indicate the photo they correspond to.
1. *wakes up / Seoul*
2. *breakfast / sister*
3. *bus / glued to their screens*
4. *train*
5. *school / robot helper*

3 Have students underline key words in the questions and use them to find the information in the text.

Reading Comprehension Questions

4 Before students discuss the questions, write *connection* on the board and elicit the technology connections that they use regularly (e.g., *phone, Internet, text messaging*).

Teacher Support Hub pxlv

Class Challenge

The word *robot* means "something that has to work" and comes from the Russian / Chinese / **Czech** language.

Learn to Learn

Understanding onomatopoeic words (i.e., words that sound like the sound they refer to) will help to increase students' comprehension of texts, especially fiction, so that they may find it easier to read for pleasure.

5 Point out to students that the words sound like the sounds they refer to. Ask: *Are there any words like this in your language?*

6 Encourage students to practice saying the words out loud to guess their meaning.

Students can collaborate digitally through *Collaboration Plus*, where you can assign, track, and assess their work. Students can also share and showcase their work and comment on each other's projects.

Explore It!

Alternatively, ask students to work in groups to make a short "South Korea quiz." The groups then swap questions or read the questions aloud for the whole class.

Culture Project

See Project Book p46 for further information and activities.

LEARN TO LEARN

Words that Describe Sounds

There are many English words that sound similar to the sounds they describe.

5 Find words in the article for these sounds.

1. three sounds that a smartphone makes (paras 1, 2, and 3) *buzzes* ping beep
2. the sound of water coming out fast (para. 1) gushes
3. two loud sounds when one thing hits another (para. 3) bangs crashes
4. the sound of a machine working quietly (para. 5) whir

6 Work in pairs. Say the words in the box and discuss what sounds you think they describe. Then use a dictionary to check.

crack	hiccup	hiss	meow	pop	splash	woof

a

Explore It!

Guess the correct answer.

South Korea has the world's fastest …

a internet speeds. b trains. c ferries.

Find another interesting fact about South Korea. Then write a question for your partner to answer.

b

c

d

e

SHAPE IT!

CULTURE PROJECT

A 3-D Room Plan

A room plan shows the design of a room and the furniture inside it. Make a plan of a room with modern technology.

Teacher's Resource Bank

Lesson Aim: I can review what I have learned and reflect on my progress.

The aim of this page is for students to review the grammar and vocabulary from the unit. You can either do it in class, as a timed progress test, or assign it for homework.

Vocabulary

1 In groups, students brainstorm vocabulary related to technology and communication before completing the exercise. Write appropriate words on the board to help them.

2 ★★★ Alternatively, ask students to close their books. Read each sentence aloud to the class, replacing the options with a *Beep!* The first team to shout *Buzz!* and give the correct answer wins a point.

Grammar in Action

3 ★ Before students attempt the task, review with them the form of the present perfect (*have/has* + past participle) and the past participle of the verbs in parentheses if needed.

4 Challenge fast finishers to prepare an extra sentence with three options. Elicit these after feedback for the whole class to complete.

Unit Quiz Review

7 REVIEW

VOCABULARY

1 Complete the crossword.

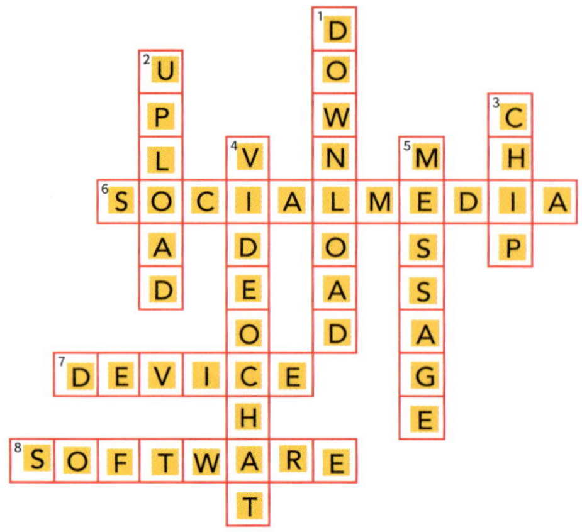

Across

6 *Facebook* and *Instagram* are examples of this.
7 A general word for an electronic gadget.
8 All the programs that tell a computer what to do.

Down

1 Take a file, photo, video, etc. from the Internet and put it onto your device.
2 Put a file from your device onto the Internet.
3 The "brain" inside your computer or phone.
4 This is when you see and talk to someone using your computer or phone.
5 A short text that you send to someone.

2 Circle the correct words.

1 Eva (caught) / *went by* the bus outside the bank.
2 Jo traveled from Boston to New York *on* / (*by*) train.
3 Nina went to the library *by* / (*on*) foot.
4 Zehra got (*off*) / *out* the tram at the last stop.
5 Luke (*took*) / *caught* a taxi from home and got (*out*) / *off* at the airport.

GRAMMAR IN ACTION

3 Complete the sentences with the present perfect form of the verbs in parentheses.

1 How annoying! My phone is on silent and I just realized that I **'ve missed** five calls. (miss)
2 You don't need to call a taxi. I **'ve booked** one with this app. (book)
3 I don't know what Dina's brother looks like. She **hasn't shared** any photos of him. (not share)
4 I **haven't downloaded** their new album. I heard it isn't very good. (not download)

4 Circle the correct answers.

1 The bus … leave at 10:02 exactly. It's never late.
a may (b) will c won't
2 They … be able to do it, but they're trying.
a can't b might (c) may not
3 Hamza bought some tools … his bike.
a fix (b) to fix c for fix
4 We don't have enough ink … the photos.
(a) to print b for to print c for print

Self-Assessment

I can talk about communication and technology.
I can talk about getting around.
I can use the present perfect to make affirmative and negative sentences and questions.
I can use *will/won't*, *may*, and *might* to make predictions.
I can use *to* + infinitive to talk about purpose.

Review the Unit Theme

Remind students of the unit title: *Are you connected?* Put students into pairs. Have them discuss the following questions: *How does technology help us communicate? What are the advantages and disadvantages of modern technology? How do forms of transportation connect us?* Share answers as a class.

Teacher Support Hub pxlvii

Self-Assessment

Encourage students to ask you for extra homework for each language area they weren't completely happy with.

Homework

Workbook pp62–63

Lesson Aim: I can make and use flashcards.

One drawback of flashcards is that they can be more difficult to store and therefore can be lost. If appropriate, you may want to adapt this page to train students to use online flashcard apps, which have the advantage of being easily accessible, especially if students have smartphones.

Warmer

Start by showing the students a flashcard (or, if appropriate, a flashcard app), and elicit how the students feel about using them instead of other ways of recording vocabulary.

1 Ask students, in pairs, to cover the green cards and guess what they might say before matching the cards' fronts and backs.

2 Allow students time to do this individually and then check in pairs.

3 If the students are using flashcard software, introduce them to extra features and options, such as adding pictures, translations, automatic definitions, and so on.

SHAPE IT!

4 As students guess the information on each other's cards, reassure them that a good card will be memorable but doesn't necessarily need to have an obvious answer for everyone. Some guessing is to be expected, as in the example.

5 During feedback, elicit students' feelings about using flashcards, and point out that different learners will prefer different ways of recording vocabulary.

LEARN TO LEARN

LEARN TO ... MAKE AND USE FLASHCARDS

You can use flashcards to learn collocations and phrases with prepositions.

1 Match the front and back of the flashcards.

1 use a messaging ______
2 get into / ______ a car
3 ______ addition
4 ______ / download photos
5 ______ instance

a upload
b app
c for
d get out of
e in

2 Match the flashcards in Exercise 1 with the different types of flashcard a–c below.

a a phrase with the preposition missing **3** **5**
b a collocation with one word missing **1**
c opposite collocations with one of them missing **2** **4**

3 Choose five collocations or phrases with prepositions from Unit 7. Use them to make the different types of flashcards in Exercise 2.

SHAPE IT!

4 Show the front of your flashcards from Exercise 3 to your partner. Can they guess what is on the back of each flashcard?

______ device

Mobile ... Voice-activated ...

No, it begins with the letter "e."

Electronic device?

Yes! That's right!

5 Discuss the questions with your partner.

Which are ...

1 easier to make: flashcards with phrases with prepositions or flashcards with collocations?
2 easier to remember with flashcards: phrases with prepositions or collocations?

Warmer

In groups, students look at the photo and brainstorm adjectives that might describe how the girl is feeling.

Teacher Support Hub ppxxxiv–xxxv

Start It!

Unit Quiz

1 & 2 Use the photo to elicit the meaning of *achievement* /əˈtʃiv·mənt/. Elicit that it's something very good and difficult that someone has succeeded in doing.

3 Brainstorm why fire has changed human society with the whole class before playing **video 8.1**.

4 Give students a minute of thinking time, and then allow group discussions before eliciting ideas with the whole class.

Video Comprehension Questions

Flipped Class

Prepare for **Explore It!** (p95). Students research an interesting fact about an amazing achievement.

8 What is success?

LEARNING OUTCOMES

I can ...

- understand comments on a web page and a talk about a young inventor
- answer questions in a job interview
- write a competition entry
- understand how to use present perfect for experience, and reflexive and indefinite pronouns
- talk about exceptional jobs and qualities, and achievements
- form people words take notes, and make a vocabulary plan
- manage my time and create a timeline

Start It!

1 Look at the photo. What did the girl and her mother do? — They won medals in a race / sports event.
2 Before you watch, think of three great human achievements.
3 Why do people say fire is a great human achievement? Watch and check. — Fire changed how people live.
4 Think of three personal achievements for you.

Watch video 8.1 | Grammar in Action 8.2 p97 | Grammar in Action 8.3 p99 | Everyday English 8.4 p100

94 WHAT IS SUCCESS? | UNIT 8

Unit Aims

Skills

I can ...

- understand online comments p96
- answer questions in a job interview p100
- write a competition entry p101
- create a timeline pp102–103

Language

I can ...

- talk about exceptional jobs and qualities p95
- understand how to use the present perfect for experience p97
- use phrasal verbs to talk about achievement p98
- understand how to use reflexive and indefinite pronouns p99

Learn to Learn

I can ...

- form people words p95
- take notes p98
- make a vocabulary study plan p105

Extra Resources

- Finished? Student's Book p125
- Vocabulary Bank, Student's Book p135
- Workbook pp64–71
- Grammar Reference and Practice, Workbook pp102–103
- Teacher Support Hub, Teacher's Book ppxxxiv–xlvii

Digital Resource Pack

(on Cambridge One)

- *Teacher's Resource Bank* for word lists, differentiated worksheets, *Culture Projects*, and many other extra resources
- *Practice Extra, Presentation Plus, Test Generator,* and *Digital Collaboration Space*

8.01–8.02 Audioscripts ppT141–142

1 8.01 ★★★ Alternatively, Student A chooses a job from the box and mimes it. The first student to guess the word wins a point and mimes the next one.

Target Vocabulary

athlete ˈæθ·lit
businessman/ businesswoman ˈbɪz·nɪs·mæn / ˈbɪz·nɪs·wʊm·ən
composer kəmˈpoʊ·zər
engineer en·dʒəˈnɪər
inventor ɪnˈven·t̬ər
mathematician ˌmæθ·məˈtɪ·ʃən
scientist ˈsaɪ·ən·tɪst
writer ˈraɪ·t̬ər

Extra Vocabulary Practice

2 8.02 ★ Before the activity, write the target vocabulary on the board. In small groups, students discuss the meaning of the words they know. For any words they don't know, get different students to look them up in a dictionary and teach them to the group.

Vocabulary Bank SB p135

Learn to Learn

Point out that there is no difference in pronunciation between *-er* and *-or*, which are pronounced as /ər/. You could also mention that *-person* can also be used with some jobs when we don't want to say that it's a man or a woman (e.g., *businessperson*).

VOCABULARY
Exceptional Jobs and Qualities

1 8.01 **Match the jobs with the photos. Listen, check, and repeat.**

athlete	5	inventor	8
businessman/ businesswoman	7	mathematician	6
composer	3	scientist	2
engineer	1	writer	4

2 8.02 **Circle the correct words. Then listen and check.**

1. Athletes like runners and swimmers have incredible *creativity* / *strength*.
2. The scientist Albert Einstein was famous for his great *intelligence* / *strength*.
3. At just four years old, Mozart showed a lot of *skill* / *determination* as a composer.
4. J. K. Rowling's *creativity* / *intelligence* as a writer made her famous around the world.
5. Ada Lovelace was an English mathematician. Her *talent* / *creativity* for math helped to make the modern computer possible.
6. The inventor Thomas Edison worked with a lot of *determination* / *talent* over many years to make his light bulb work.

LEARN TO LEARN
Word Formation: People Words

To form nouns to describe people, we often add extra letters to a verb or a noun. We sometimes need to change other letters.

3 Complete the chart with words from Exercise 1.

Verb / Noun	Suffix	People Word
invent	-or	1 inventor
compose write	-er	2 composer 3 writer
mathematics	-ian	4 mathematician
science	-ist	5 scientist
business	-man -woman	6 businessman 7 businesswoman

4 Test your partner. Ask who ...?

Who writes music? *A composer.*

Use It!

5 Choose three jobs from Exercise 1. Take notes about the special qualities the jobs need.

1 ______
2 ______
3 ______

6 Discuss your ideas.

I think a writer needs a lot of talent and creativity.

Explore It!

Guess the correct answer.

How old was Louis Braille when he invented his famous alphabet for the blind?

a 10 b 15 c 25

Find another interesting fact about an amazing achievement. Then write a question for your partner to answer.

UNIT 8 | WHAT IS SUCCESS? 95

3 & 4 ★★★ Students test each other's spelling in pairs. Student A asks a question (e.g., *Who writes music?*). Student B writes down the answer, and Student A checks the spelling.

Famous People Job Quiz

5 & 6 Remind students to think of reasons why a job needs particular qualities. Encourage them to discuss each other's ideas, saying if they agree or disagree.

Explore It!

After feedback, ask students, in groups, to discuss the achievements they talked about and choose the most amazing one, justifying their answer during feedback.

Homework

Workbook p64

Lesson Aim: I can understand online comments.

Warmer

In groups, students discuss the social media that they use and whether they often write or respond to comments.

Teacher Support Hub ppxlii–xliii

1 Encourage students to use the qualities from SB p95 when they discuss the questions.

2 8.03 To encourage faster reading, give students two minutes to read the text.

3 EXAM Encourage students to tell each other, in pairs, where they found the information.

Reordering Sentences

4 After feedback, students test each other in pairs. Student A says an expression from one of the columns, and Student B says *do* or *make*.

5 Allow some thinking time for students to form an opinion. Encourage them to research teenagers' achievements online if possible.

Extend It!

Ask students to copy the chart from Exercise 4 in their notebooks. Brainstorm other expressions with *do* (e.g., *your homework*) and *make* (e.g., *a mistake*) and get students to add these to the chart.

Class Challenge

Blaise Pascal was <u>16</u> / 22 / 35 when he invented his first calculator.

Finished?

Students turn to p125 and do Exercise 1.

READING
Online Comments

1 Look at the photos and discuss the questions.
1 Are the people successful?
2 What do you need to be successful in these areas?

8.03 2 Read the online comments. In which area is each person successful? 1 science 2 business 3 music

Teenagers Taking the World by Storm

Yesterday's article about teenagers' achievements has <u>made a big impression</u>. We've never had so many comments!

1 Krtin Nithiyanandam is only 17, but the intelligence and creativity of this British teen are amazing. He hasn't been to college, but he's <u>done laboratory research</u> into Alzheimer's disease and is the inventor of a new test for it. He's worked with Cambridge University scientists and has won awards. Genius!
smartypants 11 m ago

2 Have you ever heard of Mikaila Ulmer? This Texas kid has won one of the U.S.A.'s most famous game shows, has <u>made a fortune</u>, and has even met the president. She started a lemonade business and entered a TV competition for entrepreneurs. She won and <u>made a deal</u> worth millions of dollars. I haven't tried her lemonade, but it's called BeeSweet. Mikaila gives money to charities that protect bees, and she's even written a book. For a 13-year-old businesswoman, she's <u>doing pretty well</u>!
Marion_T 56 m ago

3 We've heard about some incredible prodigies, but how about Alma Deutscher? She's an incredible 12-year-old musician from England. Home-schooled, Alma started playing the piano at two and showed talent even then. She's given concerts all over the world, and she's also a composer. She's composed pieces for whole orchestras and has even written an opera. I'm <u>doing my best</u> to learn the violin, so when I saw Alma on television, I was amazed. With all that skill, I wonder … has she ever played a wrong note? I doubt it!
Bowfrog 1h 10 m ago

3 EXAM Read the comments again. Then mark (✓) the correct column.

Who …	Krtin	Mikaila	Alma
1 is only 12 years old?			✓
2 is 17 years old?	✓		
3 invented a medical test?	✓		
4 sold lemonade?		✓	
5 plays the piano?			✓
6 helps protect bees?		✓	

4 Find and <u>underline</u> phrases in the comments with *do* or *make*. Complete the chart with two more examples for each.

Do	*Make*
laboratory research	a big impression
pretty well	a fortune
my best	a deal

Voice It!

5 Discuss the questions.
1 Who do you think has had the most effect on people's lives: Krtin, Mikaila, or Alma? Why?
2 Do you know of another young person who has achieved a lot?

Finished? p125 Ex. 1

Flipped Class

Ask students to watch **video 8.2** and do **Video Worksheet 8.2** in the *Teacher's Resource Bank* in preparation for the next lesson.

Homework

Workbook p65

Lesson Aim: I can understand how to use the present perfect for experience.

Warmer

▶ Play **video 8.2**, if it was not assigned for homework, and ask students to raise their hands when the vlogger mentions an activity they have also done. Elicit that Joann has never lost an art competition and that she's been to the UK, Spain, and Portugal.

8.06 Audioscript pT142

1 Point out that *ever* has the meaning of "at any time up to now." Then elicit that *never* has the meaning of "not at any time."

Get It Right!

Explain that *ever* is used in questions while *never* is not common in questions.

Pronunciation

8.04–8.05 Students can turn to SB p142 for practice of intonation in questions.

2 8.06 Before the activity, tell students that a woman named Maya is cycling around the world for charity, and elicit a few questions they could ask her.

3 Fast finishers can write extra questions about other high-achieving teenagers that were mentioned in the last lesson. Elicit these during feedback and ask the class for the answers.

Extra Grammar Speaking Practice

4 Tell students that they can make more questions using their own ideas, as well as those in the box.

5 Encourage students to ask follow-up questions to find out more about each other's experiences.

GRAMMAR IN ACTION

Present Perfect for Experience

Watch video 8.2
Has Joann ever lost an art competition? Which countries has Joann been to?

	I/We/You/They	He/She/It
+	We**'ve heard** about some incredible prodigies.	He**'s worked** with Cambridge University scientists.
–	I **haven't tried** her lemonade. We**'ve** [1] *never* **had** so many comments.	He **hasn't been** to college.
?	**Have** you [2] ever **heard** of Mikaila Ulmer? Yes, I **have**. / No, I **haven't**.	**Has** she [3] ever **played** a wrong note? Yes, she **has**. / No, she **hasn't**.

Pronunciation p142

1 Complete the examples in the chart above with *ever* or *never*. Use the online comments on page 96 to help you.

Get It Right!

We use an affirmative verb with **never**.

I've never played golf. **NOT** ~~*I haven't never played golf.*~~

8.06 **2** Maya Flynn is cycling around the world for charity. Complete the interview with the present perfect form of the verbs. Then listen and check.

PAUL How far [1] *have you cycled* (you / cycle), Maya?

MAYA [2] I've ridden (I / ride) 15,000 km so far. I have another 12,000 to go!

PAUL How many countries [3] have you crossed (you / cross)?

MAYA [4] I've been (I / be) to three continents so far, and [5] I've visited (I / visit) 12 countries.

PAUL [6] Have you had (you / have) any funny experiences along the way?

MAYA Well, an emu chased me in the Australian outback. [7] I've never experienced (I / never experience) that before!

PAUL No, not many people have! And how [8] has your bicycle been (your bicycle / be)?

MAYA [9] It hasn't had (it / not have) any problems at all. It's a great bike.

PAUL So how much money [10] have you made (you / make)?

MAYA [11] I haven't reached (I / not reach) my target, but [12] I've made (I / make) $30,000 so far.

PAUL That's amazing! Good luck with the rest of your journey.

3 Write questions and short answers about the people in the online comments on page 96.

1 Krtin / work / in a laboratory?
Has Krtin worked in a laboratory?
Yes, he has.

2 Mikaila and Alma / be / to college?
Have Mikaila and Alma been to college?
No, they haven't.

3 Marion_T / try / BeeSweet lemonade?
Has Marion_T tried BeeSweet lemonade?
No, she hasn't.

4 Bowfrog / hear / Alma play?
Has Bowfrog heard Alma play?
Yes, he/she has.

Use It!

4 Use the words in the box and write questions with the present perfect and *ever* in your notebooks.

be on TV	climb a mountain	
perform in a concert	raise money for charity	
win a competition	win a race	

5 Ask and answer your questions.

Have you ever won a competition?

Yes, I have. I won an art competition in elementary school.

Finished? p125 Ex. 2

Grammar Game

Students write down three experiences they have had, using the present perfect. One of them should be a lie. Students say their three experiences, and their group asks questions to guess which one is the lie. Monitor closely to check students are switching to the simple past when discussing the details of the events.

Finished?

Students turn to p125 and do Exercise 2.

Homework

Workbook p66

Lesson Aim: I can use phrasal verbs to talk about achievement.

Warmer

Students discuss the meaning of of the advice *Never give up. Don't quit. Keep trying.*

Teacher Support Hub ppxxxviii–xxxix

8.08 Audioscript pT142

1 8.07 After feedback, if appropriate, ask students to make flashcards (see SB p93) to test each other on the phrasal verbs.

Target Vocabulary

come up with kʌm ʌp wɪð
give up gɪv ʌp
keep up with kip ʌp wɪð
look up to lʊk ʌp tu
set up set ʌp
show off ʃoʊ ɔf
take part in teɪk pɑrt ɪn
work out wɜrk aʊt

Extra Vocabulary Practice

2 Put students into small groups and encourage them to ask follow-up questions to find out more about each other.

3 ★ Write these prompts on the board to help students guess the situation: *homework, no electricity, candle, dark, no batteries, flashlight.*

4 8.08 Remind students that they are listening for the general idea and should not worry if they don't understand all the details at this point.

Vocabulary Bank SB p135

Learn to Learn

At this stage, students should be learning to write concise and clear notes, omitting articles and other small grammar words.

VOCABULARY AND LISTENING

Phrasal Verbs: Achievement

8.07 **1 Listen and repeat the verbs in the box. Complete the sentences with the correct form of the verbs. Then match them with the pictures.**

~~come up with~~	give up	
keep up with	look up to	set up
show off	take part in	work out

1 The professor was so happy when he finally _came up with_ the answer! g
2 Marcus loves to **take part in** charity races. e
3 Martha is nearly at the top. She isn't going to **give up** now! d
4 The others can't **keep up with** Grandma. f
5 My brother **set up** his own business when he was ten. h
6 Thalia really **looks up to** her mom. She wants to be just like her one day. a
7 The math problem is hard to **work out**. c
8 Aiden likes **showing / to show off** on the court! b

Use It!

2 Use phrasal verbs from Exercise 1 to write three examples from your own life. Compare with a partner.

1 ______
2 ______
3 ______

I wasn't very good at the piano, but I didn't give up.

A Talk

3 Discuss the questions.

1 What is the girl doing? 2 What is difficult for her?

The girl is doing her homework. It's difficult because she doesn't have electricity (and can't afford batteries for her flashlight).

8.08 **4 Listen to a talk. Were your ideas right?**

LEARN TO LEARN

Taking Notes

Write key words when you listen. Then use your notes to remember the ideas that you heard.

8.08 **5 Listen again and take notes for each heading.**

Personal details
1 Ann Makosinski – 20 – Canadian (parents Polish/Filipino)
Her flashlight – how it works
2
Why she thought of the idea
3
Her achievements
4
Her E-Drink mug – how it works
5

Possible answers:
2 heat from hand – energy – no battery
3 friend, Philippines – no electricity – couldn't afford batteries
4 science competition – 1st prize $25,000 – TV, newspapers
5 mug – heat from coffee – charges phone

6 Explain how Ann's inventions work. Use your notes from Exercise 5.

5 8.08 Allow students, in pairs, to discuss what they remember under each heading, taking notes on the side so that they may check their ideas when they listen again.

6 Allow students time to rehearse alone and ask you questions if necessary. Students then take turns explaining the inventions.

Flipped Class

Ask students to watch **video 8.3** and do **Video Worksheet 8.3** in the *Teacher's Resource Bank* in preparation for the next lesson.

Homework

Workbook p67

Lesson Aim: I can understand how to use reflexive and indefinite pronouns.

Warmer

▶ Play **video 8.3**, if it was not assigned for homework, and elicit that (according to the vlogger) everyone should learn to speak English, and everyone should know or understand himself or herself.

8.09–8.10 Audioscripts pT142

1 Explain that we often use reflexive pronouns when the subject and the object of the verb are talking about the same person (e.g., *I saw myself*, not *I saw me*).

2 For question 3, elicit that the reflexive pronoun is used to mean "on her own" or "without anyone's help."

3 8.09 ★ Guide students to circle the subject of each sentence before they attempt the task.

4 Allow students a minute of thinking time to form opinions and make notes before speaking.

5 After feedback, point out that we use *someone/something/somewhere* and *anyone/anything/anywhere* to mean "one person," "one thing," "one place." However, we use *some-* in positive statements and *any-* in negative statements and questions.

6 8.10 Point out that *no-* means "not one" and *every-* means "all." Ask students to compare answers in pairs and explain all their choices during feedback.

Extra Grammar Practice

7 Explain that after these pronouns, we use the verbs in the third person singular (e.g., *everyone is*). Change pairs often to allow students to practice the task more than once.

GRAMMAR IN ACTION

Reflexive Pronouns

Watch video 8.3
What skill should everyone learn?
Who does the vlogger say that everyone should know?

Singular	I → [1]myself	you → yourself	he → himself	she → [4] herself	it → itself
Plural	we → [2] ourselves	you → [3] yourselves	they → themselves		

1 Complete the examples in the chart above.

2 Complete the sentences about the talk on page 98 with reflexive pronouns.

1 Ann taught *herself* the science she needed.
2 Ann's flashlight switches itself off.
3 Ann made the flashlight herself.
4 Her inventions don't need batteries. They power themselves in other ways.
5 If we believe in ourselves, we can achieve anything.

8.09 3 Match 1–6 with a–f. Then listen and check.

1 I surprised *c*
2 John and I introduced a
3 Jane, make sure that you take care of f
4 Mike has taught e
5 You and Vicky should make d
6 Stan and Ollie prepared b

a ourselves to the new neighbors.
b themselves well for the match.
c myself when I did so well on my exams.
d yourselves some sandwiches for lunch.
e himself Spanish and French.
f yourself while I'm away.

Use It!

4 Discuss the questions.

1 Have you taught yourself a skill? What?
2 How do you reward yourself when you've done something good?
3 Where do you imagine yourself ten years from now?

I taught myself to swim when I was eight.

Indefinite Pronouns

People	Things	Places
someone (somebody) everyone (everybody) no one (nobody) anyone (anybody)	[1] something everything [2] nothing anything	somewhere [3] everywhere nowhere [4] anywhere

Ann Makosinski is **someone** I really look up to.
Anything is possible.
No one has thought of these ideas before.

5 Complete the columns in the chart above.

8.10 6 Circle the correct words in the article. Then listen and check.

TEENAGER SAILS INTO RECORD BOOKS

Dutch teenager Laura Dekker has become the youngest person ever to sail solo around the world. Laura is only 16 years old. [1]*No one* / *Anyone* so young has achieved this before. Sailing is [2]*something* / *nothing* her whole family is crazy about, and Laura learned [3]*anything* / *everything* she knows about it from her parents. By the time she was 13, there wasn't [4]*anywhere* / *nowhere* she couldn't sail by herself. [5]*Everyone* / *Someone* has a dream, and Laura's achievement shows that [6]*something* / *nothing* is impossible if you want it enough.

Use It!

7 Complete the sentences. Then compare with your partner.

Everyone in my family likes ________________
I don't know anyone who has ________________
Something I really want to do is ________________
________________ is somewhere I want to visit one day.

Finished? p125 Ex. 3

Grammar Game

Divide the class into two teams. On the board, write *Does anyone on the other team …?* Read one of the phrases below. The teams must guess if *someone/no one/everyone* in the other group does that activity. They win a point if they guess correctly.

know how to swim
go horseback riding
ride/cycle to school
watch soccer
have family in another country
speak Spanish
play the guitar
dislike ice cream

Finished?

Students turn to p125 and do Exercise 3.

Homework

Workbook p68

Lesson Aim: I can answer questions in a job interview.

Warmer

In small groups, students share ideas about what jobs they might have in the future. Elicit different ideas from the whole class.

Teacher Support Hub ppxl–xli

8.11 Audioscript pT143

1 8.11 ★★★ Challenge students to listen and answer the question with their books closed.

2 8.11 After feedback, review the use of the present perfect by eliciting that it is used to talk about past actions with a clear consequence in the present.

3 ▶ Play **video 8.4** and drill the pronunciation of the target phrases, focusing students' attention on sentence stress.

4 If appropriate, encourage students to think of equivalent phrases in their own language.

Everyday English Practice

5 Encourage personalization here by allowing students to choose a job they mentioned in the warmer rather than the ones in the box. Monitor closely to correct mistakes with grammar, and assist with vocabulary when needed.

6 If appropriate, encourage students to record their conversations on their smartphones and listen to the recording, giving them time to repeat the task if necessary.

7 Put pairs together in groups of four. While each pair performs their conversation, one student from the other pair takes notes on content and the other student is responsible for noticing any language mistakes.

SPEAKING
An Interview

1 8.11 **Listen to the conversation. What does Angie want to do?**

a learn to cook very well (circled)

b organize a team

JO	So, Angie, why do you want to join our training program?
ANGIE	Well, [1] I'm passionate about food. I've taught myself a lot about it, but the training will give me the chance to learn new skills.
JO	So have you ever worked in a kitchen?
ANGIE	Yes, [2] I've had plenty of experience working in a restaurant. My grandparents run a restaurant, and I help them on weekends.
JO	Oh, really? And what skills have you developed?
ANGIE	[3] I've learned the basics of cooking. But the main thing is [4] I've learned how to be a good team player.
JO	That's interesting. Tell me more.
ANGIE	Well, I also help the wait staff, you know. We take orders from customers and that kind of thing.

2 8.11 **Complete the conversation with the phrases from the *Useful Language* box. Then listen and check.**

Useful Language

I've learned the basics of …
I'm passionate about …
I've had plenty of experience …
I've learned how to …

3 Look at the *Everyday English* box. Find and underline the phrases in the conversation.

Watch video 8.4 Everyday English

Tell me more. | that kind of thing
the main thing is | you know

4 Match the *Everyday English* phrases with their uses.

You want to …

1 get more information. Tell me more.
2 refer to similar examples. that kind of thing
3 say your most important point. the main thing is
4 check the person understands. you know

PLAN

5 Work with a partner. In your notebook, take notes on questions to ask in a job interview for one of these jobs.

computer programmer | fashion designer | gardener | photographer | zookeeper

SPEAK

6 Practice the interview with your partner. Remember to use the present perfect to talk about experiences, vocabulary from this unit, and phrases from the *Useful Language* and *Everyday English* boxes.

CHECK

7 Work with another pair. Listen to their interview and complete the notes.

What questions did the interviewer ask?

____

____

What experience does the interviewee have?

____

Should the person get the job? ____________

Flipped Class

In preparation for the next class, ask students to take notes on their greatest achievement.

Lesson Aim: I can write a competition entry.

Warmer

In groups, students discuss the achievements they thought about for homework. Monitoring this will give you an indication of whether the students will have enough ideas to write about later on, or whether the activity will need to be adapted.

Teacher Support Hub ppxlii–xliii

1 Write the questions on the board, and then ask students to look at the advertisement for five seconds before closing their books. Students check in pairs before feedback.

2 To encourage faster reading, give students two minutes for this and disallow the use of dictionaries.

3 Ask students to underline the parts of the text where the answers can be found and check their answers in pairs before feedback.

4 If possible, elicit further ways of expressing the same ideas (e.g., 1 *I recommend getting a teacher. You could get a teacher.*).

Useful Language Practice

5 If, during the warmer activity, students seemed to lack ideas, allow them to make up an achievement. They can be creative as long as they take the task seriously.

WRITING

A Competition Entry

1 Read the advertisement. What sort of competition is this? What is the prize?

It's a writing competition. The prize is ten lessons in hang-gliding, rock climbing, or scuba diving.

CALLING ALL HIGH-FLYERS!

Write to us about your greatest achievement and you might win this month's incredible prize:

10 hang-gliding, rock climbing, or scuba diving lessons.

Tell us:

- what you have achieved
- what advice you have for others.
- how you achieved it

2 Read Ajani's competition entry. What has he achieved?

He's learned English. He's won a national story writing competition.

My name is Ajani. My family came to the UK from Afghanistan when I was seven.

My greatest achievement is learning English. When I first arrived, I couldn't understand anyone. At school, I couldn't read or write, and everything was very difficult. However, after a lot of effort, I've managed to learn English. I've even won a national story-writing competition.

How did I do it? First of all, I had a wonderful teacher named Mrs. Connor. She helped me to develop my writing skills. But I also taught myself. I've read plenty of books in English, I've watched a lot of lessons on the Internet, and I've practiced speaking with friends.

If you want to learn a language, my advice to you is to believe in yourself and never give up.

3 Read Ajani's entry again. Are the sentences *T* (true) or *F* (false)?

1 Ajani is not from England. T
2 He came to the UK by himself. F
3 He still doesn't speak much English. F
4 He speaks English when he's with friends. T
5 He thinks you need determination to succeed. T

Useful Language

after a lot of effort	My advice to you is …
How did I do it?	my greatest achievement

4 Rewrite the sentences using the phrases in the *Useful Language* box. You might need to write two sentences.

1 I think you should get a teacher.
My advice to you is to get a teacher.

2 The team worked hard and won the prize.
After a lot of effort, the team won the prize. / The team won the prize after a lot of effort.

3 Do you want to know how I learned to fly a plane?
I learned to fly a plane. How did I do it?

4 Learning French was the best thing I have done.
Learning French was my greatest achievement. / My greatest achievement was learning French.

PLAN

5 Plan your own competition entry. In your notebook, take notes for four paragraphs about one of your achievements.

1 Introduce yourself.
2 Explain the achievement.
3 Explain how you achieved it.
4 Give advice for other people.

WRITE

6 Write your competition entry. Remember to include the present perfect, reflexive pronouns, vocabulary from this unit, and phrases from the *Useful Language* box.

CHECK

7 Do you …

- have four paragraphs?
- explain your achievement clearly?
- give useful advice?

Finished? p125 Ex. 4

6 & 7 Make sure students include the language from the unit, giving them time to redraft their text if needed. Then ask students to display their texts around the room and read as many as possible. The class then votes for the three greatest achievements.

Finished?

Students turn to p125 and do Exercise 4.

Homework

Workbook p69

Lesson Aim: I can create a timeline.

Warmer

Give students a minute to think about an important invention from the last 20 years, and then ask them to share their ideas in groups. Elicit contrasting ideas and encourage students to give reasons.

Project Book

For more information and activities, see the Project Book p50.

8.12 Audioscript pT143

1 Disallow the use of dictionaries and translation software, and encourage students to guess the meaning of unknown words from context.

2 Ask students to discuss the questions in pairs before rereading the text.

How to Manage Your Time

At this stage, students should start reflecting on their time-management skills, making decisions about how they are going to manage their time effectively and in collaboration with other people.

3 After feedback, ask students to brainstorm real-life tasks where time-management skills are important (e.g., essay writing for school, projects at work). Elicit these with the whole class, together with the potential consequences of not following steps a–h in the box.

4 8.12 After the first listening, hand the audioscript to students, if possible, and play the audio again.

TECHNOLOGY PROJECT

A Timeline

1 **Read texts 1–6 on the timeline quickly. Then match them with the pictures (A–F).**

1 C 2 B 3 E 4 D 5 A 6 F

2 **For each question, choose the correct inventor. Some questions have more than one answer.**

Which inventor or inventors …

1 worked with a brother? d, f
2 studied how birds fly? b
3 had an accident? a, c
4 wasn't European? f
5 didn't fly the machine himself? b, d
6 designed an aircraft with an engine? e, f

a Eilmer of Malmesbury
b Leonardo da Vinci
c Denis Bolor
d Joseph-Michel Montgolfier
e Jules Giffard
f Orville Wright

How to Manage Your Time

3 **Look at some ideas to think about before you start a project. Mark (✓) the ideas connected to planning your time.**

a Decide on a topic for the project. ☐
b Think about all the tasks you need to do in the time available. ✓
c Prioritize tasks – decide what's most and least important. ✓
d Include some extra time. ✓
e Decide who will do what. ☐
f Set long-term deadlines. ✓
g Set short-term deadlines. ✓
h Review your project regularly to see if you are keeping to your deadlines. ✓

4 8.12 **Listen to two students planning a project. Which ideas in Exercise 3 do they talk about?**

b c d f g

1
Eilmer of Malmesbury, England, has had a great idea. He ties himself to a pair of wings and jumps off the top of a tower. Eilmer flies for 200 meters. No one has ever flown so far. However, Eilmer hasn't thought about the landing! He hurts himself badly, but also gets himself a place in the history books.

1010

4
French businessman Joseph-Michel Montgolfier and his brother, Jacques-Étienne, have invented the world's first hot-air balloon. Now they make a second flight with passengers. But they don't put themselves on board. The three lucky passengers are a hen, a duck, and a sheep!

1783

5
French engineer Jules Giffard connects a steam engine to a huge balloon. It's the first "airship." People have never seen anything like it before. It's the first aircraft that someone can steer. However, the first time Giffard sets off in his airship, it flies around in circles. He can't steer it against the strong Paris winds!

1852

Class Challenge

The first ever passenger flight took off in St. Petersburg and landed in Tampa, U.S.A., in 1841 / **1914** / 1941.

5 Given the scope of the project, you may want to give students time to make decisions and discuss the time-management aspect of the project before carrying out their tasks at home. Allow time for project updates during the following lessons until the groups are ready to present their work.

6 & 7 Ask groups to double-check their work before displaying it, and then have one student from each group stand next to their display, answering questions, while all the others walk around the room looking at other displays and asking questions.

Students can collaborate digitally through *Collaboration Plus*, where you can assign, track, and assess their work. Students can also share and showcase their work and comment on each other's projects.

For more work on technology, students can turn to SB p140. See pT126 for teaching notes.

Extend It!

Encourage students to reflect critically on their time-management and collaboration skills. Shuffle the groups and ask students to share how they managed their time in their groups, what worked well, and what they should change next time. Elicit positive and less positive experiences from the whole class.

SHAPE IT!

HIGH (AND NOT SO HIGH) ACHIEVERS

THE EARLY HISTORY OF FLIGHT

2 The brilliant Italian scientist and inventor Leonardo da Vinci has looked into how birds fly. Using his discoveries, he designs the world's first flying machine – the Ornithopter. But he has the intelligence not to try it himself! Later, other people try out similar designs, but no one gets very far.

1485

3 Frenchman Denis Bolor has come up with his own flying machine that uses wings with springs. Poor Bolor tries to show off his idea and kills himself when the springs break.

1536

6 It's 10.35 a.m. on December 17. American engineer Orville Wright has lifted himself into the air. He's flying the Wright Flyer, a motor-powered airplane he designed with his brother Wilbur. Orville keeps the Flyer in the air for 12 seconds and travels 37 meters. It isn't a long-distance flight, but it has changed the world forever.

1903

A

B

C

D

E

F

PLAN

5 **Work in groups. Plan a timeline. Choose one of the inventions in the box or choose your own. Then complete the steps below.**

the Internet	the bicycle
the computer	the skyscraper

- Decide what tasks you need to do to complete your timeline and how long each will take.
- Set long-term and short-term deadlines and include some extra time.
- Decide who will do each task.
- Research the information you need.
- Find or make pictures for your timeline.

PRESENT

6 **Display your timeline on the classroom wall. Remember to include important dates, people and events, interesting pictures, and the tips in *How to Manage Your Time*.**

CHECK

7 **Look at your classmates' timelines. Which ones have interesting facts? Discuss in your group.**

UNIT 8 | WHAT IS SUCCESS? 103

Lesson Aim: I can review what I have learned and reflect on my progress.

The aim of this page is for students to review the grammar and vocabulary from the unit. You can either do it in class, as a timed progress test, or assign it for homework.

Vocabulary

1 ★ Invite students to review the vocabulary on SB p95 before attempting this task. Elicit the vocabulary on the board for the students to use as they complete sentences 1–7.

2 Before students attempt the task, give them one minute, in pairs, to combine words in the two boxes to make phrasal verbs. Elicit what each phrasal verb means (e.g., *give up* means "to stop doing something").

Grammar in Action

3 ★★★ Challenge students to explain why the verb changes to the simple past in 1, 3, 4, and 5 (the focus turns to the details of the past event, not the result in the present).

4 Before the activity, ask students to review reflexive pronouns and indefinite pronouns on SB p99.

Unit Quiz Review

8 REVIEW

VOCABULARY

1 Complete the sentences with the words for jobs and qualities.

1 She's going to succeed. She's got plenty of d**etermination**.
2 You need a lot of s**kill** to be a concert pianist.
3 C**reativity** is important if you want to be a good designer.
4 I don't have enough s**trength** in my arms to do rock climbing.
5 Nick has written some brilliant songs. I think he'll be a professional c**omposer**.
6 I am terrible at math. I could never be a m**athematician**!
7 I could be an i**nventor**. I have a lot of ideas for new machines.

2 Complete the sentences with words from both boxes. Use the correct form of the verbs. Use some words more than once.

come give keep set work

off out up with

1 I did ballet for three years, but I **gave up** because I wasn't good at it.
2 Mira is running too fast for me. I can't **keep up with** her.
3 We'll need to arrive early to **set up** our cookie table at the market.
4 Do you know the answer? I can't **work** it **out**.
5 Amol has **come up with** a brilliant idea for our team project.

GRAMMAR IN ACTION

3 Complete the questions with *ever* and the verbs in the box. Then write the short answers.

have ride see try visit

1 A **Have** you **ever seen** a snake?
B **Yes, I have**. I saw one in our yard.
2 A **Has** your brother **ever had** an accident in his car?
B **No, he hasn't**. He's a very careful driver.
3 A **Have** your parents **ever visited** the U.S.A.?
B **Yes they have**. They went there six years ago.
4 A **Have** you **ever tried** to invent something?
B **Yes, I have**, but it wasn't successful!
5 A **Has** Fiona **ever ridden** a horse?
B **Yes, she has**. Unfortunately, she fell off!

4 Circle the correct words.

1 Dan set up a business *themselves* / *(himself)*.
2 We built our house *myself* / *(ourselves)*.
3 You won't achieve *(anything)* / *anywhere* if you don't try.
4 This computer has taught *(itself)* / *myself* to play chess.
5 Is there *no one* / *(anyone)* who knows Patrick's address?

Self-Assessment

I can talk about exceptional jobs and qualities.
I can use phrasal verbs to talk about achievement.
I can use the present perfect to talk about experiences.
I can use reflexive pronouns.
I can use indefinite pronouns.

104 REVIEW | UNIT 8

Review the Unit Theme

Remind students of the unit title: *What is success?* Put students into pairs. Have them discuss the following questions: *What does it mean to be exceptional? What experiences and achievements make you unique? Where do you see yourself in 20 years?* Share answers as a class.

Teacher Support Hub pxlvii

Self-Assessment

Ask students to look back at the Review page and the rest of the unit to decide how confident they feel about each topic. Encourage students to ask for extra practice materials on any topics they don't feel comfortable with.

Homework

Workbook p70

Students should be starting to reflect on their learning practices outside the classroom, taking steps toward becoming responsible for their own learning routines.

Warmer

With the whole class, discuss how students usually learn vocabulary and what techniques they are using.

1 Allow students time to complete the quiz, but ask them to cover the results at the bottom.

2 Students work in pairs. Encourage them to add relevant information and develop the quiz into a conversation.

3 Encourage students to discuss the results in pairs or small groups, and elicit a few reactions.

4 Discuss the ideas as a whole class and elicit some opinions.

5 Refer students back to SB p93 for instructions and ideas on making flashcards.

SHAPE IT!

6 Give students a vocabulary test after ten days have passed. After feedback, encourage them to compare their results and their study plans in groups.

LEARN TO LEARN

LEARN TO ... MAKE A VOCABULARY STUDY PLAN

You can learn vocabulary better by studying it more than once. A study plan can help you do this.

1 Do the quiz. Circle your answers and find out your score.

Do you need a vocabulary study plan? FIND OUT!

Do you ...

1 write new vocabulary in your notebook?
always / sometimes / never

2 use flashcards to learn vocabulary?
always / sometimes / never

3 look at your vocabulary notes when you do your homework?
always / sometimes / never

4 study your vocabulary notes before a test?
always / sometimes / never

5 study your vocabulary notes more than three times a week?
always / sometimes / never

Results

always = 2 points sometimes = 1 point never = 0 point

8–10: Well done! You study vocabulary well, but why not try a new study plan?

4–7: Not bad, but a study plan can help you.

0–3: Oh, no! You really need a study plan!

2 Ask your partner the quiz questions. Underline their answers.

3 Compare scores with your partner. Do you both agree with what it says about you?

4 Match 1–3 with a–c. Which sentence surprises you most? Discuss with your partner.

1 We remember vocabulary better when we study it once and b

2 When you use flashcards to learn vocabulary, c

3 It's necessary to see, hear, or say a word a

a 17 times before we remember it well.

b then a few days later (but not the next day).

c you remember it better.

5 Make a list of eight words from this unit that you want to learn. Make flashcards.

________ ________ ________
________ ________ ________
________ ________

SHAPE IT!

6 Follow steps 1–4 to make a 10-day vocabulary study plan.

1 Write the dates on the plan, starting with tomorrow's date.

2 On the shaded days, test yourself with your flashcards from Exercise 5.

3 When you finish studying each day, write "Yes!" in the "Done?" box.

4 On day 11, answer the question and circle "a lot" or "a little."

Day	1	2	3	4	5	6	7	8	9	10	11
Date											How much has the plan helped me learn vocabulary? *a lot / a little*
Done?											

Unit 9 How do you express yourself?

Lesson Aim: I can talk about music and dance.

Warmer

Students look at the photo and make a list of all the dance styles they know (e.g., *hip-hop, ballet, waltz*). Elicit a few ideas from the class.

Teacher Support Hub ppxxxiv–xxxv

Start It!

Unit Quiz

1 & 2 Ask students to discuss how the man feels. Elicit that he's dancing.

3 Ask students: *Is it possible to enjoy music if you can't hear it?* Elicit ideas before playing **video 9.1**. Elicit that the people can feel the music.

4 Use this as an opportunity to find out what students know about musical instruments, which will be covered in the next lesson.

Video Comprehension Questions

Flipped Class

Prepare for **Explore It!** (p107). Students research an interesting fact about music.

9 How do you express yourself?

LEARNING OUTCOMES

I can ...

- understand texts about music
- make polite refusals
- write a review
- understand how to use *going to*, *will*, the present continuous for the future, and the simple present for the future
- talk about and describe musical instruments and genres, and dance styles
- recognize stress patterns, distinguish between speakers, use referencing, and practice your English during vacation

Start It!

1 Look at the photo. What do you think the man is doing?
2 Before you watch, how does music make you feel?
3 How do people who can't hear enjoy music? Watch and check. They feel the music.
4 What instruments do you play or do you want to play?

Watch video 9.1 | p109 Grammar in Action 9.2 | p111 Grammar in Action 9.3 | p112 Everyday English 9.4 | p114 Globetrotters 9.5

Unit Aims

Skills

I can ...

- understand texts about music p108, p114
- make polite refusals p112
- write a review p113

Language

I can ...

- talk about musical instruments and genres p106
- understand how to use *going to* and *will* for the future p109
- talk about dance styles p110
- understand how to use the present continuous and simple present for the future p111

Learn to Learn

I can ...

- recognize stress patterns p107
- distinguish between speakers p110
- use referencing in texts p115
- practice English during vacation p117

Extra Resources

- Finished? Student's Book p126
- Vocabulary Bank, Student's Book p136
- Workbook pp72–79
- Grammar Reference and Practice, Workbook pp104–105
- Teacher Support Hub, Teacher's Book ppxxxiv–xlvii

Digital Resource Pack

(on Cambridge One)

- *Teacher's Resource Bank* for word lists, differentiated worksheets, *Culture Projects*, and many other extra resources
- *Practice Extra, Presentation Plus, Test Generator*, and *Digital Collaboration Space*

Lesson Aim: I can talk about musical instruments and genres.

Warmer

In groups, students discuss what type of music and which bands/singers they like. Write appropriate vocabulary on the board.

9.01–9.02 **Audioscripts pT143**

1 9.01 ★★★ Alternatively, students cover the boxes and work in pairs to guess the instruments and genres. Then have them look at the boxes to check their answers.

Target Vocabulary

Genres
classical ˈklæ·sɪ·kəl
folk foʊk
hip-hop ˈhɪp·hɑp
jazz dʒæz
reggae ˈre·geɪ
rock rɑk

Instruments
bass beɪs
drums drʌmz
guitar ɡɪˈtɑr
keyboard ˈki·bɔrd
microphone ˈmaɪ·krə·foʊn
saxophone ˈsæk·sə·foʊn
trumpet ˈtrʌm·pɪt
violin ˌvaɪəˈlɪn

Extra Vocabulary Practice
Famous Musicians Quiz

2 Give students three minutes to brainstorm as many genres and instruments as possible, and write them on the board.

Vocabulary Bank SB p136

Get It Right!

Explain that *the* is generally used with an instrument after *play*.

VOCABULARY
Musical Instruments and Genres

9.01 **1** Match the words in the boxes with the genres (1–6) and musical instruments (7–14) in the pictures. Listen, check, and repeat.

classical	6	hip-hop	4	reggae	3
folk	1	jazz	2	rock	5

bass	13	microphone	12
drums	11	saxophone	9
guitar	8	trumpet	14
keyboard	10	violin	7

2 How many other musical instruments and genres can you think of?

Get It Right!
We say **play football**, **tennis**, **golf**, etc.
And we also say **play the piano**, **the guitar**, **the trumpet**, etc.

LEARN TO LEARN
Stress Patterns

It's important to learn which syllable is stressed when you learn a new word.

9.02 **3** Complete the chart with the words in Exercise 1. Then listen and check. Can you add one more word to some groups?

O	folk, jazz, rock, bass, drums (rap, blues, flute, harp)
Oo	hip-hop, reggae, keyboard, trumpet (techno, country, organ, banjo)
oO	guitar (new wave, bassoon)
Ooo	classical, microphone, saxophone (opera, piccolo, triangle)
ooO	violin (mandolin, double bass)

4 Take turns clapping the rhythm of a word from Exercise 1. Your partner guesses the word.

Use It!

5 Discuss the questions.
1 What kind of music do you like listening to?
2 Can you or your friends or family play a musical instrument? Which one?
3 Which instruments do you like the sound of?

Explore It!

Guess the correct answer.
Chicago rapper Twista is one of the fastest rappers in the world. What's the fastest he can rap?

a 10 syllables per second
b 20 syllables per second
c 30 syllables per second

Find another interesting fact about music. Then write a question for your partner to answer.

UNIT 9 | HOW DO YOU EXPRESS YOURSELF? 107

Learn to Learn

Point out that, unlike some other languages, stress in English words can go in different places, and not just on the first syllable. If you don't pronounce an English word with the stress on the correct syllable, it can make you difficult to understand.

3 9.02 ★ Play the audio once and drill each word, asking students to raise both hands (or jump, if appropriate) when pronouncing the stressed syllable.

4 If you wish to make the activity quieter, you can ask students to hum the word instead.

5 Allow students a few minutes of thinking time to prepare their answers.

Explore It!

Ask students to use information they found out for homework.

Homework

Workbook p72

Lesson Aim: I can understand texts about music.

Warmer

In small groups, students discuss whether they have ever been to a concert or live music event, using vocabulary from SB p107 if possible.

Teacher Support Hub ppxxxvi–xxxvii

1 ★ Ask students to look at the box in Exercise 2 to predict the genres being shown in the pictures.

2 9.03 To encourage faster skimming, give students two minutes to read the text and disallow the use of dictionaries at this stage.

3 During feedback, elicit further information (e.g.,
1 *Who is the performer?*
2 *What's the instrument?*
3 *Which people?*
4 *Who plays the violin?* etc.).

4 ★★★ Fast finishers find another unknown word in the text and look up the meaning. Elicit these during feedback.

Extra Vocabulary Practice

5 Allow time for students to form an opinion. You may want to take this opportunity to quickly review comparative and superlative adjectives.

READING
An Events Guide

1 Look at the photos of four musicians. What kind of music do you think they play?

9.03 **2** Read the events guide. Match musicians 1–4 with the genres that they are going to perform.

blues	2	pop	4
country	3	raga	1

3 Match concerts A–D with these features. Sometimes there is more than one concert.

1 A has only one performer
2 B includes an electronic instrument
3 B is free for some people
4 B, C has more than two performers
5 C, D includes a violin
6 B, C starts before eight o'clock
7 A, C is cheaper for college students
8 D starts the latest

4 Find adjectives in the guide that mean …

1 alone — solo
2 very excited — thrilled
3 famous — well-known
4 very unusual — unique
5 surprising — unexpected
6 talented — gifted

Voice It!

5 Put the concerts in the events guide in order from most interesting to least interesting. Explain your choices to your partner.

Finished? p126 Ex. 1

WATERSIDE ARTS CENTER **What's on at the Waterside**

A Tuesday 8 p.m.
Bunny Scraggs
$8.00, $3.00 (student discount)
We think this show will surprise reggae fans. The Dubster Brothers' bassist also plays blues piano, and he's going to share that talent tonight. In this solo performance, Bunny's going to play and sing his favorite blues classics. However, if you want to hear some of the Dubster Brothers' hits, we're sure Bunny won't disappoint!

B Thursday 7 p.m.
Janet Glyndebourne and the Donuts
$5, no charge for under 16s
We're thrilled to welcome Janet Glyndebourne to Waterside. However, the well-known opera star isn't going to sing Mozart. Instead, she's going to join Kim Green on synthesizer and Bod on percussion, and they're going to play a concert of pure pop. We're sure it will be a great evening!

C Saturday 7:30 p.m.
Dr Jay and the Rodeo Band
$10.00, $4.00 (student discount)
For one night only, hip-hop artist Dr. Jay is going to lead country favorites the Rodeo Band (Helen Smith on banjo and vocals, Liam Jones on double bass, Lucy-Anne Flynn on violin). Are you really going to miss this unique event? We're sure you won't want to!

D Sunday 9:30 p.m.
Angus Beardsley Plays Raga
$15.00, $7.00
Rock legends Axel Heads have announced that they aren't going to tour again. Their fans will miss them, but we have some unexpected news! The band's bass player, Angus "The Beard" Beardsley, is also a gifted violinist. On Saturday he's going to team up with sitar player Jagjit Rakha to perform Indian raga. But is "The Beard" going to sing in Hindi, too? Come and find out!

Extend It!

Ask students to walk around the class, speaking to as many classmates as possible, to find someone who has put the four events in the same order. Students then work with this new partner to discuss their favorite music and bands.

Finished?

Students turn to p126 and do Exercise 1.

Flipped Class

Ask students to watch **video 9.2** and do **Video Worksheet 9.2** in the *Teacher's Resource Bank* in preparation for the next lesson.

Homework

Workbook p73

Lesson Aim: I can understand how to use *going to* and *will* for the future.

Warmer

▶ Play **video 9.2** if it was not assigned for homework. Elicit that Fiona is going to the All-Stars Festival (featuring hip-hop and electronic dance music). Evita is going to listen to rock music. Ask students to discuss, in pairs, which music they would prefer to listen to.

9.04 Audioscript pT143

1 Challenge students to complete the chart before checking on SB p108.

2 ★ Guide students to decide if the subjects of the sentences are singular or plural and to choose if they need *is* or *are going to*.

3 9.04 Ask students to work in pairs and complete the exercise orally before filling in the missing phrases.

Get It Right!

Remind students that we use *will* when we believe we know what will happen. An *intention* is a plan we have made for something in the future.

Extra Grammar Practice

4 & 5 Ask students to compare answers in pairs before checking with the whole class.

6 ★ Draw a chart with two columns, *intentions* and *predictions*. Write *go to the movies* under *intentions* and elicit *I am going to go to the movies*. Then allow time for students to make their own chart before discussing it in pairs.

Watch video 9.2
Which music festival is Fiona going to?
What music is Evita going to listen to?

GRAMMAR IN ACTION

Going To

	I/He/She/It	You/We/They
+	He [1] *'s going to* **share** that talent tonight.	They [3] 're going to **play** a concert of pure pop.
–	Janet **isn't going to sing** Mozart.	Axel Heads [4] aren't going to **tour** again.
?	[2] Is "The Beard" going to **sing** in Hindi?	**Are** you really **going to miss** this unique event?

1 Complete the examples in the chart above with the correct form of *going to*. Use the events guide on page 108 to help you.

2 Complete the sentences about the events guide with the correct form of *going to*.

1 The concerts *aren't going to start* (not start) before 7 p.m.
2 Two concerts are going to take (take) place on the weekend.
3 Bunny Scraggs is going to play (play) blues piano.
4 Janet Glyndebourne isn't going to perform (not perform) classical music.

9.04 **3** Complete the conversation with the correct form of *going to*. Then listen and check.

AMY Hi, Josh. [1] *Are you going to go* (you / go) out tomorrow evening?
JOSH No, [2] I'm going to stay (I / stay) at home and watch a movie. What about you?
AMY Yeah. Dr. Jay is at the Waterside. [3] I'm not going to miss (I / not miss) that.
JOSH Wow! Really?
AMY Yeah, really. [4] I'm going to buy (I / buy) my ticket this morning.
JOSH Hmm. Sounds interesting. [5] Is Aneta going to join (Aneta / join) you?
AMY No! [6] She isn't going to come (she / not come). She can't stand Dr. Jay. Why don't you come?
JOSH OK, you've convinced me. But how [7] are we going to get (we / get) there? [8] We aren't going to walk (we / not walk), are we?
AMY [9] My dad's going to give (my dad / give) us a ride.

Will and Going To

Get It Right!

We often use **will** for predictions and **going to** for intentions.

We're sure it ***will*** *be a great evening.*
Bunny ***is going to*** *play his favorite blues classics.*

4 Decide if these sentences are *P* (predictions) or *I* (intentions). Then complete the sentences and check your answers on page 108.

1 We think this show *will* surprise reggae fans. *P*
2 We're sure Bunny won't disappoint! P
3 She 's going to join Kim Green. I
4 Dr. Jay is going to lead the Rodeo Band. I

5 Complete Lia's message to Max. Use the verbs in the box with *going to* or *will*.

be buy fail ~~go~~ like not be able play

Hey Max. [1] *Are* you and Mo *going to go* to Jo's party? I think it [2] 'll / will be fun. Jo's brother has a band, and they [3] 're going to play at the party. I'm sure you [4] 'll / will like them. [5] Are you going to buy tickets for the Z Men concert? I probably [6] won't be able to go. We have a test that week, and I [7] 'll / will fail it if I don't study.

Use It!

6 Tell your partner about your intentions and predictions for the weekend.

Finished? p126 Ex. 2

Grammar Game

Put students in pairs. They take turns writing down an activity they are going to do on the weekend. Their partner can ask up to ten questions to guess the activity (e.g., *Are you going to do this at home or outside?*). They win a point if they guess correctly.

Finished?

Students turn to p126 and do Exercise 2.

Homework

Workbook p74

Lesson Aim: I can talk about dance styles.

Warmer
In groups, students discuss whether they can dance, which types of dance they have tried, and which they'd like to try.

Teacher Support Hub ppxxxviii–xxxix

9.05–9.06 Audioscripts pT144

1 9.05 After feedback, if some students feel confident, ask for volunteers to mime a type of dance for the rest of the class to guess.

Target Vocabulary
ballet dancing
bæˈleɪ ˈdæn·sɪŋ
ballroom dancing
ˈbɔl·rum ˈdæn·sɪŋ
breakdancing
ˈbreɪkˌdæn·sɪŋ
disco dancing
ˈdɪs·koʊ ˈdæn·sɪŋ
folk dance foʊk dæns
modern dance
ˈmɑ·dərn dæns
salsa dancing
ˈsɑl·sə ˈdæn·sɪŋ
swing swɪŋ
tap dancing tæp ˌdæn·sɪŋ
Zumba ˈzʌm·bə

2 Put students into groups. Encourage them to discuss different possibilities or make guesses if they are not sure about something.

Extra Vocabulary Practice

3 9.06 Remind students that they should focus mainly on key ideas and not worry too much about understanding all the details.

Vocabulary Bank SB p136

VOCABULARY AND LISTENING
Dance Styles

9.05 **1** **Match the words in the box with the photos. Listen, check, and repeat.**

ballet dancing	5	modern dance	6
ballroom dancing	1	salsa dancing	8
breakdancing	7	swing	2
disco dancing	10	tap dancing	3
folk dance	4	Zumba	9

Use It!

2 **Discuss the dance styles in Exercise 1.**
1 What type of music accompanies the styles?
2 What do people usually wear for these styles?
3 Which dance style do you think looks best? Why?

A Discussion

9.06 **3** **Listen to a conversation between four students. What are they talking about?**
a a show they have seen
(b) a show they are planning

LEARN TO LEARN
Distinguishing Between Speakers
When you listen to a group of people speaking, but you cannot see them, it can be difficult to understand who says what. For each person, consider these things:
- Are they male or female?
- Are they old or young?
- Do they say any names?

9.06 **4** EXAM **Listen again and match the people with the tasks. There are two extra tasks.**

		a	recording the show
1 Imogen	c	b	meeting the dancers
2 Marta	f	c	writing the program
3 Adam	d	d	organizing the music
4 Jack	a	e	selling tickets
		f	putting out the seats

Voice It!

5 **Discuss the questions.**
1 Have you ever helped organize a school show or a similar event?
2 What do you think is the most difficult part of organizing a show?

Learn to Learn
Listening to a conversation between a group of speakers is one of the most difficult challenges for listeners, so students shouldn't feel demotivated if they have trouble with this. They should instead use these techniques to support them.

4 9.06 EXAM ★ Write the four names on the board and play the audio again. Point to the names on the board as the speakers talk, and pause the audio after each answer is mentioned.

5 ★★★ Ask students to discuss how difficult it might be to become a professional dancer.

Flipped Class
Ask students to watch **video 9.3** and do **Video Worksheet 9.3** in the *Teacher's Resource Bank* in preparation for the next lesson.

Homework
Workbook p75

Lesson Aim: I can understand how to use the present continuous and simple present for the future.

Warmer

▶ Play **video 9.3** if it was not assigned for homework. Elicit that Paulo is going to a family party on Saturday night. The movie begins at 7:30 p.m. (and also 9:30 p.m.).

9.06–9.08 **Audioscripts pT144**

1 Elicit that the actions in the chart refer to the future and that we use the present continuous for arrangements in the future. Elicit a few examples from students.

Pronunciation

9.07 Students turn to SB p142 for practice of sentence stress.

2 9.06 During feedback, encourage students to use the contracted forms (e.g., *aren't*) that are more common in speaking.

3 9.08 ★ Ask students to decide if the subjects of the sentences are singular or plural and to decide if they need *is* or *are*.

4 & 5 Explain that the simple present is used to talk about future events that are fixed and scheduled, such as movie showtimes, travel departures, and store hours.

Extra Grammar Practice

6 Extend this activity by allowing students to talk about other events that might be planned, such as a school trip or exam.

GRAMMAR IN ACTION

Present Continuous for Future

Watch video 9.3
What is Paulo doing on Saturday night? What time does the movie begin?

Present Continuous for Future Plans

I [1] __'m__ **writing** the program.
I [2] __'m__ **not doing** anything on Friday afternoon.
[3] __Are__ you **recording** the show, Adam?

Pronunciation p142

1 Complete the examples in the chart above.

9.06 **2** Listen again to the conversation between Imogen and her friends on page 110. Correct the sentences.

1 The teachers are having a party on Friday afternoon.
They aren't having a party. They're having a meeting.
2 Ten dance groups are performing.
Ten dance groups aren't performing. Six dance groups are performing.
3 Jack is recording the show on his phone.
He isn't recording the show on his phone. He's recording it on his sister's video camera.

9.08 **3** Complete Lilia's post with the present continuous form of the verbs in the box. Then listen and check.

bring come leave meet not do perform play ~~return~~

Thank you, New Haven! You were a fabulous audience last night! We [1] *'re returning* in April, so I hope we'll see some of you again. Later today, we [2] __'re leaving__ for Hartford. We [3] __'re performing__ a new play there called *The Bell*, and I [4] __'m playing__ a girl who has the power to see the future. Hey, Hartford! If you [5] __aren't doing / 're not doing__ anything on Friday night, come along. Guess who [6] __'s coming__ to see us on our first night – Jennifer Lawrence! She [7] __'s bringing__ some friends, and we [8] __'re meeting__ them backstage after the performance. Wow!

Simple Present for Future

Simple Present for Scheduled Events

It [1] __begins__ (begin) at seven-thirty.
The doors [2] __don't open__ (open) until seven o'clock.
What time [3] __does__ the show __start__ (start)?

4 Complete the examples in the chart above with the correct form of the verbs in parentheses.

5 Complete sentences 1–4 using the simple present for the future.

DANCE-FEST

Barnsley Dance Festival, Saturday, June 21

12:30–2:00: African Beat Workshop
Learn traditional African dances.

3:00–4:00: The Langley Dance School
Watch the world's favorite ballet, *Swan Lake*.

6:15–7:00: Tarantella Talk
Gianna Romano gives a talk about one of Italy's most famous dances.

7:30–9:00: The Bronx River Combo
See this New York street dance group doing hip-hop, krumping, and more.

end last ~~start~~ take

1 The festival *starts* at lunchtime.
2 African Beat __takes__ place first.
3 The ballet __doesn't last__ for more than an hour.
4 The Bronx River Combo's performance __doesn't end__ until 9 p.m.

Use It!

6 Ask and answer the questions about each event at Dance-Fest.
1 What time does it start and end?
2 What is happening in the event?

Finished? p126 Ex. 3

Grammar Game

Students write a future plan on a piece of paper (e.g., *I'm traveling to Rome*). It doesn't need to be a true plan. They give it to another student who must show it to the rest of the group but must not read it. Then that student has to guess what their plan is by asking questions (e.g., *Am I going somewhere?*).

Finished?

Students turn to p126 and do Exercise 3.

Homework

Workbook p76

Lesson Aim: I can make polite refusals.

Warmer

In groups, students make a list of reasons why they might want to refuse (i.e., say that you will not accept) an invitation to an event (e.g., *I think it's boring. I'm tired.*), and a list of excuses (e.g., *I have to do homework. My mom doesn't want me to.*).

Teacher Support Hub ppxl–xli

9.09 Audioscript pT144

1 9.09 ★★★ Challenge students to listen and answer the question with their books closed. Elicit that Harry's going to a jazz festival. Jess can't go on Saturday because her cousin Helen is visiting her and Helen can't stand jazz. She can't go on Friday because she has a guitar lesson.

2 9.09 Go through the phrases with students and elicit that *feel like* means "want to."

Useful Language and Everyday English Practice

3 Play **video 9.4** and drill the pronunciation of the target phrases, focusing students' attention on which words are stressed.

4 Encourage students, if appropriate, to think of equivalent phrases in their own language.

5 ★★★ Tell students that they can make the conversation humorous, as this might make the language more memorable. For example, the event could run over many days and the invitee could keep refusing, finding an excuse for every day.

SPEAKING
Making Polite Refusals

9.09 **1** Listen to the conversation. What event is Harry going to? Why can't Jess go?

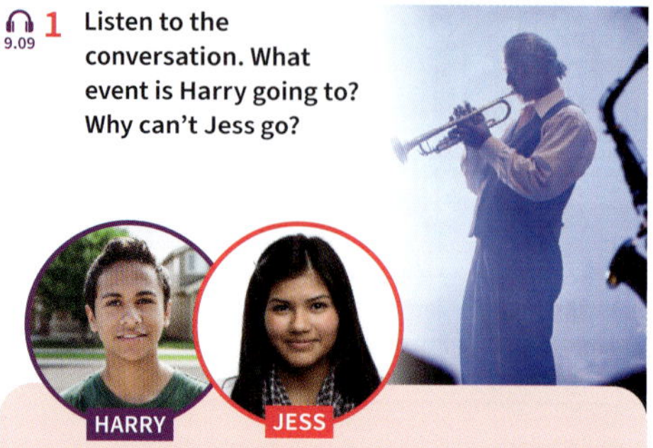

HARRY Hi, Jess. I'm going to book tickets for the jazz festival on Saturday. [1] *Do you feel like* coming along?

JESS [2] **I'd love to, but** my cousin Helen's visiting me, and I'll be with her all day long.

HARRY [3] **She's welcome to** join us if she wants.

JESS That's really nice of you, Harry, but Helen can't stand jazz!

HARRY Oh, that's too bad. Look, they're playing for two nights. What are you up to on Friday? [4] **Would you like to** come then instead?

JESS Hmm. What time does it start?

HARRY 7:30.

JESS Oh, that's no good either, Harry. I have a guitar lesson and it starts at 7:15.

HARRY OK. Never mind, Jess. Maybe another time.

JESS Sure. [5] **Thanks for asking, though**. I'm sure it'll be a great concert.

9.09 **2** Complete the conversation with phrases from the *Useful Language* box. Then listen and check.

Useful Language

Do you feel like ...?
(She's) welcome to ...
Would you like to ...?
I'd love to, but ...
Thanks for asking, though

3 Look at the *Everyday English* box. Find and underline the phrases in the conversation.

Watch video 9.4
Everyday English

all day long Never mind. That's no good.
That's too bad. What are you up to?

4 Match the phrases in the *Everyday English* box with their meanings.

1 That isn't convenient. **That's no good.**
2 It doesn't matter. **Never mind.**
3 for the whole day **all day long**
4 That's sad. **That's too bad.**
5 What plans do you have? **What are you up to?**

PLAN

5 Work with a partner. Think of an event to go to and reasons why one of you can't go.

SPEAK

6 In pairs, practice a converstion making polite refusals. Remember to use *going to*, *will*, the simple present and present continuous, vocabulary from this unit, and phrases from the *Useful Language* and *Everyday English* boxes.

CHECK

7 Work with another pair. Listen to their conversation and complete the notes.

What event do they talk about?

______

Why can't one of them go?

______

______

6 Ask students to repeat the conversation at least twice in order to promote fluency as well as accuracy in the use of the target language.

7 Monitor and choose one or two conversations that include examples of good language use, and ask students to perform these for the whole class.

Flipped Class

In preparation for the next lesson, ask students to find out about music events happening soon in their area.

Lesson Aim: I can write a review.

Warmer

In groups, students share the information they researched for homework about music events happening in their area.

Teacher Support Hub ppxlii–xliii

1 Set a strict time limit to encourage faster reading.

2 Allow students to discuss the sentences in pairs before reading again and checking their ideas.

3 ★★★ During feedback, brainstorm extra adjectives and synonyms that students could use, such as *hilarious*, *wonderful*, or *disappointing*.

4 Point out that reviews are more successful when they use interesting and engaging language like the phrases in the *Useful Language* box.

Useful Language Practice

5 Put students into pairs and give them up to five minutes to discuss concerts or shows they have been to and what they thought about them. Then ask students to decide alone what they are going to write about.

6 & 7 After writing their reviews, students can swap reviews with a partner and discuss their strengths and things that could be improved. Allow students to write a second draft if there is time.

WRITING
A Review

1 Read the review quickly. Which dance styles can you see in this show? hip-hop and ballet (hiplet)

"Hiplet" – A New Dance Experience!

Crash Dance Crew is a dance group from London. Their show, *City Dreams*, tells the story of three teenagers who have come to the city to make a new life for themselves. The show is a unique mix of hip-hop and ballet called hiplet. Three musicians on keyboards, vocals, and turntable play a mix of rap and electro funk.

It's an action-packed story, but there are some very funny moments, too. The costumes are colorful, and I was impressed by the music. However, the highlight of the show is the dancing. The mix of styles works well. On the downside, tickets are expensive and there's no student discount.

Crash Dance Crew play at the Miami Olympia Theater next week. After that, they're touring other cities in the U.S.A. All in all, if you love dance, this superb show is a must-see.

2 Read the review again and correct these sentences.

1 The performers are from Miami.
The performers are from London.

2 An orchestra plays the music for the show.
Three musicians play the music for the show.

3 The writer liked the music most.
The writer liked the dancing most.

4 Tickets are cheaper for students.
Tickets aren't cheaper for students. / There's no student discount.

5 The show is only happening in Miami.
The show is happening in other cities in the U.S.A.

3 In a review, it's a good idea to use lots of adjectives. Find and underline all the adjectives in the dance show review. Discuss with a partner what they describe.

new – life, unique – the mix of music, action-packed – the story, funny – moments in the story, colorful – the costumes, expensive – the tickets, superb – the show

4 Find and underline the *Useful Language* phrases in the review. Then match them with phrases a–e.

Useful Language

[1]All in all d
[2]If you love (dance), this (show) is a must-see. e
[3]I was impressed by ... b
[4]On the downside c
[5]The highlight of the show is ... a

a The best part is
b I loved
c It's disappointing that
d In summary
e Fans of (dance) will love this

PLAN

5 Plan a review of a concert or show you have seen. Take notes for three paragraphs in your notebook.

1 A general description of the show
2 Details about the dancing, music, costumes, etc. and your opinions of them
3 A summary of your opinion of the show

WRITE

6 Write your review. Remember to give your opinions and to include adjectives, the simple present to describe the show, and phrases from the *Useful Language* box.

CHECK

7 Do you ...
- use three paragraphs?
- say what you liked and didn't like?
- summarize your opinions at the end?

Finished? p126 Ex. 4

Extend It!

Students display their reviews around the classroom and then read each other's reviews. Elicit from the class which event sounds most interesting and why.

Finished?

Students turn to p126 and do Exercise 4.

Flipped Class

In preparation for **Explore It!** (p115), students research three interesting facts about Spanish traditions.

Homework

Workbook p77

Lesson Aim: I can understand texts about music.

Background Information

Cultures all over the world have traditional regional dances. Students may be familiar with some of these, such as tango (Argentina), samba (Brazil), danzon (Cuba), Russian squat dance, Indian classical dance, and many others. In the United States, square dancing, swing, and hula are included in traditional folk dance genres.

Warmer

▶ Play **video 9.5** and ask students to discuss the questions in groups. Elicit that the dance comes from Bavaria, a region of Germany.

Video Comprehension Questions

Put students into groups. Give them two minutes to list all the facts they know about Spain. They should not use the ones they researched for homework, as these will be used later for the *Explore It!* activity. Elicit any interesting facts and share them with the class.

Class Challenge

In Spain, there is a festival every August, where people throw oranges / **tomatoes** / money at each other.

1 Draw a chart with two columns on the board, *what we know* and *what we would like to know*. Elicit ideas from students and add them to the chart.

2 9.10 Ask students to read the text, using the chart on the board as a guide to what to find. Elicit how much information from the board is actually in the text.

3 Allow students, in pairs, to discuss where they might find the answers to questions 1–7 in the text before rereading.

4 Write *cultural expression* on the board. In groups of four, students brainstorm art forms that their culture is known for and ways people participate in and celebrate that culture. Elicit a few ideas on the board before letting students discuss the questions.

Teacher Support Hub pxlv

AROUND THE WORLD

READING
A Travel Article

1 Look at the photo of the dance on page 115. Discuss the questions.

1 What do you know about this dance?
2 What more would you like to know about it?

2 (9.10) Read the article. Does it mention any of your ideas from Exercise 1?

3 Read the article again and answer the questions in your notebook.

1 How long does the Festival de Jerez last? *Two weeks*
2 Who goes to the festival?
3 What can you do at the festival?
4 What traditions does flamenco come from?
5 When did performers start using guitars?
6 What mistake do people often make about flamenco?
7 What part of a flamenco performance can the audience take part in?

2 people from over 30 different countries
3 watch flamenco performances and take flamenco lessons
4 Roma, Spanish, Jewish, and North African traditions
5 in the 19th century
6 They think it's only dancing.
7 the shouting

Voice It!

4 Discuss the questions.

1 Folk dance is a form of cultural expression. Is folk dance an important part of your culture?
2 How is cultural expression important for a community?

Globetrotters
Watch video 9.5
The Schuhplattler

- Which dances from other countries do you know?
- Where is the *Schuhplattler* dance from?

Festival de Jerez: A Flamenco Heaven

by Dan Philips

Every year, the Spanish city of Jerez puts on a festival of flamenco dance that lasts for two wonderful weeks. For me and flamenco fans around the world, [1]it's the highlight of the year. People from over 30 different countries will show up here, all crazy about flamenco.

Every day, there are performances of flamenco. [2]Some take place in the beautiful Villamarta Theater, but most happen in the small flamenco clubs all around Jerez, known as *peñas*. And if you're interested in taking it up yourself, the greatest flamenco teachers from around the world are going to give classes.

The festival begins on February 23 and ends on March 10. Don't miss out!

SOME HISTORY

Flamenco is typically Spanish, but it has a long international history. Over five centuries ago, the Roma came to Europe from India and brought their traditional music. [3]Their traditions mixed with local traditions from the south of Spain and [4]those of Jewish and North African immigrants, and the result was flamenco.

The 19th century was the "golden age" of flamenco. The first flamenco schools opened [5]then, in Seville, Cádiz, and Jerez. Performers began to use guitars, and dance became more important. Flamenco became the art we know today.

A GUIDE FOR BEGINNERS

Instruments: The two most important of [6]these are the guitar and the castanets, but you might see performances with trumpets, violins, or even a whole orchestra.

Songs: People often think that flamenco is only dancing. In fact, the songs, called *cante*, are the real heart of it. The words are often by Spain's most famous poets.

Dance: *Zapateado* is the dance that flamenco dancers do. They stamp their feet and click their castanets in fast, complicated rhythms. Nobody nods off during a flamenco concert!

***Jaleo*:** This is the hand-clapping and shouting that make flamenco so exciting. The clapping, called *palmas*, is much more difficult than it looks. But anyone can join in the shouting, so don't be shy!

Learn to Learn

At this level, students should be able to read longer texts that have more complex sentences and understand how information is organized. Part of this involves recognizing cohesive devices, such as pronouns and determiners to refer to people, things, and actions mentioned earlier in the text.

5 If possible, display the text on the board and ask strong students to draw arrows on the text to help other students better visualize the references.

6 ★ Ask students to try to infer the meaning of the phrasal verbs from context, but then allow them to use a dictionary to check their guesses. Remind them to check the whole phrasal verb, not just part of it.

Focus on Phrasal Verbs

Students can collaborate digitally through *Collaboration Plus*, where you can assign, track, and assess their work. Students can also share and showcase their work and comment on each other's projects.

Explore It!

Remind students to use the facts about Spanish traditions that they researched for homework. Monitor closely and pick the most interesting facts. Ask the students who wrote these questions to ask them for the class to answer.

Culture Project

See Project Book p54 for further information and activities.

LEARN TO LEARN

Referencing

Writers often use words such as *this* and *that* to refer back to something they have already mentioned in the text.

5 What do underlined words 1–6 in the article refer to?

1 the festival
2 performances
3 the Roma's
4 traditions
5 in the 19th century
6 instruments

6 Find and underline six phrasal verbs in the article with the verbs below. Complete the sentences using the correct form.

join ~~miss~~ nod put show take

1 Buy tickets early so you don't miss out.
2 My mom took up flamenco guitar last year.
3 They put on the biggest concerts in the Villamarta Theater.
4 This music is so boring – it's making me nod off.
5 We showed up late and couldn't get into the concert.
6 Would you like to join in the dance with us?

Explore It!

Guess the correct answer.

Jerez is also home to a world-famous … school.

a rock climbing
b horseback riding
c film

Find three more interesting facts about Spanish traditions. Choose your favorite fact and write a question for your partner to answer.

SHAPE IT!

CULTURE PROJECT

A Webpage

A webpage gives important information in an attractive, organized way. Design a webpage about a festival.

Teacher's Resource Bank

UNIT 9 | HOW DO YOU EXPRESS YOURSELF? 115

Lesson Aim: I can review what I have learned and reflect on my progress.

The aim of this page is for students to review the grammar and vocabulary from the unit. You can either do it in class, as a timed progress test, or assign it for homework.

Vocabulary

1 After feedback, ask students to look back at SB p107. In groups, one student chooses an instrument and mimes playing it. The first student to guess wins a point and mimes the next instrument.

2 After feedback, have students describe the dance genres and say whether or not they like them.

Grammar in Action

3 ★ Guide students to decide which actions are predictions and which are intentions before getting them to do the task.

4 ★ Ask students to decide which actions are plans and which are scheduled events before they complete the sentences.

Unit Quiz Review

Extend It!

In pairs, students make two fill-in-the-blank sentences that require *will*, *going to*, the present continuous, or the simple present to talk about the future. Pairs swap sentences and complete them before checking their answers in groups. Elicit the best ones for the whole class to attempt.

9 REVIEW

VOCABULARY

1 Write the names of the musical instruments.

1  saxophone

2  keyboard

3  violin

4  trumpet

5  drums

6  guitar/bass

2 Complete the dance styles.

1 F**olk** dances are old, traditional dances.
2 Couples usually wear formal clothes for b**allroom** dancing.
3 You can hear a dancer's steps when they're t**ap** dancing.
4 B**reak** dancing is a street dance that often goes with hip-hop music.
5 People need to train for years to become professional b**allet** dancers.

GRAMMAR IN ACTION

3 Complete the sentences with the verbs in the box. Use the correct form of *going to* or *will*.

be enjoy learn meet not be not visit show tour

1 My favorite band **is going to tour** the U.S.A., but they probably **won't visit** my town.
2 Erin thinks we **won't be** able to learn these dance steps, but we **'re going to show** her that we can.
3 James has decided he **'s going to learn** the piano, and I think he **'ll enjoy** it.
4 I **'m going to meet** Rosie at the salsa class, but I'm sure she **'ll be** late, as usual!

4 Complete the sentences with the simple present or present continuous form of the verbs.

1 Adriana **is bringing** (bring) her guitar to the party on Saturday.
2 We need to hurry. The show **starts** (start) in five minutes.
3 Sara and Jeb **aren't coming** (not come) to the theater tomorrow. They have too much homework.
4 There's a bus that **gets** (get) to the concert hall at 7:15.
5 The concert **doesn't end** (not end) until 11 o'clock. That's pretty late.
6 What **are** you **doing** (do) tomorrow night? Do you want to come to my concert?

Self-Assessment

I can talk about musical instruments and genres.
I can talk about dance styles.
I can use *will* and *going to* to talk about predictions and intentions.
I can use the present continuous and the simple present to talk about future plans and scheduled events.

Review the Unit Theme

Remind students of the unit title: *How do you express yourself?* Put students into pairs. Have them discuss the following questions: *How can people use music to express themselves? Do you prefer to make music or listen to music? Explain. What dance styles are you familiar with? Why do you think people like to dance?* Share answers as a class.

Teacher Support Hub pxlvii

Self-Assessment

Encourage students to think about how difficult the activities on this page were for them in order to circle the appropriate emoji. Supply extra homework from the Workbook to students who circled some sad emojis.

Homework

Workbook pp78–79

Lesson Aim: I can practice my English during vacation.

It is important at this stage that students work toward becoming more independent and autonomous in their learning. This lesson will help raise awareness of different strategies they can try to continue developing their English during vacation.

Warmer

In groups, students brainstorm ideas about what they could do to continue practicing English during vacation. Elicit relevant ideas from the class.

1 After feedback, explain the phrase *Use it or lose it!*, which means that if any skill is not practiced, it can easily be forgotten.

2 Monitor closely and assist where necessary. After feedback, ask students, in groups, to say which ideas they would like to try, and why.

3 Elicit ideas from the whole class and write them on the board. Again, ask students to say which ideas they would like to try, and why.

SHAPE IT!

4 & 5 You may want to add a reward element. Ask students to add in their plan a reward for each of the activities they plan to do (e.g., *Every time I record a voice message for my aunt, I will ask my mom if I can play video games for half an hour.*).

LEARN TO LEARN

LEARN TO … PRACTICE YOUR ENGLISH DURING VACATION

It's important to practice English during vacation, especially when the vacation is long.

1 **Read the conversation between Egor and Polina. Then circle the correct answers.**

EGOR Two months without English classes!
POLINA But if we don't practice, we'll forget everything.
EGOR I don't want that! We've learned a lot this year.
POLINA Well, why don't we make a list of things we can do in English during the vacation?
EGOR That's a great idea!

1 They're speaking … the school year.
a during (b) at the end of

2 They don't want to … their English.
(a) forget b use

3 They're going to …
a ask for help. (b) think of ways to practice.

2 **Egor and Polina begin their list. What do ideas 1–6 practice? Write *S* (speaking), *L* (listening), *R* (reading), or *W* (writing).**

Things to Do in English over the Summer

1 Podcasts (easy ones on English online) L
2 Keep a scrapbook of places we visit. R, W
3 Change the language of our phone apps to English. R
4 Pay attention to station and airport announcements in English when we travel. L
5 Send messages to each other in English! R, W
6 Help a tourist who speaks English. S, L
7 ______
8 ______
9 ______
10 ______

3 **Work in pairs. Think of four more ways to practice English during vacation – one for speaking, listening, reading, and writing. Write them in Egor and Polina's list (7–10).**

SHAPE IT!

4 **Make a plan for practicing English during vacation.**

1 Choose four of the ten ideas from the list and write them under "Ideas" in the chart.
2 Decide when or how often you are going to do these things. Complete the chart.

	Ideas	When? / How Often?
Speaking	*Record a voice message for my aunt in English.*	*Once a week.*
Listening	*Listen to airport announcements.*	*When I fly to see my cousin.*
Speaking		
Listening		
Reading		
Writing		

5 **Tell your partner what you're going to do. Are there any things you can do together?**

For speaking, I'm going to record a voice message for my aunt once a week.

Why don't you record one for me, too? Then I can send you one back!

Great idea! That will help our listening as well!

FINISHED? ANSWER KEY

The aim of these pages is to allow students who have already finished the lesson to practice the target language for the corresponding Student's Book page in a game-like way.

Unit 1 SB p118

1 **2** soap operas
3 cooking shows
4 the news
5 cartoons

2 In A, David is reading. In B, he's playing the guitar.
In A, Julie and Sandro are drinking coffee/tea. In B, they're watching TV.
In A, Azra is sleeping / lying on the sofa.
In A, Kerem and George are laughing. In B, they're shouting/arguing.

3 **2** slowly
3 well
4 hard
5 clearly

4 **1** costume
2 director
3 artist
4 engineer
5 operator
6 lights
Mystery word: script

Unit 2 SB p119

1

P	E	T	V	W	A	R	M	C
S	H	O	C	E	G	H	K	L
N	D	H	O	T	O	I	R	O
O	F	E	L	O	L	C	U	U
W	I	N	D	Y	P	Y	I	D
Y	P	P	O	S	U	N	N	Y

2 **2** ate – eat
3 swam – swim
4 drank – drink
5 heard – hear
6 took – take

3 **Suggested answers:**
There weren't any students in the classroom.
There wasn't any money in the wallet.
There were some children in the park.
There was a sofa in the living room.
Other possible answers:
There weren't any students in the living room.
There wasn't any money in the room/classroom.

4 comb, cup, spoon, knife, hairbrush, bowl, scissors, toothbrush, plate

Unit 3 SB p120

1 **2**

e	o	l
r	n	s
l	e	r
y	s	v

lonely

4

e	d	r
y	i	f
r	g	a
o	n	s

angry

3

u	s	u
n	e	o
t	r	v
i	d	e

nervous

5

e	l	u
u	s	p
m	e	r
t	b	a

upset

2 **Possible answers:**
They were texting / playing games on their phones.
Theo was coming out of the shower / walking across the bathroom.
Mr. and Mrs. Lopez were sitting on the sofa. They were sleeping.
Grandma was walking/coming into the room. She was listening to music.

3 Were you studying for an exam two days ago?
Did you go shopping with friends last Saturday?
How many selfies did you take yesterday?
Who were you sitting next to in your last class?
Students' own answers

4 **2** down
3 past
4 across
5 up
6 over
7 down
8 into
9 peanut

Unit 4 SB p121

1

A	O	S	E	L	L	C	N	J	D
W	C	O	F	R	E	A	S	V	O
B	O	R	R	O	W	Y	P	Y	C
S	S	Y	G	W	R	P	E	U	H
C	T	E	H	E	A	R	N	I	A
P	L	P	N	H	N	T	D	S	N
D	S	A	V	E	W	M	R	N	G
N	V	Y	D	P	L	E	N	D	E

2 **2** 502,000 m^2 **3** 1,200 **4** 15 million

3 **Possible answers:**
2 There isn't / There's not enough water. / The plant/pot/soil is too dry.
3 There isn't enough pizza / They don't have enough pizza.
4 The shoes are too big (for him).

4 **Possible answers:**
2 She's a (preschool) teacher. She's reading a story to the children.
3 She's a volunteer. She's picking up trash. / They're volunteers. They're picking up trash.
4 He's a police officer. He's talking to two/some children.

Unit 5 SB p122

1 **Across**
5 fridge
6 shelves
7 armchair

Down
1 drawers
3 carpet
4 sink
5 floor

2 **2** as comfortable as; large enough – an armchair
3 as soft as; big enough – a carpet
4 as long and wide as; tall enough – the ceiling

3 **Possible answers:**
I don't have to eat a lot of chocolate.
I don't have to watch TV shows for five hours.
I have to work hard at school.
I have to sleep for eight hours every night.

4 loading the dishwasher
doing the dishes
making your bed
cleaning the bathroom
vacuuming the stairs

Unit 6 SB p123

1 **2** hit
3 tripped
4 fell
5 sprained
6 burned
The boy's name is Stefan.

2 **2** a movie theater
3 (security at) an airport
4 a forest

3 **2** two
3 Mary
4 a towel
5 an egg

4 **2** teeth/mouth
3 forehead
4 toes
5 elbow
6 cheek

Unit 7 SB p124

1 **2**

d	o	b
f	w	f
l	n	l
d	a	o

download

3

t	d	e
a	e	v
s	c	i
j	e	p

device

4

h	d	a
n	u	o
l	p	l
w	v	q

upload

5

h	m	e
e	g	s
n	a	s
e	g	p

message

2 **2** charged
3 lost
4 smashed
5 has had

3 **2** We will/won't/might/may have 3D-printers to make furniture at home.
3 We will/won't/might/may have hoverboards to get around town.
4 We will/won't/might/may have hologram teachers to teach us at home.
5 We will/won't/might/may have translator headsets to understand and speak any language.

4 ferry, bus, train, plane, taxi, tram, catch, take, get into, go by

Unit 8 SB p125

1 **2** scientist
3 athlete
4 businessman
5 mathematician
6 composer
7 engineer
Mystery word: inventor

2 **2** written a book?
3 seen an elephant?
4 met anyone famous?

3

l	y	o	u	r	s	e	l	f	s	w	i	e	x	c
t	k	o	s	o	m	e	o	n	e	b	v	i	v	q
o	e	s	e	v	e	r	y	o	n	e	v	s	a	v
m	y	s	e	l	f	a	e	c	r	d	e	j	b	q
t	s	h	u	o	e	y	n	a	v	r	e	v	m	n
h	m	e	n	u	o	t	g	y	e	t	t	q	e	o
e	p	r	a	r	t	w	o	h	t	e	h	r	y	t
m	w	s	n	s	z	k	w	w	a	h	e	g	r	h
s	f	e	y	e	s	o	m	e	t	h	i	n	g	i
e	m	l	w	l	n	a	w	i	w	g	w	n	u	n
l	c	f	h	v	p	s	b	y	t	v	h	w	g	g
v	o	h	e	e	z	e	r	r	p	s	s	v	s	h
e	o	j	r	s	v	e	k	y	g	y	e	u	m	f
s	s	g	e	v	v	d	p	b	b	x	n	l	b	g
e	h	t	h	e	h	i	m	s	e	l	f	h	f	t

4 **2** part **3** with **4** work **5** give/set **6** set/give
7 keep **8** show

Unit 9 SB p126

1 **Instruments:**
2 bass (guitar)
3 keyboard
4 violin
5 drums

Possible genres:
2 rock
3 hip-hop
4 classical
5 reggae

2 Chloe isn't going to play the guitar. She's going to play the keyboard.
Pablo isn't going to take up ballroom dancing. He's going to take up tap dancing.
Olivia and Leo aren't going to learn tap dancing. They're going to learn ballroom dancing.

3 **1** (I'm meeting my friends on Saturday) evening and we're going to see a movie at the theater.
2 Ben and I are going to a rock concert in Chicago. Our train leaves at three o'clock.

4

B	A	L	L	E	T	D	A	N	C	I	N	G	E	O	D	O	G	J	W	A	E	M	U
J	T	A	P	D	A	N	C	I	N	G	L	A	C	I	S	S	A	L	C	B	J	N	Y
Z	A	G	U	R	U	G	N	I	C	N	A	D	K	A	E	R	B	V	Y	M	I	L	F
S	G	Z	E	O	W	O	G	Q	F	P	B	X	H	W	S	W	I	N	G	U	U	L	O
Q	G	V	Z	C	L	E	S	E	L	F	M	R	A	R	Z	T	J	Y	K	Z	F	F	L
K	P	B	M	K	G	Q	F	O	R	Y	B	S	X	I	V	B	K	S	O	N	C	O	K

VOCABULARY BANK ANSWER KEY

The aim of the Vocabulary Bank pages is to offer students more practice of the unit vocabulary. They can be assigned as homework, as a class test, or as further tasks for fast finishers.

Starter Unit SB p127

1 **1** go
2 goes
3 play
4 take
5 do

2 **1** F **2** F **3** T **4** F **5** T **6** T

3 Students' own answers

Unit 1 SB p128

1 Students' own answers

2 **1** makeup artist
2 costumes
3 script
4 sound engineer
5 director

3 Students' own answers

Unit 2 SB p129

1 **1** snowy
2 rain
3 sunny
4 cloud
5 dry
Mystery word: windy

2 **1** knife
2 pillow
3 plate
4 toothbrush
5 mirror

3 **Possible answers:**
1 bedroom: blanket, comb, hairbrush, lamp, mirror, pillow
2 kitchen: bowl, cup, fork, knife, plate, scissors, spoon
3 bathroom: comb, hairbrush, mirror, toothbrush

Unit 3 SB p130

1 **1** tired
2 bored
3 upset
4 lonely
5 surprised

2 **1** c **2** e **3** b **4** a **5** d

3 Students' own answers

Unit 4 SB p131

1 **1** pays
2 spend/save
3 earn
4 borrow
5 cost

2 **1** T **2** F **3** F **4** T **5** F

3 **1** Ooo
2 ooOo
3 oO ooo
4 ooO
5 Oo ooo

Unit 5 SB p132

1 sink, picture, floor, cupboard, ceiling, carpet, bookcase, wardrobe

2 **1** dishes
2 dishwasher
3 bed
4 furniture
5 carpet

3 Students' own answers

Unit 6 SB p133

1 **1** My dad burned his hand on the stove.
2 Lena fell off her horse and broke her leg.
3 Sara tripped and sprained her ankle.
4 Dan hit his head on a cupboard door.
5 I got stung on my neck by a bee.

2 **1** cheek
2 forehead
3 teeth
4 neck
5 knee
6 chest

3 Students' own answers

Unit 7 SB p134

1 **1** c **2** e **3** b **4** a **5** d

2 Students' own answers

3 **1** You should get **off** the bus near the museum.
2 Dad goes to work on **foot**. / Dad goes to work **by** train.
3 We got **into** a taxi and went to the airport.
4 They **caught** / **took** a plane to Japan. / They went **by plane** to Japan.
5 Get **on** the train at Portland station.

Unit 8 SB p135

1 Students' own answers

2 **1** looks up to
2 give up
3 came up with
4 keep up with
5 set up

3 Students' own answers

Unit 9 SB p136

1 **1** drum(s)
2 microphone
3 keyboard
4 trumpet
5 violin

2 **1** T **2** F **3** F **4** T **5** T

3 Students' own answers

Lesson Aim: I can understand a text about history.

Warmer

Write *legend* on the board and elicit the meaning (a very old story about famous people or places). Invite students, in groups, to discuss any legends they know about their country. Elicit their ideas, assisting with relevant vocabulary. Point out to students that using English to talk about history is a useful way of developing their ability to use past tenses and to explain events.

1 If students have never heard of this, ask them what language it comes from (Spanish), and tell them that it refers to a place made of gold. Ask students to make further guesses.

2 2.12 ★★★ Give students four minutes to read the text and disallow the use of dictionaries and translation software at this point. Instead, encourage students to guess the meaning of any unknown words. Elicit that El Dorado is a mythical city made of gold, which people believed was somewhere in the Amazon jungle.

3 Suggest that students quickly scan the text again and circle all the dates they can find, as this will help them complete the exercise.

4 Allow students a few minutes of thinking time to form an opinion and look up relevant vocabulary in a dictionary. Monitor the discussions closely and elicit opinions, writing appropriate ideas on the board for the rest of the class to see.

2 HISTORY

1 Look at the title and picture and discuss the questions.

1 Have you heard of El Dorado?
2 What and where do you think it is?

2 Read the text. Check your answers to Exercise 1. (2.12)

3 Complete the sentences with years.

1 1520s – Spanish conquistadors first heard about the Muisca people.
2 1617 – Sir Walter Raleigh failed to find El Dorado.
3 1545 – They searched Lake Guatavita for gold.
4 1537 – They first went to look for "El Dorado."
5 1803 – Alexander von Humboldt proved the site at Lake Parime did not exist.

4 Why did the Europeans want to explore and control the Americas? Discuss with a partner.

5 Match the words in bold with the definitions.

1 a long search for something that may not exist or is difficult to find quest
2 a small flat boat, often made of wood raft
3 a traditional story myth
4 a fight during a war, usually to take control of a place battle

Explore It!

Guess the correct answer.

People once believed there was gold worth … in Lake Guatavita.

a $1 million b $50 million c $300 million

Find another interesting fact about a legend. Then write a question for your partner to answer.

The Legend of El Dorado

In the 1500s, Europeans were discovering and trying to take control of the Americas. In the 1520s, Spanish conquistadors heard about the Muisca people, who lived in what is now Colombia.

The stories suggested that the Muisca had a huge amount of gold. When they chose a new chief, they covered him in gold and sailed him on a **raft** into the middle of Lake Guatavita. The chief put all the gold into the lake as a gift for the gods.

In 1537, the Spanish decided to look for the chief, who they named "El Dorado," but without success. Then in 1545, they looked for gold in Lake Guatavita. They discovered a few objects, and they became sure that there was a whole city of gold somewhere in the Amazon jungle. People started to refer to the golden city as El Dorado.

Many people looked for El Dorado over the centuries. These included the British explorer Sir Walter Raleigh. In 1617, on his second expedition to South America, he fought a **battle** with the Spanish on the Orinoco River, as both the British and the Spanish searched for El Dorado. The British king was unhappy about this conflict and executed Raleigh on his return.

The **myth** of El Dorado continued to grow. Maps in the seventeenth and eighteenth centuries even showed the city next to a legendary lake, Lake Parime. But nobody ever found it, and in 1803 the German explorer Alexander von Humboldt disproved the existence of this site.

After hundreds of failed expeditions, people finally realized that El Dorado never existed. The phrase "looking for El Dorado" means to go on a hopeless **quest**.

UNIT 2 | CLIL 137

5 After feedback, ask students, in pairs, to find another unknown word in the text and find its definition. They then teach this word to another pair.

Students can collaborate digitally through *Collaboration Plus*, where you can assign, track, and assess their work. Students can also share and showcase their work and comment on each other's projects.

Explore it!

If appropriate, allow students to search for information online. If this isn't possible, ask students to work in groups to share ideas and create questions.

Lesson Aim: I can understand a text about social studies.

Warmer

Ask students, in pairs, to discuss what they remember spending money on in the last week and whether they're happy with what they bought. Elicit some ideas, along with relevant vocabulary (e.g., *unnecessary, a must, regret, good value*).

1 Allow students a minute of thinking time before discussing their ideas in pairs, and then elicit relevant ideas on the board.

2 4.12 To encourage faster reading, allow three minutes to read the text.

3 Students discuss the statements in pairs, according to what they remember of the text, before reading again and checking their answers in pairs.

4 After feedback, students, in pairs, find another unknown word in the text, find its meaning, and write an example sentence with it. Elicit a few examples from different pairs.

Students can collaborate digitally through *Collaboration Plus*, where you can assign, track, and assess their work. Students can also share and showcase their work and comment on each other's projects.

Explore It!

Alternatively, students, in pairs or groups, can write a question about teen spending and then find the answer for homework. Elicit the information in the following lesson.

4 SOCIAL STUDIES

The Best Things in Life Are (Almost) Free

There is no doubt that money is **essential** to daily life. People earn money to buy food, pay the **bills**, or save for something special like a vacation or a present. Life becomes extremely difficult for people when there isn't enough money for their basic needs.

However, many people spend too much money on items they do not need. Marketing and advertising **encourage** people to buy an enormous range of products and services, and these days, with 24-hour internet access, it is easier than ever to spend money at the touch of a button.

How American teenagers spend their money, according to a recent survey

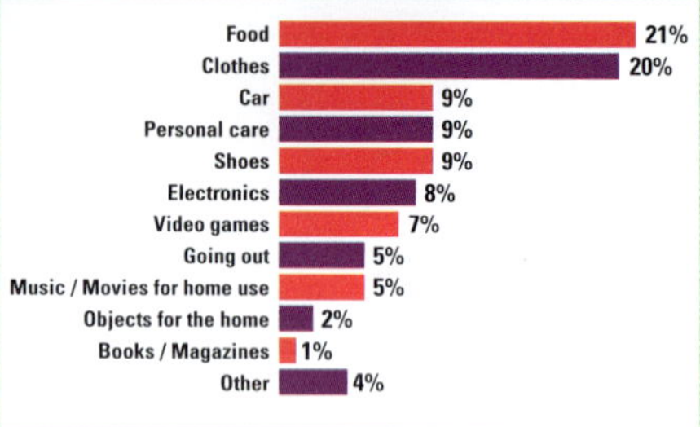

Some people believe that consuming so much is unhealthy, and we should make an effort to find interests that do not cost anything at all. If you want to do this, there are a number of options, and a good way to start is by looking at local websites. There are many free events for local communities, and you just need to select an activity that interests you. You could choose from music, dance, sports, art, tourism, walking, and many, many more.

Of course, you need access to a computer or phone to check a website. That costs money, but if it helps you to save money in the long run, then it is a good **investment**. Why not take a look today? It may be the first step in reducing your spending and starting a new low-cost life.

1 Discuss the questions.

1 Why do we need money?
2 What kinds of things can we do in our free time without money?

4.12 **2 Read the article. Are your ideas from Exercise 1 mentioned?**

3 Are the sentences *T* (true) or *F* (false)?

1 People need money for their basic needs. T
2 Teenagers don't need vacations or presents. F
3 U.S. teenagers spend less than a quarter of their money on clothes. T
4 We can use technology to find free events. T
5 If you want to save money, you sometimes have to spend a little first. T

4 Complete the sentences with the words in bold.

1 I bought a cheap phone to save money, but it was a bad investment because it broke and I had to buy a new one.
2 That video game isn't an essential item. I think you should save your money.
3 Please don't encourage Ben to buy any more sneakers. He already has plenty of pairs.
4 Lisa has almost no money left each month after she pays the bills.

Explore It!

Guess the correct answer.

The average U.S. household spends more money on … than on food.

a transportation b entertainment c healthcare

Find another interesting fact about spending in your country. Then write a question for your partner to answer.

Extend It!

Students look at the graph and discuss, in groups, whether the data is similar to the way they spend money.

Lesson Aim: I can understand a text about science.

Warmer

In groups, students have two minutes to brainstorm animals that can poison people. If necessary, explain that *poison* is something that can make people extremely sick if they eat or drink it or if it gets into their blood. The team with the most animals wins.

1 Point out that being able to read scientific texts in English is very useful, as a large amount of research is published in this language. Elicit students' ideas about the article title and photo, and write them on the board so that students can use them as a reference while reading the text later.

2 6.13 Give students three minutes to read the text, and encourage them to circle key words that helped them check their ideas from Exercise1. Elicit these during feedback.

3 Encourage students to discuss the missing information with a partner before reading again to check their answers.

4 ★★★ Fast finishers work together to write an extra half-sentence using information from the text. Elicit these after feedback and ask the rest of the class to complete the sentences.

5 After feedback, students, in pairs, find another unknown word in the text, find its meaning, and write an example sentence with it. Elicit a few examples from different pairs.

6 SCIENCE

SMALL BUT DEADLY

Imagine you are trekking through a rainforest. You're amazed at the rich variety of wildlife, although you're nervous about meeting a jaguar or a boa constrictor. Suddenly, you see something bright and yellow on a plant. You move closer and realize that it is a tiny frog. "Frogs aren't dangerous," you think, and you hold out your hand …

Stop! The animal in front of you is *Phyllobates terribilis*, or the golden poison frog. It is the most poisonous land animal in the world.

The golden poison frog is an amphibian that lives in the rainforests of Colombia. It is only about 5 cm long and weighs less than 25 grams. It is a **carnivore**, and it eats ants, beetles, and centipedes that only live in the rainforest. Scientists believe this specific diet produces the poison that the frogs secrete from their backs. If a human touches a golden poison frog, it can cause **swelling**, nausea, paralysis, or even death.

Incredibly, these frogs may also be good for humans. Scientists are investigating how they can use frog poisons in medicines to treat heart conditions. However, **deforestation** and pollution mean the golden poison frog is in danger. If we do not protect the tropical rainforests, this beautiful but **deadly** animal will soon disappear.

So, if you see one of these creatures in the jungle, keep your distance and leave it alone. Then you will both stay safe.

1 Look at the title and photo. What information can you guess about this frog?

6.13 **2 Read the article. Were your ideas correct?**

3 Complete the fact file about the golden poison frog.

SCIENTIFIC NAME:	1 Phyllobates terribilis
TYPE OF ANIMAL:	2 amphibian
SIZE:	3 5 cm
WEIGHT:	4 less than 25 grams
DIET:	5 ants, beetles, centipedes
HOME:	6 rainforests of Colombia

4 Complete the sentences.

1 The golden poison frog can hurt people if they touch it.
2 It can help people because its poison might go into medicines to treat heart conditions.

5 Complete the sentences with the words in bold.

1 This snake has a deadly bite. It can kill you.
2 There was swelling on his toe where he was stung. His toe was bigger than usual.
3 Because of deforestation, a lot of animals have lost their homes.
4 An animal that eats meat (for example, a cat) is a carnivore.

Explore It!

Guess the correct answer.

The golden poison frog has enough poison to kill …

a a cat. (b) 20,000 mice. c an elephant.

Find another interesting fact about a dangerous animal. Then write a question for your partner to answer.

Students can collaborate digitally through *Collaboration Plus*, where you can assign, track, and assess their work. Students can also share and showcase their work and comment on each other's projects.

Explore It!

Allow students to work in groups to create a question. Collect and read the questions aloud. The groups discuss and write down their answers together. To check answers, ask each group to stand up and explain the answer to the question they wrote.

Lesson Aim: I can understand a text about technology.

Warmer

In groups, students brainstorm famous inventions for two minutes. Elicit a few on the board, and elicit any extra information about them that students might know. Point out that reading technology-themed texts in English is a good way to pick up vocabulary that can be useful for describing projects, results, and ideas.

1 If students don't know what the object is, invite them to read the title and subheading of the text, and elicit what "small screen" means.

2 8.13 To encourage faster skimming, allow students three minutes to read the text. Disallow the use of dictionaries and translation software.

3 Encourage students to discuss the order of the events with a partner before rereading the text to check.

4 Allow a few minutes of thinking time for students to form an opinion and search for relevant vocabulary in a dictionary, if available. Then monitor closely and take note of useful vocabulary and grammar to point out during feedback.

5 Challenge students to explain how they were able to guess the meaning of the words in bold (e.g., with *crops*, the clue in the text is *farm*).

Students can collaborate digitally through *Collaboration Plus*, where you can assign, track, and assess their work. Students can also share and showcase their work and comment on each other's projects.

8 TECHNOLOGY

1 Look at the photos. Do you know what the invention is and who invented it?

2 Read the article. Check your answers to Exercise 1.
television; Philo Farnsworth (and other inventors)

3 Put the events in order.

a 1 Farnsworth entered invention competitions.
b 3 He went to college.
c 2 He had an idea while he was working on his family's farm.
d 6 Businesses took up his ideas.
e 5 He produced the first version of a fully electronic television.
f 4 He had to get a job.

4 Imagine you're going to spend 24 hours without looking at any type of screen. How can you spend your time? Discuss your ideas with a partner.

5 Match the words in bold with the definitions.

1 plants that farmers grow crops
2 change slowly over a long time evolve
3 stop doing something before you have completely finished drop out
4 first example of an invention prototype

Explore It!

Guess the correct statement.

a After his invention, Philo Farnsworth had a television in every room of his house.
b Philo Farnsworth became one of the first television news presenters.
(c) Philo Farnsworth didn't like television and didn't allow his family to watch it.

Find another interesting fact about television. Then write a question for your partner to answer.

Philo Farnsworth:
A Big Influence on the Small Screen

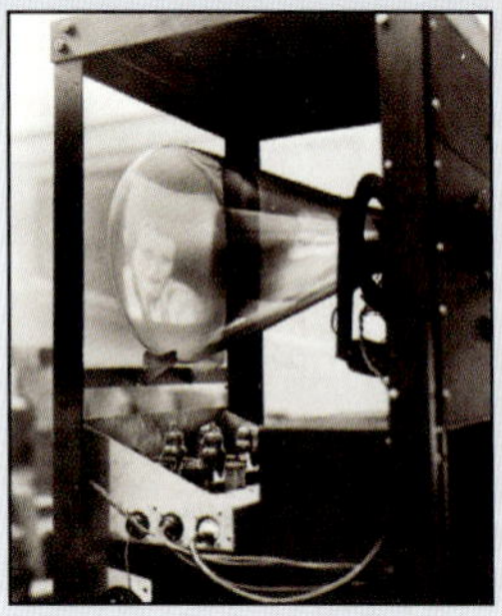

The television is probably the world's most popular form of entertainment. On average, people around the world watch three hours of television per day, and in Europe and North America, it is closer to four hours. But who is responsible for this amazing invention?

It isn't an easy question to answer because, over the years, different people developed different types of televisions. One of these was Philo Farnsworth, a farmer's son from Utah in the U.S.A. He built the first all-electronic TV set. This young man's creativity and determination made a big difference in the development of the small screen.

Farnsworth was always interested in inventions. As a young teenager, he took part in invention competitions and made mechanical gadgets that helped with household chores. In 1921, at the age of 15, he came up with the basic idea for a totally electronic television. He was looking at the parallel lines of **crops** on his family's farm when he realized that he could separate images into parallel lines of light, which he could transform into television images.

Farnsworth was a brilliant student and started college, but he was forced to **drop out** and work after his father died. However, he continued to work on his invention. Finally, in 1928, he finalized his **prototype** TV. His invention continued to **evolve** and improve, and throughout his career, different companies produced different versions of it. The television continues to evolve quickly – today's flat-screen smart TVs will surely look old-fashioned to future generations.

Explore It!

If appropriate, ask students to search for the information online using their smartphone or tablet. If this is not possible, students can work in small groups to create a question.

Extend It!

Students research an inventor from their country and what they invented. They then prepare a short presentation about the inventor in groups.

Unit 1: Tip

We join the pronouns (*I*, *you*, *he*, etc.) to the auxiliary verb *to be* to make a contraction of one syllable. *We're listening* has four syllables with the stress on the beginning of the main verb. Have students practice the sentences with the correct stress and pronouncing the contractions as one word.

Unit 2: Tip

Ask students to guess the rules for the pronunciation of *-ed* endings. Share the chart below with them.

/ɪd/	/t/	/d/
T wanted	C danced	B robbed
D needed	CH watched	G tagged
	GH laughed	L called
	K looked	M seemed
	P helped	N opened
	SH washed	R cleared
	SS missed	S used
	X fixed	V loved
		Z amazed

Words that end in a vowel sound use the /d/ pronunciation for *-ed* (e.g., *enjoyed, followed, played, tried*).

Unit 3: Tip

Tell students that with two-syllable adjectives, the stress often falls on the first syllable but is sometimes on the second.

Have students look up words they find difficult to pronounce in an online dictionary and listen to the recordings of the pronunciation. Many students struggle with *tired* and *bored*. Remind them that these are both one-syllable words with a soft *r* sound.

PRONUNCIATION

UNIT 1
Contractions: *To Be*

1.04 **1 Listen and repeat.**

1 **I am** sitting in my bedroom. > **I'm** sitting in my bedroom.
2 **He is** taking a selfie. > **He's** taking a selfie.
3 **You are** walking on the moon. > **You're** walking on the moon.
4 **We are** listening to music. > **We're** listening to music.

1.05 **2 Listen and (circle) the option you hear. Practice saying the sentences.**

1 (*They are*) / *They're* listening to music.
2 *She is* / (*She's*) reading a blog.
3 (*He is*) / *He's* skiing in France.
4 *You are* / (*You're*) watching TV.
5 (*It is*) / *It's* eating.

UNIT 2
/t/, /d/, and /ɪd/

2.03 **1 Listen and repeat.**

1 /t/ walk**ed** 2 /d/ liv**ed** 3 /ɪd/ want**ed**

2 Write the verbs in the correct column.

~~agreed~~ arrived changed cooked decided helped looked survived traveled wanted

1 /t/ or /d/	2 /ɪd/
agreed, arrived, changed, cooked, helped, looked, survived, traveled	decided, wanted

2.04 **3 Listen and check.**

UNIT 3
Word Stress in Adjectives

1 How many syllables do these adjectives have?

afraid	2	angry	2	bored	1
nervous	2	excited	3	lonely	2
upset	2	surprised	2	tired	1

3.02 **2 Listen and check.**

3 Match the words in Exercise 1 with their stress patterns. Complete the chart.

1 oO	2 Oo	3 oOo	4 O
afraid, upset, surprised	nervous, angry, lonely	excited	bored, tired

3.03 **4 Listen and repeat the sentences.**

1 Sam's afraid of dogs.
2 My best friend is very upset.
3 I'm worried about exams.
4 I studied all night and I'm very tired.
5 I feel embarrassed when I forget someone's name.

UNIT 4
-er Ending Sounds

4.06 **1 Listen and repeat.**

/ər/ garbage collect**or** preshool teach**er** fitt**er** bett**er**

4.07 **2 Listen and repeat the sentences.**

1 My sister's a firefighter.
2 The teacher is happier than the actor.
3 Life is better when you're healthier.

UNIT 5
Have: /f/ vs /v/

5.08 **1 Listen and (circle) the option you hear: /f/ or /v/.**

1 Jenny and Peter **have** to make their beds every day. (/f/) / /v/
2 I **have** a new bed. /f/ / (/v/)
3 George and Helen **have** to make dinner every Saturday. (/f/) / /v/
4 Tom doesn't **have** to help in the house. (/f/) / /v/
5 Do you **have** an extra pencil? /f/ / (/v/)
6 Sam and Dan don't **have** to do much. (/f/) / /v/

PRONUNCIATION 141

Unit 4: Tip

Even though the spelling at the ends of these words can be *-or* or *-er*, the sound you say is exactly the same.

Unit 5: Tip

Ask students when the pronunciation is /hæf/ (in *have to*) and when it is /hæv/ (when *have* is the main verb). This is a good moment to have students practice the *v* sound. Have them place their top front teeth just behind their bottom lip and make it vibrate. When they say *f*, they should blow air through their top teeth, and there is no vibration.

Unit 6: Tip

It can be difficult to tell the difference between these two sounds. To make the /ʌ/ sound, the mouth is open and the jaw is dropped. The sound comes from the throat. Have students say several words that contain this sound (e.g., *mother, brother, uncle, son, cousin*). Alternatively, have them practice these sentences: *My uncle is my mother's brother. My cousin is my uncle's son. It's fun to have lunch on Sunday in London.*

To make the /ʊ/ sound, the mouth doesn't open as wide, and the lips make a round shape (e.g., *cook, look, book; I could look in the cookbook.*). In Exercise 4, the sentences mix the two sounds. Have students write the sounds above the words in the sentences.

She cut (/ʌ/) her foot (/ʊ/), but (/ʌ/) she couldn't (/ʊ/) call her cousin (/ʌ/).
I must (/ʌ/) put (/ʊ/) some books (/ʊ/) in the cupboard (/ʌ/).

Unit 7: Tip

Ask students which words contain a long *i* sound (words with /aɪ/) and which have a short *i* sound (/ɪ/).

Show them the lists of minimal pairs below.

bit	*bite*
fin	*fine*
lick	*like*
lit	*light*
pin	*pine*
rim	*rhyme*
sit	*sight*

Ask them if they can detect any patterns with the spellings that let us know what the sound is (e.g., the words ending in *-e* and *-ight* tend to have the /aɪ/ sound).

2 (5.09) **Listen and repeat the sentences.**

1 I **have** to do the gardening this weekend.
2 My brothers **have** a really big wardrobe.
3 We don't **have** to go to school on Monday.
4 We **have** a bookcase in the living room.
5 Does Jake **have** to do the dishes?

UNIT 6
/ʌ/ and /ʊ/

1 (6.04) **Listen and repeat.**

1 /ʌ/ must must not
2 /ʊ/ should cook full

2 Write the words in the correct column.

~~brother~~ could cousin cut foot put stung

1 /ʌ/	2 /ʊ/
brother, cousin, cut, stung	could, foot, put

3 (6.05) **Listen, check, and repeat.**

4 (6.06) **Listen and repeat the sentences.**

1 She cut her foot, but she couldn't call her cousin.
2 I must put some books in the cupboard.

UNIT 7
The Letter *i*

1 (7.03) **Listen and repeat.**

1 /ɪ/ chip film kick
2 /aɪ/ like online hi

2 Write the words in the correct column.

bike device ~~Internet~~ online printer video Wi-Fi will write

1 /ɪ/	2 /aɪ/
Internet, printer, video, will	bike, device, online, Wi-Fi, write

3 (7.04) **Listen, check, and repeat.**

4 (7.05) **Listen and repeat the sentences.**

1 James can't get Wi-Fi, so he doesn't have Internet.
2 I can watch videos online on my new device.

UNIT 8
Intonation in Questions

1 (8.04) **Listen and repeat.**

1 Was Mozart a scientist?
2 Where do you live?
3 Have you cycled 100 kilometers?
4 What did you do last night?

2 Circle the question endings where Nick's voice goes up. Underline the endings where it goes down.

NICK How long have you been a teacher?
MR. K Well, Nick. It's been 20 years now.
NICK Really? That's a long time! Do you like it?
MR. K Yes, but some days are harder than others.
NICK What do you like best about it?
MR. K The best thing is seeing students improve.
NICK That's great. Do you think you'll be a teacher for the next 20 years?
MR. K Well, I hope so!

3 (8.05) **Listen, check, and repeat.**

UNIT 9
Sentence Stress

1 How many syllables do these sentences have? Then underline the words you think are stressed.

1 We're going to play jazz. 6
2 We'll buy a new guitar. 6
3 Is Jake playing the drums? 6
4 We're going to a free concert. 8

2 (9.07) **Listen, check, and repeat.**

3 Clap the rhythm of these sentences.

1 She often sings in a band.
2 Is the piano your favorite instrument?
3 The concert starts at eight o'clock.
4 Adam is organizing the music.

142 PRONUNCIATION

Unit 8: Tip

We pronounce open questions differently from *yes/no* questions. Have students identify which questions are open (asking for information) and which are *yes/no* questions.

Unit 9: Tip

Remind students that stress is important when speaking English if you want people to understand you. Ask students what type of words they need to stress in English (main verbs, adjective, and nouns).

STUDENT'S BOOK AUDIOSCRIPTS

Starter Unit

S.01
1 read books, read magazines
2 chat online
3 go shopping
4 go for a bike ride
5 hang out with friends
6 listen to music
7 make cookies, make videos
8 play an instrument
9 take photos
10 write a blog

S.02
1 [musical instrument]

2	A	Ready? Say cheese!
	B & C	Cheeeeese!
3	A	Aiden … Aiden …
	B	Sorry! I can't hear you. Hang on a minute.
4	A	OK, are we ready?
	B	Yes, we are! Let's go!
5	A	Let's go to the sports store now.
	B	Good idea. We can look at the sneakers.

6 This is my favorite recipe: cinnamon chocolate chip cookies. They're delicious! Now, let's see. What's next?

7 This one is about movies. There are a lot of reviews and interviews in it. I buy it every week. But I also get a sports one that comes out every month.

S.03
1 gymnastics
2 rugby
3 sailing
4 track and field
5 swimming
6 basketball
7 table tennis
8 hockey

Not in the pictures: volleyball, windsurfing

S.05
I like my new school. I don't know all the students in my class yet, but I sit next to a boy named Jorge in my English class. He plays basketball every day, but he doesn't like other sports. Do you get a lot of homework? Our teachers don't give us a lot. I go to homework club on Wednesdays. Some of the older students help us. They're nice. After homework club, I don't get home until about 6:30 p.m.

S.06
1 tablet
2 headphones
3 money
4 bus pass
5 portable charger
6 keys
7 phone
8 passport
9 camera
10 laptop

S.07

ALEX	Hi … Is this the coding club?
EMMA	Sorry. This is the photography club. I'm Emma, by the way.
ALEX	Hi, I'm Alex.
EMMA	Are you new here?
ALEX	Yes, I am, and I'm lost. I don't have a map of the school.
EMMA	Don't worry! I love helping people. Do you want to come to the photography club? Look … we have two new cameras this semester. I hate using my phone for photos, and these cameras are really cool.
ALEX	No, thanks. I want the coding club. I don't like taking photos.
EMMA	Oh, that's too bad.
ALEX	Do you like taking photos?
EMMA	I love it, so this is the club for me. OK … coding club … let me see … Oh, there's Libby. She goes to the coding club every week. Libby! Libby, this is Alex. He's new here. Alex, meet Libby.
ALEX & LIBBY	Hi.
EMMA	So Libby, Alex wants to go to the coding club.
LIBBY	No problem. Follow me. So, do you have your own laptop?

ALEX Uh … no … I don't, but I have a tablet. Is that OK?

LIBBY Don't worry! They have a lot of laptops there. You can borrow one.

ALEX So, what's the teacher like?

LIBBY Mr. Adams? He's great. He sometimes thinks he's Bill Gates, and he loves telling stories.

ALEX Do you have your own computer?

LIBBY Yes, I do. I like writing computer programs for it.

ALEX Wow! That's cool.

LIBBY Yes, it is, but I'm really busy and I don't have much free time. I want to write more! I don't mind helping you write some programs.

ALEX Really? Thanks, Libby. What's the club like?

LIBBY It's fun! OK, here we are …

S.08 We have a new student in our class. Her name's Paola. What do we have in common? A lot! She has brown hair and blue eyes – just like me!

Does she have any brothers and sisters? Yes, she does. She has two little sisters, just like me. She doesn't have any brothers. We have the same phones and headphones!

We don't have school today because it's a holiday. I'd like to call Paola – but I don't have her phone number. It's annoying!

Unit 1

1.01 **1** soap opera
2 drama
3 reality show
4 talk show
5 documentary
6 cartoon
7 streaming series
8 game show

Not in the photos: comedy, cooking show, sports show, the news

1.02 **1 A** So, what do you think of *Laugh a Minute*?

B I love it! I can't stop laughing. Look …

2 Oh, I hope she can win the money, but I'm not sure she can do it … Oh, come on!

3 A So, have you watched the latest episode yet?

B No, not yet.

A Oh … well, guess what happens? I can tell you. It's so exciting!

B No, be quiet. Don't tell me now. I want to watch it tonight.

A OK, well be prepared for a surprise … a big surprise.

4 A OK, so what's happening now? Can you explain?

B Well, Miguel is meeting Veronica, but Xavier doesn't know. Xavier isn't happy with Miguel, so they aren't speaking to each other and …

A OK, OK, stop! I think I get it now.

5 A Oh, no … now those bugs are moving all over him. NO! Now he's eating them … that's disgusting!

B I bet they taste delicious with some salt!

6 A So, do you like that show?

B No way! That's for little kids.

A True, but it's really funny and it makes me laugh.

1.05 **1** They are listening to music.
2 She's reading a blog.
3 He is skiing in France.
4 You're watching TV.
5 It is eating.

1.06 **ROSA** What are you doing right now, Toni?

TONI I'm talking to you.

ROSA Ha, ha. Very funny! Are you studying for the math test?

TONI No, I'm watching a talk show. Why are you calling me?

ROSA Well, this math homework is giving me a headache. Can you help me?

TONI Sorry, Rosa. I can't talk now. They're interviewing Ed Sheeran. I'll call you back, OK? Bye.

ROSA Great. Thanks a lot, Toni.

1.07 **1** set
2 lights
3 actor
4 camera
5 sound engineer
6 makeup artist
7 camera operator
8 script
9 costume
10 director

1.08 **MATT** Hi! I'm Matt and I'm from New Zealand. I live in the capital – Wellington – on the North Island. More than three million people visit the locations for movies like *The Lord of the Rings* here every year. Today, I'm visiting a movie workshop with my media studies class. We're waiting for our guide. Ah, here she is now.

CLARA Hi. I'm Clara, your guide. If you have any questions or I'm not explaining things clearly, let me know! Listen carefully – there's a quiz at the end and a prize! Yes …

GIRL What do you do here?

CLARA We make costumes, we design and build models, and we design movie sets. First stop, costumes. Do you recognize any of these?

MATT There's Thor's helmet from *Thor* and Frodo's shirt from *Lord of the Rings* – wow!

CLARA Do you want to hold it?

MATT Yes, please! I can't believe I'm touching this. It's very light.

CLARA Yes, it is. It's because it isn't metal – it's plastic. Next, let's look at the bigatures.

GIRL The bigatures? What are they?

CLARA They're really large models of buildings or landscapes used for the filming of a movie. Some of them are nine meters high.

GIRL Why do you use bigatures?

CLARA To create scenes in places that don't exist in real life. So we take photos of the bigature, for example a castle, and then we put the images together with actors in front of them to create the scene. OK, let's move on. There's Martin. He's one of our camera operators, and he's working hard today. Shh … talk quietly, please. Martin is working.

MATT What is he doing?

CLARA He's taking a photo of a model for one of the new *Avatar* movies.

MATT No way! *Avatar*'s my favorite movie!

CLARA OK, follow me … Next, I'm taking you to see …

1.09 Media studies is my favorite subject at school. I love it! This week, we're studying the history of film. We're learning all about talkies, CGI, and lots more! I don't know much about it. It takes a long time and a lot of people to make a movie.

Sorry! Time to go! My little brother is making a lot of noise downstairs. I think he's watching his favorite comedy with my mom and dad. They all love it, and they always laugh a lot.

What are you doing at school this week?

1.10 **EVA** What are you doing?

ALEX I'm watching the second episode of this new comedy series.

EVA But it's lunchtime.

ALEX I'm not having lunch today. Lunch can wait.

EVA So, what do you think of the show?

ALEX I love it! Do you like comedies?

EVA No, I don't. I'm not really into them. I prefer watching documentaries and dramas.

ALEX Everyone's watching this one. It's really cool! Why don't you watch it with me?

EVA I'm not sure.

ALEX I think you'll really like it.

EVA OK. Let's see.

ALEX Well? What do you think of it?

EVA Actually, it's not bad!

Unit 2

2.01 **1** dry, hot, and sunny
2 cold and snowy
3 cloudy and windy
4 foggy
5 rainy, warm, and wet

Not in the photos: icy, stormy

2.04 **1** /t/ or /d/ agreed arrived changed cooked helped looked survived traveled

2 /ɪd/ decided wanted

2.05 On September 6, 1620, 102 people left England to travel 4,500 km to North America. They didn't agree with some of the religious views in Europe at that time, so they decided to start a new life.

They traveled on a ship called the *Mayflower*, and the journey took 66 days. The first half of the journey went well. Then the weather changed, and it was very cold and stormy. People got sick and some of them didn't survive.

In December, they arrived in Plymouth Bay. They didn't know anything about this new land, but the local Wampanoag people helped them find food and build houses.

2.06

1 fork

2 scissors

3 knife

4 blanket

5 toothbrush

6 comb

7 mirror

8 plate

9 bowl

10 pillow

11 hairbrush

12 spoon

13 lamp

14 cup

2.07 **1** [toothbrush]

2 Be careful. Try to cut the paper neatly.

3 Stop it! Hey! Ouch …

4 **DAD** Stand still, please.

GIRL Ow! That hurts.

5 Mmm. That's delicious soup.

6 [knife]

2.08 **RADIO HOST** Good afternoon and welcome to *The History Hour*. Last week, there was an exhibition in Copenhagen about a special teenager, and I went along to find out more from Ingrid Noren – a Danish historian.

RADIO HOST Wow! So here she is.

INGRID Yes. This is the Egtved girl. She's 3,000 years old! Archaeologists found her body in 1921 in Egtved, a small village in southern Denmark.

RADIO HOST What's special about her?

INGRID Before we found her, there wasn't really any information about clothes that people wore at that time.

RADIO HOST Really? What did you learn about her?

INGRID We know she died in 1370 BCE when she was between 16 and 18 years old. And we know she died in the summer because there were some summer flowers with her body.

RADIO HOST Ah! Were there any other things from the Bronze Age with her body?

INGRID Yes, there were. There was a blanket, a comb, a belt, some jewelry, and a cup.

RADIO HOST Why did she have those things?

INGRID We're not sure – we're working on that.

RADIO HOST I can imagine. So, what about her clothes?

INGRID Until we found the Egtved girl, there weren't any Bronze Age clothes to examine, and we didn't know much about Bronze Age fashion! When scientists examined her skirt and top, they discovered the wool didn't come from Danish sheep – there weren't any sheep in Denmark with that type of wool.

RADIO HOST Was she Danish?

INGRID No, she wasn't. She probably came from southern Germany – about 800 km from Egtved.

RADIO HOST Wow! That's a long way from home. Why was she in Denmark?

INGRID At that time, people traveled a lot, and there were a lot of people in northern Europe from different countries. Germany and Denmark were two very powerful countries, so we think she was there to marry.

RADIO HOST Well, Ingrid, it was fascinating to talk to you today, now I'd like to …

2.09 1 There were some humans in Africa 250,000 years ago. But they started to leave Africa in small groups about 120,000 years ago.

2 There wasn't an alphabet with letters in Aztec society. But there was an alphabet – it had pictures instead of letters. Amazing!

3 There were some university courses for students in Oxford in 1095. The courses were expensive, so they were mainly for rich people.

4 There weren't any forks for eating food in ancient Greece. People used knives, spoons, and their hands! The first fork probably appeared in the eighth or ninth century in rich homes in Persia.

5 There was a famous Roman cook named Apicius. He wrote one of the first recipe books in the first century CE. You can still make his recipes today!

2.10 **CARLA** Hi, Andy. How was your weekend?

ANDY It was OK, thanks.

CARLA What did you do?

ANDY I went to the country for my grandpa's 70th birthday.

CARLA Cool! What was the weather like?

ANDY It was cold, wet, and windy.

CARLA That's a shame. Where did you stay?

ANDY We stayed on my grandpa's farm.

CARLA What was it like?

ANDY Well, there wasn't any Wi-Fi, and there were a lot of noisy sheep outside.

CARLA Really?

ANDY Yes, really. That region has more sheep than people.

CARLA Wow. You learn something new every day!

ANDY What about you? What did you do?

CARLA Nothing much. I watched TV and made some cupcakes.

ANDY Sounds good!

2.11 **SOPHIE** Wow, Leo. The school history festival was a great idea. Everyone's displays are really interesting!

LEO Oh, hi, Sophie. Yes! I really liked Oliver's display about Viking ships.

SOPHIE Me, too! There were colorful pictures and surprising facts. I didn't know Vikings sailed all the way to Canada!

LEO Did the display say what year that happened?

SOPHIE I don't think so.

OLIVER Hey, guys!

SOPHIE Oh, hi, Oliver! We were just talking about your Viking ship display!

OLIVER What did you think?

LEO We both really like it.

SOPHIE It's very interesting. You found some cool facts!

OLIVER Oh, I'm glad you liked it. … Is there anything I should change about it?

LEO Hmm. Well, actually, I'd like to know when the Vikings sailed to Canada.

OLIVER Oh, I have that in my notes, but I forgot to write it in my text. Do you think I have time to add it before the parents arrive?

SOPHIE I think so! It's really good! I'm going to look at some of the other displays.

LEO Me, too.

OLIVER OK, have fun! See you later!

Unit 3

3.01 1 She isn't bored. She's angry.

2 He isn't embarrassed. He's tired.

3 She isn't worried. She's surprised.

4 He isn't tired. He's lonely.

5 He isn't afraid. He's upset.

6 She isn't excited. She's nervous.

3.05 One day, a hare was telling the other animals how fast he could run. At that moment, a tortoise was walking past. He heard the hare, and he offered to race him.

The race began. At first, the hare was running very fast and the tortoise was going very slowly. The hare was soon near the end of the race. The other animals weren't watching, so he decided to stop for a rest. He soon fell asleep. The tortoise continued to walk slowly while the hare was sleeping.

Finally, just as the tortoise was finishing the race, the hare woke up. The tortoise was the winner!

The moral of the story is: don't be too sure that something is easy. Sometimes things are more difficult than you think.

3.06

1 down	**5** into	**9** up
2 out of	**6** under	**10** through
3 over	**7** off	**11** along
4 between	**8** past	**12** across

3.07

1 Be careful! Don't fall down the stairs.

2 Who is that coming out of Bruno's house? Is it Carla?

3 Let's jump into the water together! Are you ready?

4 Don't cross the road between those cars! It's dangerous!

5 Why don't we swim across the lake to the other side? It isn't far.

6 Laura walked past me without saying hello.

3.08

RADIO HOST Good evening and welcome to this week's edition of *What's Your Story?* Today is Local Heroes' Day, so we want you to call us and share your stories. Do you have a story about a local hero? What did they do? So, first let's talk to Melissa. Hi there!

MELISSA Hi.

RADIO HOST So, Melissa, what's your story?

MELISSA It's not my story because it didn't happen to me, but I read about it and I think it's great. A man saved a boy's life on his wedding day in a park near my house.

RADIO HOST No way! What were the bride and groom doing in a park?

MELISSA Well, a photographer was taking photos of Clayton and Brittany Cook after their wedding. While the photographer was preparing his camera, Clayton noticed three children, two boys and a girl, behind them.

RADIO HOST What were the children doing?

MELISSA They were playing in the park, but they were bored. Clayton was watching them because they were standing close to the lake.

RADIO HOST Uh-oh. What happened next?

MELISSA Well, while the photographer was taking photos of Brittany on her own, one of the children pushed another one into the water. There was a loud splash! The children were shouting because one of the boys was in the lake. When Clayton saw the boy, it was obvious that he couldn't swim and was having trouble.

RADIO HOST What did Clayton do?

MELISSA He immediately jumped into the water and pulled the boy out. The boy was upset, but he was OK.

RADIO HOST Thank goodness! And was Clayton wearing his wedding clothes when he jumped into the water?

MELISSA Yes, he was. They got very wet!

RADIO HOST I'm sure he didn't mind. What an amazing story, and what a hero Clayton was! A real-life Superman! Thanks for sharing. Now, next …

3.09

1 A Were you watching TV at 8 p.m. last night?

B Yes, I was.

2 A What were you wearing yesterday?

B I was wearing jeans and a hoodie.

3 A Was your brother chatting online at 5 p.m. yesterday?

B No, he was wasn't. He was playing basketball.

4 A Where were Alice and her family living in 2017?

B They were living in Mexico City.

3.10 I was walking to the bus stop one afternoon when I fell down on the icy street. I was carrying a heavy bag with all my school things, and I broke my glasses. I felt very embarrassed.

Other people were waiting for the bus, but they didn't help me. However, one woman picked up my bag and glasses, and she found an empty seat for me. While I was sitting there, she cleaned my face and gave me some water. But when I looked for her a few minutes later, there was no one there.

3.11 **DAVID** Guess what happened yesterday.

LAURA No idea. What?

DAVID Well, it didn't happen to me; it happened to Adrian.

LAURA Go on.

DAVID He was at the new shopping mall.

LAURA You're kidding! What was he doing at a shopping mall? He hates shopping.

DAVID He was looking for new sneakers.

LAURA Really?

DAVID Yes, really. Now please stop interrupting. While he was looking at the sneakers, someone bumped into him.

LAURA Who was it?

DAVID It was LeBron James!

LAURA No way! That's amazing!

DAVID I know.

LAURA Did he take a photo?

DAVID No, he didn't. He was too embarrassed. Can you believe it?

LAURA What a great story!

Unit 4

4.01 borrow change cost earn lend owe pay save sell spend

4.02 **1 CASHIER** OK, so your total is $14.40. Cash or card? OK, that's ready for you now … insert your card here.

2 BOY Dad, I don't have enough money to go to the movies with Jack tonight. Do you have some money I can use?

DAD Yes, I do. You can have some, but I want it back on the weekend.

BOY Of course!

3 GIRL 1 Wow! Look at those sneakers. They're really cool and they aren't very expensive. Why don't you get them?

GIRL 2 No, I can't. I want to have enough money for my trip to Greece next summer.

4 TELLER Hi, can I help you?

WOMAN Yes, I have U.S. dollars, but I need Polish zloty.

TELLER Sure, let's just see how much you can get today …

5 SELLER Come on! Delicious fresh fruit, it's a bargain! We have apples, bananas, pears, pineapples … go on, you know you want to …

4.04 It's the fourth Friday in November and it's Black Friday. It's the busiest shopping day of the year. Things are cheaper than usual today. Shoppers can get the best prices for the latest gadgets or the most stylish sneakers. In my opinion, Black Friday is the worst day of the year. People seem to be more interested in shopping than anything else! I think we could all be happier without spending money all the time.

4.05 **1** vet

2 lawyer

3 firefighter

4 garbage collector

5 preschool teacher

6 nurse

7 police officer

8 surgeon

Not in the photos: caregiver, lifeguard, paramedic, volunteer

4.08 **1** I don't work now – I'm retired – so I have enough time to do something useful. You're never too old to help in a place like this. I serve meals at the homeless shelter three times a week, and sometimes we collect clothing and blankets for the people who come here.

The best thing: You feel like you're making a difference, really helping people.

The worst thing: Sometimes people need more help than we can give. But you do what you can.

2 I love my job, but it can be very busy. Sometimes I'm too busy to have lunch! We mostly take care of dogs and cats, but sometimes people bring birds and lizards in. Once, we even treated a pet tarantula!

The best thing: Helping people's pets feel better.

The worst thing: Seeing pets when they're very sick.

3 I'm 15. I work at the local swimming pool. I'm the one with red shorts, sitting near the diving board. And I'm there to make sure you stay safe. I only work during the summer, so I still have enough time to have fun with my friends.

The best thing: I have the skills to save someone's life, and I have enough money to buy things.

The worst thing: When younger kids make too much noise, or when they break the rules, running or splashing other people.

4 I'm not a doctor or a nurse, but I might save your life if you have a health emergency. I drive an ambulance and I wear a special uniform, and I can work during the day or at night.

The best thing: When you save someone's life.

The worst thing: The work can be very stressful.

4.09 I'm too young to have a full-time job, but every Saturday I'm a volunteer with a local vet. I help the receptionist when she doesn't have enough time to do everything. Last week, there were too many people in the waiting room – we didn't have enough chairs for them to sit on! Sometimes it gets too noisy for me, especially when there are too many animals and there isn't enough space in the waiting room.

The best thing: I love animals and I can spend all day with them!

The worst thing: Sometimes there's too much information for me, and I don't understand it all.

4.10

BILLY Hey, Rita. What's up? You look worried.

RITA I am. Could you do me a favor?

BILLY It depends. What do you need?

RITA Would you mind lending me $20?

BILLY Oh. I'm sorry, I can't. I spent too much money on the weekend.

RITA OK, no problem. What about you, Greg?

GREG Maybe. What's it for?

RITA I want to buy a bag for Maisie's birthday. There's a really cute one that I want to get her, but I don't have enough money.

GREG When's her birthday?

RITA Yesterday! Please, Greg.

GREG Sure, since you asked so nicely. There you go.

RITA Thanks, Greg. You're the best! I owe you one.

GREG Actually, you owe me 20!

4.11

YUSUF OK, so we have enough time, and we all want to volunteer. What's the best way for us to volunteer in our community? Lara?

LARA Let's go to the after-school sports club – that's the easiest thing to do. We could watch the younger students and take care of them. That isn't too much work for us.

YUSUF That's an interesting idea. But I think we can do something that isn't at school. Also …

THIAGO Excuse me Yusuf, can I make a suggestion?

YUSUF Sure, go ahead, Thiago.

THIAGO What about going to the nursing home and teaching the older people how to use computers and tablets?

YUSUF That's not a bad idea. Lara, what do you think?

LARA I'm not sure. We need permission to do that, and I don't know who to ask. I think it needs too much organization.

YUSUF Do you have any other ideas, Thiago?

THIAGO Yes, how about cleaning the park?

YUSUF I think that's a great idea. We all know the park isn't very clean, so people aren't using it. It's too dirty to play soccer or basketball there. What do you think, Lara?

LARA Yes, I like that idea, too. How about doing it on Saturday mornings? I think we all have enough time then. We can make a poster and ask other people to help us, too.

YUSUF OK, so we don't want to work with the younger students, and we aren't into the nursing home idea. Do we think the park is the best idea? Are there any more ideas? So we all agree: we clean the park and make it a better place for the whole community.

STUDENTS Yes!

YUSUF That's good enough for me! Let's get started and make a poster!

Unit 5

5.01
1 ceiling
2 cupboard
3 fridge
4 sink
5 floor
6 shelves
7 wardrobe
8 desk
9 chest of drawers
10 picture
11 bookcase
12 armchair
13 carpet

5.02
1 This is a bright, sunny room, and my sister and I spend a lot of time here. My sister sleeps above me. We have a big chest of drawers and a big wardrobe for our clothes, which we share.

2 This was a nice room. It had a pretty wood ceiling and a big mirror on the wall. There was a nice big bath, but the sink was tiny and the toilet didn't work very well. So we built a new one!

3 I have a lot of pictures of my family on the wall, and there's a nice warm carpet on the floor. I have a large wood desk and lots of shelves with books and papers. I work from home, so I spend a lot of time in this room.

4 This room is very small, but my whole family likes spending time in here. There isn't a table or chairs, but there's a new fridge – it's really tall. And there are lots of cupboards. Above the sink, there's a window with a view of the yard.

5.04
Kids' toys aren't cheap these days, but not many toys are as expensive as the Astolat Dollhouse Castle. It's as tall as a small Christmas tree and as heavy as a horse. The castle was the idea of an American artist, Elaine Diehl, and it took thirteen years to build. It isn't really a toy. It's a work of art, and it's good enough to be in a museum.

The furniture is small enough to fit in your hand, and it's as beautiful as the furniture in a real palace. The tiny sofas and beds are as soft as the real things. The books on the shelves aren't large enough to read, but they have real pages. One thing that isn't small is the price – over eight million dollars! Are you rich enough to buy it?

5.05
1 make the bed
2 do the laundry
3 do the ironing
4 sweep the floor
5 mop the floor
6 vacuum the carpet
7 do the dishes
8 load the dishwasher, empty the dishwasher
9 dust the furniture

5.06
Hi, kids. Can you please help with some things around the house while I'm out?

Ollie: Please mop the kitchen floor and load the dishwasher with the plates and cups from breakfast. Can you also dust the furniture in the living room, please, and vacuum the carpet?

Mia: Make your bed and sweep the floor in your bedroom. Then can you please do the ironing for me?

Thanks, kids. I'll see you this evening.

Love, Dad

5.07
REPORTER Yesterday, I read that only half of teenagers in the United States help at home with household chores. Can this be true? Do American children have to help at home? To find out, I talked to some teenagers here in Houston, Texas.

Hello. We're doing a survey about how much teenagers help at home. Can I ask you a few questions?

CINDY Sure.

REPORTER Thanks. What's your name, by the way?

CINDY I'm Cindy.

REPORTER OK, Cindy. So, do you help out with household chores?

CINDY Well … yes, I do, but not much. I have to help in the kitchen, for example.

REPORTER Cooking?

CINDY No, I can't cook! I have to clean the kitchen after dinner, that's all.

REPORTER And do you have to do the dishes?

CINDY Yes, but at least I don't have to sweep and mop the floor. That's my brother's job.

REPORTER Hi there. What are your names, and do you have to help much at home?

KIM Hi, I'm Kim and this is my sister, Maisie. Well, we don't have to help on school days because we have to do a lot of homework for school and also I have to practice the piano. But on Saturday morning, we help with the housework. I do a lot of chores, actually.

REPORTER Really?

KIM Yeah! For example, I have to vacuum the living room. I hate that!

REPORTER Hello, what's your name?

ADAM I'm, Adam, and this is my little brother Jake.

REPORTER So, do you and Jake have to help your parents at home?

ADAM Well, Jake doesn't have much to do. He's only five. He has to clean his room and make his bed, but that's all.

REPORTER What about you, Adam?

ADAM Yes, I have to do some other chores around the house, but it isn't a problem. I don't mind.

REPORTER Do you have a favorite chore?

ADAM Well, yes. I prefer doing the ironing because you don't have to move around. So, I can listen to music or watch TV at the same time. Yeah, ironing is cool!

5.10 Do you have to help with the housework? Do you have to make your bed or clean the kitchen? Martha Pinter and her brother, Ben, have to do more than most young people their age. They live on a farm in Queensland, Australia, and the whole family has to share the work. Martha has to get up early to milk the cows. In spring, she also has to take care of the new lambs – that's her favorite job. Ben has to collect the hens' eggs before breakfast. But Martha and Ben don't have to catch the bus to school every day. There isn't a school near their farm, so they have to have all their lessons at home.

5.11 **OSCAR** Hey, Nina. Look at this photo – it's Liam's bedroom in his new house.

NINA Oh! It looks big enough for two people. Does he have to share it?

OSCAR No, it's all his. Actually, it isn't as big as it looks. There's a large mirror in the background, so it looks bigger.

NINA Oh, yes, I see. What's that thing on the wall?

OSCAR It's a clock. What do you think of the color of the walls?

NINA Hmm. I'm not convinced.

OSCAR Really? I think it looks awesome! I don't think much of those curtains, though.

NINA Me neither. And what's that at the bottom? Is it a carpet?

OSCAR Yes, I think so. I like it. And I love those pictures on the left.

NINA Me, too. They look great.

Unit 6

6.01
1 cut your finger
2 slip
3 get stung by a bee
4 get bitten by a mosquito
5 hit your head
6 burn your hand
7 scratch your arm
8 break your leg
9 trip over a chair
10 fall off your horse
11 sprain your ankle
12 bruise your leg

6.02
1 [stung by a bee] Ow!
2 [fall off a bike] Ouch!
3 [trip over a cat]
4 [slip on the ice]
5 [burn hand on match]

6.05
1 /ʌ/ brother cousin cut stung
2 /ʊ/ could foot put

6.07 Hi everyone,

Now that spring is here, I think you should all think about walking or cycling to school if you can.

Cycling is fun and healthy, but you must be careful. For example, you shouldn't ride when the weather is bad, and you must wear a helmet. That's extremely important. However, you also must not forget that there are rules on the road for cyclists, and you must learn these rules.

The school website has some good advice, such as which clothes you should wear when riding your bike, and I think all cyclists should read it carefully.

One more thing: we need to know which students are cycling to school, so you must tell Mrs. Jones if you plan to ride your bike. That's a school rule, so you must not forget!

6.08

1 forehead	**5** neck	**9** elbow
2 cheek	**6** shoulder	**10** knee
3 teeth	**7** chest	**11** heel
4 chin	**8** wrist	**12** toe

6.09 **STEVE** Hi, and welcome back. Today we are talking about dangerous animals. A lot of dangerous animals live near or in the water, so you should always be careful when you're near the ocean or a river or a lake. Today we're going to talk about crocodiles! OK, you won't see any crocodiles if you're on vacation in Spain. But Australia is different. That's dangerous crocodile country. Photographer Pam Krommer works in Queensland and knows a lot about crocodiles. Welcome, Pam.

PAM Hello, Steve.

STEVE So, Pam. How often do crocodiles hurt people?

PAM Well, it happens, but not very often. There are usually fewer than three crocodile attacks per year in Australia. If you swim in safe places, you won't be in any danger from crocodiles. But you must not swim if there are warning signs.

STEVE And when a crocodile gets you, that's the end, right?

PAM Not always. For example, a few years ago, a man named Jamie Verdi was fishing in Queensland, and suddenly a crocodile appeared and grabbed his leg in its mouth.

STEVE That's scary. All of his leg?

PAM As far as his knee.

STEVE So what did Jamie do?

PAM Well, he used his hands to hold onto a tree, but crocodiles are very strong. After a few minutes, the crocodile pulled Jamie into the water, right up to his neck.

STEVE And if that happens, you're in trouble!

PAM Oh, yes! But Jamie knew this: a croc sometimes opens its mouth if you hit it in the eye. It's your only chance, and it might not work, but you have to try it. So he hit the croc in the eye, it opened its mouth, and it swam away. The crocodile's teeth hurt Jamie's leg, and it also bit his arm badly, but he was alive!

STEVE Wow – what a story!

6.10 So you're going to visit Queensland. Great idea! If you like beaches and forests, you'll love Port Douglas. It's amazing. It usually takes about an hour to get there if you take a bus from the airport. Buses are frequent, so if you miss one, you won't have a long wait. Of course, if you don't mind spending more money, there are always taxis at the airport, too! If you visit Four Mile Beach, you'll have a great time surfing. But be careful! If you don't see anyone else in the water, it probably means there are sharks or jellyfish in the ocean! Have fun and take care!

6.11 **DAN** Awesome mountain bike, Hayley!

HAYLEY Thanks, Dan.

DAN I'd like to get one, too. Do you think I should buy one online?

HAYLEY Not really. Some online stores aren't reliable. Their bikes aren't very safe. Anyway, make sure you don't buy one without trying it first. Why don't you try The Bike Shack in town? They're really good.

DAN OK. I'll have a go at it.

HAYLEY And you should definitely buy a good helmet, too. You can really hurt yourself if you fall off, so you must not ride without one.

DAN Good idea. I think I should find some buddies to ride with, too. What do you think?

HAYLEY Sure. How about joining my bike club? We go out every weekend.

DAN Yeah! Good job, Hayley. I'll do that.

6.12 **JOHN** Hi. My name's John, and my group worked like this: each person in our group wrote about a different topic. I wrote about desert animals. Josh wrote about the weather. Vicky wrote about the problems people have in the desert, and Sophie wrote all the other facts about deserts. Then we put it all together.

ISLA Hello, I'm Isla. My group worked like this: I looked on the Internet to get all the information, Zara found all the pictures, and Martin wrote the texts. Then Harry checked the texts for mistakes and put everything together into a poster.

POPPY Hi, I'm Poppy and I was in a group with Leo, Daisy, and Max. This is how my group worked: first, we all made our own posters and showed them to the group. We read everyone's work and then used the best parts of all the posters to make our final group poster.

Unit 7

7.01
1 upload
2 download
3 screen
4 app
5 chip
6 device
7 video chat
8 software
9 social media
10 message
11 emoji

7.02
1 My phone fell out of my pocket this morning and the screen broke.
2 I can't do a video chat with you right now. I don't have a camera on my laptop.
3 Most of my friends upload photos to social media sites like Instagram.
4 Look at this app – it's great for practicing new English words. Why don't you download it, too?

7.04
1 /ɪ/ Internet printer video will
2 /aɪ/ bike device online Wi-Fi write

7.07
1 one trillion
2 one billion
3 one million
4 one thousand
5 one hundred

7.08 **JACK** What's wrong, Kim?

KIM I've lost my phone. Do you know where it is?

JACK No, I don't. I haven't heard it ring, either. Maybe it's in your coat pocket.

KIM I've looked in all my pockets. It's not there.

JACK Maybe you've left it in Mom's car.

KIM No, I don't think so. I used it this afternoon, but I can't remember where I left it.

JACK Maybe Mom's put it somewhere.

KIM No, I've asked her and she says she hasn't seen it. Jack, can you call me?

JACK I think so. I haven't charged my phone, but I think it has enough power left. Hang on … OK, I'm calling you …

KIM Here, look! I've found it. It was in my bag all the time.

7.09
1 go on foot
2 get on a train
3 go by tram
4 catch a plane, take a plane
5 get out of a car
6 take a taxi, get into a taxi
7 get off a bus

7.10 **JIM** Welcome to *The Science Show*. Today's show is all about the future of transportation, and with me in the studio is Professor Annie Walker from the University of New Hampshire. Hello, Professor Walker.

ANNIE Hello, Jim.

JIM Annie, a lot of us catch a bus to go to work, but it takes hours because of the traffic. To solve the problem, some people think we should invent flying cars. Should we?

ANNIE No, I don't think so, Jim. Believe it or not, the first flying cars do actually exist. But you can't just get in your car and fly away. They need a runway to take off.

JIM So in your view, we won't see a lot of flying cars in the sky soon?

ANNIE No. Also, it won't be very safe if everyone is flying around in their own car.

JIM OK. So what about jetpacks? Scientists haven't created those for us yet, but we might not need to wait much longer.

ANNIE In my opinion, that won't ever happen, Jim. You see, it takes a lot of energy to lift a person off the ground, and the rockets on your back will be very heavy. I don't think we'll be able to stay in the air for more than a few minutes.

JIM So we may have them one day just for fun, but they may not be useful for getting to work.

ANNIE No, you won't take a jetpack to work, I'm afraid.

JIM Well, I think the future sounds quite disappointing, Professor. What's the good news?

ANNIE The good news is the hyperloop. It's a completely new kind of transportation, and in my opinion, it will really change our lives.

JIM What is it?

ANNIE It's similar to the subway in New York, but much, much faster. The trains don't have wheels. Instead they travel on something that is similar to skis, on a cushion of air. In a hyperloop, trains can travel more than a thousand kilometers per hour.

JIM That's amazing. But is this just science fiction?

ANNIE No, scientists have made a lot of progress. I think we might see hyperloops between big cities in the next twenty years.

JIM I can't wait! Thanks, Professor Walker.

7.11 What will transportation be like in the future? I think some things will change, but some things won't change. For example, I'm sure we'll have cars in the future, but they might be less noisy and dirty than they are now. But I also think every family will have a flying car. That will be fun. I'm not so sure about jetpacks, though. We might have jetpacks just for fun, but they won't be useful for most people. I mean, children won't go to school with a jet pack. I think there will be hyperloops, but I don't think everyone will travel on them. Some people might not want to travel on a hyperloop. They may be too scared. But I'll want to. I'm sure of that!

7.12 **TOM** So, Dad, before you start, switch the camera to video mode. Have you done that?

DAD Like this?

TOM Yes, that's right. It needs to be in video mode to record a video. Now, look at this little screen.

DAD I can't see anything.

TOM Ah. Remember not to put your hand in front of the camera!

DAD Is this better?

TOM Not quite. Look, you need to keep your fingers here. That's it. Now, do you see this button?

DAD This one?

TOM No, not that one. This one here. It's really important that it's turned on if you want to record sound. Oh, and make sure that the light is red. That means you're recording. Got it?

DAD Yes, I think so. Thanks, Tom!

Unit 8

8.01

1 engineer
2 scientist
3 composer
4 writer
5 athlete
6 mathematician
7 businesswoman
8 inventor

8.02

1 Athletes like runners and swimmers have incredible strength.

2 The scientist Albert Einstein was famous for his great intelligence.

3 At just four years old, Mozart showed a lot of skill as a composer.

4 J. K. Rowling's creativity as a writer made her famous around the world.

5 Ada Lovelace was an English mathematician. Her talent for math helped to make the modern computer possible.

6 The inventor Thomas Edison worked with a lot of determination over many years to make his light bulb work.

8.06

PAUL How far have you cycled, Maya?

MAYA I've ridden fifteen thousand kilometers so far. I have another twelve thousand to go!

PAUL How many countries have you crossed?

MAYA I've been to three continents so far, and I've visited twelve countries.

PAUL Have you had any funny experiences along the way?

MAYA Well, an emu chased me in the Australian outback. I've never experienced that before!

PAUL No, not many people have! And how has your bicycle been?

MAYA It hasn't had any problems at all. It's a great bike.

PAUL So how much money have you made?

MAYA I haven't reached my target, but I've made thirty thousand dollars so far.

PAUL That's amazing! Good luck with the rest of your journey.

8.08

Ann Makosinski is a brilliant young inventor, and she's someone I really look up to. When I think about myself in five or ten years from now, I hope I will be as successful as she is.

Ann's dad is Polish and her mom is Filipino, but she's Canadian and grew up in Victoria. She came up with her first invention when she was only fifteen. Her idea was a flashlight that uses the heat from your hand for energy instead of batteries. The flashlight switches itself on when you hold it, and it switches itself off when you put it down. It doesn't need a battery, so it can keep working for years and never runs out of energy. It's really simple, but also really clever.

How did Ann come up with this idea? Well, she has a friend who lives in the Philippines. This friend was having problems doing her homework because she didn't have electricity at home, and she couldn't afford batteries for her flashlight. So Ann looked into ways of making a flashlight that uses human body heat for power. She taught herself all the science behind the idea and figured out how to build it. Soon she had a working prototype, and she decided to take part in an international science competition called the Google Science Fair. She won first prize, worth twenty-five thousand dollars!

This great achievement has changed her life. She's been on TV and in newspapers around the world. She's also come up with another invention. She calls it the E-Drink, and it's a mug that uses the heat from your coffee to charge your phone. It's simple, clever, and kind to the environment. It's amazing that no one has thought of these ideas before. And that's why I look up to her so much. But can anyone be like Ann Makosinski? Yes, if we believe in ourselves, anything is possible. However, you can't achieve anything without hard work.

8.09

1 I surprised myself when I did so well on my exams.

2 John and I introduced ourselves to the new neighbors.

3 Jane, make sure that you take care of yourself while I'm away.

4 Mike has taught himself Spanish and French.

5 You and Vicky should make yourselves some sandwiches for lunch.

6 Stan and Ollie prepared themselves well for the match.

8.10

Teenager Sails into Record Books

Dutch teenager Laura Dekker has become the youngest person ever to sail solo around the world. Laura is only sixteen years old. No one so young has achieved this before. Sailing is something her whole family is crazy about, and Laura learned everything she knows about it from her parents. By the time she was thirteen, there wasn't anywhere she couldn't sail by herself. Everyone has a dream, and Laura's achievement shows that nothing is impossible if you want it enough.

8.11 **JO** So, Angie, why do you want to join our training program?

ANGIE Well, I'm passionate about food. I've taught myself a lot about it, but the training will give me the chance to learn new skills.

JO So have you ever worked in a kitchen?

ANGIE Yes, I've had plenty of experience working in a restaurant. My grandparents run a restaurant, and I help them on weekends.

JO Oh, really? And what skills have you developed?

ANGIE I've learned the basics of cooking. But the main thing is, I've learned how to be a good team player.

JO That's interesting. Tell me more.

ANGIE Well, I also help the wait staff, you know. We take orders from customers and that kind of thing.

8.12 **BOY** It's June 7 today. When do we need to get the whole project finished?

GIRL Let's give ourselves two weeks. So that's June 21.

BOY There's a lot to do. We need to research the topic, find pictures …

GIRL Or draw them ourselves.

BOY Yes, or draw them ourselves. We also need to write the text, of course.

GIRL And check it for mistakes.

BOY Right. And if we're making a web page, someone needs to do the technical part!

GIRL That's a lot of things to do, and we don't have a lot of time.

BOY So what's the most important?

GIRL Well, doing research is really important because we need good ideas.

BOY OK. What about getting pictures?

GIRL Well, I think we can leave that to the end. It's not so important.

BOY Don't you think so? Hmm, I don't agree. Don't forget that if we want to make a web page …

GIRL How long do you think it will take us to write the text?

BOY Oh, I don't know. Perhaps two days?

GIRL Two days? Hmm … You're probably right, but let's say three, just in case something goes wrong. I mean, if we get lots of other homework, for example, we might need more time for the project text.

GIRL OK, so let's start with research. We can do that today and tomorrow.

BOY Right. Let's finish all our research by the end of tomorrow. What next?

Unit 9

9.01

1 folk	**6** classical	**11** drums
2 jazz	**7** violin	**12** microphone
3 reggae	**8** guitar	**13** bass
4 hip-hop	**9** saxophone	**14** trumpet
5 rock	**10** keyboard	

9.02 folk jazz rock bass drums hip-hop reggae keyboard trumpet guitar classical microphone saxophone violin

9.04 **AMY** Hi, Josh. Are you going to go out tomorrow evening?

JOSH No, I'm going to stay at home and watch a movie. What about you?

AMY Yeah. Dr. Jay is at the Waterside. I'm not going to miss that.

JOSH Wow! Really?

AMY Yeah, really. I'm going to buy my ticket this morning.

JOSH Hmm. Sounds interesting. Is Aneta going to join you?

AMY No! She's not going to come. She can't stand Dr. Jay. Why don't you come?

JOSH OK, you've convinced me. But how are we going to get there? We're not going to walk, are we?

AMY My dad's going to give us a ride.

9.05
1 ballroom dancing
2 swing
3 tap dancing
4 folk dance
5 ballet dancing
6 modern dance
7 breakdancing
8 salsa dancing
9 Zumba
10 disco dancing

9.06

IMOGEN OK, everyone, so the dance show is this Friday night. You all know that, don't you?

GROUP Yes, we know that.

IMOGEN Good. So we only have a few days to get ready.

JACK What time does the show start, Imogen?

IMOGEN It begins at 7:30. The teachers are having a meeting at five o'clock that ends at six, and our show begins at 7:30. Everyone is performing in the gymnasium.

MARTA How many different dance groups are performing?

ADAM I think there are six groups. Ballroom, breakdancing, modern dance, tap dancing, salsa … What's the last one?

JACK Irish dancing!

ADAM Uh, yes, that's right.

IMOGEN Great! Now, the doors open to let the audience in at seven o'clock, so we need all the seats ready before then. Marta, can you put out the seats?

MARTA Sure, I'm not doing anything on Friday afternoon. I can come in early and put the seats out.

IMOGEN That's great. Thanks, Marta.

MARTA Is anyone recording the show?

IMOGEN Oh, yes, good point. Are you recording the show, Adam?

ADAM No, I'm not good with cameras. You're doing that, aren't you, Jack?

JACK Yep, that's me. I'm going to borrow my sister's video camera. She has a really good one.

IMOGEN Great. Now, what else? Oh, the music. Adam, you're organizing that, right?

ADAM Yes. I'm going to download all the tracks for the different groups tonight. It won't take me long.

IMOGEN Good. Thanks, Adam. So, that's almost everything, isn't it? No, wait! What about programs? Who's writing the program? I've forgotten.

GROUP You are!

IMOGEN I am? Oh, yes. *I'm* writing the program!

9.08

LILIA Thank you, New Haven! You were a fabulous audience last night! We're returning in April, so I hope we'll see some of you again.

Later today, we're leaving for Hartford. We're performing a new play there called *The Bell*, and I'm playing a girl who has the power to see the future. Hey, Hartford! If you're not doing anything on Friday night, come along. Guess who's coming to see us on our first night – Jennifer Lawrence! She's bringing some friends, and we're meeting them backstage after the performance. Wow!

9.09

HARRY Hi, Jess. I'm going to book tickets for the jazz festival on Saturday. Do you feel like coming along?

JESS I'd love to, but my cousin Helen's visiting me, and I'll be with her all day long.

HARRY She's welcome to join us if she wants.

JESS That's really nice of you, Harry, but Helen can't stand jazz!

HARRY Oh, that's too bad. Look, they're playing for two nights. What are you up to on Friday? Would you like to come then instead?

JESS Hmm. What time does it start?

HARRY 7:30.

JESS Oh, that's no good either, Harry. I have a guitar lesson and it starts at 7:15.

HARRY OK. Never mind, Jess. Maybe another time.

JESS Sure. Thanks for asking, though. I'm sure it'll be a great concert.

WORKBOOK ANSWER KEY

Starter Unit pp4–7

VOCABULARY AND READING

1 b 6 c 11 d 8 e 9 f 4

2 2 rugby
3 track and field
4 sailing
5 hockey
6 gymnastics
7 volleyball
8 basketball
9 swimming
10 windsurfing

3 making pizza

4 2 doesn't cycle
3 good
4 speaks
5 eating

EXPLORE IT!

1 cm

GRAMMAR IN ACTION AND VOCABULARY

1 2 goes
3 don't see
4 write
5 makes

2 2 What sports does Carla do? Carla plays hockey and does gymnastics.
3 Where does Nico's father work? Nico's father works in a pizzeria.
4 What does Nico know a lot about? Nico knows a lot about pizza.

3 2 Iris is never late for hockey practice.
3 Paul always takes great photos.
4 Molly sometimes sits next to her friend.
5 Do you usually listen to loud music?

4

T	N	O	H	M	C	H	S	A	L	J	N
A	Z	Q	S	O	I	B	C	D	S	G	H
B	U	R	R	N	O	A	L	H	S	S	J
L	Y	D	K	E	Y	S	H	E	F	C	H
E	F	M	W	Y	R	P	S	A	O	H	G
T	V	L	S	I	E	T	D	D	P	A	C
F	K	S	C	P	A	S	S	P	O	R	T
K	V	W	J	H	D	S	U	H	R	G	O
L	A	P	T	O	P	D	B	O	T	E	S
O	B	U	P	N	L	P	D	N	A	R	A
U	C	A	M	E	R	A	C	E	B	R	L
T	E	Y	N	J	A	N	W	S	L	E	G
D	S	K	L	H	Q	L	D	A	E	D	F
B	U	S	P	A	S	S	P	N	M	O	V

LISTENING AND GRAMMAR IN ACTION

1 bus stop

2

	Gymnastics Class	Running Club	Photography Club	Play Video Games
Hannah	✓	✗	✓	✗
Joe	✗	✓	✗	✓

3 2 F 3 T 4 F 5 T 6 F

4 2 playing 3 speaking 4 using 5 writing
6 helping

5 2 Does, have; he does 3 Do, have; they don't
4 Do, have; you don't 5 Do, have; we do
6 Does, have; she does.

6 2 have 3 Do we have 4 do 5 has 6 listening
7 has 8 doesn't have 9 sharing 10 love

WRITING

1 on Sundays

2 2 T 3 F 4 F 5 F

3 **Possible answers:**
1 Victor's favorite free-time activity ... (paragraph 2)
2 My name's ...; Victor's nine ... (paragraph 1)
3 He practices on Mondays, Wednesdays, Fridays, and Saturdays! (paragraph 2)

4 My friend Mason has a big family. He has two brothers, two sisters, and 35 cousins. They all live on the same street! In Mason's house, there are a lot of pets. They have two dogs, three cats, four rabbits, and a parrot! They have a big house and a big yard, so there's lots of space!

5, 6 and 7 Students' own answers

Unit 1 pp8–15

VOCABULARY

1 **2** sports show **3** documentary **4** drama **5** game show **6** talk show **7** soap opera **8** the news **9** comedy **10** cooking show **11** cartoon **12** reality show

2 **2** cooking **3** talk show **4** comedy **5** the news **6** cartoons

3 **2** the news **3** sports show **4** cartoon **5** game show **6** reality show

4 **2** cooking shows **3** comedies **4** talk shows **5** soap operas **6** streaming series

EXPLORE IT!

60

READING

1 Manny Ellis

2 **2** fact **3** billion **4** live **5** support

3 **2** a comedy show **3** at her friend's house **4** soccer **5** a documentary about the Olympics **6** on the side of the road / at the *Vuelta a España*

4 Students' own answers

GRAMMAR IN ACTION

1 **2** is making **3** are watching **4** is sitting **5** isn't eating **6** Are you waiting

2 **2** 's/is preparing **3** 're/are waiting **4** 's/is making **5** aren't/are not crying; 're/are laughing **6** 'm not/am not watching; 'm/am working

3 **b** What is Anita doing on the computer? 1
c Why are you all standing there? 3
d What is Miguel doing in the park? 4
e Why is Paul working late tonight? 2
f What are you watching on TV? 6

4 **2** Are we listening to the instructor? No, we aren't.
3 Is she waiting for the next episode? Yes, she is.
4 Are they enjoying the show? No, they aren't.
5 Are you sending a message to a friend? No, I'm not.
6 Am I helping you? Yes, you are.

5 **2** 'm using **3** 'm writing **4** Are, taking **5** 'm preparing **6** 're learning **7** 're working **8** 'm looking forward to

VOCABULARY AND LISTENING

1

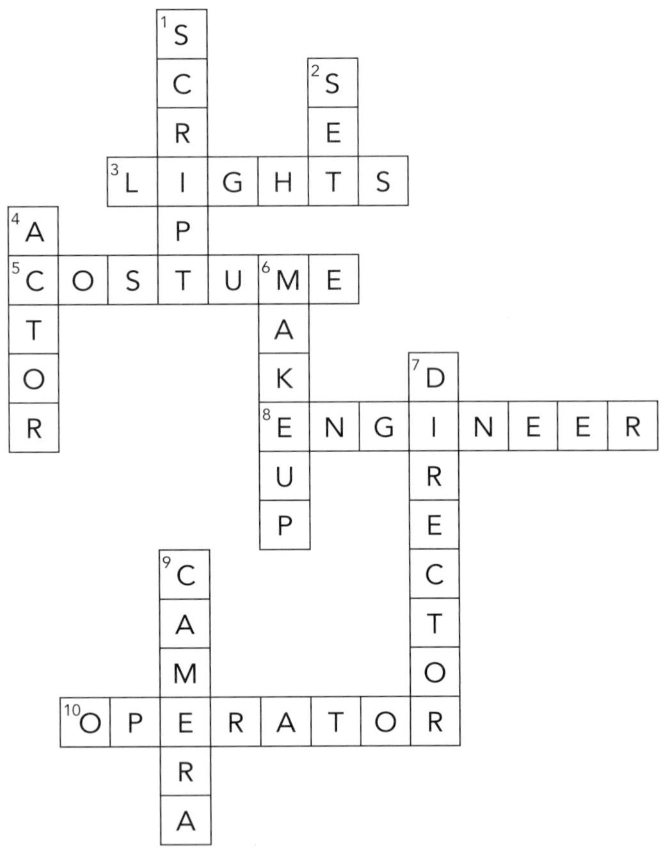

2 **2** e **3** d **4** a **5** c

3 **1** Sydney, Australia **2** four **3** New Road

4 **2** b **3** a **4** b **5** c **6** c

5 Students' own answers

GRAMMAR IN ACTION

1

Present Simple	Present Continuous
always every day every week never	at the moment right now this afternoon today

2 **2** love **3** takes **4** 're watching **5** don't come **6** make

3 **2** I'm watching a good TV drama at the moment.
3 We sometimes eat our lunch outside in the summer.
4 The sound engineer never talks to the actors.
5 Are you listening to your teacher right now?
6 My sister is taking a guided tour of Sydney now.

4 **2** Their little brothers are playing happyly. happily
3 Our parents teach us to say "thank you" nice. nicely
4 Be carefully! That camera is very expensive! careful
5 You're doing your homework very good at the moment. well
6 She's playing the guitar beautiful now. beautifully

5 **2** quietly **3** slowly **4** loudly **5** hard **6** badly

WRITING

1 because his stories are funny, but they are never mean or offensive

2 **1** Australia **2** 15 million people
3 He laughs so much that he cries.

3 **a** 2 **b** 3 **c** 1

4 **1** and; c **2** but; a **3** or; b

5, 6, and 7 Students' own answers

REVIEW 1

1 **1** h **2** f **3** e **4** d **5** a **6** g **7** b **8** c

2 **1** camera operator **2** script **3** costume **4** director **5** lights **6** set **7** makeup artist **8** sound engineer **9** actor **10** digital camera

3 **1** are you doing **2** 'm/am writing **3** 's/is working **4** Is he filming **5** 's/is traveling **6** 's/is cooking **7** are you sending **8** 'm/am hoping

4 **1** 'm/am writing, email **2** watch, 're /arelistening **3** 's/is saving, needs **4** Are, looking; sits **5** doesn't go, 's/is working **6** are swimming, prefer **7** Are, waiting; doesn't … arrive **8** 'm/am cooking, make

5 **1** quiet **2** nice **3** happily **4** loudly **5** quickly **6** well **7** beautifully **8** pretty

6 **1** b **2** c **3** a **4** a **5** b **6** c **7** c **8** a **9** b **10** c **11** a **12** c

Unit 2 pp16–23

VOCABULARY

1 foggy cold windy hot icy cloudy rainy warm sunny wet stormy dry

2 **2** icy **3** rainy **4** foggy **5** cloudy **6** windy

3 **2** wet; a **3** foggy; d **4** snowy; b **5** windy; c **6** sunny; e

4 **2** dry **3** warm **4** hot 5 rainy 6 snowy

5 **2** cloud 3 ice 4 sun 5 wind 6 snow 7 fog 8 storm

EXPLORE IT!

180

READING

1 nothing

2 **2** bury **3** hides **4** secret **5** treasure **6** clues

3 **2** F **3** F **4** T **5** T **6** F

4 Students' own answers

GRAMMAR IN ACTION

1 **2** took **3** enjoyed **4** read **5** wrote **6** were

2 **b** hike; 1 **c** Were; 6 **d** enjoy; 3 **e** did; 2 **f** write; 5

3 **2** Did you swim in the ocean? No, I didn't.
3 Did you all go in the pool? Yes, we did.
4 Did your friends like the food? Yes, they did.
5 Did Tomas take lots of photos? Yes, he did.
6 Did Susie want to come home? No, she didn't.

4 **2** We didn't enjoyed the bus trip. enjoy
3 Did you found a good tour guide last week? find
4 I did went out in the stormy weather. went
5 They stoped for food and drink. stopped
6 Did she be late for class yesterday? Was she

5 **2** decided **3** didn't have **4** Did, ride **5** stayed **6** took care of **7** returned **8** wrote **9** became **10** traveled

VOCABULARY AND LISTENING

1 **2** lamp **3** blanket **4** spoon **5** knife **6** pillow **7** bowl **8** fork **9** comb **10** plate **11** scissors **12** cup **13** hairbrush **14** toothbrush

2 b 12 c 5 d 11 e 2 f 4

3 Possible answers

Kitchen	Bathroom	Bedroom
bowl spoon fork plate scissors cup	comb hairbrush scissors mirror toothbrush	comb mirror lamp hairbrush pillow

4 museum, comb, jewelry, mirror

5 **2** (just) 24 **3** 1930s **4** bed **5** head **6** (house) key

6 Students' own answers

GRAMMAR IN ACTION

1 **2** There was **3** Were there **4** There wasn't **5** Was there **6** There were **7** There weren't

2 **2** There weren't any interesting things in the display.
3 Were there many people at the exhibition?
4 There was an old woman with a baby.
5 Was there any jewelry in the box?
6 There were hundreds of tourists in Naples.

3 **2** f **3** d **4** a **5** b **6** c

4 **2** a **3** a **4** an **5** some **6** some **7** any **8** an

5 **2** There were **3** some **4** any **5** a **6** some **7** an **8** some **9** an **10** There was **11** there weren't **12** some

WRITING

1 c

2 **2** At first, **3** The weather was **4** there were a lot of problems **5** Finally,

3 **1** England to Scotland **2** weeks **3** good **4** Sven

4 **2** d **3** f **4** c **5** a **6** e

5, 6, and 7 Students' own answers

REVIEW 2

1 **1** foggy **2** rainy **3** cold **4** icy **5** warm **6** stormy/snowy **7** cloudy **8** dry **9** hot **10** snowy **11** wet; windy **12** sunny

2 **1** scissors **2** lamp **3** comb; hairbrush **4** toothbrush **5** fork; spoon **6** blanket **7** bowl; plate **8** cup **9** pillow **10** mirror

3 **1** worked **2** set **3** wanted **4** traveled **5** was **6** was **7** took **8** arrived

4 **1** There weren't any mirrors in the bathroom.
2 Was there any information about Egyptian mummies?
3 There were some interesting books in the museum
shop.
4 There was an article about dinosaurs in the newspaper.
5 Were there any good exhibitions in Berlin?
6 There wasn't a clear answer to my question.
7 There weren't any bowls in the kitchen.
8 There were some visitors from Portugal in our school.

5 **1** c **2** b **3** c **4** a **5** b **6** a **7** c **8** c **9** b **10** a **11** c **12** b

Unit 3 pp24–31

VOCABULARY

1

	1 L	O	N	11 E	L	Y						
				M								
				2 B	O	R	E	D				
				3 A	F	R	A	I	D			
		4 N	E	R	V	O	U	S				
		5 W	O	R	R	I	E	D				
				6 A	N	G	R	Y				
				7 S	U	R	P	R	I	S	E	D
		8 U	P	S	E	T						
				9 E	X	C	I	T	E	D		
10 T	I	R	E	D								

11 Students' own answers

2 **2** angry **3** lonely **4** bored **5** embarrassed

3 **2** nervous **3** tired **4** upset **5** excited

4 Students' own answers

EXPLORE IT!
horses

READING

1 **1** c **2** a **3** b

2 **2** chief **3** melts **4** rescue **5** beat **6** giant

3 **2** F **3** F **4** F **5** T **6** T

4 Students' own answers

GRAMMAR IN ACTION

1 **2** was making **3** wasn't sleeping **4** were sitting **5** was looking **6** weren't shopping

2 **2** They weren't texting. They were talking.
3 He wasn't sleeping. He was watching TV.
4 We weren't sitting on the bus. We were waiting for the bus.

3 **2** was playing **3** was listening **4** wasn't dancing **5** was feeling **6** were jumping **7** were sleeping

4 **2** was snowing **3** wasn't wearing **4** was standing **5** wasn't feeling **6** was talking/speaking **7** wasn't listening/speaking **8** was playing

VOCABULARY AND LISTENING

1 **2** up **3** across **4** past **5** out of **6** through **7** into **8** between **9** down **10** along **11** over **12** off

2 **2** under **3** over **4** through **5** off **6** into

3 **2** into **3** between **4** under **5** over **6** across

4 Students' own answers

5 Students' own answers

6 **2** c **3** c **4** b **5** b **6** c

7 Students' own answers

GRAMMAR IN ACTION

1 **2** Was the woman wearing a long coat?
3 Were your friends skating down the street?
4 How many people were walking through the park?
5 Where were the children jumping into the river?
6 Why were the passengers getting off the bus?

2 **2** Was he carrying a black bag? Yes, he was.
3 Were alarm bells ringing in the bank? Yes, they were.
4 Was the police officer riding a motorcycle? No, he wasn't.
5 Were the people helping the police officer? No, they weren't.
6 Were the dogs running after the man? No, they weren't.

3 **2** was looking, found
3 didn't hear, was standing
4 were cycling, started
5 had, was doing
6 Were they sitting, hit

4 **2** My friend was looking at her phone when the teacher was seeing her. saw
3 While we were eating dinner, the cat was jumping onto the table and surprised us! jumped
4 He was playing football when he was breaking his leg. broke
5 Weren't you answering the phone when it rang? Didn't you answer

5 **2** was standing **3** didn't see **4** walked **5** was playing **6** stole **7** wasn't looking **8** was leaving **9** took

WRITING

1 Students' own answers

2 **2** F **3** T **4** T **5** F

3 a 7 b 1 c 3 d 5 e 4 f 2 g 6

4 a 2 b 6 c 4 d 3 e 5 f 1

5, 6, and 7 Students' own answers

REVIEW 3

1 **1** worried **2** embarrassed **3** bored **4** nervous **5** afraid **6** surprised **7** lonely **8** angry **9** excited **10** tired **11** upset

2 **1** f **2** c **3** e **4** b **5** a **6** d

3 **1** under **2** down **3** over **4** through **5** out of **6** up

4 **1** were talking **2** were singing **3** were laughing **4** were discussing **5** were thinking

5 **1** was she feeling nervous?
2 were they talking about?
3 was he visiting?
4 were you camping?
5 were you running?
6 was she waiting (for)?

6 **1** were waiting, started **2** heard, was sitting **3** called, were taking **4** returned, was playing **5** ended, was crying/cried **6** was looking, found

7 **1** c **2** b **3** a **4** c **5** a **6** c **7** a **8** b **9** a **10** c **11** a **12** c

Unit 4 pp32–39

VOCABULARY

1 **2** change **3** earn **4** borrow **5** spend **6** sell **7** pay **8** lend **9** save **10** owe

2 **2** lend **3** cost **4** earns **5** owing **6** sold

3 **2** cost **3** pay **4** sell **5** change **6** spend

4 **2** borrow **3** owe **4** lend **5** save **6** sell **7** cost

5 **1** borrows **2** sells, buy **3** save, spend **4** earn, win

EXPLORE IT!

True. They print approximately $974 million of real money and $30 billion of Monopoly money.

READING

1 Students' own answers

2 **2** pressure **3** part-time, common **4** employer

3 **2** T **3** F **4** F **5** T

4 Students' own answers

GRAMMAR IN ACTION

1 **2** a **3** d **4** c **5** f **6** b

2 **Possible answers**
2 When I was six, I could/couldn't count to ten in English.
3 When I was six, I could/couldn't ride a skateboard / skateboard/go skateboarding.
4 When I was six, I could/couldn't swim (100 meters).
5 When I was six, I could/couldn't make / bake a cake.
6 When I was six, I could/couldn't use a cell phone / smartphone.

3 **2** happier **3** the most important **4** the most difficult **5** shorter **6** more helpful

4 **2** Was your phone more expensive than mine?
3 What's worse than losing your wallet?
4 Monday is the quietest day in town.
5 These are the cheapest jeans in the store. / These jeans are the cheapest in the store.
6 Yesterday was the best day of my life.

5 **2** older **3** the richest **4** more exciting **5** the most successful **6** the most expensive

VOCABULARY AND LISTENING

1

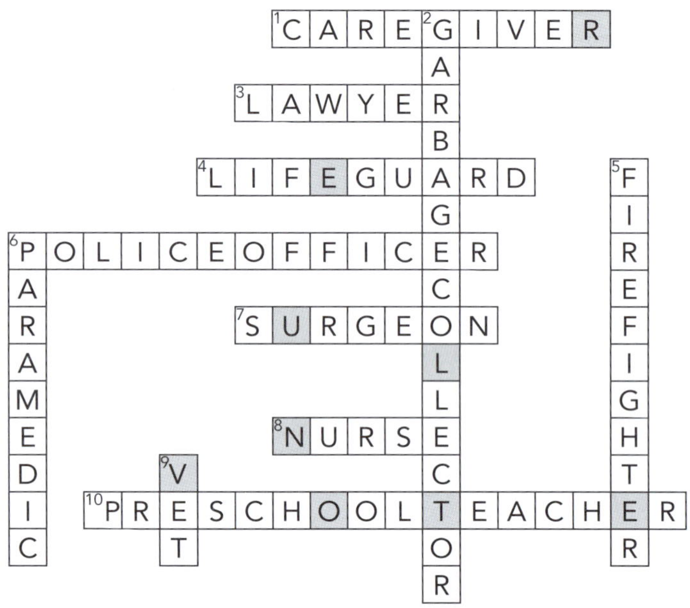

The gray letters make the word "volunteer."

2 **2** vet **3** police officer **4** firefighter **5** caregiver

3 a hospital

4 **2** a **3** c **4** a **5** c

5 Students' own answers

GRAMMAR IN ACTION

1 **2** too expensive **3** too young **4** too hot **5** too busy **6** too hard

2 **2** many **3** much **4** much **5** many **6** much

3 **2** too much **3** too **4** too much **5** too **6** too many

4 **2** There is enough food in the world for everyone. / There is enough food for everyone in the world.
3 Are there enough volunteers in your organization?
4 We don't have enough information at the moment.
5 Is there enough space in this classroom?

5 **2** It's too noise in here for me; please be quiet. noisy
3 The teacher gave us too much options to think about. many
4 There wasn't information enough on the poster. enough information
5 She was much young to be a caregiver. too

6 **2** too many **3** too much **4** too many **5** too **6** enough

WRITING

1 No, he doesn't.

2 **2** First of all **3** Personally, I think **4** In conclusion **5** I believe that

3 **1** working in a supermarket or a café
2 If teens are doing these jobs, adults can't do them, and they need money more than teens.
3 sleep longer and get up later
4 enjoying free-time activities

4 **a** 2 **b** 4 **c** 1 **d** 3

5, 6, and 7 Students' own answers

REVIEW 4

1 **1** h **2** e **3** f **4** b **5** a **6** g **7** d **8** c

2 **1** paramedic **2** caregiver **3** lifeguard **4** surgeon **5** volunteer **6** lawyer

3 **1** couldn't **2** could **3** couldn't **4** couldn't **5** could **6** couldn't

4 **1** worse **2** angrier **3** more worried **4** most upset **5** most hard-working / hardest-working **6** harder **7** more difficult **8** easiest

5 **1** too **2** enough **3** too much **4** too many **5** enough **6** too

6 **1** b **2** b **3** c **4** c **5** a **6** c **7** b **8** a **9** c **10** c **11** a **12** c

Unit 5 pp40–47

VOCABULARY

1 **2** chest of drawers **3** ceiling **4** shelves **5** picture **6** bookcase **7** desk **8** floor **9** cupboard **10** wardrobe **11** carpet **12** fridge **13** sink

2 **2** floor **3** armchair **4** desk **5** pictures **6** wardrobe

3 **2** picture **3** chest of drawers **4** floor **5** cupboard **6** sink

EXPLORE IT!

7,500

READING

1 Students' own answers

2 **2** row **3** canal **4** barge **5** path **6** crowd

3 **2** a **3** a **4** a **5** c **6** b

4 Students' own answers

GRAMMAR IN ACTION

1 **2** n't as noisy as **3** n't as slow as **4** as old as **5** n't as tall as **6** n't as colorful as

2 **2** is as big as **3** is as good as **4** isn't as busy as **5** isn't as fast as **6** is as old as

3 **2** safe **3** hot **4** old **5** well

4 **2** e **3** b **4** c **5** f **6** a

5 **2** as tall as **3** soft enough **4** as comfortable as **5** as expensive as **6** as nice as

VOCABULARY AND LISTENING

1 **2** do **3** make **4** dust **5** load **6** do **7** sweep **8** vacuum **9** do

2 **2** vacuum the carpet **3** do the dishes **4** do the laundry **5** load the dishwasher **6** make the bed

3 Milo

4 **2** laundry **3** pay **4** some **5** likes **6** their homework

5 Students' own answers

GRAMMAR IN ACTION

1 **2** has to **3** don't have to **4** don't have to **5** have to

2 **2** have to make **3** don't have to shop **4** doesn't have to do **5** don't have to wash **6** has to help

3 **2** Do you have to help around the house?
3 Does the dog have to sleep outside?
4 Do you have to vacuum the bedroom carpet?
5 Do the children have to be in bed by nine?
6 Does Owen have to leave before breakfast?

4 **2** don't have to mop
3 doesn't have to help/do
4 has to make
5 has to vacuum, doesn't have to do
6 has to make

5 **2** have to clean up **3** have to put **4** don't have to mop **5** has to do **6** doesn't have to carry **7** has to take

WRITING

1 house b

2 **2** too **3** as well **4** too **5** as well as

3 **2** F **3** T **4** T

4 a 2 **b** 3 **c** 1

5, 6, and 7 Students' own answers

REVIEW 5

1 **1** armchair **2** cupboard **3** wardrobe **4** shelves **5** sink **6** floor **7** chest of drawers **8** carpet **9** fridge **10** desk

2 **1** make the bed **2** mop the floor **3** empty the dishwasher **4** do the dishes **5** sweep the floor **6** load the dishwasher **7** do the ironing **8** dust the furniture **9** vacuum the carpet

3 **1** is as big as my house.
2 isn't as cold as (the weather/it was) yesterday.
3 isn't as relaxed as Jack.
4 isn't old enough to watch that movie.
5 is big enough (for me).
6 isn't as strong as Frank (he is).
7 sweet enough?
8 is as tall as her mother.

4 **1** don't have to **2** have to **3** doesn't have to **4** don't have to **5** don't have to **6** has to **7** don't have to **8** have to

5 **1** b **2** c **3** b **4** a **5** b **6** a **7** c **8** c **9** b **10** c **11** c **12** c

Unit 6 pp48–55

VOCABULARY

1 **2** hit **3** bruise **4** sprain **5** cut **6** get stung **7** burn **8** fall off **9** slip **10** scratch **11** break **12** trip over

2 **2** sprain **3** get cut **4** break

3 **2** f **3** b **4** a **5** c **6** d

4 **2** scratched **3** burn **4** get bitten **5** cut **6** hit

5 **2** sprained **3** didn't break **4** tripped over **5** hit **6** bruised

EXPLORE IT!

Only female

READING

1 **1** Burns **2** Do Not Eat or Drink! **3** Things Up Noses **4** Falls

2 **2** candles **3** poison **4** risky **5** ladder **6** stuck

3 **2** A candle near a curtain can start a fire.
3 a top bathroom cupboard
4 They think it's funny.
5 people over 65 and kids under 15
6 A young child can fall from it.

4 Students' own answers

GRAMMAR IN ACTION

1 **2** shouldn't **3** should **4** should **5** shouldn't **6** should

2 **2** should send **3** should be **4** shouldn't laugh **5** should do **6** shouldn't drink

3 **2** shouldn't drink **3** should listen **4** shouldn't watch **5** should leave/put **6** should turn/switch

4 **2** must not take photos
3 must not use your cell phone / must switch/turn off your cell phone

4 must wear a hat/helmet
5 must not cycle / ride your bike here
6 must wash your hands

5 2 should 3 must 4 must not 5 must 6 must

VOCABULARY AND LISTENING

1

A	K	E	E	H	C	C	L	V
R	W	D	O	C	H	I	N	N
F	O	R	E	H	E	A	D	M
Y	B	K	J	T	S	F	K	E
U	L	C	P	E	T	M	N	C
L	E	E	H	E	X	Z	E	I
A	C	N	S	T	T	O	E	A
W	R	I	S	T	V	N	W	N
R	E	D	L	U	O	H	S	R

2 2 cheeks 3 heel 4 neck 5 chests 6 knee 7 toes 8 wrist

3 a 3 b 5 c 1 d 6 e 2 f 4

4 2 F 3 T 4 T 5 F 6 T

5 Students' own answers

GRAMMAR IN ACTION

1 2 get, are 3 cuts, touch 4 get, stay 5 falls, turns 6 stings, hurts

2 2 If we study hard, we do well on our tests.
3 When Helena feels sick, she doesn't come to school.
4 My little brother falls down if he runs too fast.
5 I feel really bad when I forget my friends' birthdays.
6 If you call the doctor after nine, nobody answers.

3 2 get, eat 3 doesn't rain, die 4 fall, walk 5 go, break

4 2 won't be 3 snows 4 aren't 5 runs

5 2 'll get 3 feel 4 'll think 5 make 6 will, know 7 look 8 will, recognize 9 will be 10 pack

WRITING

1 Students' own answers

2 1 make sure 2 If you ask me, 3 I'd say 4 That's why

3 1 B 2 S 3 K

4 2 b 3 b 4 c 5 c

5, 6, and 7 Students' own answers

REVIEW 6

1

			1 S											
2 S	L	I	P											
			R											
	4 B		A		5 G		6 G		3 F					
7 B	R	U	I	S	E		E		A					
	E		N		T		T		L			8 S		
	A				S		B		L			C		
	K				9 T	R	I	P	O	V	E	R		
					U		T		F			A		
		10 B	U	R	N		T		F			T		11 C
					G		E					C		U
							N					12 H	I	T

2 1 forehead 2 heel 3 elbow 4 knee 5 chin 6 neck 7 chest 8 shoulder 9 cheek 10 teeth 11 wrist 12 toe

3 2 ✓ 3 ✓ 4 must 5 ✓ 6 must 7 must not

4 1 If you get stung by a bee, it hurts.
2 We won't get cold if we wear warm clothes.
3 If I see a red flag, I won't go swimming.
4 Nikita won't be happy if you wake him up.
5 When it rains, we usually play soccer indoors.
6 It is safer to wear a helmet when you go cycling.

5 1 c 2 a 3 b 4 c 5 b 6 c 7 b 8 a 9 b 10 c 11 a 12 c

Unit 7 pp56–63

VOCABULARY

1 upload download app chip social media device video chat emoji screen software

2 **2** video chat **3** device **4** software **5** social media **6** screen

3 **2** download **3** app **4** emoji **5** screen **6** chip

4 send a message/photos, electronic devices/media, computer software/screen, upload photos/software, social media

5 **2** screen **3** download **4** apps **5** message **6** video chatting

EXPLORE IT!
False. It's 110 times.

READING

1 Students' own answers

2 **2** expert **3** properly **4** innovation **5** major **6** minds

3 **2** F **3** T **4** T **5** T **6** F

4 Students' own answers

GRAMMAR IN ACTION

1 **2** changed **3** chosen **4** done **5** heard **6** learned **7** designed **8** seen

2 **2** has changed **3** has been **4** 've seen **5** have chosen **6** 've done **7** 've designed **8** has heard

3 **2** Sergey hasn't forgotten his password.
3 Wanda hasn't broken her watch.
4 We haven't bought a new computer.
5 They haven't turned on the TV.

4 **2** Alex hasn't read anything about Silicon Valley.
3 We've looked for some better information.
4 They've bought a new computer online.
5 He's used the latest software.
6 The boys haven't called their parents.

5 **2** have bought **3** 've downloaded **4** 've decided **5** 've started **6** have written **7** 's chosen **8** haven't recorded

VOCABULARY AND LISTENING

1 **2** get on a train **3** get off a bus **4** get out of a car **5** get into a taxi **6** go by tram **7** take a plane

2 **2** e **3** a **4** b **5** f **6** c

3 **2** by **3** on **4** taken **5** on **6** on **7** catch **8** of

4 No

5 **2** b **3** b **4** c **5** c **6** a

6 Students' own answers

GRAMMAR IN ACTION

1 **2** will **3** won't **4** won't **5** will

2 **2** won't **3** may **4** may **5** will

3 **2** c **3** c **4** a **5** b **6** c

4 **2** First, my sister went online to check the train times.
3 We walked to the station to buy the tickets (there).
4 I left the house at 6 a.m. to catch the first train.
5 My sister wanted to stop at a store to buy some sandwiches.
6 We got on the train quickly to get the best seats.

5 **2** to go **3** may buy **4** will travel **5** to drive **6** might fly

WRITING

1 a

2 **2** more **3** example **4** as **5** addition

3 **2** e **3** b **4** a **5** c

4 **a** 3 **b** 1 **c** 2

5, 6, and 7 Students' own answers

REVIEW 7

1 **1** app **2** video chat **3** emoji **4** upload **5** social media **6** software **7** screen **8** chip **9** download **10** device **11** message

2 **2** getting on a train / taking the subway
3 taking/getting on/catching a plane
4 getting out of a/the car **5** getting into a taxi
6 getting off a bus

3 **1** haven't played **2** 've finished **3** 've made **4** 've sent **5** hasn't replied **6** 's flown **7** 've checked **8** haven't heard

4 **1** to print **2** might/may not have **3** 'll buy **4** to get **5** won't take **6** to play **7** might/may be able to **8** to edit **9** 'll be

5 **1** a **2** a **3** c **4** a **5** c **6** c **7** b **8** a **9** c **10** a **11** a **12** b

Unit 8 pp64–71

VOCABULARY

1

		[1]B	U	S	I	N	E	S	S	M	A	N				
		[2]D	E	T	E	R	M	I	N	A	T	I	O	N		
					[3]I	N	V	E	N	T	O	R				
								[4]A	T	H	L	E	T	E		
					[5]E	N	G	I	N	E	E	R				
								[6]C	O	M	P	O	S	E	R	
							[7]C	R	E	A	T	I	V	I	T	Y
					[8]S	C	I	E	N	T	I	S	T			
								[9]W	R	I	T	E	R			
[10]I	N	T	E	L	L	I	G	E	N	C	E					
								[11]S	K	I	L	L				
									[12]T	A	L	E	N	T		
					[13]S	T	R	E	N	G	T	H				

The word in gray is "mathematician."

2 **2** creativity **3** determination **4** intelligence
5 strength

3 **2** inventor, Tim Berners-Lee **3** Adele, composer
4 Marie Curie, scientist **5** Usain Bolt, athlete
6 writer, Suzanne Collins

EXPLORE IT!
200

READING

1 creative

2 **2** wheelchair **3** face **4** extreme **5** tricks

3 **2** DS **3** F **4** DS **5** T **6** F

4 Students' own answers

GRAMMAR IN ACTION

1 **2** has won **3** has not been **4** hasn't seen
5 've raised **6** has cycled

2 **2** c **3** f **4** e **5** b **6** a

3 **2** **A** Has Fiona ever sung in a band?
B No, she hasn't, but she's sung in the bath tub/ shower.
3 **A** Have they ever swum in the ocean?
B No, they haven't, but they've swum in a swimming pool.
4 **A** Has your dad ever made a cake?
B No, he hasn't, but he's made bread.

4 **2** They <u>never have</u> been to the U.S. have never
3 <u>Never you have</u> ridden a horse. You have never
4 <u>Have</u> she ever broken her phone? Has
5 <u>Stayed you ever</u> in a five-star hotel?
Have you ever stayed
6 I'm happy to say I have <u>ever</u> lost my house keys.
never

5 **2** 've never explored **3** have been
4 've never surfed **5** have, ever tried **8** 's done

VOCABULARY AND LISTENING

1 **2** a **3** h **4** c **5** f **6** d **7** b **8** g

2 **2** give up, b **3** looks up to, f **4** shows off, d
5 keep up with, c **6** taking part in, a

3 a shine, reflect b mold, Petri dish, bacteria

4 They were both (happy) accidents.

5 **2** the middle of the road **3** an animal **4** bacteria
5 on vacation **6** killing

6 Students' own answers

GRAMMAR IN ACTION

1 **2** yourselves **3** yourself **4** itself **5** ourselves
6 themselves

2 **2** take care of themselves **3** taught ourselves
4 entered / has entered himself **5** made herself
6 imagine ourselves

3 **2** She's looked everywhere for her phone.
3 Nobody knows what will happen tonight.
4 There was nowhere to sit on the bus.
5 Someone has broken my new camera.
6 Is there anything I can do to help?

4 **2** e **3** f **4** a **5** c **6** d

5 **2** everyone **3** somewhere **4** himself
5 something **6** Nobody **7** everywhere
8 themselves

WRITING

1 You have to describe how you have helped someone who has faced a challenge.

2 He's made friends and is a drummer in their band.

3 **1** greatest achievements **2** a lot of effort **3** did I do **4** advice to you

4 **1** He has learning difficulties. **2** because he was very shy **3** a drum **4** three

5, 6, and 7 Students' own answers

REVIEW 8

1 **1** athlete **2** inventor **3** engineer **4** mathematician **5** scientist **6** composer **7** writer **8** businesswoman

2 **1** creativity **2** talent **3** strength **4** intelligence **5** determination

3 **1** keep up **2** look up to **3** take part in **4** work out **5** set up **6** come up with, give up

4 **1** Have, heard **2** 've, read **3** 's, broken **4** Has, seen **5** Have, been

5 **1** My cat has taught myself to open the fridge door. Itself/himself/herself
2 Mrs. Howe is nobody who I've always looked up to. somebody
3 Mary Ann saw themselves in a video clip on *YouTube*. herself
4 We've looked anywhere for our lost door keys. everywhere
5 You often talk to ourselves when you're alone. I've heard you! yourself
6 I think there's anything wrong with my computer. something
7 I've noticed that my brother looks at herself in the mirror a lot. himself
8 There was anybody in the house; it was empty. nobody

6 **1** b **2** c **3** a **4** b **5** b **6** c **7** a **8** b **9** a **10** c **11** a **12** b

Unit 9 pp72–79

VOCABULARY

1

Instruments	Genres
violin bass guitar saxophone drums trumpet keyboard	folk classical rock hip-hop jazz

2 **2** bass **3** guitar **4** trumpet **5** saxophone **6** violin **7** keyboard **8** microphone

3 **2** hip-hop **3** folk **4** classical **5** jazz **6** reggae

4 **1** reggae **2** guitar **3** violin

5 Students' own answers

EXPLORE IT!

13

READING

1 Students' own answers

2 **2** set **3** provide **4** available **5** latest **6** mix

3 **1** $4 **2** indoors **3** fruit juice **4** They can ask him to play a song. **5** because he's the geography teacher **6** They play a lot of musical instruments.

4 Students' own answers

GRAMMAR IN ACTION

1 **2** She's going to watch TV.
3 He isn't going to answer the phone.
4 Faye's going to play the piano.
5 They're going to record a song.

2 **2** aren't going to tell **3** 's going to bring **4** 're going to see **5** 's going to be

3 **2** I'm going to study singing.
3 Lily's/She's going to enter a talent competition.
4 Finn and Livvy are / They're going to run a marathon.
5 Max and I are / We're going to get free concert tickets.

4 **2** won't **3** will **4** Will **5** won't

5 **2** are you going to, 'll **3** 's going to, 'll **4** aren't going to, won't

6 **2** 'm going to meet **3** 'm going to ask **4** 'll get **5** 'm going to try **6** 'll learn

VOCABULARY AND LISTENING

1 **2** tap dancing **3** ballroom dancing **4** breakdancing **5** folk dance

2 **2** Salsa **3** Swing **4** modern **5** Zumba

3 **1** four
2 two males and two females
3 two are native speakers (Jessica and Ralf), and two are non-native speakers (Enzo and Camila)

4 **2** F **3** T **4** F **5** T **6** F

5 Students' own answers

GRAMMAR IN ACTION

1 **2** is helping **3** is teaching **4** is writing
5 'm not playing **6** Are, coming

2 **2** They're performing three evening concerts in July.
3 A journalist is interviewing the lead singer later.
4 A TV camera operator is recording tomorrow's show.
5 The drummer isn't playing with the band tonight.
6 He's flying to New York next week to study music there.

3 **2** are watching **3** 'm cooking **4** isn't coming
5 are, arriving **6** aren't doing

4 **2** arrive **3** leaves **4** doesn't end

5 **2** do the singers arrive?
3 does our train leave the next morning?
4 does tomorrow's rehearsal end?

6 **2** are meeting **3** 's coming **4** Aren't you watching
5 're getting **6** does the show end **7** ends
8 're going **9** 're buying

WRITING

1 in the auditorium

2 **2** if you love **3** highlight **4** a must-see
5 downside **6** All in all

3 **2** the story **3** the costumes **4** the makeup
5 Chris Randall **6** Chris's voice
7 the dancers' songs **8** the set

4, 5, and 6 Students' own answers

REVIEW 9

1 **1** violin; classical **2** folk, guitar **3** hip-hop, microphone **4** drums, trumpet **5** bass, keyboard
6 saxophone, jazz

2 disco salsa tap ballroom breakdancing
Zumba swing folk ballet modern

3 **1** are going to go **2** 're going to meet
3 'm going to finish **4** 's going to bring
5 will cost **6** won't rain **7** will be **8** 'll have

4 **1** 'm not doing **2** starts **3** are arriving
4 Are you using **5** 's writing **6** opens
7 is happening **8** doesn't end

5 **1** b **2** a **3** c **4** b **5** c **6** a **7** b **8** a **9** b
10 b **11** c **12** c

EXAM PRACTICE

Reading Practice p81

1 **2** What day does Tom prefer playing tennis with his brother?
3 Why does Mason think art classes are difficult?
4 Who prefers studying alone to studying with other people?
5 How did Eva feel on the morning of her exam?
6 What, according to Josh, is the best thing about eating lunch at home?

2 **1** What's Ben doing with his friends now?
2 What did Ben do last weekend with his aunt?
3 Where did Ben arrange to see his friend last week?
4 What does Ben do Monday to Friday after school?
5 Where does Ben go on Saturdays?
1 C **2** E **3** A **4** B **5** D

3 **2** B; was nervous – felt worried **3** A; were tired – didn't have much energy **4** C; are upset – aren't very happy

4 **2** with no difficulty **3** with care **4** show **5** right **6** scared

Reading Practice p83

1 **2** preposition **3** possessive adjective **4** verb **5** determiner **6** question word **7** conjunction

2 **1** a **2** off **3** his **4** have/need **5** much **6** Where **7** because

3 **1** an **2** won **3** his **4** run **5** at/in **6** better **7** as **8** in

4 **2** a **3** c **4** b **5** c **6** a

5 **2** very, really **3** What, Which **4** need, have **5** Can, Could **6** on, off

Listening Practice p85

1 **1** because they are both in the band / because they're happy to be in the band
2 musical instruments, types of music
3 at school / in a classroom

2 **2** c **3** a **4** c **5** b

3 **2** jobs **3** accidents and injuries **4** transportation **5** furniture

4 **1** a, d **2** b, d **3** a, d **4** b, d **5** b, c

GRAMMAR PRACTICE

Grammar Practice Starter

1 **2** gets up **3** goes **4** watches **5** flies **6** tries

2 **2** does **3** play **4** studies **5** catches

3 **2** Harry reads the school magazine every week.
3 My sister doesn't hang out with friends in the evening.
4 My friends love my new blog.
5 Laura and Luis don't play hockey on Saturdays.
6 We do homework at the homework club.

4 **2** Does Dan read your blog? No, he doesn't.
3 Do you play computer games with your friends? Yes, I/we do.
4 Does your sister write good stories? No, she doesn't.
5 Do Ruth and Ben go to the same school? Yes, they do.

5 **2** are often **3** usually go **4** sometimes get **5** is never **6** usually listens

6 **2** Molly doesn't mind getting up early.
3 We like going to the gym.
4 My dad hates listening to the radio.
5 Jen doesn't mind doing homework.

7 **2** has **3** doesn't have **4** has **5** have **6** have **7** Do, have **8** Does, have

Grammar Practice Unit 1

1 **2** walking **3** taking **4** writing **5** running **6** shopping

2 **2** 'm looking for **3** 's sitting **4** isn't drinking **5** is making **6** aren't chatting

3 **2** Are Rory and Holly watching a movie? Yes, they are.
3 Is Alicia watching a movie? No, she isn't.
4 Is Jack studying grammar? Yes, he is.
5 Are Rory and Holly studying grammar? No, they aren't.
6 Is Alicia studying grammar? Yes, she is.

4 **2** My mom always makes the costumes for the show.
3 We aren't studying English today.
4 My best friend doesn't want to go to the movies.
5 I chat online with my friends on the weekend. / On the weekend, I chat online with my friends.
6 I'm helping my mom at the moment.

5 **2** 'm not doing **3** visit **4** listens **5** makes **6** isn't talking

6 **2** quickly **3** slowly **4** badly **5** well **6** carefully

Grammar Practice Unit 2

1 **2** stayed **3** liked **4** smiled **5** cried **6** studied **7** planned **8** stopped

2 **2** Joanna didn't go to school last week.
3 Megan and Sarah didn't feel tired after the trip.
4 The trip took ten hours!
5 I bought some new shoes.

3 **2** Did Beth eat pizza? Yes, she did.
3 Did Maria and Sam go to the movies? Yes, they did.
4 Did Maria and Sam eat pizza? No, they didn't.
5 Did Ivan go to the movies? Yes, he did.
6 Did Ivan eat pizza? No, he didn't.

4 **2** did he go? **3** did they start school? **4** did she meet? **5** did he eat? **6** did they stay at home?

5 **2** there weren't **3** there were **4** there wasn't **5** There were **6** there was **7** There weren't

6 **2** an **3** any **4** a **5** a **6** some

7 **2** Were there **3** Was there **4** Was there **5** Were there

Grammar Practice Unit 3

1 **2** was taking **3** were chatting **4** were watching **5** was getting **6** were hiding

2 **2** wasn't writing **3** weren't sitting **4** weren't riding **5** wasn't eating **6** weren't making

3 **2** Where were they going last night?
3 Who was she talking to?
4 Why was he laughing at me?
5 Where were you and your mom staying?
6 What were your friends saying?

4 **2** weren't **3** wasn't **4** was **5** were **6** was

5 **2** was going, rang **3** fell, was walking **4** arrived, was dancing **5** was taking, arrived **6** was chatting, came

6 **2** saw **3** was going **4** heard **5** was trying **6** shouted

Grammar Practice Unit 4

1 **2** couldn't take **3** couldn't buy **4** could answer **5** couldn't hear **6** could ride

2 **2** Could his brother speak Spanish?
3 Could Amy and David understand his accent?
4 Could Jeff skate when he was six?
5 Could you understand the science class yesterday?

3 **2** better **3** bigger **4** worse **5** more intelligent

4 **1** B more dangerous **2** A best B better **3** A the easiest B easier

5 **2** My mom has too much work.
3 I have too many clothes in my wardrobe.
4 I don't have enough money to buy a new laptop.
5 She doesn't have enough time to study.

6 **2** too many **3** n't enough **4** too **5** too much **6** enough

Grammar Practice Unit 5

1 **2** as big as **3** isn't as beautiful as **4** are as expensive as **5** isn't as light as **6** aren't as wide as

2 **2** b **3** e **4** a **5** c

3 **2** big enough **3** as big as **4** as comfortable as **5** as small as

4 **2** have to **3** doesn't have to **4** don't have to **5** have to **6** don't have to

5 **2** Do **3** has to **4** doesn't have to **5** don't have to **6** Does, does

Grammar Practice Unit 6

1 **2** shouldn't go **3** should open **4** shouldn't stay **5** should go **6** shouldn't wear

2 **2** must get up **3** must not eat **4** must not talk **5** must not stand **6** must brush

3 **2** must wear **3** must look **4** must not walk **5** must take **6** must not climb

4 **2** d **3** a **4** f **5** b **6** e

5 **2** We'll, we go **3** they swim, they'll be **4** don't come, I won't be **5** he sees, he'll be

6 **2** doesn't have **3** 'll call **4** won't go **5** eat

Grammar Practice Unit 7

1 **2** changed **3** studied **4** tried **5** dropped **6** planned

2 **2** done **3** ridden **4** written **5** forgotten **6** seen

3 **2** 's/has **3** 's/has **4** 've/have **5** 's/has **6** 've/have

4 **2** 've forgotten **3** hasn't made **4** has broken **5** has bought **6** have changed

5 **2** 'll study **3** will be **4** will be **5** will do **6** 'll work

6 **2** might **3** will **4** may **5** may not **6** will

7 **2** to change **3** to have **4** to speak **5** to take **6** to show

Grammar Practice Unit 8

1 **2** never **3** Have, haven't **4** ever, has

2 **2** Has Christina ever sprained her ankle?; has
3 Has Tony ever eaten Japanese food?; hasn't
4 Have your parents ever traveled to a different country?; haven't
5 Has your sister ever learned a new language?; has
6 Have you ever spent too much money?; have

3 **2** I've never <u>invent</u> anything! invented
3 Has your brother ever <u>win</u> a prize? won
4 She <u>haven't</u> been to a different country. hasn't
5 I <u>haven't never</u> seen a waterfall. have never

4 **2** himself **3** themselves **4** ourselves **5** myself **6** itself

5 **2** herself **3** myself **4** themselves **5** himself **6** ourselves

6 **2** nothing **3** everywhere **4** Someone **5** nothing **6** anywhere

Grammar Practice Unit 9

1 **2** isn't going to work **3** 's going to perform **4** are going to buy **5** aren't going to go

2 **2** is Tina going to work **3** are your parents going to start **4** is your brother going to do **5** Are you going to learn **6** Is your sister going to buy

3 **2** are going to **3** are going to **4** will **5** will

4 **2** Jess is watching ballet this weekend.
3 Marta and Adam are going out for pizza with their friends tonight.
4 Marta and Adam are going to a concert this weekend.

5 **2** 'm having **3** are going **4** are, going **5** 'm meeting **6** 's making

6 **2** does, begin **3** lasts **4** has **5** ends **6** does, open

NOTES

NOTES

NOTES

NOTES

SHAPE IT! 2

PROJECT BOOK

Simon Cupit

CAMBRIDGE
UNIVERSITY PRESS

CAMBRIDGE
UNIVERSITY PRESS & ASSESSMENT

Shaftesbury Road, Cambridge CB2 8EA, United Kingdom

One Liberty Plaza, 20th Floor, New York, NY 10006, USA

477 Williamstown Road, Port Melbourne, VIC 3207, Australia

314–321, 3rd Floor, Plot 3, Splendor Forum, Jasola District Centre, New Delhi – 110025, India

103 Penang Road, #05–06/07, Visioncrest Commercial, Singapore 238467

Avenida Paulista, 807 conjunto 2315, 01311–915, São Paulo, Brazil

Torre de los Parques, Colonia Tlacoquemécatl del Valle, Mexico City C.P. 03200, Mexico

Cambridge University Press & Assessment is a department of the University of Cambridge.

We share the University's mission to contribute to society through the pursuit of education, learning and research at the highest international levels of excellence.

www.cambridge.org
Information on this title: www.cambridge.org/9781108923453

First published 2020

20 19 18 17 16 15 14 13 12 11 10 9 8 7

Printed in Malaysia by Vivar Printing

A catalogue record for this publication is available from the British Library.

ISBN 978-1-108-92345-3 Shape It! Teacher's Book & Project Book with Digital Pack Level 2
ISBN 978-84-9036-882-4 Collaborate Project Book Level 2

Additional resources for this publication at www.cambridge.org/shapeit/resources

CONTENTS

AN INTRODUCTION TO PROJECT WORK

Welcome back to school! Your students are eagerly awaiting new challenges. How are you going to help them develop their skills this year?

Your class has now experienced project work. Students have worked together in groups to produce and present their projects to the class. At the same time, they have used and developed their language skills to communicate real meaning. The projects in Level 2 are designed to help your students expand their learning possibilities and stay motivated.

This book will guide you on how to make the most of your projects so your students can continue to work successfully both in and out of the classroom.

What Is Project Work?

Imagine you and your class have just finished Unit 6 (*How Can I Stay Safe?*). Your students have learned vocabulary for parts of the body and practiced making suggestions to avoid accidents and injuries. How can you review and expand on this topic? In this case, your students make an information pamphlet about a remote place or habitat, including suggestions for how to stay safe.

As you know, this is project work: students taking ownership of their work and making decisions together. There is a realistic final outcome and a series of stages to follow that allows groups to explore how they can achieve their goals. The final aim is always a presentation stage. Presentation Ideas p18 Your role is to facilitate how this happens. As a result, students learn by doing and have a shared, memorable experience to look back on.

Throughout the project work process, students develop a number of **life skills**. They learn to:

BENEFITS AND ADVANTAGES OF PROJECT WORK

Personal Advantages

- encourages **creativity** by promoting **lateral thinking**
- increases **motivation** through challenge
- develops **autonomy** and a **sense of responsibility**
- increases natural **curiosity**
- improves **self-knowledge** through **self-evaluation**
- improves **communication skills** through teamwork
- involves family and friends in the **learning process**
- improves **interpersonal** relationships
- develops **life skills**

Academic Advantages

- allows teachers to deal with **mixed-ability** classes
- motivates whole-team / cooperation / group work and promotes chances to **learn from one another**
- develops **planning** and **organizational skills**
- permits a "**flipped classroom**" approach
- **consolidates learning** through research and opportunities for deep thinking
- increases opportunities to **integrate cross-curricular** and **cultural topics**
- encourages **peer teaching** and **correction**
- enables students with **different learning styles** to help one another

Language Learning

- provides opportunities to **use language authentically**
- integrates all **four skills** (reading, writing, listening, and speaking)
- allows for the use of **self- and peer-evaluation language**
- encourages research and **use of English out of the class**
- is learner-centered: students **learn language from one another**
- practices both **fluency** and **accuracy** through different types of presentations

Project Work and the Cambridge Framework for Life Competencies

How can we prepare our students to succeed in a rapidly changing world? We see the need to help students develop transferable skills, to work with people from around the globe, to think creatively, analyze sources critically, and communicate their views effectively. However, how can we balance the development of these skills with the demands of the language curriculum?

Cambridge has developed the Cambridge Framework for Life Competencies. This Framework reinforces project work, helping teachers recognize and assess the many transferable skills that project work develops alongside language learning.

The Framework provides different levels of detail, from six broad Areas of Competency to specific Can Do Statements. We have grouped the different competencies into six main areas, which are supported by three foundation layers.

Creative Thinking	Critical Thinking	Learning to Learn	Communication	Collaboration	Social Responsibilities
EMOTIONAL DEVELOPMENT		DIGITAL LITERACY		DISCIPLINE KNOWLEDGE	

It then defines specific competencies in each Area. For example, here are the Competencies for Collaboration :

- Taking personal responsibility for own contribution to a group task
- Listening respectfully and responding constructively to others' contributions
- Managing the sharing of tasks in a project
- Working toward a resolution related to a task

Finally, there is a Can Do statement for each Competency. These will differ depending on the age of the students.

Area of Competency:
Collaboration

↓

Competency:
Managing the sharing of tasks in a project

↓

Can Do Statements:

- Follows the instructions for a task and alerts others when straying from them.
- Explains reasons for suggestions and contributions.
- Takes responsibility for completing tasks as part of a larger project.

For more information, go to: cambridge.org/elt

Level 2 Projects	Area of Competency	Competency	Can Do Statements
Culture Project: An Infographic Teacher's Resource Bank Unit 1	Creative Thinking	Creating new content from own ideas or other resources	*Communicates personal response to creative work from art, music, or literature.*
	Learning to Learn	Reflecting on and evaluating own learning success	*Selects and uses a wide range of mind maps and other tools to organize thoughts; Identifies what needs to be revisited before identifying new learning goals.*
History Project: A Museum Display Student's Book Unit 2 pp30–31	Collaboration	Listening respectfully and responding constructively to others' contributions	*Listens to / acknowledges different points of view respectfully; Evaluates contributions from other students with appropriate sensitivity.*
	Communication	Managing conversations	*Can use simple techniques to start, maintain, and close conversations of various lengths; Uses appropriate strategies to develop a conversation (e.g., showing interest).*
Culture Project: A Comic Strip Teacher's Resource Bank Unit 3	Critical Thinking	Synthesizing ideas and information	*Selects key points from diverse sources to create a new account.*
	Social Responsibilities	Taking active roles including leadership	*In group work, makes consultative decisions; Encourages others to participate and contribute to projects.*
Social Studies Project: A Poster Student's Book Unit 4 pp54–55	Social Responsibilities	Understanding personal responsibilities as part of a group and in society	*Understands various aspects of society (e.g., volunteering); Gets involved in collective action in the school (e.g., through volunteering).*
	Creative Thinking	Using newly created content to solve problems	*Employs new ideas and content in solving a task or activity; Makes an assignment original by adding new angles.*
Culture Project: A Poster Teacher's Resource Bank Unit 5	Learning to Learn	Practical skills for participating in learning	*Participates sensibly and positively in learning activities in class; Understands essential grammatical terms and concepts.*
	Collaboration	Managing the sharing of tasks in a project	*Ensures that work is fairly divided among members in group activities; Offers to help others finish a task.*
Science Project: An Information Pamphlet Student's Book Unit 6 pp78–79	Critical Thinking	Understanding and analyzing links between ideas	*Compares points and arguments from different sources; Identifies the basic structure of an argument.*
	Communication	Managing conversations	*Uses appropriate language to negotiate meaning: to show understanding; to signal lack of understanding; to seek clarification.*
Culture Project: A 3-D Room Plan Teacher's Resource Bank Unit 7	Critical Thinking	Evaluating ideas, arguments, and options	*Examines possible solutions to a given problem and states how effective they are; Assesses strengths and weaknesses of possible solutions.*
	Collaboration	Working toward a resolution related to a task	*Is aware when others have divergent views and ideas for completing a problem or task; Is able to propose solutions that include views and ideas other than their own.*
Technology Project: A Timeline Student's Book Unit 8 pp102–103	Learning to Learn	Practical skills for participating in learning	*Uses metacognitive strategies (e.g., time management) to maximize learning; Takes effective notes in class and from homework reading.*
	Creative Thinking	Creating new content from own ideas or other resources	*Writes or tells an original story, given prompts or without prompts; Responds imaginatively to contemporary or historical events and ideas.*
Culture Project: A Webpage Teacher's Resource Bank Unit 9	Communication	Managing conversations	*Uses appropriate language to negotiate meaning: to check own understanding; to check interlocutors' understanding; Invites contributions from interlocutors in a conversation.*
	Social Responsibilities	Understanding and describing own and others' cultures	*Makes informed comparisons between their own society and other societies; Understands the contributions of different cultures to their own lives.*

HOW TO USE THE *PROJECT* BOOK

See learning outcomes at a glance, as well as the skills students will develop and the resources and evaluation tools you may wish to use.

Manage student roles and responsibilities.

Monitor and assess the skills that project work develops, mapped to the Cambridge Framework for Life Competencies.

Print and/or digital references will help you locate the material that you need.

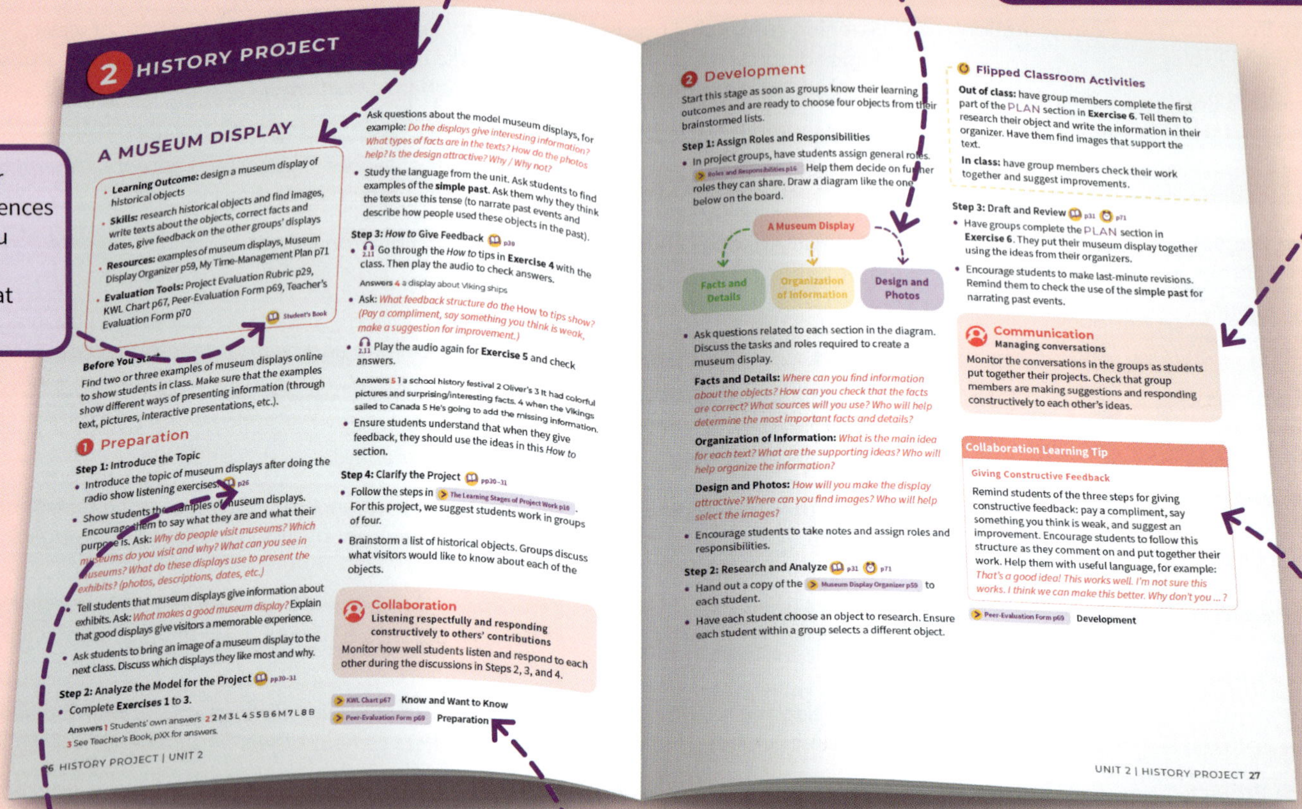
2 HISTORY PROJECT

A MUSEUM DISPLAY

- **Learning Outcome:** design a museum display of historical objects
- **Skills:** research historical objects and find images, write texts about the objects, correct facts and dates, give feedback on the other groups' displays
- **Resources:** examples of museum displays, Museum Display Organizer p59, My Time-Management Plan p71
- **Evaluation Tools:** Project Evaluation Rubric p29, KWL Chart p67, Peer-Evaluation Form p69, Teacher's Evaluation Form p70

Student's Book

Before You Start

Find two or three examples of museum displays online to show students in class. Make sure that the examples show different ways of presenting information (through text, pictures, interactive presentations, etc.).

1 Preparation

Step 1: Introduce the Topic

- Introduce the topic of museum displays after doing the radio show listening exercises. p26
- Show students the examples of museum displays. Encourage them to say what they are and what their purpose is. Ask: *Why do people visit museums? Which museums do you visit and why? What can you see in museums? What do these displays use to present the exhibits? (photos, descriptions, dates, etc.)*
- Tell students that museum displays give information about exhibits. Ask: *What makes a good museum display?* Explain that good displays give visitors a memorable experience.
- Ask students to bring an image of a museum display to the next class. Discuss which displays they like most and why.

Step 2: Analyze the Model for the Project pp30–31

- Complete **Exercises 1** to **3**.

Answers 1 Students' own answers 2 2 M 3 L 4 S 5 B 6 M 7 L 8 B 3 See Teacher's Book, pXX for answers.

- Ask questions about the model museum displays, for example: *Do the displays give interesting information? What types of facts are in the texts? How do the photos help? Is the design attractive? Why / Why not?*
- Study the language from the unit. Ask students to find examples of the **simple past**. Ask them why they think the texts use this tense (to narrate past events and describe how people used these objects in the past).

Step 3: *How to* Give Feedback p30

- 2.11 Go through the *How to* tips in **Exercise 4** with the class. Then play the audio to check answers.

Answers 4 a display about Viking ships

- Ask: *What feedback structure do the How to tips show? (Pay a compliment, say something you think is weak, make a suggestion for improvement.)*
- 2.11 Play the audio again for **Exercise 5** and check answers.

Answers 5 1 a school history festival 2 Oliver's 3 It had colorful pictures and surprising/interesting facts. 4 when the Vikings sailed to Canada 5 He's going to add the missing information.

- Ensure students understand that when they give feedback, they should use the ideas in this *How to* section.

Step 4: Clarify the Project pp30–31

- Follow the steps in The Learning Stages of Project Work p18. For this project, we suggest students work in groups of four.
- Brainstorm a list of historical objects. Groups discuss what visitors would like to know about each of the objects.

Collaboration
Listening respectfully and responding constructively to others' contributions

Monitor how well students listen and respond to each other during the discussions in Steps 2, 3, and 4.

KWL Chart p67 Know and Want to Know
Peer-Evaluation Form p69 Preparation

26 HISTORY PROJECT | UNIT 2

2 Development

Start this stage as soon as groups know their learning outcomes and are ready to choose four objects from their brainstormed lists.

Step 1: Assign Roles and Responsibilities

- In project groups, have students assign general roles. Roles and Responsibilities p16 Help them decide on further roles they can share. Draw a diagram like the one below on the board.

A Museum Display → Facts and Details / Organization of Information / Design and Photos

- Ask questions related to each section in the diagram. Discuss the tasks and roles required to create a museum display.

Facts and Details: *Where can you find information about the objects? How can you check that the facts are correct? What sources will you use? Who will help determine the most important facts and details?*

Organization of Information: *What is the main idea for each text? What are the supporting ideas? Who will help organize the information?*

Design and Photos: *How will you make the display attractive? Where can you find images? Who will help select the images?*

- Encourage students to take notes and assign roles and responsibilities.

Step 2: Research and Analyze p31 p71

- Hand out a copy of the Museum Display Organizer p59 to each student.
- Have each student choose an object to research. Ensure each student within a group selects a different object.

Flipped Classroom Activities

Out of class: have group members complete the first part of the PLAN section in **Exercise 6**. Tell them to research their object and write the information in their organizer. Have them find images that support the text.

In class: have group members check their work together and suggest improvements.

Step 3: Draft and Review p31 p71

- Have groups complete the PLAN section in **Exercise 6**. They put their museum display together using the ideas from their organizers.
- Encourage students to make last-minute revisions. Remind them to check the use of the **simple past** for narrating past events.

Communication
Managing conversations

Monitor the conversations in the groups as students put together their projects. Check that group members are making suggestions and responding constructively to each other's ideas.

Collaboration Learning Tip

Giving Constructive Feedback

Remind students of the three steps for giving constructive feedback: pay a compliment, say something you think is weak, and suggest an improvement. Encourage students to follow this structure as they comment on and put together their work. Help them with useful language, for example: *That's a good idea! This works well. I'm not sure this works. I think we can make this better. Why don't you ... ?*

Peer-Evaluation Form p69 Development

UNIT 2 | HISTORY PROJECT 27

Identify the corresponding pages of the Students Book.

Find useful photocopiable resources.

Get useful tips for monitoring collaborative skills.

A photocopiable graphic organizer helps students organize their notes in the developmental stage of each project.

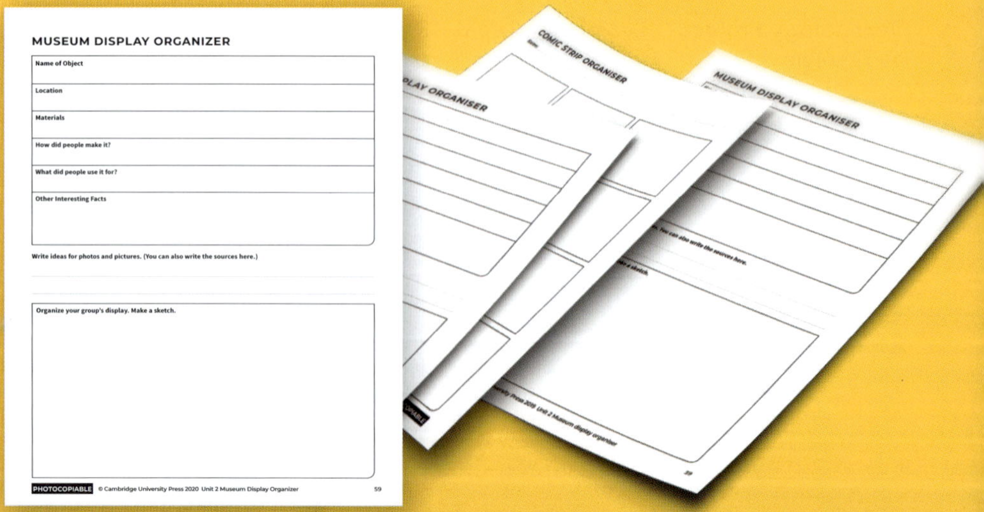

Get ideas for extra differentiated practice in each project; perfect for mixed abilities!

See clear guidelines for identifying and assessing student performance.

Identify the other vital skills that project work develops.

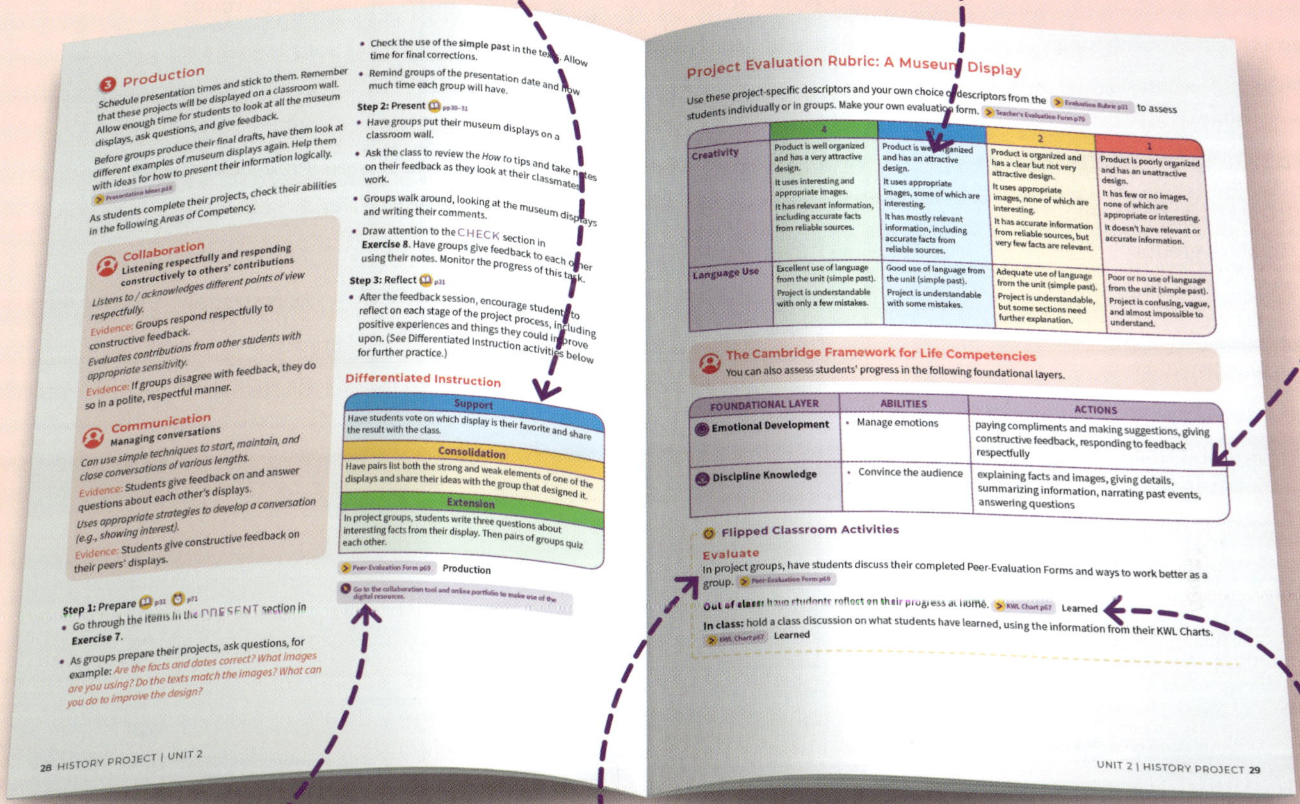

Students can work together on their projects in the digital collaboration space, and teachers can track and assess their work. Students can also share and comment on each other's work in the portfolio.

Help students evaluate themselves and their peers.

Get flipped classroom ideas for carrying out the activities both in and out of class.

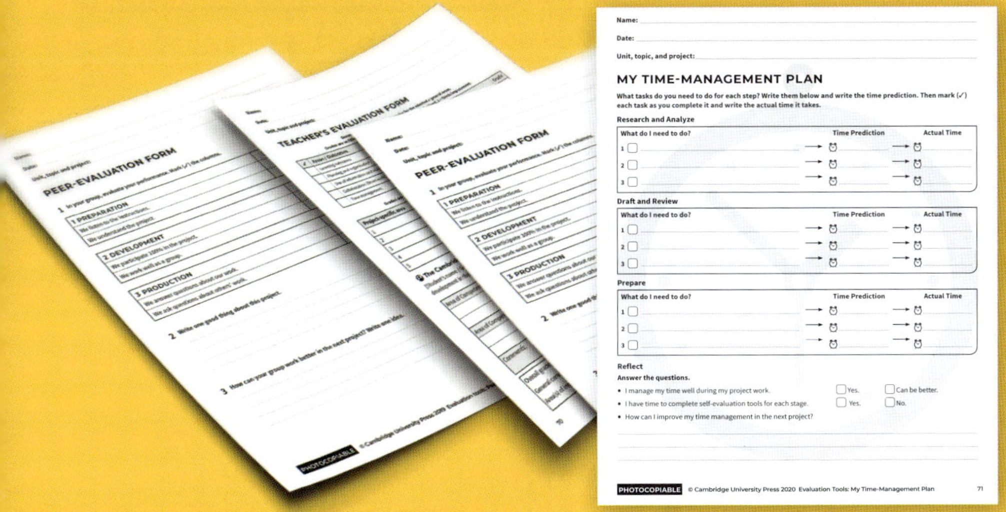

Photocopiable assessment and time-management sheets help students work more independently.

THE LEARNING STAGES OF PROJECT WORK

1 Preparation

Facilitators

Step 1: **Introduce** the topic

Step 2: **Analyze** the model for the project

Step 3: **Go through** the *How to* tips

Step 4: **Clarify** the project

- Organize groups
- Review the learning outcomes and skills
- Brainstorm ideas
- Focus on key information
- Have groups make decisions about content

2 Development

Project Groups

Step 1: **Assign** roles and responsibilities

Step 2: **Research** and **analyze**

Step 3: **Draft** and **review**

- Put together work
- Peer-correct
- Express opinions and make choices

3 Production

Project Groups

Step 1: **Prepare**

- Decide how the project will look and who will speak
- Practice

Step 2: **Present**

- Take turns presenting
- Ask questions and give feedback

Step 3: **Reflect**

- Discuss all stages of the process

Pre-Evaluation (Self-Evaluation)

Tools for students:
KWL Chart, My Learning Diary, Peer-Evaluation Form

Tools for teachers:
Teacher's Evaluation Form

> Evaluation Tools pp67–70

Formative Evaluation (Self-Evaluation, Peer-Evaluation, Observation)

Tools for students:
KWL Chart, My Learning Diary, Graphic Organizers, Peer-Evaluation Form

Tools for teachers:
Teacher's Evaluation Form

> Evaluation Tools pp67–70

Formative and Summative Evaluation

Tools for students:
KWL Chart, My Learning Diary, Peer-Evaluation Form

Tools for teachers:
Teacher's Evaluation Form, Evaluation Rubric

> Evaluation Tools pp67–70

> Evaluation Rubric p21

Reflection (You and Students)

1 Have *student-to-student*, *student-to-teacher,* and *teacher-to-student* discussions on evaluation grades.

2 Identify areas for improvement in future projects using the Evaluation Tools.

> Evaluation p20

L1 IN PROJECT WORK

Many teachers believe that the only way for students to learn English effectively is by using it at all times in class. They feel that any time students spend using their own language is a missed opportunity.

Do you allow L1 use in your classroom? If you do, don't worry: there is little evidence to support the above idea (Kerr, 2016).[1] In fact, there are occasions when allowing students to use L1 is beneficial. This is particularly true of project work.

We can exploit the potential of L1 in different steps of the project cycle. Take *Clarifying the project* as an example (Preparation stage, Step 4). If students fail to understand the project's objectives, they won't carry it out properly. Allowing L1 use is not a "missed opportunity" here. It ensures a richer project experience.

Of course, this doesn't mean you should use students' own language *all* of the time. You have to consider factors like age, level, the complexity of the project, and its outcomes. The question is not *if* you should use students' own language, but *when*, *how*, and *how much*.

At Level 2, we suggest you allow own-language use for in-depth explanations, discussions, and reflection. However, students should be using more English in the development and presentation stages.

Tips for L1 Use

- Set rules for when students can use L1.
- Encourage groups to monitor their own-language use and explore English equivalents.
- Allow students "own-language moments" (Kerr, 2014: 26–29),[2] such as preparing for speaking activities. Remember that the students' goal is to produce English in the Production stage of project work.

OL = Own Language, E = English, ■ shows suggested language

THE LEARNING STAGES OF PROJECT WORK		
1 Preparation	**OL**	**E**
Introducing and discussing the topic	□■	■□
Analyzing the model for the project	□■	■□
Going through the *How to* tips	□■	■□
Clarifying the project	■■	■□
2 Development	**OL**	**E**
Assigning roles and responsibilities	□■	■■
Researching and analyzing	□■	■□
Drafting and reviewing	□■	■■
3 Production	**OL**	**E**
Preparing the final presentation	□■	■□
Presenting the project	□□	■■
Reflecting on the process	■■	■□

[1] Kerr, Philip (2016). The learner's own language. Explorations in English Language and Linguistics. 3.1:1-7.
[2] Kerr, Philip (2014). Translation and Own-Language Activities. Cambridge: Cambridge University Press.

MIXED ABILITIES IN PROJECT WORK

How can you teach in ways that suit each type of learner? Projects offer a great advantage in this area, as students can explore different ways of completing them.

Mixed-ability class characteristics can depend on individual differences, such as motivation, ability, age, and experience. Allow your students to express their ideas in different ways, and remember that no one will benefit from a project that is too difficult or too easy.

Studies have shown that adolescence is the best time for instructed language learning. Teenagers are faster at learning and are ready to observe and use rules (DeKeyser, 2010).[1] Your activities should reflect this learning phase, which means getting to know your students and their differences in the following four areas:

Cognitive Maturity

Your students' ages and experiences affect their ability to understand and follow instructions.

→ Adapt instructions according to level and avoid complicated words and phrases with beginners and elementary students.

Proficiency

Every member of your class will have a different language level.

→ Make sure tasks involve an appropriate degree of difficulty and are suitably challenging. Provide the levels of support needed.

Interests

Teenagers have a wide variety of interests and skills.

→ Allow students to take roles within a project that help them develop their personal interests and relate to the main task. Encourage them to expand their knowledge.

Learning Preferences

Everyone has different learning preferences, such as reading, taking notes, asking questions, listening, moving around, or watching videos.

→ Use a variety of modalities in your classroom, such as visual, kinesthetic, auditory, multimodal, or text.

The Roles of the Facilitator

Give Feedback

Is it a mouse?

Ask for and Give Reasons

Why? Because ...

Encourage Participation

What do you think?

Listen Actively

That's interesting! Really?

[1] DeKeyser, R., Alfi-Shabtay, I., & Ravid, D. (2010). Cross-linguistic evidence for the nature of age effects in second language acquisition. Applied Psycholinguistics, 31(3), 413-438.

Classroom Suggestions

Challenge	Suggestion
When working in groups, more proficient students solve the problems, while others stay quiet.	Allow time for "think-pair-share" activities, where students think individually first, discuss ideas with a partner, then share their ideas with another pair.
When less proficient students are put in groups according to ability, they become labeled as "less proficient," which affects their motivation and self-esteem.	Vary groupings to ensure all students benefit and contribute in different contexts.
High-ability students do not feel challenged.	Give extension work and higher-level input.
Lower-proficiency students do not complete tasks.	Give additional support and adapted activities.

Differentiated Instruction

We provide a specific suggestion for differentiated instruction in each project. Each one has three categories:

1 *Support* activities help students better understand the tasks and concepts.

2 *Consolidation* activities reinforce what students are learning.

3 *Extension* activities provide additional challenges for more proficient students.

1 PREPARATION		
Support	**Consolidation**	**Extension**
Suggest ways to record and keep notes. Extend time limits. Give students specific goals related to competencies.	Have students organize ideas. Provide students with specific tasks to improve competencies. Give extra roles and responsibilities.	Suggest alternative ideas. Focus on additional competencies. Set additional goals.

2 DEVELOPMENT		
Support	**Consolidation**	**Extension**
Provide more examples of models. Suggest sources for research. Give essential information that helps with students' roles. Ask specific questions about findings.	Analyze different models. Have students share opinions. Make additional notes of findings. Assess validity of sources. Give extra responsibility in line with roles.	Produce another model for the project. Analyze opinions. Look for different points of view. Allow for peer-teaching.

3 PRODUCTION		
Support	**Consolidation**	**Extension**
Ensure level-appropriate participation during presentation. Allow feedback in own language. Suggest ways to improve.	Encourage feedback in English. Have students discuss self-evaluation. Encourage suggestions for ways to improve.	Give all feedback and evaluation in English. Have students interview each other about what they learned. Encourage suggestions for ways to improve.

TIME MANAGEMENT IN PROJECT WORK

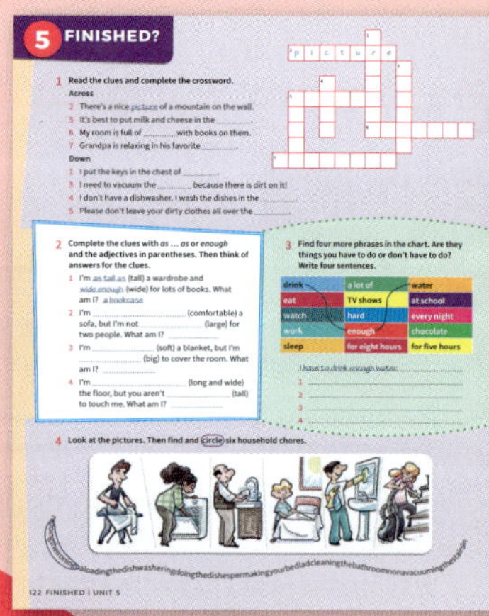

① Be Prepared

Take a look at the project before you start the unit.

② Divide the Project into Smaller Tasks

Every project is comprised of a number of smaller tasks, such as research, preparation, organizing notes, and brainstorming. Ask yourself:

- *How long will each task take?*
- *Can the task be done in class or out of class?*
- *At what stage of the unit can students complete each step?*
- *What language do they need?*

By approaching the project this way, you will see that the steps may not take up too much class time.

③ Prioritize and Set Short-Term Goals

Think about how the project groups can best use class time. Should they brainstorm, draw pictures, or organize sentences? Be clear about what you want the groups to achieve by the end of each session.

④ Help Students Plan Out-of-Class Assignments

Ensure the groups understand that the out-of-class tasks are just as important as the in-class ones when preparing a project. Set goals and give time limits. Encourage them to use their My Time-Management Plans when you see this icon: ⏰

> My Time-Management Plan p71

⑤ Be Flexible Between Projects

How much time you give students for each task will vary from project to project. It may depend on factors such as previous knowledge, level of language difficulty, or access to information.

⑥ Set a Time for the Presentation

Make sure you allow sufficient class time for the presentation step, including its evaluation. If the steps leading to the final product have been distributed and completed in an organized way, it's likely there will be more time for presenting it.

It is important that groups present their projects when they expect to do so. It can be demotivating if you run out of time before they present.

CHALLENGES AND IMPLICATIONS

Now in their second year, most of your students are familiar with the school environment and have experienced working in groups. While many will still prefer to work individually, they will have also seen the benefits of a well-organized project group.

Your second-year students will continue to go through social, emotional, and physiological changes. They will also probably have more responsibilities and academic pressure.

What are some changes and challenges to expect?

Change	Challenge
Academic: more workload and responsibilities	Organizing time, planning when to study, doing homework, staying motivated
Environment: different teachers and expectations	Getting used to new ways of learning, building trust
Social: new friends or social groups (some students will change friends or clubs)	Dealing with peer pressure, resolving conflicts, building good relations
Self growth: physiological, emotional, and moral changes	Building self-confidence, developing empathy, providing emotional support
Personal: more complex personal issues, new interests	Sharing personal problems, maintaining open communication

All these changes and their challenges have implications for how to use project work in your classroom. You can encourage successful collaboration by:

- describing how you are going to organize your classes
- explaining how much guidance you will give and your expectations
- making students feel excited about how they can work (using the Internet, online programs, the library, etc.)
- observing group dynamics
- organizing group work from the start
- making sure no one is isolated
- developing different skills through varied ways of working (e.g., reflection, peer-evaluation, listening to others)
- continuing to pay attention to each student as an individual

COLLABORATION

Collaborative Skills	Behaviors	Level 2 Projects
Peer-Tutoring	Correcting and editing each other's work	**An Infographic:** match the text with the images; check content; suggest additions
Giving Constructive Feedback	Commenting on group members' work	**A Museum Display:** make a compliment on and suggest an improvement to each other's sections
Resolving Conflicts	Reaching a compromise and making final decisions	**A Comic Strip:** choose a story; agree on key events; select the best way to represent events
Using Social Skills	Giving opinions, persuading, compromising, agreeing	**A Poster:** agree on content; express opinions politely
Encouraging Responsibility	Completing tasks on time to finish a project together	**A Poster:** find information individually; prepare own section; check each other's work
Listening Actively	Responding to others' work or suggestions	**An Information Pamphlet:** plan information together; share first drafts and give opinions
Disagreeing Appropriately	Giving opinions politely to come to a solution	**A 3-D Room Plan:** decide on modern technology and furniture; comment on labels and diagrams
Sharing Tasks	Ensuring all group members have a task and role	**A Timeline:** identify the main tasks and roles; set long-term and short-term deadlines; review the project regularly
Sharing Resources	Helping group members complete or improve work	**A Webpage:** find and share online templates, images, and information; help each other find these resources

Roles and Responsibilities

Each project has specific roles; however, here are some general roles that you can apply at any time.

The **group leader** supervises, communicates with the teacher, and manages participation.

The **coordinator** tracks time and makes sure individuals complete their tasks.

The **diary keeper** records decisions and tracks roles and responsibilities.

The **resource manager** takes care of resources and keeps the final product for presentation.

The **inspector** verifies and edits information.

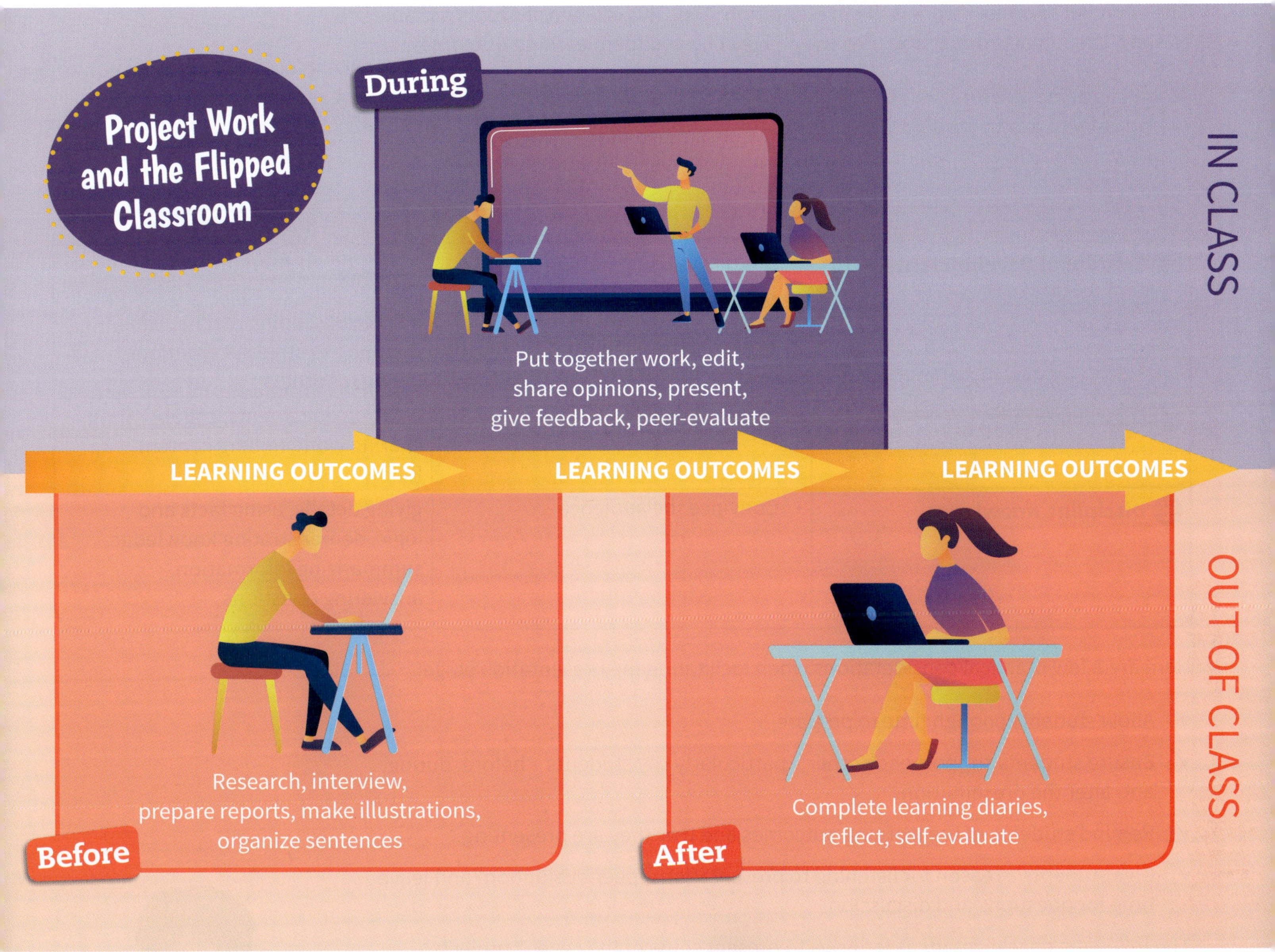

Each project in this book contains at least one flipped classroom idea. Students are still collaborating when they use this approach. They have to assign roles, get things ready on time, share information and resources, and check one another's work. Ensure students plan out-of-class project work and use their My Time-Management Plans. > My Time-Management Plan p71

How Well Did I Collaborate?

At the end of the process, have students answer a few questions about how well they collaborated.

Collaboration

Did I ...
help my group?
share information?
do the tasks for my role?

Was I motivated?

Did we ...
trust each other in my group?
share opinions in my group?
share materials in my group?

What can I do to be a better group member?

PRESENTATION IDEAS

The end goal of project work is the presentation step. This is when students are able to show their final product and how they have achieved their learning outcomes.

As well as being a natural way to end the project process, this stage also gives you an opportunity to assess students' progress in the foundational layers of The Cambridge Framework for Life Competencies. > The Cambridge Framework for Life Competencies p6

FOUNDATIONAL LAYER	ABILITIES	EXAMPLE ACTIONS
Emotional Development	• Identify and understand emotions • Manage emotions • Empathize and build relationships	reflecting on strengths and weaknesses, verbalizing emotions, employing coping mechanisms, adapting to stressful emotions, caring for others
Digital Literacy	• Use digital tools	creating documents, collaborating, sharing work, finding content, following safe practices
Discipline Knowledge	• Convince the audience	giving details, using facts and logic, demonstrating knowledge, summarizing information, answering questions

Here are a few practical considerations when facilitating the presentation stage:

- ✓ Allow students enough time to prepare.
- ✓ Ensure students support each other – particularly shy students – before, during, and after the presentation.
- ✓ Remind students of the learning outcomes and *why* they are presenting.
- ✓ Give students a reason for listening to presentations (peer-evaluation) and leave time for questions and discussion.

The following page gives ideas for ways to present some of the Level 2 projects. However, they are only suggestions. Where possible, let students choose modes of presentation that are most suitable for their projects and the classroom context.

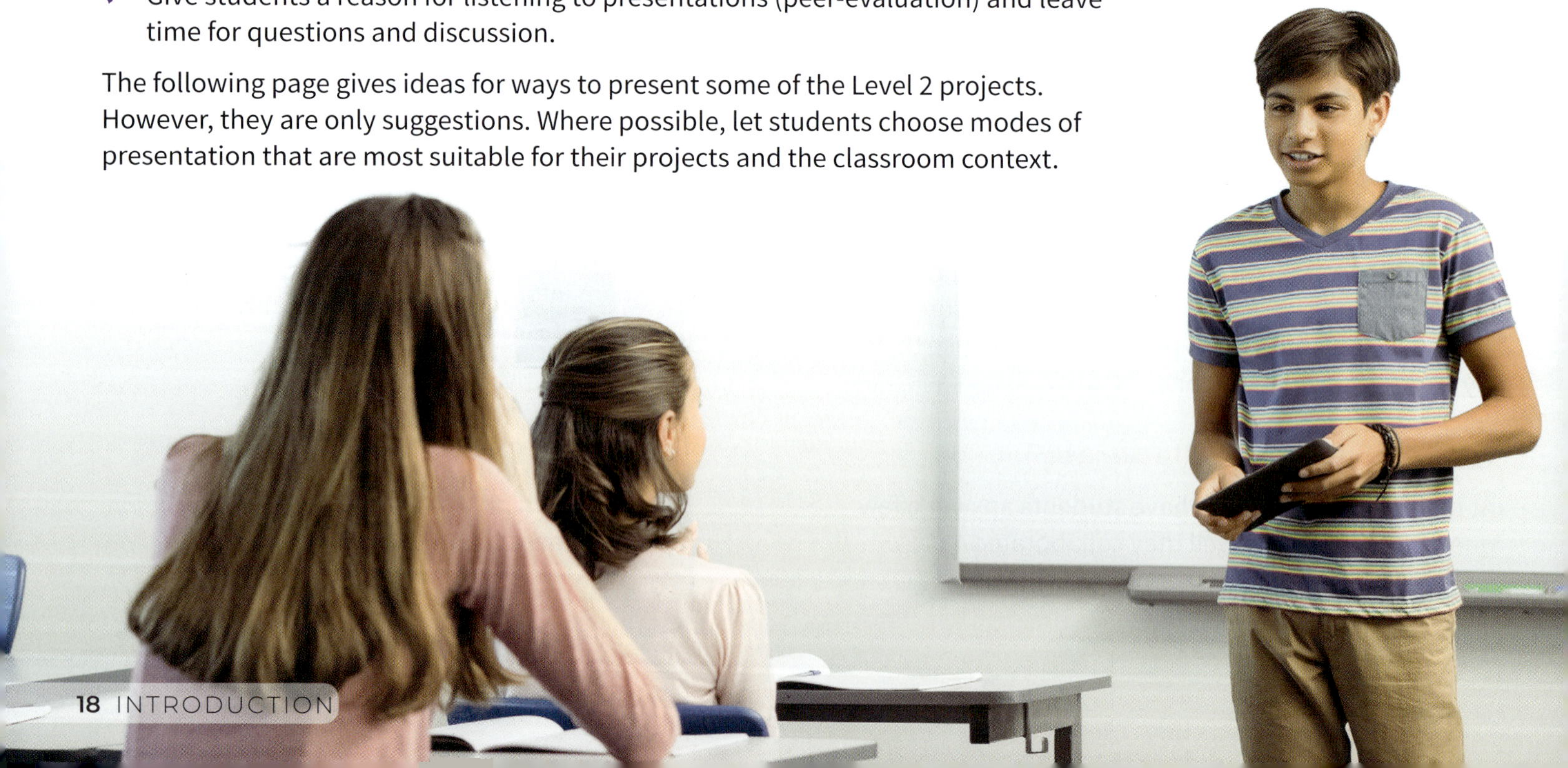

1 Infographics

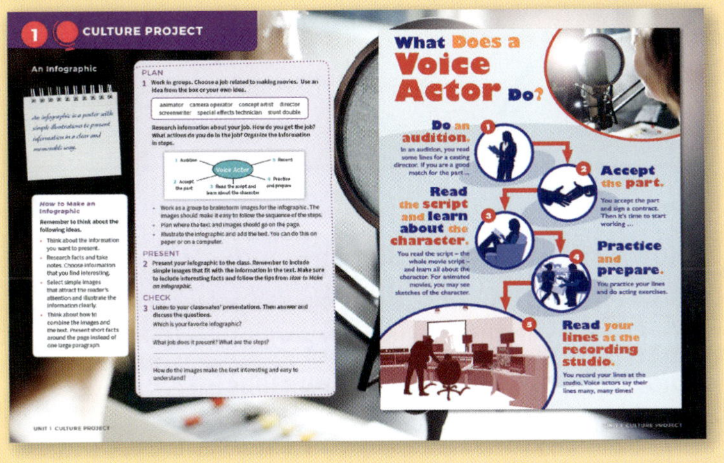

Have students use word-processing programs to make infographics and room plans online.

1. **Create a template** (a blueprint to place text and images)
2. **Find or draw images for the infographic** (photos, illustrations, or drawings)
3. **Write the text** (describe each step)
4. **Check that the images match the text**
5. **Add extra features** (borders, decorative backgrounds, etc.)
6. **Put it all together** (check, correct, and edit final version)

2 3-D Room Plans

1. **Choose** an area. Draw an outline and take measurements.
2. **Add** fixed features (doors, windows, sinks, etc.)
3. **Add** furniture. Use simple shapes.
4. **Label** the plan. Add descriptions in call-out boxes where necessary.
5. **Check** spelling and grammar. Make sure the room plan is easy to understand.

3 Webpages

1. **Look at** an example of a **wireframe** (show students the elements of a webpage).
2. **Research** more examples of webpage designs and make own sketches.
3. **Choose** a favorite webpage design and arrange the information into the relevant sections.
4. **Find** an online webpage template similar to the design chosen.
5. **Follow** the online steps to complete the product this way.

EVALUATION

What?

Product

How well did students achieve their **learning outcomes**?

How well did they demonstrate these?

How did they **evaluate options** and make **decisions**?

Process

How well did students **plan** the product?

How well did students **develop** the project (roles and responsibilities, research and analysis)?

Did students develop **life competencies**?

Who?

Self-Evaluation

Peer-Evaluation

Teacher–Student Evaluation

When?

Preparation

After groups are formed: clarifying learning outcomes, brainstorming ideas, identifying key information, making decisions about content

Development

After each step: evaluating roles and responsibilities, researching and analyzing findings, drafting and reviewing

Production

Before presentation: deciding on mode of presentation

During presentation: practicing presentation skills

After: giving feedback and self-evaluating

How?

Informal Evaluation Tools

KWL Chart, My Learning Diary, Peer-Evaluation Form

> Evaluation Tools pp67–69

Formal Evaluation Tools

Project Evaluation Rubrics, Evaluation Rubric, Teacher's Evaluation Form

> Evaluation Rubric p21

> Teacher's Evaluation Form p70

EVALUATION RUBRIC

The rubric below covers areas you can evaluate in every project. You can select some or all of these for each project when you feel it is necessary. There are also two project-specific rubrics with adapted evaluation descriptors in each unit.

Exceeds expectations (4): students show they are ready to go further and can take extra challenges in certain areas.

Very good (3): students complete the tasks successfully and as expected.

Good (2): students complete the tasks reasonably well with some aspects done better than others.

Needs improvement (1): students show room for improvement in most areas evaluated.

	4	3	2	1
Learning Outcomes	Completes all stages to successfully achieve the overall learning outcomes.	Completes most stages effectively. Largely achieves overall learning outcomes.	Has missed some stages. Partially completes overall learning outcomes.	Hasn't successfully completed any of the stages. Overall learning outcomes unachieved.
Planning and Organization	Product is well organized, interesting, and easy to follow. It follows the model for the project and no details are missing.	Product is well organized and easy to follow. Some details are incorrect or missing.	Product is similar to the model for the project but is missing essential information. It follows the model with difficulty.	Product does not look or sound anything like the one specified in the task. There is little or no sequence to ideas.
Use of Information and Resources	Uses a wide range of resources to get information relevant to the product.	Uses different resources to get information relevant to the product, with some gaps.	Most information is relevant and useful, but only comes from one or two resources.	There is little evidence of research and hasn't used appropriate resources.
Collaboration (Teamwork)	Collaborated in all stages and understood roles and responsibilities.	Collaborated in all stages and understood responsibilities. There was minor confusion about roles and responsibilities.	Collaborated in most stages, but there was some confusion about roles and responsibilities.	There was little or no collaboration throughout all stages. Didn't recognize roles and responsibilities.
Time Management	Completed everything on time. Revised and corrected project.	Completed everything on time, with one or two steps at the last minute. Revised and corrected project.	Completed all steps but at the last minute. There was little time for revision or correction.	Did not finish project. Missed steps in the process.
Creativity	Product is very original and interesting. All ideas are well developed.	Product is interesting and very creative. Most ideas are well developed.	There is some evidence of creativity that could have been developed. Product is a mixture of original and copied ideas.	Little imagination or creativity. Most ideas copied and pasted from other sources.
Problem-Solving Skills	All group members participate and listen actively to solve problems effectively at all times.	Most group members are actively involved to solve most problems.	Some evidence of problem solving but not by all group members.	Little or no evidence of problem solving, either individually or in groups.
Language Use	Excellent use of language. Project is clear and understandable with only a few mistakes.	Good use of language. Project is clear and understandable with some mistakes.	Adequate use of language. Project is understandable, but some sections need further explanation.	Random words are used in a confusing and vague way. Project is almost impossible to understand.
Presentation Skills	All group members participate. Presentation is well put together and is clear and interesting throughout.	All group members participate. Presentation is mostly clear and interesting.	All group members participate, but the method of presentation is sometimes inappropriate or not engaging.	None of the group members fully participate. Inappropriate and uninteresting method of presentation.
Final Product	Exceeds expectations	Very good	Good	Needs improvement

AN INFOGRAPHIC

- **Learning Outcome:** make an infographic about a movie-making job
- **Skills:** research information and make a spidergram to organize it, brainstorm images, combine text and pictures to present information clearly
- **Resources:** two or more infographics about jobs, Infographic Organizer p58, My Time-Management Plan p71
- **Evaluation Tools:** Project Evaluation Rubric p25, My Learning Diary p68, Peer-Evaluation Form p69, Teacher's Evaluation Form p70

Student's Book Teacher's Resource Bank Unit 1

Before You Start

Find two or three examples of infographics, either in print or online, to show students in class.

1 Preparation

Step 1: Introduce the Topic

- Introduce the topic of infographics after doing the vocabulary exercises. p14 Ask: *What is the purpose of an infographic? What types of infographics have you seen?*
- Show students the infographic examples. Ask: *What is the infographic about? How is the information organized? Do the pictures make the information easier to understand?*
- Explain that infographics use pictures and text to convey information or to explain how to do something in a way that is easy to understand. Ask: *How is the information usually presented? (As a series of steps.)*
- Ask students to bring an example of an infographic about a job to the next class (in their own language or English). They can discuss them and say if the information is interesting, helpful, and easy to understand.

Step 2: Analyze the Model for the Project Unit 1

- Look at the model infographic with the class. Ask: *What job is this infographic about? What steps can you see? What do the pictures show? Would you like to do this job?*
- Ask students to imagine the infographic is about a movie or TV actor instead of a voice actor. Ask: *What step would be different? (Step 5 would be on a movie/TV set.) What other steps might an on-screen actor need to take? (Get fitted for costumes, have hair and makeup done, rehearse scenes with other actors, etc.)*

Creative Thinking

Creating new content from own ideas or other resources

Monitor students' participation during the class discussion in Step 2.

Step 3: *How to* Make an Infographic Unit 1

- Go through the *How to* tips with the class. Have different students say why each tip is important.
- Discuss where students can find suitable images. Explain that for infographics, it can be helpful to sketch images before finding them.
- Ensure students understand that when they make their infographics, they should use the tips in this *How to* section.

Step 4: Clarify the Project Unit 1

- Follow the steps in The Learning Stages of Project Work p10.
- Brainstorm different jobs related to making movies and write them on the board.
- Have groups discuss where they can find more information about movie-making jobs.

My Learning Diary p68 Preparation

Peer-Evaluation Form p69 Preparation

2 Development

Start this stage as soon as groups know their learning outcomes and have brainstormed a list of movie-making jobs.

Step 1: **Assign Roles and Responsibilities**

- In project groups, have students assign general roles. > Roles and Responsibilities p16 Help them decide on further roles they can share, such as those in the diagram.

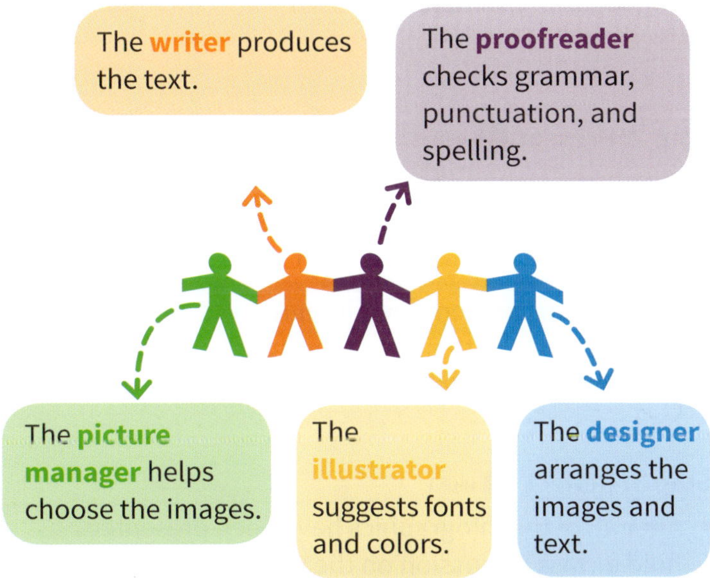

Step 2: **Research and Analyze** Unit 1 p71

- Have groups start the PLAN section in **Exercise 1**. Have them choose a movie-making job from the list. Alternatively, they can choose one idea from the list they brainstormed previously.
- Point to the model spidergram and ask what type of information it has.
- Hand out a copy of the > Infographic Organizer p58 to each student.

Flipped Classroom Activity

Out of class: have students research information about their job and fill in the spidergram on their graphic organizers.

In class: group members compare their findings. Ask: *What kinds of images did you find? Are they effective? Do the images make the text easier to understand?* Students choose the best ideas for their infographic.

Step 3: **Draft and Review** Unit 1 p71

- Hand out a copy of the > Infographic Organizer p58 to each student.
- Group members complete the rest of the PLAN section. Ask them to brainstorm ideas for images and decide on a layout for their organizers. Assign each group member a section of the infographic to work on.

Flipped Classroom Activities

Out of class: students write their sections of the infographic in their organizers (alternatively, groups can work together on the whole infographic in class). Encourage them to use the **simple present** and **present continuous**.

In class: group members put their sections together in the correct order to create their infographics and review their work.

Learning to Learn

Reflecting on and evaluating own learning success

Monitor progress of the tasks in Steps 2 and 3, ensuring group members use their spidergrams and organizers effectively. (See Differentiated Instruction activities below for further practice.)

Differentiated Instruction

Support
Help students review their infographic section, checking to make sure it contains all the necessary information.
Consolidation
Encourage students to check each other's sections and make sure the images fit with the text.
Extension
Allow students to make final decisions about corrections and the placement of text and images.

> My Learning Diary p68 **Development**

> Peer-Evaluation Form p69 **Development**

3 Production

Schedule presentation times and stick to them, ensuring all groups present their infographics. Spread the presentations over a few classes, if necessary. Allow enough time for each presentation and for questions.

Before groups present their final infographics, check that they have followed and completed the relevant steps.

> Presentation Ideas p18

As students complete their projects, check their abilities in the following Areas of Competency.

Creative Thinking

Creating new content from own ideas or other resources

Communicates personal response to creative work from art, music, or literature.

Evidence: Students assess different infographics and vote for the most effective one.

Learning to Learn

Reflecting on and evaluating own learning success

Selects and uses a wide range of mind maps and other tools to organize thoughts.

Evidence: Students use their spidergrams and infographic organizers to put together key information.

Identifies what needs to be revisited before identifying new learning goals.

Evidence: Group members check each other's work and suggest improvements.

Step 1: Prepare Unit 1 p71

- Go through items in the PRESENT section in **Exercise 2**.
- As groups prepare their project, ask questions, for example: *Do the images work with the text? Are the steps presented in a logical order? Is the information easy to understand?*
- Check grammar and spelling. Remind students to use the **simple present** for facts and the **present continuous** for actions in progress.
- Remind groups of the presentation date and how much time each group will have.

Collaboration Learning Tip

Peer-Tutoring

Monitor group members as they correct and edit each other's work. Explain that this includes checking spelling, punctuation, and language as well as ensuring that the images are simple and work with the text. Encourage students to suggest improvements or additions to each other's work and make changes where necessary. Help with useful language, for example: *Why don't you ... ?, You could ... , Maybe you should change this.*

Step 2: Present Unit 1

- Draw attention to the CHECK section in **Exercise 3**. Ask the class to think about these questions as they listen to their peers' presentations.
- Have groups present their infographics. Remind speakers to take their time and speak clearly. They should describe each image and how the text relates to it.

Step 3: Reflect Unit 1

- After all of the infographics have been presented, hold a class discussion on the CHECK questions in **Exercise 3**.
- Discuss different steps of the project process and the final result. Ask: *How well did you work in your group? What did you find difficult / interesting? Would you like to do any of the movie-making jobs?*
- Have students vote on their favorite infographic.
- Encourage students to reflect on each stage of the project process, including positive experiences and things they could improve upon.

> Peer-Evaluation Form p69 **Production**

Go to the collaboration tool and online portfolio to make use of the digital resources.

Project Evaluation Rubric: An Infographic

Use these project-specific descriptors and your own choice of descriptors from the Evaluation Rubric p21 to assess students individually or in groups. Make your own evaluation form. Teacher's Evaluation Form p70

	4	3	2	1
Creativity	Product is well organized with creative and interesting ideas. It contains interesting information, and steps are presented in a logical order. It uses simple, attractive images that clearly illustrate all of the steps.	Product is organized with interesting ideas. It contains fairly interesting information, and steps are presented in a logical order. It uses simple, attractive images that mostly illustrate all of the steps.	Product has interesting ideas but lacks organization. It presents steps in a logical order, but the information is not very interesting. It includes simple, attractive images, but some of the images do not illustrate the steps.	Product lacks interesting ideas and organization. The steps are not in order or some are missing, and the information is not interesting. The images are in the incorrect order or do not illustrate the steps.
Language Use	Product shows excellent use of grammar, punctuation, and spelling. Excellent use of language from the unit (simple present and continuous). Project is understandable with only a few or no mistakes.	Product shows good use of grammar, punctuation, and spelling. Good use of language from the unit (simple present and continuous). Project is understandable with some mistakes.	Product shows adequate use of grammar, punctuation, and spelling. Adequate use of language from the unit (simple present and continuous). Project is understandable, but some sections need further explanation.	Product shows poor use of grammar, punctuation, and spelling. Poor or no use of language from the unit (simple present and continuous). Project is confusing, vague, and almost impossible to understand.

The Cambridge Framework for Life Competencies

You can also assess students' progress in the following foundational layers.

FOUNDATIONAL LAYER	ABILITIES	ACTIONS
Digital Literacy	• Use digital tools	finding content on various websites, downloading images, sharing work online, assessing online material
Discipline Knowledge	• Convince the audience	presenting ideas, summarizing information, describing images, answering questions

Flipped Classroom Activities

Evaluate

In project groups, have students discuss their completed Peer-Evaluation Forms and ways to work better as a group. Peer-Evaluation Form p69

Out of class: have students reflect on their progress at home. My Learning Diary p68 **Production**

In class: hold a class discussion on what students have learned, using the information from their learning diaries. My Learning Diary p68 **Production**

A MUSEUM DISPLAY

- **Learning Outcome:** design a museum display of historical objects
- **Skills:** research historical objects and find images, write texts about the objects, correct facts and dates, give feedback on the other groups' displays
- **Resources:** examples of museum displays, Museum Display Organizer p59, My Time-Management Plan p71
- **Evaluation Tools:** Project Evaluation Rubric p29, KWL Chart p67, Peer-Evaluation Form p69, Teacher's Evaluation Form p70

Student's Book

Before You Start

Find two or three examples of museum displays online to show students in class. Make sure that the examples show different ways of presenting information (through text, pictures, interactive presentations, etc.).

1 Preparation

Step 1: Introduce the Topic

- Introduce the topic of museum displays after doing the radio show listening exercises. p26
- Show students the examples of museum displays. Encourage them to say what they are and what their purpose is. Ask: *Why do people visit museums? Which museums do you visit and why? What can you see in museums? What do these displays use to present the exhibits? (photos, descriptions, dates, etc.)*
- Tell students that museum displays give information about exhibits. Ask: *What makes a good museum display?* Explain that good displays give visitors a memorable experience.
- Ask students to bring an image of a museum display to the next class. Discuss which displays they like most and why.

Step 2: Analyze the Model for the Project pp30–31

- Complete **Exercises 1** to **3**.

Answers **1** Students' own answers **2** 2 M 3 L 4 S 5 B 6 M 7 L 8 B **3** See Teacher's Book, pXX for answers.

- Ask questions about the model museum displays, for example: *Do the displays give interesting information? What types of facts are in the texts? How do the photos help? Is the design attractive? Why / Why not?*
- Study the language from the unit. Ask students to find examples of the **simple past**. Ask them why they think the texts use this tense (to narrate past events and describe how people used these objects in the past).

Step 3: *How to* Give Feedback p30

- 2.11 Go through the *How to* tips in **Exercise 4** with the class. Then play the audio to check answers.

Answers **4** a display about Viking ships

- Ask: *What feedback structure do the* How to *tips show? (Pay a compliment, say something you think is weak, make a suggestion for improvement.)*
- 2.11 Play the audio again for **Exercise 5** and check answers.

Answers **5** 1 a school history festival 2 Oliver's 3 It had colorful pictures and surprising/interesting facts. 4 when the Vikings sailed to Canada 5 He's going to add the missing information.

- Ensure students understand that when they give feedback, they should use the ideas in this *How to* section.

Step 4: Clarify the Project pp30–31

- Follow the steps in The Learning Stages of Project Work p10. For this project, we suggest students work in groups of four.
- Brainstorm a list of historical objects. Groups discuss what visitors would like to know about each of the objects.

Collaboration

Listening respectfully and responding constructively to others' contributions

Monitor how well students listen and respond to each other during the discussions in Steps 2, 3, and 4.

KWL Chart p67 Know and Want to Know

Peer-Evaluation Form p69 Preparation

2 Development

Start this stage as soon as groups know their learning outcomes and are ready to choose four objects from their brainstormed lists.

Step 1: Assign Roles and Responsibilities

- In project groups, have students assign general roles. > Roles and Responsibilities p16 Help them decide on further roles they can share. Draw a diagram like the one below on the board.

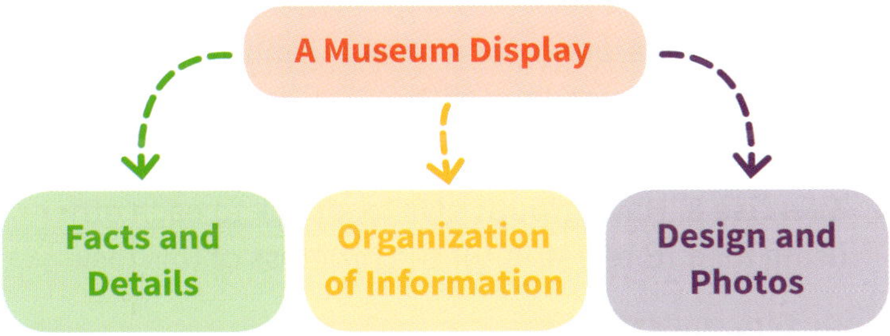

- Ask questions related to each section in the diagram. Discuss the tasks and roles required to create a museum display.

  Facts and Details: *Where can you find information about the objects? How can you check that the facts are correct? What sources will you use? Who will help determine the most important facts and details?*

  Organization of Information: *What is the main idea for each text? What are the supporting ideas? Who will help organize the information?*

  Design and Photos: *How will you make the display attractive? Where can you find images? Who will help select the images?*

- Encourage students to take notes and assign roles and responsibilities.

Step 2: Research and Analyze p31 p71

- Hand out a copy of the > Museum Display Organizer p59 to each student.
- Have each student choose an object to research. Ensure each student within a group selects a different object.

Flipped Classroom Activities

Out of class: have group members complete the first part of the PLAN section in **Exercise 6**. Tell them to research their object and write the information in their organizer. Have them find images that support the text.

In class: have group members check their work together and suggest improvements.

Step 3: Draft and Review p31 p71

- Have groups complete the PLAN section in **Exercise 6**. They put their museum display together using the ideas from their organizers.
- Encourage students to make last-minute revisions. Remind them to check the use of the **simple past** for narrating past events.

Communication
Managing conversations

Monitor the conversations in the groups as students put together their projects. Check that group members are making suggestions and responding constructively to each other's ideas.

Collaboration Learning Tip

Giving Constructive Feedback

Remind students of the three steps for giving constructive feedback: pay a compliment, say something you think is weak, and suggest an improvement. Encourage students to follow this structure as they comment on and put together their work. Help them with useful language, for example: *That's a good idea! This works well. I'm not sure this works. I think we can make this better. Why don't you ... ?*

> Peer-Evaluation Form p69 Development

3 Production

Schedule presentation times and stick to them. Remember that these projects will be displayed on a classroom wall. Allow enough time for students to look at all the museum displays, ask questions, and give feedback.

Before groups produce their final drafts, have them look at different examples of museum displays again. Help them with ideas for how to present their information logically.

> Presentation Ideas p18

As students complete their projects, check their abilities in the following Areas of Competency.

Collaboration

Listening respectfully and responding constructively to others' contributions

Listens to / acknowledges different points of view respectfully.

Evidence: Groups respond respectfully to constructive feedback.

Evaluates contributions from other students with appropriate sensitivity.

Evidence: If groups disagree with feedback, they do so in a polite, respectful manner.

Communication

Managing conversations

Can use simple techniques to start, maintain, and close conversations of various lengths.

Evidence: Students give feedback on and answer questions about each other's displays.

Uses appropriate strategies to develop a conversation (e.g., showing interest).

Evidence: Students give constructive feedback on their peers' displays.

Step 1: Prepare p31 p71

- Go through the items in the PRESENT section in **Exercise 7**.
- As groups prepare their projects, ask questions, for example: *Are the facts and dates correct? What images are you using? Do the texts match the images? What can you do to improve the design?*
- Check the use of the **simple past** in the texts. Allow time for final corrections.
- Remind groups of the presentation date and how much time each group will have.

Step 2: Present pp30–31

- Have groups put their museum displays on a classroom wall.
- Ask the class to review the *How to* tips and take notes on their feedback as they look at their classmates' work.
- Groups walk around, looking at the museum displays and writing their comments.
- Draw attention to the CHECK section in **Exercise 8**. Have groups give feedback to each other using their notes. Monitor the progress of this task.

Step 3: Reflect p31

- After the feedback session, encourage students to reflect on each stage of the project process, including positive experiences and things they could improve upon. (See Differentiated Instruction activities below for further practice.)

Differentiated Instruction

Support
Have students vote on which display is their favorite and share the result with the class.
Consolidation
Have pairs list both the strong and weak elements of one of the displays and share their ideas with the group that designed it.
Extension
In project groups, students write three questions about interesting facts from their display. Then pairs of groups quiz each other.

> Peer-Evaluation Form p69 Production

Go to the collaboration tool and online portfolio to make use of the digital resources.

Project Evaluation Rubric: A Museum Display

Use these project-specific descriptors and your own choice of descriptors from the > Evaluation Rubric p21 to assess students individually or in groups. Make your own evaluation form. > Teacher's Evaluation Form p70

	4	3	2	1
Creativity	Product is well organized and has a very attractive design. It uses interesting and appropriate images. It has relevant information, including accurate facts from reliable sources.	Product is well organized and has an attractive design. It uses appropriate images, some of which are interesting. It has mostly relevant information, including accurate facts from reliable sources.	Product is organized and has a clear but not very attractive design. It uses appropriate images, none of which are interesting. It has accurate information from reliable sources, but very few facts are relevant.	Product is poorly organized and has an unattractive design. It has few or no images, none of which are appropriate or interesting. It doesn't have relevant or accurate information.
Language Use	Excellent use of language from the unit (simple past). Project is understandable with only a few mistakes.	Good use of language from the unit (simple past). Project is understandable with some mistakes.	Adequate use of language from the unit (simple past). Project is understandable, but some sections need further explanation.	Poor or no use of language from the unit (simple past). Project is confusing, vague, and almost impossible to understand.

The Cambridge Framework for Life Competencies

You can also assess students' progress in the following foundational layers.

FOUNDATIONAL LAYER	ABILITIES	ACTIONS
Emotional Development	• Manage emotions	paying compliments and making suggestions, giving constructive feedback, responding to feedback respectfully
Discipline Knowledge	• Convince the audience	explaining facts and images, giving details, summarizing information, narrating past events, answering questions

Flipped Classroom Activities

Evaluate

In project groups, have students discuss their completed Peer-Evaluation Forms and ways to work better as a group. > Peer-Evaluation Form p69

Out of class: have students reflect on their progress at home. > KWL Chart p67 **Learned**

In class: hold a class discussion on what students have learned, using the information from their KWL Charts. > KWL Chart p67 **Learned**

3 CULTURE PROJECT

A COMIC STRIP

- **Learning Outcome:** make a comic strip of a traditional story
- **Skills:** identify the key events in a traditional story, sequence events, brainstorm and draw images to represent each event, add text, present the comic strip
- **Resources:** two or more comic strips, Comic Strip Organizer p60, My Time-Management Plan p71
- **Evaluation Tools:** Project Evaluation Rubric p33, My Learning Diary p68, Peer-Evaluation Form p69, Teacher's Evaluation Form p70

Student's Book Teacher's Resource Bank Unit 3

Before You Start

Collect two or three different print or online comic strips to show students in class.

1 Preparation

Step 1: Introduce the Topic

- Introduce the topic of comic strips after doing the writing exercises. p41 By this time, students will have seen a number of different text types for telling stories. Alternatively, you could introduce the topic earlier, after doing the reading exercises. p36 Ask: *Do you read comic strips? What comic strips do you like? Where do you find them?*
- Show students the comic strips. Ask: *What are the elements of comic strips?* Point out how comic strips are divided into panels using images, speech and thought bubbles, and onomatopoeia. Ask students what each element is used for.
- Expand on the comic strip definition. Unit 3 Explain that a comic strip is a sequence of drawings in panels that tells a story. Say that comic strips use speech bubbles for dialogue and other types of bubbles for thoughts and sounds.
- Ask students to bring a comic strip to the next class (in their own language or in English). They can describe the images and story and say what they like about them.

Step 2: Analyze the Model for the Project Unit 3

- Draw attention to the title of the model comic strip and ask students what they think the story is about. Then have individual students identify the key event in each picture.
- Explain that the story is an adaptation of a Turkish fairy tale, *The Boy Who Found Fear*. Ask: *What is the boy afraid of at the end of the story? (Becoming the king.)*
- Ask further questions, for example: *What speech bubbles can you see? Why is "Help!" in a different-shaped bubble? Do you like the story and pictures? Why / Why not?*
- In pairs, have students tell the story by looking at the pictures.

Step 3: *How to* Make a Comic Strip Unit 3

- Go through the *How to* tips with the class. Students look at the model comic strip to see how the tips have been followed.
- Ensure students understand that when they make their comic strips, they should use the ideas in this *How to* section.

Critical Thinking
Synthesizing ideas and information

Monitor students' understanding of the key events in the model and how they are shown in comic strip format. Ask if there are other ways to narrate the events in the story.

Step 4: Clarify the Project Unit 3

- Follow the steps in The Learning Stages of Project Work p10.
- Brainstorm traditional stories from around the world.
- Have groups discuss which stories they like and what they know about the details and the characters.

My Learning Diary p68 Preparation

Peer-Evaluation Form p69 Preparation

2 Development

Start this stage as soon as groups know their learning outcomes and have brainstormed traditional stories to research.

Step 1: Assign Roles and Responsibilities

- In project groups, have students assign general roles. > Roles and Responsibilities p16 Help them decide on further roles they can share, such as those in the diagram.

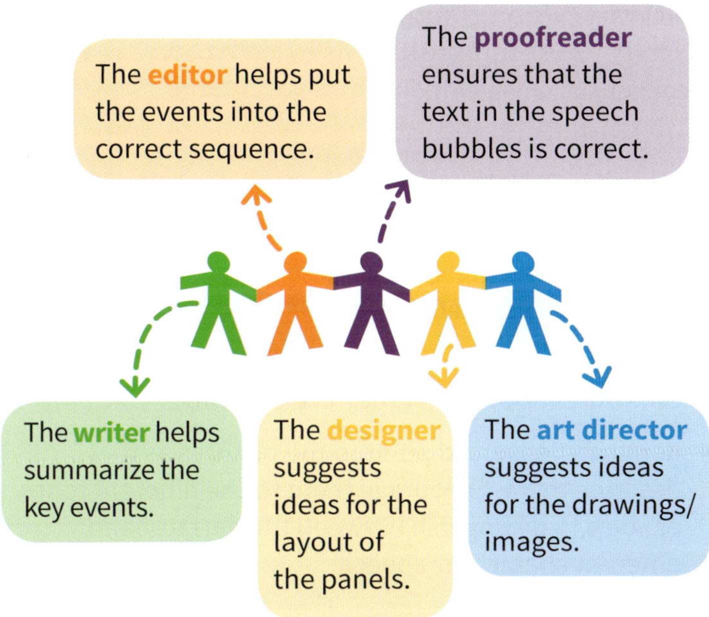

Step 2: Research and Analyze Unit 3 p71

- Have groups start the PLAN section in **Exercise 1**. They choose a story from those they brainstormed.
- Groups work together to determine the key events in their story and write a list (with a maximum of 12 events) similar to the one in the PLAN section. Remind students to use the **simple present** when writing their lists.
- Hand out a copy of the > Comic Strip Organizer p60 to each student.

Step 3: Draft and Review Unit 3 p71

- Have groups brainstorm ideas for images to represent the key events. They can write their ideas in their organizers.
- Tell groups to ensure each member has an equal number of images to draw.

Flipped Classroom Activities

Out of class: have students continue with the PLAN section at home. Ask them to draw their images in the Comic Strip Organizer. Remind them to present the key events in sequence.

In class: have groups cut out their drawings and arrange them in order on a desk or sheet of paper.

Groups prepare the final version of their comic strip on a piece of poster board and add text. Make sure groups agree on the number and order of key events. (See Differentiated Instruction activities below for further practice.)

Differentiated Instruction

Support

Help students with ideas for phrasing and sequencing key events, as well as with grammar tenses.

Consolidation

Encourage students to write dialogue and use speech and thought bubbles and onomatopoeia.

Extension

Have students come up with alternative endings for their comic strips. Encourage them to peer-review each other's comic strips and choose their favorite.

Social Responsibilities

Taking active roles including leadership

Encourage all group members to participate and make decisions about different aspects of their comic strips in line with their roles.

> My Learning Diary p68 **Development**

> Peer-Evaluation Form p69 **Development**

3 Production

Schedule presentation times and stick to them, ensuring all groups present their comic strips. Spread the presentations over a few classes, if necessary. Allow time for each presentation and for questions.

As groups produce their final comic strips, you can suggest that they follow the same steps as those they used to create their infographics. If groups want to create a digital version of their comic strip, make sure they're using an appropriate free online comic strip maker.

> Presentation Ideas p18

As students complete their projects, check their abilities in the following Areas of Competency.

Critical Thinking

Synthesizing ideas and information

Selects key points from diverse sources to create a new account.

Evidence: Students identify and illustrate the key events in their stories.

Social Responsibilities

Taking active roles including leadership

In group work, makes consultative decisions.

Evidence: Students consider each other's ideas before making final decisions.

Encourages others to participate and contribute to projects.

Evidence: All group members contribute to the project and perform their assigned roles.

Step 1: Prepare Unit 3 p71

- Go through the items in the PRESENT section in **Exercise 2**.
- As groups prepare their project, suggest that each member presents the panels they composed.
- Have group members practice their presentation. Remind them to use the pictures as prompts to tell the story and include all the key events. Check to make sure that students are using the **simple past** and **continuous** correctly when narrating the actions.

Collaboration Learning Tip

Resolving Conflicts

Encourage students to reach a compromise when making final decisions about the layout and text in their comic strip. If group members cannot come to an agreement, ask: *Can you think of an alternative / any solutions?* Have students listen actively and respond respectfully to each other's ideas. Help them with useful language, for example: *I think … ; Why don't we … ?; That's a good idea, but … ; What about … ?* Encourage students to learn how to reach a consensus when working in project groups.

Step 2: Present Unit 3

- Draw attention to the CHECK section in **Exercise 3**. Ask the class to think about these questions as they listen to their peers' presentations.
- Have groups present their comic strips. Tell the class to take notes about what they like and why.
- Remind speakers to point to the pictures as they describe them. Encourage them to use different tones of voice to distinguish between the narrator and different characters' speech.

Step 3: Reflect Unit 3

- After the presentations, hold a class discussion on the CHECK questions in **Exercise 3**.
- As students discuss their favorite comic strip, ask: *Were the stories interesting? What did you like/not like about the images? Were the key events easy to follow? Why / Why not?*
- Encourage students to reflect on each stage of the project process, including positive experiences and things they could improve upon.

> Peer-Evaluation Form p69 Production

Go to the collaboration tool and online portfolio to make use of the digital resources.

Project Evaluation Rubric: A Comic Strip

Use these project-specific descriptors and your own choice of descriptors from the > Evaluation Rubric p21 to assess students individually or in groups. Make your own evaluation form. > Teacher's Evaluation Form p70

	4	3	2	1
Creativity	Product is interesting, attractive, and easy to follow. It includes all the key events in the correct sequence. It has attractive images that match the events and help tell the story. It uses a variety of speech bubbles in an effective way.	Product is interesting, attractive, and fairly easy to follow. It includes most of the key events in the correct sequence. It has attractive images that usually match the events and help tell the story. It uses one type of speech bubble in an effective way.	Product is fairly interesting and attractive but not very easy to follow. It is missing some of the key events, and they aren't always in the correct sequence. It has images that usually match the events but are not attractive. It is missing speech bubbles in some panels.	Product isn't interesting or attractive, and it is difficult to follow. It is missing many key events, and the sequence is incorrect. The images don't match the events and aren't attractive. It is missing speech bubbles in most panels.
Language Use	Product shows excellent use of grammar, punctuation, and spelling. Excellent use of language from the unit (simple past and continuous). Project is understandable with only a few or no mistakes.	Product shows good use of grammar, punctuation, and spelling. Good use of language from the unit (simple past and continuous). Project is understandable with some mistakes.	Product shows adequate use of grammar, punctuation, and spelling. Adequate use of language from the unit (simple past and continuous). Project is understandable, but some sections need further explanation.	Product shows poor use of grammar, punctuation, and spelling. Poor or no use of language from the unit (simple past and continuous). Project is confusing, vague, and almost impossible to understand.

The Cambridge Framework for Life Competencies

You can also assess students' progress in the following foundational layers.

FOUNDATIONAL LAYER	ABILITIES	ACTIONS
Discipline Knowledge	• Convince the audience	conveying key events clearly, using images to tell a story, using appropriate tone of voice when narrating a story
Emotional Development	• Empathize and build relationships	listening actively, reaching compromises, reflecting on strengths and weaknesses, verbalizing emotions appropriately, resolving conflicts

Flipped Classroom Activities

Evaluate

In project groups, have students discuss their completed Peer-Evaluation Forms and ways to work better as a group. > Peer-Evaluation Form p69

Out of class: have students reflect on their progress at home. > My Learning Diary p68 **Production**

In class: hold a class discussion on what students have learned, using the information from their learning diaries. > My Learning Diary p68 **Production**

4 SOCIAL STUDIES PROJECT

A POSTER

- **Learning Outcome:** make a poster about volunteer work
- **Skills:** ask for and express opinions to choose an idea, research information and photos about the idea, design the poster
- **Resources:** two or more posters about volunteer or community work, Poster Organizer p61, My Time-Management Plan p71
- **Evaluation Tools:** Project Evaluation Rubric p37, KWL Chart p67, Peer-Evaluation Form p69, Teacher's Evaluation Form p70

Student's Book

Before You Start

Collect two or three different posters about volunteer or community work to show students in class.

1 Preparation

Step 1: Introduce the Topic

- Introduce the topic of volunteer work after doing the monologues listening exercises. p50
- Show students the posters. Ask: *What is the purpose of these posters? Where and when is the work? Why is this work necessary? Who can volunteer? What skills or interests do they need?*
- Explain that volunteering is an unpaid activity in which someone gives their time to help a person, group, or organization. Ask: *What kind of volunteer work can teenagers do?* Write a list on the board. *(Clean up parks, work in an animal shelter, work in a retirement home.)*
- Ask students to bring a poster about volunteering to the next class (in their own language or in English). They can discuss the posters, saying which type of work they find interesting and why.

Step 2: Analyze the Model for the Project pp54–55

- Complete **Exercises 1** and **2**.

Answers **1** b **2** 2 What? 3 Who? 4 Why? 5 When? 6 What are the benefits?

- Ask questions about the model poster: *Is the message clear? Does the poster have all the key information? How does it present the information? Would you like to volunteer at the park? Why / Why not?*
- Study the language from the unit. Ask students to find examples of **comparative** and **superlative adjectives**, ***can*** and ***could***, and ***too much*** and (***not***) ***enough*** + **noun**.

> **Social Responsibilities**
> **Understanding personal responsibilities as part of a group and in society**
> Have students discuss the poster's message: *Together we can make our park cleaner!* Ask: *Why is volunteering important?* Discuss how volunteering helps the community.

Step 3: *How to* Agree as a Group p56

- Go through the *How to* tips in **Exercise 3** with the class. Check the answer.

Possible answers **3** 1 c 2 d 3 a 4 e 5 f 6 b

- 4.11 Tell the class that they will listen to three students talking about doing volunteer work in their community. Play the audio for **Exercise 4** and check the answers. Play the audio again and have students identify words or phrases for suggesting ideas, interrupting politely, and asking for or summarizing opinions. *(Let's … , Excuse me … , Can I make a suggestion?, What about … ?, Are there any more ideas?, So we all agree …)*

Answers **4** 1 L, T 2 T 3 Y

- Ensure students understand that when they need to agree as a group to make decisions, they should use the ideas in this *How to* section.

Step 4: Clarify the Project pp54–55

- Follow the steps in The Learning Stages of Project Work p10.
- Brainstorm different types of volunteer work and say how each type of work helps the community.

KWL Chart p67 **Know and Want to Know**

Peer-Evaluation Form p69 **Preparation**

2 Development

Start this stage as soon as groups know their learning outcomes and have brainstormed different types of volunteer work.

Step 1: Assign Roles and Responsibilities

- In project groups, have students assign general roles. Roles and Responsibilities p16 Help them decide on further roles they can share. Draw a diagram like the one below on the board.

- Ask questions related to each section in the diagram. Discuss the tasks and roles required to create a poster for volunteer work:

  Message: *Who do you want to get as volunteers? What type of work do you want to do? How can you make the work interesting? What information do people need? Who will help decide on the information to include?*

  Organization of Information: *What information goes in the introduction? What sections will the poster have? Who will help organize the information?*

  Design and Photos: *How will you make the poster attractive and effective? Where can you find images? Who will help select the images?*

- Encourage students to take notes and assign roles and responsibilities.

Step 2: Research and Analyze p55 p71

- Have students read the ideas in the PLAN section in **Exercise 5** and choose a project. Alternatively, they can choose one idea from the list they brainstormed previously.
- Hand out a copy of the Poster Organizer p61 to each student.
- Have group members think of messages to attract volunteers and complete the "Introduction" part of their organizers.

Flipped Classroom Activities

Out of class: have students complete the rest of their organizers. Tell them to bring their ideas and researched images to the next class.

In class: have group members compare their notes and images. Give each group one more Poster Organizer p61 to complete with each of their best ideas and images.

Ensure groups agree on their final choices. They can refer to the ideas in the *How to* section. (See Differentiated Instruction activities below for further practice.)

Differentiated Instruction

Support
Help groups make decisions by giving them options. Help students summarize their ideas.
Consolidation
Allow students time to read the information in each other's organizers and come up with a list of final ideas.
Extension
Have group members lead the discussions about what to include and summarize the arguments for and against different options.

Creative Thinking

Using newly created content to solve problems

Monitor students as they plan their posters and look for original and creative ideas to attract volunteers.

Step 3: Draft and Review p55 p71

- Hand out a piece of poster board to each group. Students use the final ideas from their group Poster Organizer to create a final version of their poster.
- Have students add the images they chose and check language.
- Encourage peer correction. Check that groups are using language from the unit (comparative and superlative adjectives, *can* and *could*, *too much* and (*not*) *enough* + noun) in the texts.

Peer-Evaluation Form p69 Development

3 Production

Schedule presentation times and stick to them. Remember that these projects will be displayed on a classroom wall. Allow enough time for students to look at all the posters, ask questions, and give feedback.

Before groups produce their final drafts, have them look at the different examples of posters again. Help them with ideas for how to organize their information and present it logically. > Presentation Ideas p18

As students complete their projects, check their abilities in the following Areas of Competency.

Social Responsibilities

Understanding personal responsibilities as part of a group and in society

Understands various aspects of society (e.g., volunteering).

Evidence: Poster shows why volunteers are needed.

Gets involved in collective action in the school (e.g., through volunteering).

Evidence: Poster shows how people can volunteer.

Creative Thinking

Using newly created content to solve problems

Employs new ideas and content in solving a task or activity.

Evidence: Poster has a creative design and interesting content.

Makes an assignment original by adding new angles.

Evidence: Poster provides original reasons for volunteering.

Step 1: Prepare p55 p71

- Go through the items in the PRESENT section in **Exercise 6**.
- As groups prepare their project, ask questions, for example: *Is the information presented in the poster useful? How does the poster attract volunteers? What images are you using? What things did you decide together as a group?*
- Remind groups of the presentation date and how much time each group will have.

Collaboration Learning Tip

Using Social Skills

As groups finalize their projects in Step 1, encourage them to use polite language for asking for and expressing opinions, interrupting politely, and making decisions. Remind them of useful language, for example: *Let's ... , Excuse me ... , Can I make a suggestion?, What about ... ?, Are there any more ideas?, So we all agree ...*

Step 2: Present p55

- Draw attention to the CHECK section in **Exercise 7**. Ask the class to think about the question as they look at each other's posters.
- Have groups display their posters on the classroom walls.
- Ask students to walk around and look at the posters; tell them to assess which posters make them want to work as a volunteer.
- Encourage the class to ask questions and have group members explain why and how their groups came to make some decisions.

Step 3: Reflect p55

- After the display session, hold a class discussion on the CHECK question in **Exercise 7**.
- Write positive opinions about each poster on the board. Then have the class vote for their favorite poster and the best way to work as a volunteer in their community.
- Encourage students to reflect on each stage of the project process, including positive experiences and things they could improve upon.

> Peer-Evaluation Form p69 **Production**

Go to the collaboration tool and online portfolio to make use of the digital resources.

Project Evaluation Rubric: A Poster

Use these project-specific descriptors and your own choice of descriptors from the > Evaluation Rubric p21 to assess students individually or in groups. Make your own evaluation form. > Teacher's Evaluation Form p70

	4	3	2	1
Creativity	Product is well organized with creative and interesting ideas. It has a lot of persuasive messages to attract volunteers. It uses eye-catching images.	Product is organized with interesting ideas. It has some persuasive messages to attract volunteers. It uses some eye-catching images.	Product has interesting ideas but lacks organization. It has one or two persuasive messages to attract volunteers. It uses images, but they aren't very eye-catching.	Product lacks interesting ideas and organization. It doesn't have any persuasive messages to attract volunteers. It uses very few or no images.
Language Use	Product shows excellent use of grammar, punctuation, and spelling. Excellent use of language from the unit. Project is understandable with only a few or no mistakes.	Product shows good use of grammar, punctuation, and spelling. Good use of language from the unit. Project is understandable with some mistakes.	Product shows adequate use of grammar, punctuation, and spelling. Adequate use of language from the unit. Project is understandable, but some sections need further explanation.	Product shows poor use of grammar, punctuation, and spelling. Poor or no use of language from the unit. Project is confusing, vague, and almost impossible to understand.

The Cambridge Framework for Life Competencies

You can also assess students' progress in the following foundational layers.

FOUNDATIONAL LAYER	ABILITIES	ACTIONS
Emotional Development	• Empathize and build relationships	expressing opinions and interrupting politely, making decisions and agreeing as a group, verbalizing emotions appropriately
Discipline Knowledge	• Convince the audience	using persuasive language, demonstrating knowledge, giving details, answering questions

Flipped Classroom Activities

Evaluate

In project groups, have students discuss their completed Peer-Evaluation Forms and ways to work better as a group. > Peer-Evaluation Form p69

Out of class: have students reflect on their progress at home. > KWL Chart p67 **Learned**

In class: hold a class discussion on what students have learned, using the information from their KWL Charts. > KWL Chart p67 **Learned**

5 CULTURE PROJECT

A POSTER

- **Learning Outcome:** design a poster about unusual traditional homes
- **Skills:** find information about an unusual traditional home and use a spidergram to organize it; decide on a design, including photos and maps; present the poster
- **Resources:** two or more posters, Poster Organizer p62, My Time-Management Plan p71
- **Evaluation Tools:** Project Evaluation Rubric p41, My Learning Diary p68, Peer-Evaluation Form p69, Teacher's Evaluation Form p70

Student's Book Teacher's Resource Bank Unit 5

Before You Start

Collect two or three online or print posters about unusual traditional homes to show students in class. Choose posters that combine both graphics and written information about the homes, such as their history, materials, and location.

1 Preparation

Step 1: Introduce the Topic

- Introduce the topic of posters after doing the reading exercises. p60 Ask: *Which home is your favorite? Why? How are these homes different from traditional ones?*
- Show students the posters. Ask: *What is the purpose of these posters? What can you learn about each home?* Discuss which homes students like the most and why.
- Explain that informative posters combine text and graphics to get people's attention. Ask: *How do the example posters combine text and graphics? Are they effective?*
- Ask students to bring an example of an informative poster to the next class (in their own language or in English). They can discuss what the posters are about and how effective the designs are.

Flipped Classroom Activities

Step 2: Analyze the Model for the Project Unit 5

Out of class: have students read the model poster and think about these questions: *What sections does the poster have? What kind of information is in each section? What order are the sections in? How do the pictures relate to the text in each section? What types of images does the poster use?*

In class: have students discuss their answers to the questions. Then ask them to compare the model poster with the examples they brought to class.

Learning to Learn

Practical skills for participating in learning

Assess students' preparation and participation for the class discussion in Step 2.

Step 3: *How to* Design a Poster Unit 5

- Go through the *How to* tips with the class. Ask students to say if each tip is related to content or design and to explain why it is important. Stress that both content and design are equally important in posters.
- Ensure students understand that when they design their posters, they should use the ideas in this *How to* section.

Step 4: Clarify the Project Unit 5

- Follow the steps in The Learning Stages of Project Work p10.
- Brainstorm different types of unusual homes.
- Have groups discuss what resources they can use to find out information about the homes and think about how they can present the information. If they are considering a digital format, tell them to research suitable programs.

My Learning Diary p68 Preparation

Peer-Evaluation Form p69 Preparation

2 Development

Start this stage as soon as groups know their learning outcomes and have brainstormed different types of homes.

Step 1: Assign Roles and Responsibilities

- In project groups, have students assign general roles. > Roles and Responsibilities p16 Help them decide on further roles they can share, such as those in the diagram.

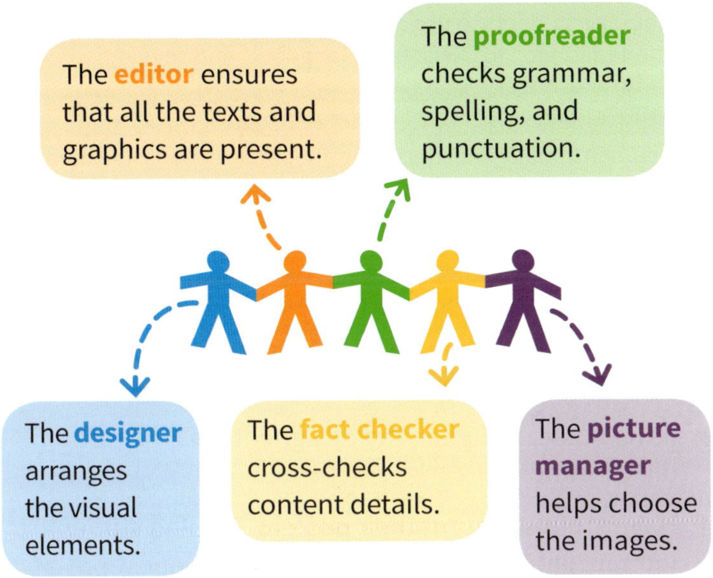

Step 2: Research and Analyze Unit 5 p71

- Have groups start the PLAN section in **Exercise 1** and choose an unusual traditional home. Hand out a copy of the > Poster Organizer p62 to each student.
- Remind students of the ideas in the *How to* box when listing and comparing ideas, choosing images, and deciding on a design.

Step 3: Draft and Review Unit 5 p71

> My Learning Diary p68 Preparation

> Peer-Evaluation Form p69 Preparation

Flipped Classroom Activities

Out of class: have each student work on their section. Remind them to check their grammar, spelling, and punctuation and to find images that support their text.

Tell students to try to include examples of language from the unit in their sections; for example, (***not***) ***as … as***, and (***not***) + **adjective** + ***enough*** for describing their home, and ***have to*** / ***don't have to*** for instructions on how to build it.

In class: have group members put their poster together and agree on final changes to the design.

Collaboration

Managing the sharing of tasks in a project

Monitor how group members are sharing roles and responsibilities in Steps 2 and 3. Check how well group members help each other in completing the tasks.

Collaboration Learning Tip

Encouraging Responsibility

Tell students it is important to complete their sections on time so that their groups can finish the project in class. Remind group members of their general roles. Discuss any problems groups may be having in keeping to the schedule. Reflect on why this is happening and encourage or suggest possible solutions.

3 Production

Schedule presentation times and stick to them, ensuring all groups present their posters. Spread the presentations over a few classes, if necessary. Allow enough time for each presentation and for questions.

Before groups produce their final drafts, discuss how they will present their information. If they choose to present it digitally, ensure they can use the available classroom technology. > Presentation Ideas p18

As students complete their projects, check their abilities in the following Areas of Competency.

Learning to Learn

Practical skills for participating in learning

Participates sensibly and positively in learning activities in class.

Evidence: Students listen actively, ask questions, and express opinions in class discussions.

Understands essential grammatical terms and concepts.

Evidence: Posters include accurate examples of language from the unit.

Collaboration

Managing the sharing of tasks in a project

Ensures that work is fairly divided among members in group activities.

Evidence: Groups divide tasks according to their roles.

Offers to help others finish a task.

Evidence: Group members work together to complete their poster on time.

Step 1: Prepare Unit 5 p71

- Go through the items in the PRESENT section in **Exercise 2**.
- As groups prepare their project, ask questions, for example: *Does your poster include photos, maps, and drawings? Is the title short and interesting? Are all the sections complete? Is the handwriting clear? Did you check the grammar, spelling, and punctuation? Are the facts correct?* Say that each group member will present their section. Give students time to practice in their groups. (See Differentiated Instruction activities above for further practice.)
- Remind groups of the presentation date and how much time each group will have.

Differentiated Instruction

Support
Help students with self- and peer-correction: check their work and point out areas that need improvement.
Consolidation
Encourage students to use different resources (websites, dictionaries, etc.) to check facts, language, and spelling.
Extension
Let students make final decisions about corrections. Encourage them to explain their logic to their group.

Step 2: Present Unit 5

- Draw attention to the CHECK section in **Exercise 3**. Ask the class to think about these questions as they listen to their peers' presentations.
- If the poster is digital, the designer takes the role of digital editor.
- Have groups present their posters. Remind students to interact with their audience and ask for questions at the end of their presentation.
- Tell the class to take notes on what they like about each poster.

Step 3: Reflect Unit 5

- After all of the posters have been presented, hold a class discussion on the CHECK questions in **Exercise 3**.
- Have students say what they like about each poster and why before voting on their favorite. Then ask: *Was planning/researching/designing your poster easy/difficult? Why/Why not?*
- Encourage students to reflect on each stage of the project process, including positive experiences and things they could improve upon.

> Peer-Evaluation Form p69 Production

Go to the collaboration tool and online portfolio to make use of the digital resources.

Project Evaluation Rubric: A Poster

Use these project-specific descriptors and your own choice of descriptors from the > Evaluation Rubric p21 to assess students individually or in groups. Make your own evaluation form. > Teacher's Evaluation Form p70

	4	3	2	1
Creativity	Product is well organized with creative ideas. It has a short and interesting title. It uses borders and includes attractive photos, maps, and drawings.	Product is organized with creative ideas. It has a short and fairly interesting title. It uses borders and includes some attractive photos, maps, and drawings.	Product has creative ideas but lacks organization. It has a title, but it's either too long or not interesting. It includes some attractive images but doesn't use borders.	Product lacks creative ideas and organization. It has no title. It doesn't use any design features, and most images are unrelated to the topic.
Language Use	Product shows excellent use of grammar, punctuation, and spelling. Excellent use of language from the unit. Project is understandable with only a few or no mistakes.	Product shows good use of grammar, punctuation, and spelling. Good use of language from the unit. Project is understandable with some mistakes.	Product shows adequate use of grammar, punctuation, and spelling. Adequate use of language from the unit. Project is understandable, but some sections need further explanation.	Product shows poor use of grammar, punctuation, and spelling. Poor or no use of language from the unit. Project is confusing, vague, and almost impossible to understand.

The Cambridge Framework for Life Competencies

You can also assess students' progress in the following foundational layers.

FOUNDATIONAL LAYER	ABILITIES	ACTIONS
Digital Literacy	• Use digital tools	finding content and cross-checking facts on various websites, using digital tools to design and present posters, sharing work online
Discipline Knowledge	• Convince the audience	explaining facts and images, demonstrating knowledge, giving details, answering questions

Flipped Classroom Activities

Evaluate

In project groups, have students discuss their completed Peer-Evaluation Forms and ways to work better as a group. > Peer-Evaluation Form p69

Out of class: have students reflect on their progress at home. > My Learning Diary p68 **Production**

In class: hold a class discussion on what students have learned, using the information from their learning diaries. > My Learning Diary p68 **Production**

6 SCIENCE PROJECT

AN INFORMATION PAMPHLET

- **Learning Outcome:** make an information pamphlet
- **Skills:** decide how the group will work together, decide on the sections and images, work individually and as a group, give feedback on first drafts
- **Resources:** two or more information pamphlets, Information Pamphlet Organizer p63, My Time-Management Plan p71
- **Evaluation Tools:** Project Evaluation Rubric p45, KWL Chart p67, Peer-Evaluation Form p69, Teacher's Evaluation Form p70

Student's Book

Before You Start

Collect two or three different types of information pamphlets to show students in class. If possible, bring in pamphlets showing a variety of formats (e.g., half-fold, bi-fold, gate fold, etc.).

1 Preparation

Step 1: Introduce the Topic

- Introduce the topic of information pamphlets after doing the reading exercises. p72
- Show students the pamphlets. Encourage them to say what they are and who they are for. Ask: *What are information pamphlets? Why do people read them? What are these pamphlets about?*
- Explain that pamphlets use short texts to provide information. For example, they can tell people about an event, are used to sell something, or they can offer suggestions and advice. Have students describe some specific examples of these types of posters.
- Ask students to bring a pamphlet to the next class (in their own language or in English). They can discuss which pamphlets they like or don't like and why.

Step 2: Analyze the Model for the Project pp78–79

- Complete **Exercises 1** to **3**.

  Answers **1** a **2** 2 T 3 F 4 F 5 T 6 T **3** Desert Animals: snakes, scorpions; Desert Weather: sandstorms; Our Bodies in the Desert: heat cramps

- Ask questions about the structure and effectiveness of the pamphlet, for example: *What information is in the Fact File? (Facts about deserts.) What sections are there? What questions are there for each section? What can you see in the photos? Who is the pamphlet for?*
- Study the language from the unit. Ask students to find examples of the **zero** and **first conditional**, ***should***, and ***must***. Ask why the pamphlet uses these structures (to give suggestions and advice).

Critical Thinking

Understanding and analyzing links between ideas

Use the questions in Step 2 to assess how well students understand the purpose of the model pamphlet and how the advice is presented.

Step 3: *How to* Work in Groups p78

- 6.12 Go through the three ways of working listed in **Exercise 4**. Say that in the audio, the students will talk about how they worked in their groups. Play the audio and check answers.

  Answers **4** 1 I 2 J 3 P

- In pairs, students discuss the questions in **Exercise 5**.
- Ensure students understand that when they work in groups, they should use the ideas in this *How to* section.

Step 4: Clarify the Project pp78–79

- Follow the steps in The Learning Stages of Project Work p10.
- Brainstorm remote places and habitats with the class.
- Have students discuss what resources they can use to research the brainstormed items (e.g., an encyclopedia, atlas, websites, etc.).

KWL Chart p67 Know and Want to Know

Peer-Evaluation Form p69 Preparation

2 Development

Start this stage as soon as groups know their learning outcomes and have discussed what resources to use.

Step 1: **Assign Roles and Responsibilities**

- In project groups, have students assign general roles. Roles and Responsibilities p16 Help them decide on further roles they can share. Draw a diagram like the one below on the board.

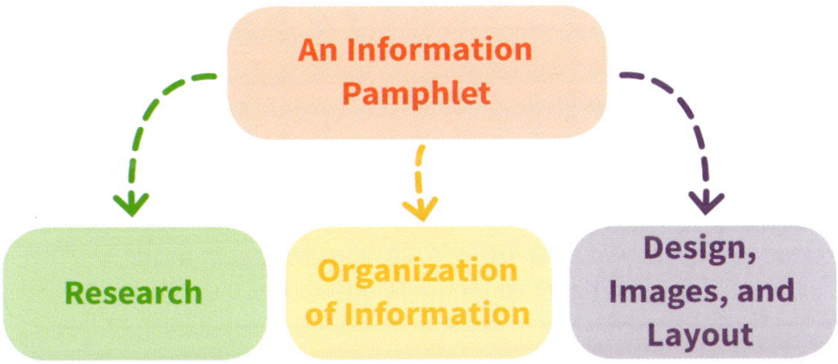

- Ask questions related to each section in the diagram. Discuss the tasks and roles required to create an information pamphlet:

  Research: *Where can you find information? How can you check that the facts are correct? How will you classify the information? Who will help organize the information and suggest which is best to use?*

  Organization of information: *What is the purpose of the pamphlet? What sections will it have? What are the main and supporting ideas? How will you present the information? Who will help organize it?*

  Design, images, and layout: *How will you make the pamphlet attractive and easy to read? Where can you find images? Who will help select the images and decide on the layout?*

- Encourage students to take notes and assign roles and responsibilities.

Step 2: **Research and Analyze** p79 p71

- Have groups start the PLAN section in **Exercise 6** and choose a remote place or habitat for their pamphlet. Remind students of the three ways of working in groups described in **Exercise 4**. Ask them to decide which way they want to work.

Flipped Classroom Activities

Out of class: have students write their sections, prepare their versions of the pamphlets, or do their assigned tasks, depending on the way of working they have chosen.

In class: have groups complete the rest of the PLAN section. Give each group a copy of the Information Pamphlet Organizer p63 to help them organize their information.

Step 3: **Draft and Review** p79 p71

- Have groups draw up a rough plan of their pamphlet. Remind them to think about the organization of information and the design and layout discussed in Step 1.
- Allow time for drafting and reviewing. Encourage students to use the language from the unit when making suggestions or giving advice.
- Have groups share their draft with another group. Tell them to exchange opinions and suggest improvements.
- Encourage group members to make revisions out of class according to their roles. Have them bring their ideas to the next class.

Communication

Managing conversations

Monitor progress of the tasks in Step 3 to check how well students understand each other's ideas and suggestions.

Collaboration Learning Tip

Listening Actively

When groups are sharing opinions about their first drafts, ensure they are listening to each other's ideas and asking questions to clarify information or get more details. Monitor to help with useful language, for example: *What do you mean? Can you repeat that? Can you explain?* Ensure students show interest and respond respectfully to suggestions and feedback.

Peer-Evaluation Form p69 Development

3 Production

Schedule presentation times and stick to them. Remember that these projects will be displayed on a classroom wall. Allow enough time for students to look at all the pamphlets, ask questions, and give feedback.

Before groups produce their final drafts, have them decide on the format and layout of their pamphlet. It could, for example, be bi-fold, tri-fold, gate fold, etc.

Presentation Ideas p18

As students complete their projects, check their abilities in the following Areas of Competency.

Critical Thinking

Understanding and analyzing links between ideas

Compares points and arguments from different sources.

Evidence: Students combine their research to produce a coherent pamphlet.

Identifies the basic structure of an argument.

Evidence: Pamphlet has a clear, logical structure with well-presented sections.

Communication

Managing conversations

Uses appropriate language to negotiate meaning: to show understanding; to signal lack of understanding; to seek clarification.

Evidence: Groups discuss different aspects of their pamphlets, and ask and answer questions in order to agree on the final product.

Step 1: Prepare p79 p71

- Go through the items in the PRESENT section in **Exercise 7**.
- As groups prepare their project, monitor how they are working together and how well they are sharing responsibilities. Remind them of the ideas in the *How to* section.
- Check the language in the pamphlets, especially the use of ***should*** and ***must*** and the **zero** and **first conditional**. (See Differentiated Instruction activities below for further practice.)
- Remind groups of the presentation date and how much time each group will have.

Differentiated Instruction

Support
Help students with language for giving suggestions. Encourage them to come up with more suggestions based on your example.
Consolidation
Elicit structures for giving advice that students can use in their pamphlets. Ask: *What are three things you should/must do?*
Extension
Have peers correct each other's work and suggest more examples of structures for giving advice.

Step 2: Present p79

- For this project, students walk around the classroom and look at the pamphlets on the wall. Group members can take turns standing by their display to answer questions.
- Draw attention to the CHECK section in **Exercise 8**. Tell groups to ask each other about how they worked together. Encourage them to discuss what went well and what didn't go very well.
- Have alternating group members present their pamphlets to the rest of the class.
- Ensure students interact with one another and that presenters respond appropriately to their classmates' ideas.

Step 3: Reflect p79

- After the presentations, hold a class discussion on the CHECK questions in **Exercise 8**.
- Encourage students to reflect on each stage of the project process, including positive experiences and things they could improve upon.

Peer-Evaluation Form p69 Production

Go to the collaboration tool and online portfolio to make use of the digital resources.

Project Evaluation Rubric: An Information Pamphlet

Use these project-specific descriptors and your own choice of descriptors from the > Evaluation Rubric p21 to assess students individually or in groups. Make your own evaluation form. > Teacher's Evaluation Form p70

	4	3	2	1
Creativity	Product has a very original and attractive design. It uses many striking images and is divided into clear sections. It includes a lot of interesting facts. All group members contributed creatively.	Product has an original and attractive design. It uses some striking images and is divided into fairly clear sections. It includes some interesting facts. Most group members contributed creatively.	Product has a clear design that largely follows the model. It uses adequate images and is divided into sections, though these are not always clear. It includes very few interesting facts. Only some group members contributed creatively.	Product has an unattractive design with little creativity, and it doesn't follow the model. It doesn't use images, and there are no clear sections. It doesn't include any interesting facts. Members didn't work as a group, and there was little creativity.
Language Use	Excellent use of language from the unit (*should, must,* zero and first conditionals). Project is understandable with only a few mistakes.	Good use of language from the unit (*should, must,* zero and first conditionals). Project is understandable with some mistakes.	Adequate use of language from the unit (*should, must,* zero and first conditionals). Project is understandable, but some sections need further explanation.	Poor or no use of language from the unit (*should, must,* zero and first conditionals). Project is confusing, vague, and almost impossible to understand.

The Cambridge Framework for Life Competencies

You can also assess students' progress in the following foundational layers.

FOUNDATIONAL LAYER	ABILITIES	ACTIONS
Emotional Development	• Empathize and build relationships	sharing roles, making decisions together, checking understanding, reflecting on strengths and weaknesses, giving advice on how to improve
Discipline Knowledge	• Convince the audience	explaining facts and images, summarizing information, giving details and advice about the topic, answering questions

Flipped Classroom Activities

Evaluate

In project groups, have students discuss their completed Peer-Evaluation Forms and ways to work better as a group. > Peer-Evaluation Form p69

Out of class: have students reflect on their progress at home. > KWL Chart p67 **Learned**

In class: hold a class discussion on what students have learned, using the information from their KWL Charts. > KWL Chart p67 **Learned**

7 CULTURE PROJECT

A 3-D ROOM PLAN

- **Learning Outcome:** design a 3-D room plan
- **Skills:** draw a diagram (digitally or on paper), decide what technology to include, invent a new technological device, describe the items in the room plan by using call-out boxes
- **Resources:** two or more room plans, 3-D Room Plan Organizer p64, My Time-Management Plan p71
- **Evaluation Tools:** Project Evaluation Rubric p49, My Learning Diary p68, Peer-Evaluation Form p69, Teacher's Evaluation Form p70

Student's Book Teacher's Resource Bank Unit 7

Before You Start

Collect two or three examples of room plans to show students in class. Use an online program or other real room plans you may have access to, such as the school's.

1 Preparation

Step 1: Introduce the Topic

- Introduce the topic of room plans after doing the vocabulary exercises p83 and once students have talked about different technological devices. Alternatively, wait until ***will/won't***, ***may***, and ***might*** have been practiced. p87
- Show students the room plans. Ask: *What are these? What do they show? Who creates room plans? What are they for?* Have students sketch a room plan of the classroom, including fixed objects, such as doors and windows, and furniture.
- Explain that a 3-D room plan is a diagram of a room or rooms in a building that shows the view from above and can include measurements, fixed objects, furniture, electric systems, and water pipes.
- Ask students to find an example of a room plan online and bring it to the next class (in their own language or in English). It can show one or more rooms in a building. Students can describe the room plans in groups.

Step 2: Analyze the Model for the Project Unit 7

- Have students describe the model room plan. Ask: *What furniture does the classroom have? How is it different from our classroom?* Students read the texts.
- Ask further questions, for example: *Which ideas do you like? Would you like some of these things in your classroom? Which ones?* Discuss how classrooms will be different in the future. (See Differentiated Instruction activities below for further practice.)

Differentiated Instruction

Support
Have students find examples of predictions in the call-out boxes. They can discuss which predictions are most likely to come true.
Consolidation
In pairs, have students take turns reading a prediction from one of the call-outs and guessing the item it refers to.
Extension
In pairs, have students cover the call-out boxes and take turns pointing to plan items, making predictions what they will do.

Step 3: *How to* Design a Room Plan Unit 7

- Go through the *How to* tips with the class. Have different students say why each idea is important.
- Ensure students understand while designing their plans, they should use ideas in this *How to* section.

Critical Thinking

Evaluating ideas, arguments, and options

Have students discuss problems they might have as they follow the *How to* tips and find solutions.

Step 4: Clarify the Project Unit 7

- Follow the steps in The Learning Stages of Project Work p10.
- Brainstorm different rooms: real or imaginary.

My Learning Diary p68 **Preparation**

Peer-Evaluation Form p69 **Preparation**

2 Development

Start this stage as soon as groups know their learning outcomes and have brainstormed different rooms to choose from.

Step 1: Assign Roles and Responsibilities

- In project groups, have students assign general roles. Roles and Responsibilities p16 Help them decide on further roles they can share, such as those in the diagram.

Step 2: Research and Analyze Unit 7 p71

- Have groups start the PLAN section in **Exercise 1**. Tell them to choose a room and brainstorm modern technology.
- Have groups draw an outline of their room. Draw attention to the model room plan notes. Ask students to plan their room, taking similar notes on technological devices, what they do, and where they go, as well as their new invention and other furniture.
- Ask groups to decide on their room plan format: either print or digital. Encourage those who have chosen a digital format to look for free programs online.
- Hand out a copy of the 3-D Room Plan Organizer p64 to each student. Tell students to copy a rough sketch of their room plan in the first part and to include all the items their groups agreed on.
- Have group members decide who will prepare which texts for each of the items.

Collaboration Learning Tip

Disagreeing Appropriately

If students cannot agree on some of the items to include in their room plans, encourage polite discussion and allow them to give their opinions and explain their reasons. Have them make alternative suggestions to come to a solution everyone is happy with. Monitor to help with useful language, for example: *I'm not sure about ... , I don't agree because ... , Why don't we ... ?, How about ... ?, Maybe we should ...*

Flipped Classroom Activities

Step 3: Draft and Review Unit 7 p71

Out of class: group members prepare their sections, taking notes in the second part of their organizers. Remind them to use language from the unit: ***will*** for predictions and the **infinitive of purpose**.

In class: group members check each other's work, paying attention to spelling and grammar.

Groups put together a final version of their room plan. If groups are creating it digitally, they may need to do this out of class.

Collaboration

Working toward a resolution related to a task

Monitor students' ability to reach compromises and make changes to the final plan as they listen to each other's ideas.

My Learning Diary p68 **Development**

Peer-Evaluation Form p69 **Development**

3 Production

Schedule presentation times and stick to them, ensuring all groups present their room plans. Spread the presentations over a few classes, if necessary. Allow enough time for each presentation and for questions.

Before groups produce their final drafts, offer help and suggest ideas for them to complete their digital or print room plans successfully. Presentation Ideas p18

As students complete their projects, check their abilities in the following Areas of Competency.

Critical Thinking

Evaluating ideas, arguments, and options

Examines possible solutions to a given problem and states how effective they are.

Evidence: Groups redraft when necessary and share opinions about new ideas.

Assesses strengths and weaknesses of possible solutions.

Evidence: Groups make decisions in order to achieve the learning outcomes.

Collaboration

Working toward a resolution related to a task

Is aware when others have divergent views and ideas for completing a problem or task.

Evidence: Students listen attentively to each other's opinions and make decisions together.

Is able to propose solutions that include views and ideas other than their own.

Evidence: Students make compromises about what to include, considering all group members' ideas.

Step 1: Prepare Unit 7 p71

- Go through the items in the PRESENT section in **Exercise 2**. Say that each group member will present their section.
- Allow time for groups to finalize their room plans. If they disagree, remind them to do so politely and to try to come to a consensus.
- Monitor to check that the room plans have a clear design, the text in the call-out boxes is clear, and the boxes correctly match the items in the diagram.
- Ask students to check spelling and grammar. Help with corrections as necessary.

Step 2: Present Unit 7

- Draw attention to the CHECK section in **Exercise 3**. Ask the class to think about these questions as they listen to their peers' presentations.
- Remind speakers to look at their audience, speak slowly and clearly, and smile. Tell them to point to the section of the room plan they are describing. If students are presenting digitally, they can zoom in on specific features.
- Have groups present their room plans.
- Tell the class to take notes on what they like about each room plan and new invention.

Step 3: Reflect Unit 7

- After all of the room plans have been presented, hold a class discussion on the CHECK questions in **Exercise 3**.
- Have the class discuss what they like about each room plan and invention and why. Ask: *What have you learned about room plans? What makes an effective room plan? What were the most interesting technological devices? Which is your favorite invention?*
- Encourage students to reflect on each stage of the project process, including positive experiences and things they could improve upon.

Peer-Evaluation Form p69 Production

Go to the collaboration tool and online portfolio to make use of the digital resources.

Project Evaluation Rubric: A 3-D Room Plan

Use these project-specific descriptors and your own choice of descriptors from the > Evaluation Rubric p21 to assess students individually or in groups. Make your own evaluation form. > Teacher's Evaluation Form p70

	4	3	2	1
Creativity	Product has a very attractive design with clear labels. Its call-out boxes show many creative ideas. It presents a new invention with a clear description of its purpose and advantages.	Product has an attractive design with clear labels. Its call-out boxes show some creative ideas. It presents a new invention with a fairly clear description of its purpose and advantages.	Product has an adequate design with mostly clear labels. Its call-out boxes show only one or two creative ideas. It presents a new invention, but its purpose or advantages are unclear.	Product has an unclear design and is either missing most labels, or these are unclear. It doesn't have call-out boxes, or these don't show any creative ideas. It doesn't present a new invention.
Language Use	Excellent use of language from the unit (*will*; infinitive of purpose). Project is understandable with only a few mistakes.	Good use of language from the unit (*will*; infinitive of purpose). Project is understandable with some mistakes.	Adequate use of language from the unit (*will*; infinitive of purpose). Project is understandable, but some sections need further explanation.	Poor or no use of language from the unit (*will*; infinitive of purpose). Project is confusing, poorly written, and vague.

The Cambridge Framework for Life Competencies

You can also assess students' progress in the following foundational layers.

FOUNDATIONAL LAYER	ABILITIES	ACTIONS
Discipline Knowledge	• Use digital tools	finding content on various websites, creating documents, sharing work online, using digital room plan programs
Emotional Development	• Manage emotions	reflecting on strengths and weaknesses, verbalizing emotions and disagreeing appropriately, finding solutions

Flipped Classroom Activities

Evaluate

In project groups, have students discuss their completed Peer-Evaluation Forms and ways to work better as a group. > Peer-Evaluation Form p69

Out of class: have students reflect on their progress at home. > My Learning Diary p68 **Production**

In class: hold a class discussion on what students have learned, using the information from their learning diaries. > My Learning Diary p68 **Production**

8 TECHNOLOGY PROJECT

A TIMELINE

- **Learning Outcome:** make a timeline about an invention
- **Skills:** research information and images; manage time: prioritize tasks, set long- and short-term deadlines, divide up tasks
- **Resources:** two or more timelines, Timeline Organizer p65, My Time-Management Plan p71
- **Evaluation Tools:** Project Evaluation Rubric p53, KWL Chart p67, Peer-Evaluation Form p69, Teacher's Evaluation Form p70

Student's Book

Before You Start

Find two or more timelines about inventions or events from magazines or online to show students in class.

1 Preparation

Step 1: Introduce the Topic

- Introduce the topic of timelines after doing the grammar exercises. p97
- Show students the timelines. Ask: *What can timelines be about? What information do these timelines have? How is the information presented?*
- Explain that timelines are lines that show a sequence of events in chronological order. Explain that a timeline helps you understand when things happened and in what order. Point out that many timelines have images to help describe events.
- Ask students to bring an example of a timeline to the next class (in their own language or in English). They can say where they found the timelines (newspapers, magazines, online, etc.) and discuss what they are about. Then they can compare the designs.

Step 2: Analyze the Model for the Project pp102–103

- Complete **Exercises 1** and **2**.

Answers **1** 2 B 3 E 4 D 5 A 6 F **2** 2 b 3 a, c 4 f 5 b, d, f 6 e, f

- Ask questions about the content and design of the model timeline, for example: *What is the purpose of this timeline? What is its shape? How do the design and shape relate to the topic? Is the timeline easy to follow?*
- Study the language from the unit. Ask students to find examples of the **present perfect for experience** and **reflexive** and **indefinite pronouns**.

Step 3: ***How to*** **Manage Your Time** p102

- Go through the ideas in **Exercise 3** with the class. Students take turns calling out the answers.

Answers **3** b, c, d, f, g, h

- As you discuss students' answers, ask questions to check comprehension, for example: *Why is it important to prioritize? What is a short- / long-term deadline?*
- 8.12 Play the audio and check answers.

Answers **4** b, c, d, f, g

- Ensure students understand that when managing their time for the project, they should use the ideas in this *How to* section.

Learning to Learn

Practical skills for participating in learning

Have students think about time-management problems they have had in past project work. Ask them to come up with another idea for effective time management.

Step 4: Clarify the Project pp102–103

- Follow the steps in > The Learning Stages of Project Work p10.
- Have groups brainstorm possible inventions for their timeline. Tell them to bring a list with their ideas to the next class.

> KWL Chart p67 **Know and Want to Know**

> Peer-Evaluation Form p69 **Preparation**

2 Development

Start this stage as soon as groups know their learning outcomes and have a list of possible inventions for their timelines.

Step 1: Assign Roles and Responsibilities

- In project groups, have students assign general roles. > Roles and Responsibilities p16 Help them decide on further roles and responsibilities they can share. Draw a diagram like the one below on the board.

- Ask questions related to each section in the diagram. Discuss the tasks and roles required to create a timeline:

  Research: *Where can you find information? How can you check facts, dates, and events? Who will help put all the information together and suggest which is best to use?*

  Organization of information: *How will you decide on the key dates and events? What facts do you need next to each date? Who will help organize the information?*

  Design, images, and layout: *What shape will your timeline have? How will you make your timeline attractive and easy to read? Where can you find images? Who will help select the images and decide on the layout?*

- Encourage students to take notes and assign roles and responsibilities.

Step 2: Research and Analyze p103 p71

- Have groups start the PLAN section in **Exercise 5**. Tell them to choose an invention. Alternatively, they can choose one idea from the list they brainstormed previously.
- Refer students to the diagram for tasks and roles from Step 1. Have groups discuss what tasks they need to accomplish to complete their timeline. If necessary, play Track 8.12 again to help generate ideas.
- Give students a long-term deadline for the whole project, and let them set short-term deadlines for the tasks they discussed.
- Remind students to use > My Time-Management Plan p71 .

Flipped Classroom Activities

Out of class: have students research information and images for their timelines. Tell them to bring their findings to the next class.

In class: have groups check their findings together and decide which information and images to use.

Step 3: Draft and Review p103 p71

- Hand out a copy of the > Timeline Organizer p65 to each group.
- Have groups use the organizer to put together the key information and ideas for images. Encourage students to think of attractive and imaginative ways to present their timeline.
- Go through the items in the PLAN section and have groups ensure their timelines include all the items mentioned.
- Have groups write and edit their timelines, using language from the unit, including examples of the **present perfect for experiences** and **reflexive** and **indefinite pronouns**.
- As groups review their projects, remind them of the time-management ideas in the *How to* section.

Creative Thinking

Creating new content from own ideas or other resources

Monitor groups' understanding of the sequence of events in their timelines, as well as their creativity when presenting this sequence visually.

> Peer-Evaluation Form p69 **Development**

3 Production

Schedule presentation times and stick to them. Remember that these projects will be displayed on a classroom wall. Allow enough time for students to look at all the timelines, ask questions, and give feedback.

As groups work on their final drafts, give them tips on how best to present their timelines with images. Tell students they can follow the steps for making an infographic. Alternatively, groups could choose to make their timelines digitally, using a free online timeline maker.

Presentation Ideas p18

As students complete their projects, check their abilities in the following Areas of Competency.

Learning to Learn
Practical skills for participating in learning

Uses metacognitive strategies (e.g., time management) to maximize learning.

Evidence: Groups share tasks and follow the ideas in the *How to* section.

Takes effective notes in class and from homework reading.

Evidence: Group members research and select the key facts about their invention.

Creative Thinking
Creating new content from own ideas or other resources

Writes or tells an original story, given prompts or without prompts.

Evidence: Timeline describes events in chronological order with visual aids.

Responds imaginatively to contemporary or historical events and ideas.

Evidence: Timeline presents information in an imaginative way.

Step 1: Prepare p103 p71

- Go through the items in the PLAN section in **Exercise 5** again.
- As groups prepare their project, ask questions, for example: *How is the design connected to the topic? Have you included all the key dates, people, and events? Do the images match the texts? Are you sharing and completing tasks on time?*
- Point to **Exercise 6** in the PRESENT section. Remind groups of the presentation date.

Step 2: Present p103

- For this project, students interact and look at the timelines. Group members can take turns standing by their display to answer questions.
- Draw attention to the CHECK section in **Exercise 7**. Tell the class to think about this question as they look at their peers' timelines. Have them write down interesting facts and features they find attractive.
- Have alternating group members present their timelines. (See Differentiated Instruction activities below for further practice.)
- Ensure students interact with one another.

Differentiated Instruction

Support
Have groups cut up their Timeline Organizers into six sections, shuffle them, and pass them to another group to reorder.
Consolidation
Ask students questions about other groups' timelines and have them find out the answers.
Extension
In project groups, have students write questions about their timelines. Then pairs of groups quiz each other.

Step 3: Reflect p103

- After the presentations, hold a class discussion on the CHECK question in **Exercise 7**. Ask students to give reasons for their ideas and to give constructive feedback.
- Have students reflect on the project process, including positive experiences and things they could improve upon.

Peer-Evaluation Form p69 Production

Collaboration Learning Tip

Sharing Tasks

As groups discuss the projects in Step 3, remind them of the time-management ideas in the *How to* section. Recap the tasks groups performed to finish their projects and how they prioritized them. Ask if everyone was able to complete their assigned task. Discuss what groups did if an aspect of the project was falling behind.

Go to the collaboration tool and online portfolio to make use of the digital resources.

Project Evaluation Rubric: A Timeline

Use these project-specific descriptors and your own choice of descriptors from the Evaluation Rubric p21 to assess students individually or in groups. Make your own evaluation form. Teacher's Evaluation Form p70

	4	3	2	1
Creativity	Product is clear and logical, with an original design that relates to the theme. It uses a wide variety of images that clearly illustrate the events. It includes a wide range of interesting facts.	Product is mostly clear and logical, with an original design that relates to the theme. It uses a variety of images that illustrate the events quite well. It includes mostly interesting facts.	Product is clear and logical only in parts. It has a good design but is only loosely related to the theme. It uses images that only illustrate some of the events. It includes relevant facts, but only a few are interesting.	Product is unclear and illogical, with a design that is not related to the theme. It uses very few or no images, and these don't illustrate the events well. It doesn't include any interesting or relevant facts.
Language Use	Excellent use of language from the unit (present perfect for experiences; reflexive and indefinite pronouns). Project is understandable with only a few mistakes.	Good use of language from the unit (present perfect for experiences; reflexive and indefinite pronouns). Project is understandable with some mistakes.	Adequate use of language from the unit (present perfect for experiences; reflexive and indefinite pronouns). Project is understandable, but some sections need further explanation.	Poor or no use of language from the unit (present perfect for experiences; reflexive and indefinite pronouns). Project is confusing, vague, and almost impossible to understand.

The Cambridge Framework for Life Competencies

You can also assess students' progress in the following foundational layers.

FOUNDATIONAL LAYER	ABILITIES	ACTIONS
Emotional Development	• Empathize and build relationships	sharing and prioritizing tasks, agreeing on and trying to stick to deadlines, giving constructive feedback
Discipline Knowledge	• Convince the audience	giving facts and details, arranging information in the correct order, presenting in a clear and logical manner (written and oral), answering questions

Flipped Classroom Activities

Evaluate

In project groups, have students discuss their completed Peer-Evaluation Forms and ways to work better as a group. Peer-Evaluation Form p69

Out of class: have students reflect on their progress at home. KWL Chart p67 **Learned**

In class: hold a class discussion on what students have learned, using the information from their KWL Charts. KWL Chart p67 **Learned**

9 CULTURE PROJECT

A WEBPAGE

- **Learning Outcome:** make a festival webpage
- **Skills:** research information and use a spidergram to organize it, research images and maps, use a webpage template
- **Resources:** two or more webpages about festivals, Webpage Organizer p66, My Time-Management Plan p71
- **Evaluation Tools:** Project Evaluation Rubric p57, My Learning Diary p68, Peer-Evaluation Form p69, Teacher's Evaluation Form p70

Student's Book Teacher's Resource Bank Unit 9

Before You Start

Research festivals from around the world. Choose two or three. Find webpages about them to show in class.

1 Preparation

Step 1: Introduce the Topic

- Introduce the topic of webpages after doing the reading exercises. p108 Draw attention to the events in the guide. Ask: *Where can we find out about arts and entertainment events?*
- Show students the webpages. Ask: *What are they about? What information is in each section? Is there any information missing? Who are the webpages for? Would you like to go to these festivals? Why / Why not?*
- Ask students which webpages they visit and what for. Ask: *Do you visit webpages about festivals?*
- Ask students to bring an example of a webpage about a festival to the next class (in their own language or in English). They can discuss the webpages in groups.

Step 2: Analyze the Model for the Project Unit 9

- Have students look at the sections, titles, and pictures on the model webpage. Ask: *What is this webpage about? Who might read it?* Have students read the webpage.
- Check comprehension. Ask: *Where is this festival? Who goes to it? What can visitors do? Where can they stay? Would you like to go to this festival? Why / Why not?*
- Ask questions about the webpage's design and purpose: *Is it attractive? What is the webpage's objective?* (See Differentiated Instruction activities for further practice.)

Differentiated Instruction

Support
In pairs, have students make true/false sentences about the webpage and then test another pair.
Consolidation
Have students list other possible festival events the webpage doesn't mention and choose the best ones.
Extension
Tell students to imagine they are going to the Jerez Festival. Have them plan three things they are going to do.

Communication
Managing conversations

Ensure students contribute to discussions while using appropriate language for each task.

Step 3: *How to* Design a Webpage Unit 9

- Ask students the question at the top of the project page: *Have you ever thought about designing one?* Then go through the *How to* tips with the class.
- Draw attention to *what a visitor will want to know* in the third tip. Stress webpages should have purposes.
- Ensure students understand while designing their webpages, they should use the ideas in this *How to* section.

Step 4: Clarify the Project Unit 9

- Follow the steps in The Learning Stages of Project Work p10.
- Brainstorm world festivals. Have groups discuss where to find more information about them.

My Learning Diary p68 Preparation

Peer-Evaluation Form p69 Preparation

2 Development

Start this stage as soon as groups know their learning outcomes and have discussed what sources to use.

Step 1: Assign Roles and Responsibilities

- In project groups, have students assign general roles. Roles and Responsibilities p16 Help them decide on further roles they can share, such as those in the diagram.

Step 2: Research and Analyze Unit 9 p71

- Have groups start the PLAN section in **Exercise 1**. Have them decide on their festival.
- Have groups take notes about their festival. Hand out a copy of the Webpage Organizer p66 to each student. Students use the spidergram to plan their notes.

Flipped Classroom Activities

Out of class: have students research interesting historical facts and think of imaginative activities. They can add the information to their spidergrams.

Have students refer to the example webpage designs in the second part of their organizers. Encourage them to look for wireframes and other online templates and sketch a webpage design in the space provided.

In class: have groups organize all the information. Then have them agree on who will prepare each section.

Collaboration Learning Tip

Sharing Resources

Have resource managers ensure all group members share useful information and resources. This can include online templates and wireframes, photos, maps, drawings, and facts about their festival. Have them encourage their peers to say how they found the information.

Flipped Classroom Activities

Step 3: Draft and Review Unit 9 p71

Out of class: have group members prepare their parts as explained in the PLAN section.

Encourage students to use their sources to check and confirm facts about their festivals.

In class: group members check each other's sections.

If they haven't done so yet, groups should decide on final design and content.

Out of class: led by the web designer, have groups work on the webpage design and share and check their work online. Remind them to use a template that matches their chosen design.

Social Responsibilities

Understanding and describing own and others' cultures

Encourage students to look for cultural information about their festivals and include it in their webpages. Ask: *How is culture important to the festival? (Use of traditional music/food/clothes, etc.)*

My Learning Diary p68 **Development**

Peer-Evaluation Form p69 **Development**

3 Production

Schedule presentation times and stick to them, ensuring, if possible, that all groups present their webpage on a big screen. Spread the presentations over a few classes, if necessary. Allow enough time for each presentation and for questions.

Before groups produce their final webpages, help them follow the online steps for the template they have chosen to complete their project. Presentation Ideas p18

As students complete their projects, check their abilities in the following Areas of Competency.

Communication

Managing conversations

Uses appropriate language to negotiate meaning: to check own understanding; to check interlocutors' understanding.

Evidence: Students make content corrections based on each other's feedback.

Invites contributions from interlocutors in a conversation.

Evidence: Group members ask each other questions about their sections.

Social Responsibilities

Understanding and describing own and others' cultures

Makes informed comparisons between their own society and other societies.

Evidence: Webpage includes cultural observations.

Understands the contributions of different cultures to their own lives.

Evidence: Students think about the cultural importance of their festival and reasons why it's relevant for them.

Step 1: Prepare Unit 9 p71

- Go through the items in the PRESENT section in **Exercise 2**.
- As groups prepare their project, ask them questions to remind them of the tasks they need to complete. Tell them that they should be ready to answer questions, particularly about their own sections.

Flipped Classroom Activities

Out of class: groups finalize their webpages by sharing tasks online. Remind them to follow the ideas in the *How to* section.

In class: groups make final corrections. Have them focus on content, making sure the webpage includes all the information visitors will need. Then have them check spelling and grammar, especially the use of tenses.

Step 2: Present Unit 9

- Draw attention to the CHECK section in **Exercise 3**. Ask the class to think about these questions as they look at their peers' webpages.
- If possible, have groups project their webpages on a big screen. Ensure each group member presents their section.
- After the presentations, students could try and use the webpages: they could click on the different features, zoom in, etc.
- Encourage students to ask questions and take notes about what they like.

Step 3: Reflect Unit 9

- After the presentations, hold a class discussion on the CHECK questions in **Exercise 3**.
- Have the class say what they like about each webpage and why. Then ask: *Which festivals would you like to go to? Why?* Finally, the class can vote on their favorite webpage.
- Encourage students to reflect on each stage of the project process, including positive experiences and things they could improve upon.

Peer-Evaluation Form p69 **Production**

Go to the collaboration tool and online portfolio to make use of the digital resources.

Project Evaluation Rubric: A Webpage

Use these project-specific descriptors and your own choice of descriptors from the > Evaluation Rubric p21 to assess students individually or in groups. Make your own evaluation form. > Teacher's Evaluation Form p70

	4	3	2	1
Creativity	Product's name is very interesting and relevant. Product is attractive and contains visuals for each description. It is easy to use and understand. It contains very interesting cultural information.	Product's name is interesting and relevant. Product is attractive and contains visuals for most descriptions. It is generally easy to use and understand. It contains some interesting cultural information.	Product's name is relevant but not interesting. Only some parts are attractive, and a few descriptions don't have visuals. Some parts are difficult to use or understand. It contains cultural information but is not very interesting.	Product's name is not interesting or relevant. Product is unattractive with very few visuals. It is impossible to use or understand. It doesn't contain any cultural information.
Language Use	Excellent use of language from the unit (future tenses). Project is understandable with only a few mistakes.	Good use of language from the unit (future tenses). Project is understandable with some mistakes.	Adequate use of language from the unit (future tenses). Project is understandable, but some sections need further explanation.	Poor or no use of language from the unit (future tenses). Project is confusing, poorly written, and vague.

The Cambridge Framework for Life Competencies

You can also assess students' progress in the following foundational layers.

FOUNDATIONAL LAYER	ABILITIES	ACTIONS
Digital Literacy	• Use digital tools	finding content, creating a webpage, sharing work online, using digital presentation techniques, adding interactive features
Discipline Knowledge	• Convince the audience	explaining facts and images, giving details, describing events, answering questions

Flipped Classroom Activities

Evaluate

In project groups, have students discuss their completed Peer-Evaluation Forms and ways to work better as a group. > Peer-Evaluation Form p69

Out of class: have students reflect on their progress at home. > My Learning Diary p68 **Production**

In class: hold a class discussion on what students have learned, using the information from their learning diaries. > My Learning Diary p68 **Production**

INFOGRAPHIC ORGANIZER

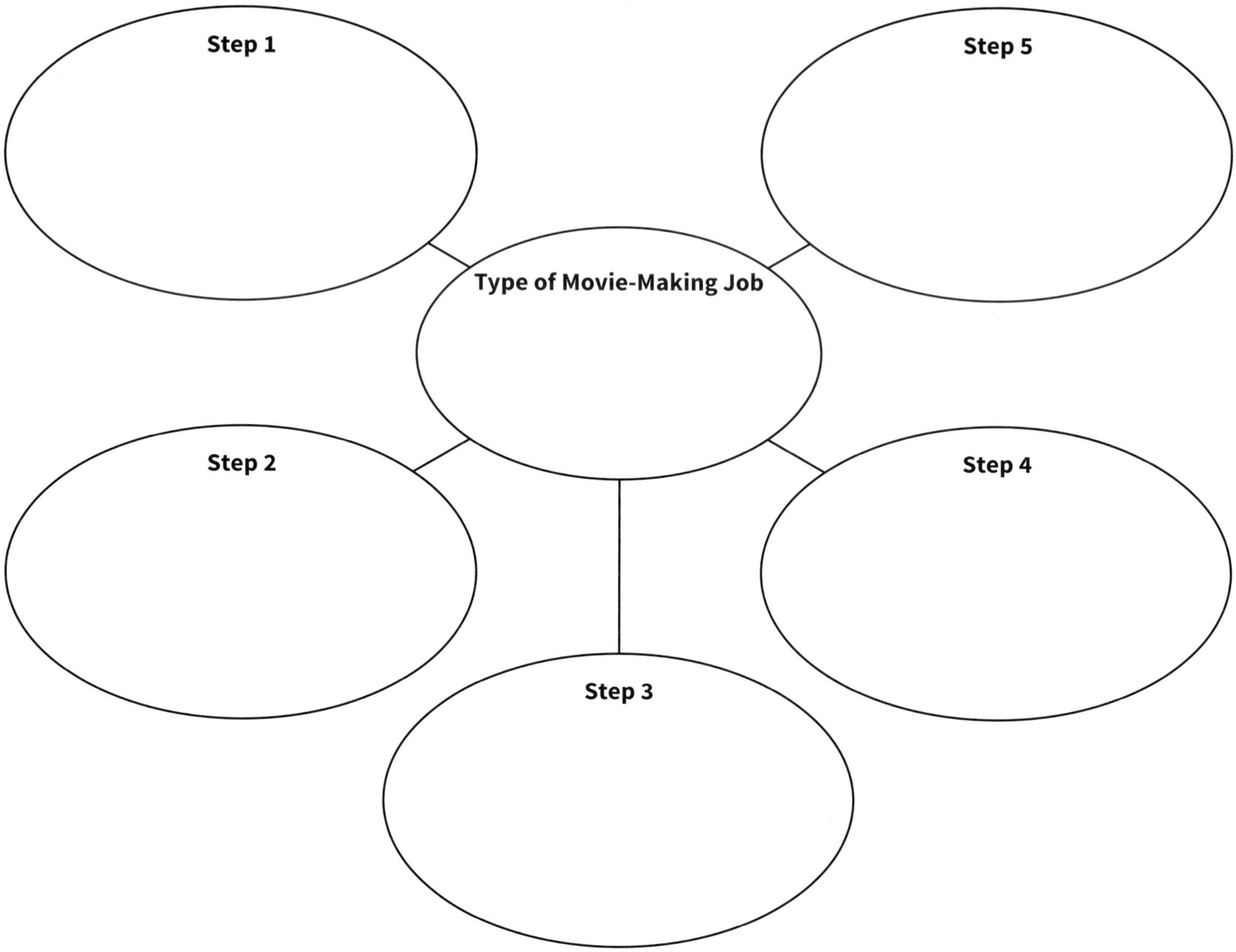

Text	Images

MUSEUM DISPLAY ORGANIZER

Name of Object
Location
Materials
How did people make it?
What did people use it for?
Other Interesting Facts

Write ideas for photos and pictures. (You can also write the sources here.)

Organize your group's display. Make a sketch.

COMIC STRIP ORGANIZER

POSTER ORGANIZER

Title	
Introduction (messages to attract volunteers: think of questions and sentences)	
Ideas for Images	
What?	**Why?**
Where?	
Who?	**What are the benefits?**
When?	

POSTER ORGANIZER: A SPIDERGRAM

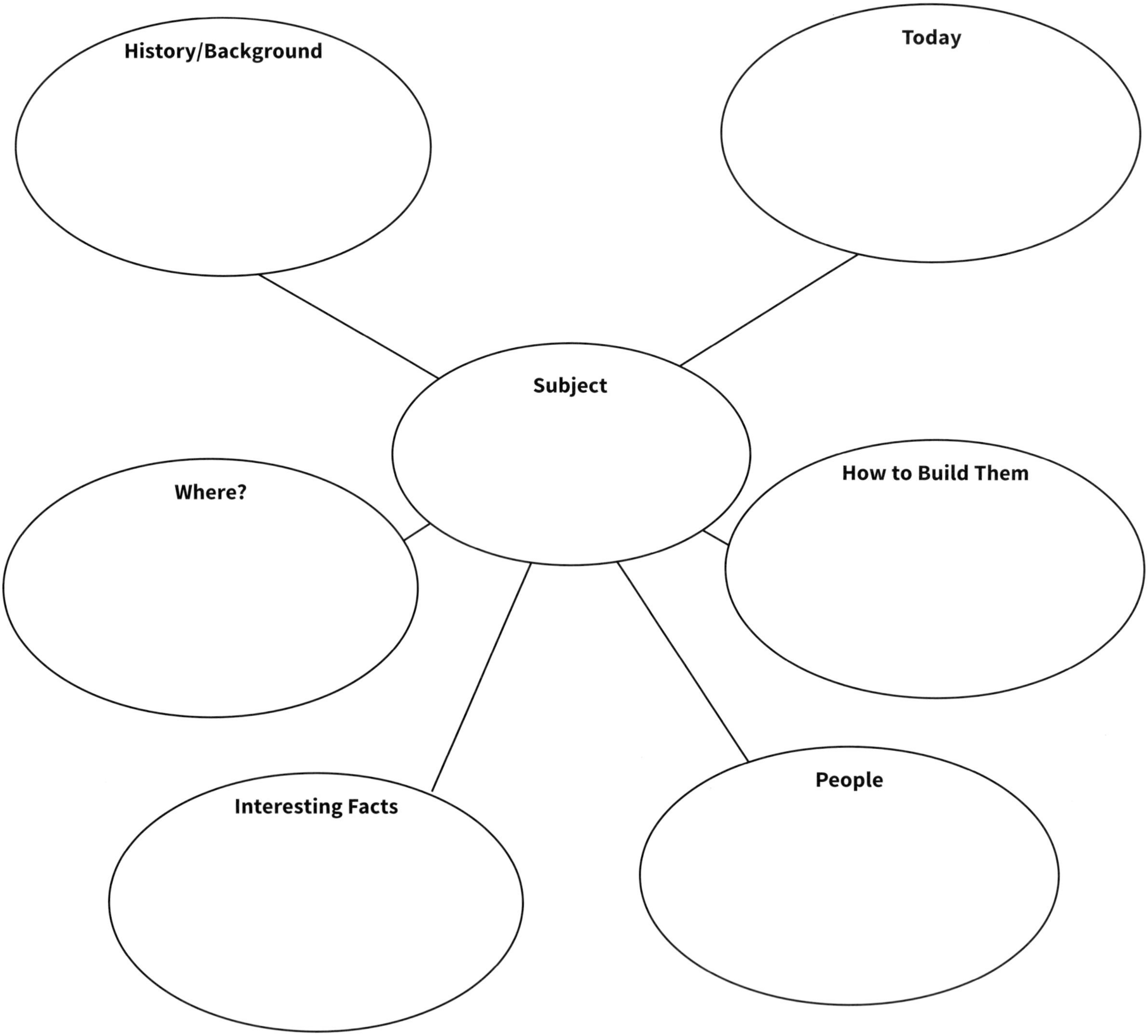

INFORMATION PAMPHLET ORGANIZER

Place or Habitat: ______________________________

Fact File:

Sections (e.g., weather, animals, dangers, etc.)

Image Ideas:		**Image Ideas:**
	Image Ideas:	

3-D ROOM PLAN ORGANIZER

Items' Names
What is each item for?
What will each item do?
What will we be able to do with each of the items?
NEW INVENTION! What is its name? What will it do?

TIMELINE ORGANIZER

Title: ____________________

Image 1

Year: ________

Image 3

Year: ________

Image 5

Year: ________

Text 1

Text 2

Text 3

Text 4

Text 5

Text 6

Image 2

Year: ________

Image 4

Year: ________

Image 6

Year: ________

Ideas for Images: ____________________

WEBPAGE ORGANIZER

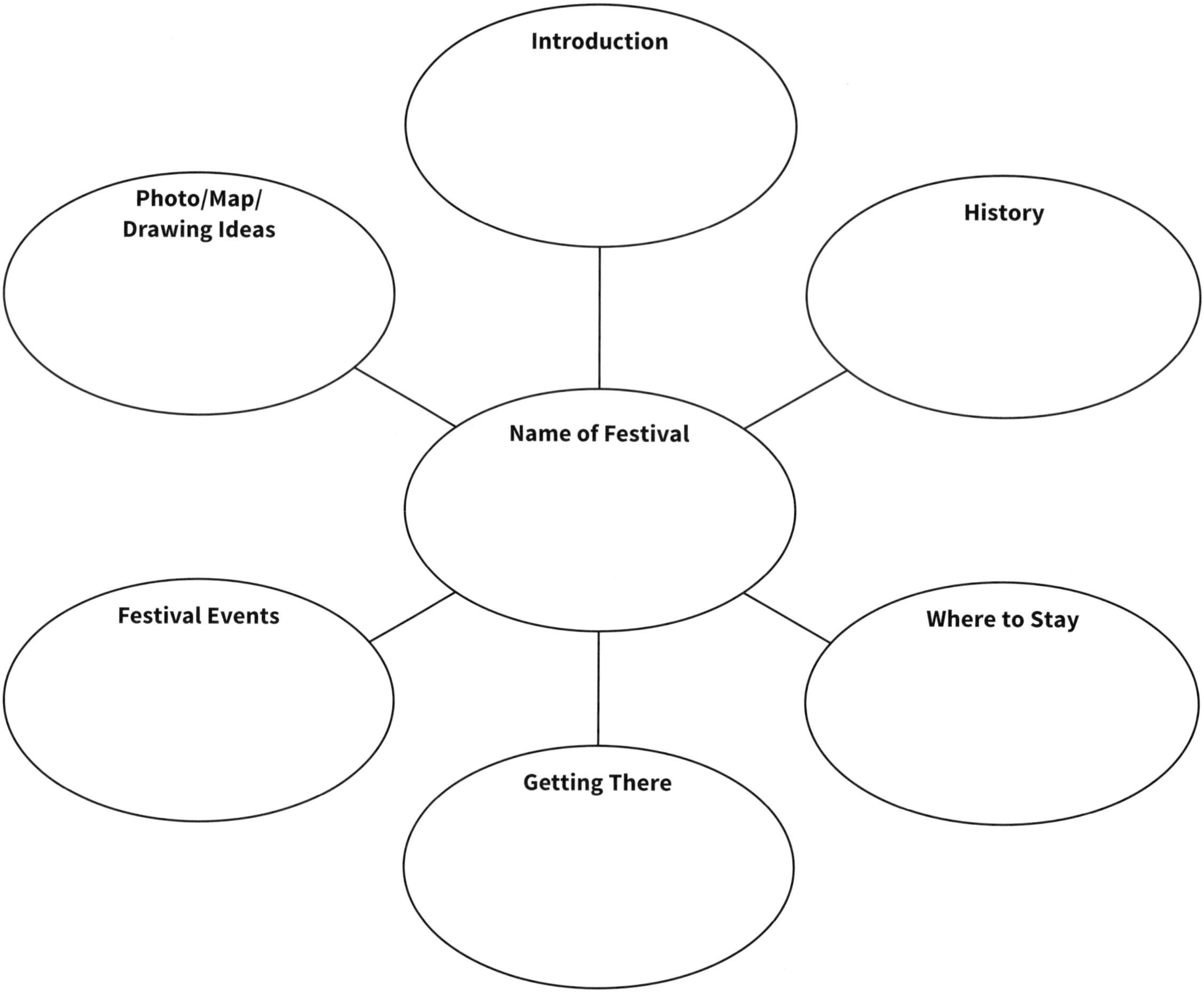

Look at the webpage designs. Then draw your own design including all the information in your spidergram.

Name: ______________________________

Date: ______________________________

Unit, topic, and project: ______________________________

KWL CHART

***K*now**	***W*ant to Know**	***L*earned (Know Now)**
What do we know about the topic?	*What do we want to know about the topic?*	*What do we know now about the topic?*
		What do we know now about the tasks?
What are our tasks?		*What can we do now as a group?*

Name: ____________________

Date: ____________________

Unit, topic, and project: ____________________

MY LEARNING DIARY

1 PREPARATION

- *What am I learning?*
- *What resources can I use? (for example, the Internet, the library, magazines, ...)*
- *Who is in my project group?*
- *What is my role in the group?*

2 DEVELOPMENT

- *What is difficult about this project?*
- *Who or what can help me?*
- *What do I like / not like?*
- *How can we make our work better?*

3 PRODUCTION

- *Is it a good presentation? Why / Why not?*
- *In the presentation, what is my role?*
- *How do I feel when I give a presentation?*

Name: ______________________________

Date: ______________________________

Unit, topic, and project: ______________________________

PEER-EVALUATION FORM

1 **In your group, evaluate your performance. Mark (✓) the columns.**

1 PREPARATION	☺	😐	☹
We listen to the instructions.			
We understand the project.			

2 DEVELOPMENT	☺	😐	☹
We participate 100 percent in the project.			
We work well as a group.			

3 PRODUCTION	☺	😐	☹
We answer questions about our work.			
We ask questions about others' work.			

2 **Write one good thing about this project.**

____

____

____

____

3 **How can your group work better in the next project? Write one idea.**

____

____

____

____

Name: ______________________________

Date: ______________________________

Unit, topic, and project: ______________________________

TEACHER'S EVALUATION FORM

Group or individual performance grades for the selected ✓ general areas.
Grades are as follows: 4 = Exceeds expectations, 3 = Very good, 2 = Good, 1 = Needs improvement.

✓	Areas / Outcomes	Grade	✓	Areas / Outcomes	Grade
	Learning outcomes			Creativity	
	Planning and organization			Problem-solving skills	
	Use of information and resources			Language use	
	Collaboration (teamwork)			Presentation skills	
	Time management			Final product	

Group or individual performance grades for the project-specific areas.
Grades are as follows: 4 = Exceeds expectations, 3 = Very good, 2 = Good, 1 = Needs improvement.

Project-Specific Area	Grade
1	
2	
3	
4	
5	

The Cambridge Framework for Life Competencies

[Student's name / Group] ______________________ showed (✓) did not show (✗) development in the following competencies and skills during this project.

Area of Competency 1	✓/✗	Foundational Layers	✓/✗
Area of Competency 2	✓/✗		
		Comments:	
Comments:			

Overall grade: __________

General comments:

Area(s) of improvement:

Name: ______________________

Date: ______________________

Unit, topic, and project: ______________________

MY TIME-MANAGEMENT PLAN

What tasks do you need to do for each step? Write them below and write the time prediction. Then mark (✓) each task as you complete it and write the actual time it takes.

Research and Analyze

What do I need to do?	Time Prediction	Actual Time
1 ☐ ______	→ ______	→ ______
2 ☐ ______	→ ______	→ ______
3 ☐ ______	→ ______	→ ______

Draft and Review

What do I need to do?	Time Prediction	Actual Time
1 ☐ ______	→ ______	→ ______
2 ☐ ______	→ ______	→ ______
3 ☐ ______	→ ______	→ ______

Prepare

What do I need to do?	Time Prediction	Actual Time
1 ☐ ______	→ ______	→ ______
2 ☐ ______	→ ______	→ ______
3 ☐ ______	→ ______	→ ______

Reflect

Answer the questions.

- I manage my time well during my project work. ☐ Yes. ☐ Can be better.
- I have time to complete self-evaluation tools for each stage. ☐ Yes. ☐ No.
- How can I improve my time management in the next project?

____

____

____

Acknowledgments

The authors and publishers acknowledge the following sources of copyright material and are grateful for the permissions granted. While every effort has been made, it has not always been possible to identify the sources of all the material used, or to trace all copyright holders. If any omissions are brought to our notice, we will be happy to include the appropriate acknowledgments on reprinting and in the next update to the digital edition, as applicable.

Key: Int = Introduction

Photography

The following photographs are sourced from Getty Images:

Int: Hero Images; Steve Debenport/E+; code6d/E+; ilyast/DigitalVision Vectors; FatCamera/E+; RobinOlimb/DigitalVision Vectors; RaStudio/iStock/Getty Images Plus; Wavebreakmedia/iStock/Getty Images Plus; pbombaert/Moment; Nina Dermawan/Moment Mobile; Wibowo Rusli/Lonely Planet Images; anactor/iStock/Getty Images Plus; Michael H/DigitalVision; Coco Flamingo/Imagezoo; portishead1/E+; mediaphotos/iStock/Getty Images Plus; Indeed; MachineHeadz/iStock/Getty Images Plus; vgajic/E+; Snapshots from *Shape It! Project Book 2* pp. 26–27; Snapshots from *Shape It! Project Book 2* pp. 59–60; Snapshots from *Shape It! Project Book 2* pp. 69–71; Snapshots from *Shape It! Student's Book 2 Culture Projects* Unit 1 & 7.

The following photographs are sourced from other libraries/sources:

Int: Kirby Wu; Malini Images/Alamy Stock Photo

Cover Design and Illustrations: Collaborate Agency

Typesetting: TXT Servicios Editoriales

American English Consultant: Mandie Drucker

Freelance Editors: Sue Costello, Mike Kemper, and Cara Norris-Ramirez